Monitored Peril

Monitored Peril

Asian Americans and the Politics of TV Representation

Darrell Y. Hamamoto

LIBRARY

 University of Minnesota Press
Minneapolis
London

Published by the University of Minnesota Press
2037 University Avenue Southeast, Minneapolis, MN 55455–3092
Printed in the United States of America on acid-free paper

Library of Congress Cataloging-in-Publication Data

Hamamoto, Darrell Y.
  Monitored peril : Asian Americans and the politics of TV
representation / Darrell Y. Hamamoto.
    p.   cm.
  Includes bibliographical references and index.
  ISBN 0-8166-2368-6 (acid-free paper)
  ISBN 0-8166-2369-4 (pbk: acid-free paper)
  1. Asian Americans in television. I. Title
PN1992.8.A78H36   1994
791.45'6520395073—dc20   93-38700

for June, for Gena

Contents

Preface

It was media historian J. Fred MacDonald who first suggested this project to me as I was in the final stages of completing a book about television situation comedy. Initially, I thought that there simply was not enough archival material to warrant a book-length discussion of Asian Americans on television. Furthermore, with the exception of public television, my past casual viewing experience told me that such representations were almost always one-dimensional and demeaning. Why belabor the obvious? As for the first assumption, I was mistaken that television programs featuring Asian Americans were too few in number for one to discern thematic and historical patterns within them. As for my skepticism about whether the project could sustain more than just a few pedestrian observations, the reader will have to decide if such concerns were justified.

As I probed deeper into the vaults of the UCLA Film and Television Archive, I discovered a wealth of programs that featured any number of Asian and Asian American characters, both peripheral and central. In addition to rare archival material generously provided by MacDonald and Associates, I managed to build an extensive private collection that spanned the whole of network television history. Although most of the Asian American figures depicted in the surveyed TV programs were indeed one-dimensional and peripheral when compared with the dominant, Euro-American lead characters, I soon realized that this fact in itself was worthy of examination. I came to conclude that racialized discourses of subordinate social identity must be accounted for historically and politically if they are ever to be subverted.

Because I wanted to discover the *material* reasons for the symbolic social subordination of Asian Americans on television, I inverted standard critical practice by relegating High Theory to a secondary position while foregrounding the study of U.S. history, culture, and

politics and its relationship to white supremacist discursive formations. I was not interested in the aestheticized *phenomenon* of television so much as its material relationship to larger structures of
political-economic and cultural *domination*. In paying close attention to the contours of postwar U.S. society, I hoped to avoid treating crucially important descriptive and explanatory concepts such as
"race" (and its chi-chi cousin, "otherness") as mere abstractions, lacking in either historical specificity or reference to politics and power
relations in U.S. society. As is often the case with psychoanalytic appropriations of the "race" concept, it simply will not do to treat one
of the fundamental organizing principles of American plural society
with a token mention of a Frantz Fanon or perhaps an Albert
Memmi. It reduces the work of politically engaged, anticolonial intellectuals to a glass-bead game of little consequence for the lives
nonwhite Americans.

Racism is not an intellectual abstraction for those who feel the
sting of its lash. For example, in a highly personal and nuanced response to the Los Angeles uprising or *sai-i-ku* (literally, April 29),
Elaine H. Kim describes the way in which network television news
and talk shows helped to heighten racial tensions between African
Americans and Korean Americans. According to Kim, Korean
Americans were exploited by the network news media "to deflect attention from the racism they inherited and the economic injustice
and poverty that had been well woven into the fabric of American
life."[1] Add to this the irony of Korean immigrants to the United
States who, while growing up in Korea, learned the lessons of
American democracy by viewing dubbed versions of *Gunsmoke*,
Knight Rider, and *MacGyver*. Despite their television introduction
to American culture and society, "they did not realize that, as immigrants of color, they would never attain political voice or visibility
but would instead be used to uphold the inequality and the racial hierarchy they had no part in creating," writes Kim.[2]

In part, the intention of the present study is to compensate for the
tendency in theoretical practice to trot out television as a purely rhetorical stalking-horse so that certain points can be made concerning
the postmodern condition.[3] The hyperaesthetic pronunciamentos of
Jean Baudrillard, for example, pretend to transcend politics and history while abolishing the social. Worse yet, his critique of contemporary media and society brings unwarranted closure to persistent
problems of capitalist relations of production, in which network television and allied industries play an integral role.[4] Although the
poetic sweep and grandeur of a Baudrillard are helpful in stimulat-
ing the critical imagination, such mundane activities as archival re-

search and empirical study are also necessary operations in gaining a full understanding of media and society.

Against the Baudrillardian tendency, I have found ideological critique to be the most productive means of interpreting the relationship between Asian American representation on television and the dominant social order. Since Foucault, it has been commonly accepted that knowledge and power inhere in discursive formations through which social roles are assigned and enforced.[5] Popular cultural forms such as network television programs are especially effective vehicles for the transmission of a racialized discourse that confers legitimacy to white supremacist social institutions and power arrangements. The following pages will lay bare core ideological asssumptions of select TV programs with an eye on destabilizing their taken-for-granted status. Once the fissures of liberal thought as embodied in dominant TV forms have been exposed, it remains for independent Asian American media artists (practicing a Foucauldian-inspired counterhegemonic "discourse politics") to drive a wedge into the cracks of the edifice.[6]

A stylistic note is in order before turning to the main work. While recognizing the substantial cultural and historical differences between Asians and Asian Americans, both groups will be treated in the present study where appropriate. There are at least three reasons for occasionally grouping Asians with Asian Americans. For one, the respective groups exist on a historical and sociocultural continuum rather than as two analytically distinct entities. Other than citizenship and nationality, there is no definitive line of demarcation that separates Asians from Asian Americans. William Dean Howell's assertion that it takes three generations to make an American notwithstanding, it is not so readily apparent at what point a distinctly Asian personal and social identity shades into that of a full-fledged American. It is more likely the case that the very idea of "Americanness" is a reified concept that serves the interests of a social and intellectual elite who have a vested interest in the perpetuation of an Anglo-Saxon monoculture.[7]

Second, there are a number of tragic examples drawn from history that demonstrate the refusal of Euro-Americans to understand and respect the distinction between Asians and Asian Americans. For Asian Americans, like other people of color, physical identifiability remains of paramount importance in the creation and maintenance of "racial meanings" in U.S. society.[8] But even so, rarely are African Americans identified as being African. And although Latinos are often assumed to be Mexican, rarely are they taken to be Spanish. This is not the case with Asian Americans. Such willful ignorance allows for "Asian Americans" — a political concept that in itself conceals the sheer diversity and fragmentation of the various Asian ethnic groups — to be considered perpetual aliens, often with disastrous consequences.

Third, large-scale political events in Asia have always had repercussions for Asian American communities.[9] Whether it be the imperialist policies of the United States in the Philippines at the turn of the century, the Indian independence movement of the 1920s, the militarism of Imperial Japan throughout the 1930s, the U.S. "loss" of China in the late 1940s, the Cold War partitioning of Korea during the 1950s, or the undeclared war against Vietnam during the 1960s through mid-1970s, each of these world-historical events has directly affected the lives of Filipino, Asian Indian, Japanese, Chinese, Korean, and Vietnamese people residing in the United States. For better or worse, the lives of Asian Americans are linked with the changing political-economic relationships between the United States and Asian nations.

One of the more gratifying aspects of the present undertaking is the interest and involvement of many friends and colleagues in its realization. As already mentioned above, Fred MacDonald was there at the genesis of this project and provided invaluable intellectual and material support. I hope he forgives me for not following his suggestion by titling this book *You'll Wonder Where the Yellow Went*, after the memorable Pepsodent jingle. I gratefully acknowledge the 1990–91 research fellowship awarded by the Rockefeller Foundation that supported the first phase of this project. Had poet, restaurateur, and *Amerasia Journal* editor Russell Leong not taken a chance on me, I never would have had the time or money to conduct the primary research for this book. I also wish to thank Don Nakanishi, director of the Asian American Studies Center at UCLA, who has graciously allowed my voice (if somewhat shrill at times) to be heard.

Is it possible to thank adequately Marina Heung, Gina Marchetti, Sumiko Higashi, Karen Leonard, Lee Meihls, David Steinman, and Bob Thompson for their giving me an occasional bucking up? Same goes for Charlie Musser, with whom I shared an eventful year. A heartfelt thanks to the faculty of the Program in Comparative Culture at UC Irvine — particularly Pete Clecak and Raul Fernandez — for providing me with an institutional home, and to both Charles Igawa and Stanley Aronowitz, whose respective influence from earlier times lingers on.

I have benefited a great deal from the multifaceted intellectual work of Doug Kellner and even more from his personal example and the advice so kindly given me. Then there is Carl Boggs, whose life force and existential self-creation are of Nietzschean proportions, whether driving the streets of L.A. or riding the TGV from Paris to Frankfurt while wondering aloud about Marilyn. Appreciation to Dave Williams, who in addition to being a longtime bandmate in a high-concept, almost nonexistent group, now happily shares in an Asian American experience of his own while continuing to play funky white-boy 9th-chord rhythms at Glenalbyn Sound Studios.

Finally, without the forgiving indulgence of June Kurata and Gena Hamamoto, work of this sort would be difficult to tackle. But in allowing me to commit spousal and parental neglect of the highest order, at least you got your names mentioned in this here book.

Chapter 1

White Christian Nation

Controlling Images

Early on in the movement of Asian labor to the United States, immigrants from the Far East were viewed by the dominant Euro-American society as a peril to a white Christian nation whose manifest destiny it was to lead the lesser races down the path of moral, political, and economic development along capitalist lines. Their massive numbers contributed greatly to national economic development and helped create the unparalleled social wealth of the United States in the early stages of its drive toward global ascendancy.[1] Needed but not necessarily wanted, Asian Americans have been often viewed as a yellow blight upon the land.

While Asians were not fully welcomed by nativists and members of the white working class, their labor was nonetheless instrumental in creating the agricultural and industrial infrastructure of the United States as it entered the advanced stages of capitalist development.[2] The simultaneous necessity and undesirability of Asian immigrant labor is a crucial political-economic contradiction that informs much of the past and present experience of Asians in the United States. The manner in which Asian immigrants have been dealt with historically by the receiving society has ranged from relative tolerance to outright exclusion.

As it concerns Asians in the United States, another no less important contradiction operates on the level of ideology. Liberal democratic ideals predicated upon individual freedom and equality of opportunity have existed in perpetual tension against the reality of a color-caste system wherein white Americans occupy the top rungs of a relatively rigid hierarchy based upon socially constructed racial identity.[3] Despite the existence of a rigid color-caste system, the relative "success" of Asian Americans has been cited often by both journalists and academic commentators as "proof" that this basic social contradiction plays no signficant role in a liberal democratic society characterized by a high degree of upward mobility and near-infinite opportunities for advancement.[4]

I have argued elsewhere that it is in the nature of television drama to embody the contradictions of the larger society. In realist drama, the narrative arc—its rise, descent, and resolution—is dependent upon conflict. More specifically, it is sociocultural and political-economic conflict that form the dramatic basis of network television programs.[5] Given this premise, a select survey of television programs that feature Asian American characters would reveal a plethora of social contradictions that give expression, sometimes unintentionally, to the meaning of their collective presence within the larger society.

Patricia Hill Collins observes that the exercise of political-economic domination by racial elites in society "always involves attempts to objectify the subordinate group."[6] The objectification of subordinate groups is achieved through the application of "controlling images" that help justify economic exploitation and social oppression on the basis of an interlocking system comprising race, class, and gender. The so-called mammy image prevalent in U.S. popular culture, for example, traditionally has been invoked to justify the exploitative use of African American women as a cheap source of labor in bourgeois Euro-American households and to stand as counterexample to the hypersexual Black "Jezebel."[7]

Racist controlling images as described by Collins form part of a larger system of "psychosocial dominance," as Donald G. Baker refers to it. Along with the threat and occasional use of coercive violence, the exercise of psychosocial dominance plays a central role in the concentration and maintenance of power among ruling elites. Beyond "coercive dominance," the psychosocial form of control is subtly effective in that subordinate groups internalize the set of dominant racial meanings that cause them to "reject their own individual and group identity."[8] In its stead, a white supremacist complex that establishes the primacy of Euro-American cultural practices and social institutions serves as the principal mechanism of subordinating or excluding those groups that do not conform to the normative profile.

Within a system of racial inequality, basic power resources such as food, education, health care, shelter, information, communication, transportation, and energy are apportioned on the basis of a given group's conformity to or deviation from the physical and behavioral norms established and enforced by the dominant Euro-American group. The gross maldistribution of power resources within a capitalist political economy is naturalized through a set of beliefs that attribute real or imagined physical and intellectual traits to "groups socially defined as races."[9] This set of beliefs forms the basis of ideological racism.

In the postwar era, television has been the principal medium by which rituals of psychosocial dominance are reenacted daily. "The technological revolution in communications has created new and complex instruments of persuasion," Dennis H. Wrong observes in his classic treatise on the nature of political power, "access to which constitutes a vitally important power resource."[10] Even the most seemingly benign TV programs articulate the relationship between race and power, either explictly or through implication. In the popular culture, it is via network television programs that the related states of unfreedom comprising racial, gender, and class formations are forcibly reconciled with the master narrative of liberal democratic ideology. This marriage of convenience is inherently unstable, however, and it remains the principal challenge to the creators of television programs to mediate social contradictions once they reach a certain level of disruptive salience within the popular culture.

Racial meanings are continually being redefined and renegotiated as they meet with challenges to their legitimacy by media watchdog groups, independent artists, journalists of the alternative press, and even academic critics. Stuart Hall issues an important reminder that it would be too easy to conceive of the media as "simply the ventriloquists of a unified and racist 'ruling class' conception of the world."[11] Although network television operates in accordance with the for-profit market imperatives of oligopoly capitalism, this is not to say that there exists a tidy one-to-one relationship between corporate-controlled media institutions and the racist undertone of many network TV programs. Not only is such a neat correlation impossible to demonstrate from the standpoint of methodology, but on a tactical level such economistic pessimism holds little hope for change and transformation. Much more fruitful is the Gramscian perspective that "allows us to view popular culture as a terrain of negotiation and exchange between classes and groups."[12] As the following pages will, I hope, demonstrate, even the most obdurate of falsehoods crumble when subjected to the combined force of interest group activism, political agitation, civil unrest, and critical study. Alternative cultural practices can also form a counterhegemonic bloc against the dominant discourse such as reproduced in network television fare. The vibrant independent Asian American media arts movement is a current example of such counterhegemonic cultural practice.[13] As Raymond Williams has observed, the popular culture of nondominant peoples (whom he calls "majorities") is "irrepressible" in nature. Their popular culture persists "under any pressures and through whatever forms, while life itself survives, and while so many people – real if not always connected majorities – keep living and looking to live beyond the routines which attempt to control and reduce them."[14]

Other Americans

In her multigenerational study of women and labor migration in the United States, Evelyn Nakano Glenn correctly observes that substantial differences separate the experiences of European ethnic groups and those of immigrants or indigenes of color.[15] Unlike "white ethnics," Asians, Chicanos, Native Americans, and African Americans have been held in check by a color-caste system that has placed them at or near the bottom of the labor employment ladder. Whereas women of color have found it difficult to move out of low-paying, low-status domestic labor, women of European immigrant groups have held such jobs as only the first step in their economic ascent.

According to Glenn, the "two-tiered" labor system is characterized not only by class and patriarchal oppression, but by institutional racism as well. Physical identifiability and ethnic-racial distinctiveness have helped to create and maintain a two-tiered labor system whereby "later cohorts of non-white immigrant groups had different labor market experiences from later cohorts of white immigrant groups."[16] The differential treatment of nonwhite ethnic-racial groups must be kept in mind, for many liberal/conservative ethnicity theorists such as Nathan Glazer, William Julius Wilson, and Charles Murray cite the example of successful European immigrant groups as an argument for the abandonment of social welfare programs that serve large numbers of the nonwhite underclass.[17] But as E. San Juan, Jr., observes, such mean-spirited arguments deny the key role of "race and racism as causal factors in the making of the political and economic structure of the United States."[18] Racial identity remains the basic dividing line in U.S. society.

Whereas liberal theorists tend to overstate the uniform nature of social discrimination supposedly endured by all immigrant groups as they move through the Parkian "race relations cycle," theorists on the left also have minimized the very real forms of racial oppression endured by nonwhite ethnic and racial minorities. Until recently, leftist sociocultural critics have favored some variant of traditional Marxian class analysis in explaining racial oppression. For too long, both liberal and radical theorists have given short shrift to the detailed study of nonwhite groups and their subordination according to ethnic or racial social identity.[19]

Like many left-liberal commentators who discuss race and ethnicity in American society, conservative thinkers such as Michael Novak have argued that white ethnics have also suffered social discrimination. Catholic Polish Americans, Italian Americans, and Jewish Americans are given as examples of European ethnic groups that were once held at bay by the Anglo-Saxon Protestant establishment through discriminatory practices. But the larger agenda of Novak's *The Rise of the Unmeltable Ethnics* (1972) was to blunt demands for redress by African Americans, who led the equality revolution of the 1960s.[20] In a sense, the Novak book was an early warning sign of the full-blown white backlash that was to be unleashed with furious vengeance during the "Reagan Revolution" of the 1980s. Erstwhile left-liberal opinion leaders such as Irving Kristol and Norman Podhoretz joined with the traditional conservative establishment to fabricate ideological justification for the war against economic, cultural, and political democracy led by nonwhite Americans.[21] Racial minorities (African Americans in particular) were called upon to pull themselves up by their own bootstraps, just like other groups have done in the past. In an era of shrinking resources, it was argued, the state could no longer guarantee entry into the middle class through its already strained social welfare provisions.

The assumption of a basic uniformity and commensurability among all ethnic groups regardless of color obscures the crucial role of race and racism in the production and maintenance of inequality in American life. Ethnic and racial difference extends far beyond superficial "cultural" trappings such as language, religion, cuisine, and mode of dress, such as is currently being touted by liberal multiculturalists. Rather, nonwhite groups such as Asian Americans are cast into the role of ethnic-racial "other" by the dominant society on the basis of arbitrary somatic norms and social behavior.

The social construction of Asian American "otherness" is the precondition for their cultural marginalization, political impotence, and psychic alienation from mainstream American life. Elaine H. Kim has described the way in which the orientalia articulated through popular literature written by whites has helped construct Asian otherness, and Eugene Franklin Wong has brought similar insights to bear in his study of the commercial cinema.[22] Just as popular literature and the cinema performed important ideological functions in their day, in the postwar era it is television that has been instrumental in the symbolic mediation of conflicts between competing claimant groups that seek to realize the substantive equality promised by American social democracy. The remainder of this chapter will offer an introductory survey of racist controlling images imposed upon Asian Pacific Americans by network television.

Bachelor Fathers

The first Asian group to arrive in the United States on a large scale were the Chinese. Between 1849 and 1930, more than 400,000 Chinese workers arrived in Hawaii and the U.S. mainland, leaving their homeland to escape poverty, widespread political conflict, and the deleterious effects of contact with Western imperialist countries.[23] Unlike European immigrants to the United States, the vast majority of Chinese immigrants were unmarried males who formed the "womanless households" characteristic of both urban and rural settlements.[24]

There are several compelling reasons a Chinese "bachelor society" developed throughout California and much of the American West. For one, social custom dictated that married women remain at home rather than accompany their husbands, many of whom viewed their visit to *Gam Saan* or "Gold Mountain" as only temporary. Second, the needs of American capitalism were served nicely by a nonpermanent alien labor force, because, "as a yellow proletariat, Chinese migrant workers would not have families in America, and America would not have a Chinese population granted citizenship by birth."[25] Finally, with the passage of successive Chinese Exclusion Acts inspired by virulent anti-Asian racism, the supply of marriageable females was all but cut off. The imbalance in gender ratio among Chinese Americans was not fully corrected until long after World War II.[26]

The politics of white racial supremacy had become an established feature of American democracy by the time of Jackson. Systematic Indian-killing campaigns, the African American slave trade, and the forced incorporation of Mexicans through territorial annexation served as precedents for the anti-Chinese agitation to follow. Thus the anti-Chinese hostility beginning during the mid-1800s in Far Western states such as California conformed to a long-established pattern of discrimination based upon color or "race." By the latter part of the nineteenth century a coalition of Republican and Democratic leadership combined with white working-class laborers ensured Euro-American supremacy by uniting around the issue of Chinese exclusion.[27] In sum, the "bachelor society" formed by early Chinese immigrants to a large extent is the material outcome of antidemocratic tendencies within American republican rule.

Just as the popular entertainment forms of the previous century helped provide ideological justification for the maintenance of inequality along racial lines, contemporary mass-mediated popular culture on television serves a similiar function.[28] For example, such diverse television programs as *Bachelor Father* (1957–62), *Have Gun Will Travel* (1957–63), *Bonanza* (1959–73), *Valentine's Day* (1964–65), *Star Trek* (1966–69), the eminently forgettable *Highcliffe Manor* (1979), and *Falcon Crest* (1981–90) all featured the stock Chinese bachelor character, a social type that has its origins in the discriminatory immigration policies of the late nineteenth century.

Bachelor Father was a situation comedy centered on lighthearted domestic problems that faced attorney Bentley Gregg (John Forsythe), who, although unmarried, was responsible for the welfare of his orphaned niece, Kelly (Noreen Corcoran). Providing the domestic touch to the Gregg family was "houseboy" Peter Tong (Sammee Tong). The neatly uniformed Peter performed traditional female functions within the household in addition to dispensing sage advice to both the teenage Kelly and her swinging bachelor father. Peter Tong's role within the Bentley household was similar to that of Hop Sing (Victor Sen Yung) in the long-running television Western, *Bonanza*.

In the prime-time soap opera *Falcon Crest*, created by Earl Hamner, a Chinese butler played by the eponymous Chao-Li Chi was surrogate father to Lance Cumson (Lorenzo Lamas). Lance was the grandson of matriarch Angela Channing (Jane Wyman), who presided over the Falcon Crest winery with an iron hand. Lance was a child of divorce whose father was usually absent from home. Therefore, Lance would often receive instruction in manhood from Chao-Li Chi. The personal relationship between the callow young white male and the sagelike older Asian male is a fairly common pattern in TV drama. It represents a power relationship wherein a social subordinate (Chao-Li) trains his superior (Lance Cumson) in skills that will allow him to achieve and maintain superordinate status after reaching maturity.

A Chinese bachelor domestic with the dehumanizing name Hey Boy (Kam Tong) was seen regularly on the highbrow TV Western *Have Gun Will Travel* during the 1957–60 seasons and then again from 1961 to 1963. Hey Boy worked in the hotel where the central character, a professional gunfighter who went by the name of Paladin (Richard Boone), conducted his business. Hey Boy was replaced by Hey Girl (Lisa Lu) during the 1960–61 season while Kam Tong pursued a more prominent dramatic role in the adventure program *Mr. Garlund* (1960–61). This short-lived CBS program is of historical interest in that its principal character, businessman Frank Garlund (Charles Quinlivan), was the foster brother of Kam Chang (Kam Tong), the only person the secretive and elusive tycoon could trust. Garlund had been raised by Kam Chang's father, Po Chang (Philip Ahn), himself a businessman. Again, it was a case of a yellow man raising a white male to adulthood.

The characters Frank Garlund and Lance Cumson conform to a common, verging on folkloric, pattern found in popular culture as it concerns yellow-white relations. In this relationship, an Asian master tutors a young white male charge and endows him with powers or gifts (such as martial arts prowess or religiomagic wisdom) that are otherwise unattainable from white mentors. Newly endowed with unconventional powers after an extended period of intense training, the white male hero is then able to prevail over both his coethnics and the "bad" Asians who threaten him. In maturity, the hero then is called upon to protect the yellow mentor from abuse at the hands of both whites and "bad" Asians in repayment for the special powers taught him. On the face of it, this form of symbolic "repayment" appears altruistic. In fact, however, this diegetic inversion restores the student to a position of social superiority over his master, thus preserving the overarching white/dominant-yellow/subordinate relationship.

The tenacity of this white-yellow power relationship on television can be seen in more recent programs as well. The June 1992 debut of the action-adventure program *Raven* conforms to the convention of the white martial artist trained by an Asian master. In an episode titled "Return of the Black Dragon," Jonathan Raven (Jeffrey Meeks) works by night as a bartender at a posh Honolulu nightclub that caters to a primarily Asian clientele.[29] By day, Raven searches for his long-lost son. As a teenager, Raven had received instruction in the martial arts from his Japanese *sensei* (master). As an adult, Raven uses his martial arts prowess to defeat the "bad" Asians and to defend the weaker "good" Asians. By this formula, the white man appropriates an Asian counterhegemonic cultural practice such as the martial arts (which originated as an unarmed response to official state power) and puts it to his own heroic use.

Rocky Sin (Jack Soo) was an "Oriental" valet employed by playboy publishing executive Valentine Farrow (Tony Franciosa) in *Valentine's Day*. Rocky Sin and Valentine Farrow had been friends in the army, where presumably they were equals. In civilian life, however, Rocky is content to receive vicarious pleasure through Val's amorous adventures. Jack Soo's career was in many ways emblematic of the struggles Asian American performers have endured.

"Soo" was born and raised in Oakland, California, as Goro Suzuki. Hoping to pursue a career in entertainment, Suzuki changed his name to the slightly less offensive Soo to overcome residual anti-Japanese hostility on the West Coast. Soo later held down the role of the world-weary figure Sergeant Nick Yemana (1975–78) in the police sitcom *Barney Miller* (1975–82) before dying of cancer in 1979.[30]

The Gene Roddenberry space opera *Star Trek* (1966–69) featured a multicultural supporting cast including an Asian named Hikaru Sulu (George Takei).[31] Mr. Sulu sat at the helm of the starship U.S.S. *Enterprise* and guided it along its five-year interplanetary mission to contact alien life-forms and civilizations. Unlike his television predecessors, Sulu did not do the crew's laundry or prepare their meals. But the controlling image of the Asian American bachelor domestic servant is so thoroughly steeped in U.S. popular culture that it was spoofed in a skit on the Fox Television comedy program *In Living Color* (1990–present). Created by filmmaker Keenen Ivory Wayans, the irreverent if sometimes sophomorically humorous program was awarded an Emmy for outstanding variety, music, or comedy series in its first season.[32]

In the skit "The Wrath of Farrakhan," Minister Louis Farrakhan (Daymon Wayans) of the Nation of Islam comes aboard the *Enterprise* to liberate its nonwhite crew members from the white command of Captain James T. Kirk (James Carrey).[33] In this confrontation, Captain Kirk orders Mr. Sulu (Kipp Shiotani) to have Minister Farrakhan removed from the spacecraft. But Farrakhan plants a mutinous seed of doubt in Sulu's mind by asking the socially and sexually repressed helmsman, "Who does the laundry around here?" Sulu turns on Kirk in anger, recalling how the skipper has called him "Buddha-head" and "pie-face."

Before turning control of the *Enterprise* over to Minister Farrakhan, Mr. Sulu lodges a final protest against his desexualization under the rule of Captain Kirk. "I've been in space all this time and I haven't had one woman yet," Sulu complains. "You even take the ugly ones, Captain. My loins are about to explode. I want to do the nasty." "Well all right then my horny Asian brother," Farrakhan says approvingly. "Warp factor five. We're going home. Destination, 125th Street." Mr. Sulu's days as an intergalactic eunuch and glorified houseboy are over. Having at last achieved his long-deferred sexual and social liberation with the help of Minister Farrakhan, Mr. Sulu will pilot the starship back to earth, to Harlem, the cultural capital of Black America.

In this otherwise silly skit, Wayans perceptively plays the controlling images of African Americans as hypersexual beasts against that of the desexualized Asian male. In her gloss on Fanon's *Black Skin, White Masks*, Mary Ann Doane poses the question, "Why is it sexuality which forms a major arena for the articulation of racism?" Leaving aside the empirically unfalsifiable psychoanalytic hypothesis she advances concerning the conflation of "fear," "desire," and "otherness" with sexuality, it nevertheless can be observed that sexuality is "indissociable from the effects of polarization and differentiation, often linking them to structures of power and domination."[34] In reference to Mr. Sulu, the yellow man's desexualization attends his social subordination by the white patriarchal power structure represented by Captain Kirk.

The desexualization of the Asian American male is closely bound with the inability to form a family with his female counterpart because of racially specific barriers erected by the state. By contrast, the hypersexuality attributed to the African American male reflects the anxiety of the master race, whose ability to affect Black family formation is much more limited. But in both cases, controlling images are useful in the reinforcement of legal-juridical constraints that selectively target nonwhite peoples.

Rising Sons

Historically, family formation along the lines of the bourgeois ideal has been difficult for Japanese Americans as well. It is therefore no coincidence that, like the Chinese, Japanese American males have been portrayed often as lone desexualized beings. Like the Chinese, many early Japanese immigrants to the United States viewed their sojourn (*dekasegi*) as temporary. It was assumed that once he had attained a certain level of wealth, the migrant laborer would return to Japan. During the first two decades of the twentieth century, however, hopes of returning to Japan faded while corresponding dreams of making a home in America took hold. As a consequence, the marriage rate accelerated and so too did the birthrate.[35]

Again, like the Chinese, Japanese immigrants were specifically targeted for social subordination and exclusion by racially motivated laws that prevented them from acquiring real property and obtaining U.S. citizenship. Factors that negatively impinged upon Japanese family formation and maintenance included the Gentlemen's Agreement (1908) negotiated between the governments of Japan and the United States, the Alien Land Law (1913) passed in California, and exclusionary legislation passed by the U.S. Congress. The Immigration Act of 1924 struck the final blow against the Japanese American community by barring entry to aliens ineligible for U.S. citizenship.

This in effect prevented a large number of immigrant bachelors from marrying and bringing wives to the United States. For at least one contemporary observer, the passage of the 1924 Immigration Act brought Japanese immigrants to the realization "that all of their efforts to adapt themselves to American society and to demonstrate their assimilability had been in vain."[36]

After four and even five generations of a Japanese American presence in U.S. society, it would seem reasonable to expect television programs to depict individuals and families who are fairly well assimilated. But this is not the case. Rather, Japanese Americans are still represented as foreigners, as aliens. Japanese immigration to the United States has fallen off drastically since the 1960s, especially in comparison with other Asian groups. Yet many television programs feature recent Japanese immigrants rather than the more assimiliated Americans of Japanese ancestry. This strategy of symbolic containment implies that Japanese Americans still occupy "probationary" status within the larger society.

One of the earliest programs that featured a Japanese American occupying a central role was *The Courtship of Eddie's Father* (1969–72). Although the Japanese POW Fuji Kobiaji (Yoshio Yoda) appeared regularly on the military sitcom *McHale's Navy* (1962–66), it was actually entertainer Miyoshi Umeki who first earned costar status in a television series. Much earlier, during the 1955 season, Umeki broke into television as a featured performer on the musical variety program *Arthur Godfrey and His Friends* (1949–57). Miyoshi Umeki replaced a Hawaiian performer named Haleloke, who had been on the program for five years (1950–55) before being fired by the autocratic Godfrey as part of a larger personnel purge.

An accomplished, versatile performer, Umeki later went on to a career in films and won an Academy Award for her role in *Sayonara* (1957). Four years later, Umeki, as "Mei Li," starred in *Flower Drum Song* (1961). Although sappy and sentimental, *Flower Drum Song*—based on the 1957 novel by Chin Yang Lee—was nonetheless the first commercial film to feature Asian Americans exclusively in singing, acting, and dancing roles. If nothing else, *Flower Drum Song* showcased the talents of Asian American performing artists who were otherwise consigned to less-than-glamorous, unchallenging positions within the entertainment field.[37]

As the soft-spoken, unassuming housekeeper in *The Courtship of Eddie's Father*, Mrs. Livingston, Umeki took care of widower Tom Corbett (Bill Bixby) and his inquisitive young son Eddie (Brandon Cruz). Although there is little direct evidence revealed in the program itself, on the basis of her Anglo-Saxon name it might be inferred that housekeeper Mrs. Livingston was a war bride at one point in her life. In any case, it was obvious that Mrs. Livingston was born and raised in Japan, given her accent, geishalike demeanor, and propensity for offering tidbits of "Oriental" wisdom to her employer and his son.

Asian exotica on TV has not abated in more recent years. Programs such as *Happy Days* (1974–84), *Mr. T. and Tina* (1976), *Gung Ho* (1986–87), and *Davis Rules* (1991–92) continued to portray Japanese Americans as newly arrived foreigners. Even Lieutenant Ohara (Pat Morita) of the Los Angeles Police Department in the detective drama *Ohara* (1987–88) was shown solving crimes through Zen-like meditation techniques practiced in front of a shrine at home. The ascetic Japanese American detective was without a wife (deceased), which left him with few material or earthly attachments that could interfere with his transcendental pursuit of the bad guys. After solving a difficult case, Ohara would sometimes be seen engaging in some form of exotic activity, such as cooking a meal using a Chinese wok, as in the tag scene of the episode "Seeing Something That Isn't There."[38]

Although almost always cast in the role of the alien Asian on television, Pat Morita is an American-born entertainer who began his career as a stand-up comedian. During a late 1960s appearance on *The Tonight Show* (1954–present) with guest host Flip Wilson, Morita, billed as the "Hip Nip," jokes about the common perception among whites that people of Asian heritage in the United States are not truly Americans.[39] Like only the best comedians, Morita reaches deep into existential issues and mines them as source material for humor. Still, it is not certain whether the audience "gets it," as a fidgety Morita puffs nervously on a cigarette while tossing off one-liners to a not-quite-comprehending studio audience. On the basis of his starring role in the popular feature film *The Karate Kid* (1984) and its sequels *The Karate Kid, Part II* (1986) and *The Karate Kid, Part III* (1989), Pat Morita began appearing in both TV and print media ads as the "Colgate Wisdom Tooth" in early 1989. In the course of his career as a performer, Morita had graduated from being the self-professed "Hip Nip" to an "Oriental" wise man who fights tooth decay by recommending liberal applications of Colgate Tartar Control Formula.

Pioneering Asian American performers such as Pat Morita set the stage for new talent, including stand-up comedian Henry Cho, a second-generation Korean American born and raised in Knoxville, Tennessee. Cho has appeared on a number of television comedy programs and talk shows in addition to doing guest shots on the sitcoms

Designing Women (1986–93) and *Lenny* (1990–91). But like Pat Morita's thirty years before him, Cho's work as a stand-up comedian is
constrained by his Asian American ethnicity. Cho always prefaces
his comedy routine with reference to his ethnic background before
moving into the heart of the act itself.⁴⁰

The characters Matsuo "Arnold" Takahashi (Pat Morita) in
Happy Days and Taro "Mr. T." Takahashi (Pat Morita) in *Mr. T.
and Tina* both depict the Japanese American population as a "foreign" presence. Mr. T. is a Japanese inventor with two children who
has moved with his family from Tokyo to Chicago and lives with his
sister-in-law Michi (Pat Suzuki). Vice-principal Elaine Yamagami
(Tamayo Otsuki) in the situation comedy *Davis Rules* is also a Japanese immigrant. With her thick accent, the somewhat scatterbrained
school administrator utters strings of malapropisms and misinter-
prets culture-specific information, which blesses Yamagami with an
endearing naive honesty. The likelihood of a recent Japanese immigrant occupying such a key position in a public school is, to say
the least, remote. Yet, in their wisdom, the *Davis Rules* producers
chose to cast stand-up comedian Tamayo Otsuki in the role when
they could have just as easily selected a Japanese American actor who
possessed competence in the English language. Given the prepon-
derance of immigrant characters in the shows discussed, it might be
inferred that such controlling images of Japanese Americans as recent arrivals, as "aliens," are meant to perpetuate the notion of their
radical unassimilability.

"Little Brown Brothers"

In addition to convenient lapses in historical memory, contemporary
cheerleaders for the Asian American success story often suffer from
selective perception when it comes to groups that do not fit precon-
ceived images of control. The lives of Filipino Americans, for example, differ markedly from those of other Asian American groups owing to the nearly century-long imperial relationship between the
Philippines and the United States. Yet the legacy of military conquest, colonial exploitation, and continued economic underdevelopment is conveniently overlooked in the case of Filipino Americans.⁴¹

Like other Asian groups, early Filipino male immigrants to the
United States faced barriers erected by antimiscegenation laws, occupational discrimination, and social isolation. Family formation
was also made difficult for Filipinos. During the 1920s and throughout the 1940s, the rate of marriage among Filipino Americans was
quite low given the fourteen to one gender ratio between men and
women. Because the few marriages that did take place between Pi-

noys and Pinays "were not enough to provide a permanent base for Pinoy communities," interracial marriages (often between other minority groups members) were not so infrequent as was the case with other Asian American groups.[42]

In comparison to other Asian American groups, there are surprisingly few Filipino Americans to be found on commercial television programs. Juvenile black belt karate expert Ernie Reyes, Jr., co-starred in the cop drama *Sidekicks* (1986–87) as a ten-year-old orphan named Ernie Lee who helped his unofficial father Sergeant Jake Rizzo (Gil Gerard) solve crimes and beat up criminals. The young martial artist had been given over to Rizzo by the boy's dying grandfather, Sabasan (Keye Luke), who passed on supernatural Asian powers to the junior crime fighter. As in the earlier Asian martial arts-oriented program *Kung Fu* (1972–75), Sabasan would reappear in a flashback whenever his grandson Ernie was in need of help.

Hawaiian-born Tia Carrere was "discovered" at a local market by the parents of a producer, who cast the Filipino American actress in the surprisingly progressive teen-oriented movie *Aloha Summer* (1988). Carrere then appeared for two years on the long-running soap opera *General Hospital* (1963–present) as Jade Soong. In a non-Filipino role, Carrere played Venus Poon, the mistress of Hong Kong drug lord Four Finger Wu (Khigh Deigh) in the four-part miniseries *Noble House* (1988), based on the popular novel by James Clavell. The hit movie *Wayne's World* (1992), directed by Penelope Spheeris, featured Carrere's singing talents and won her enough attention to be named among *People* magazine's "50 Most Beautiful People in the World 1992" (May 4, 1992). The only other Asian included in that list was actress Joan Chen, who played the mysterious Jocelyn "Josie" Packard in David Lynch's *Twin Peaks* (1990–91). In keeping with their collective desexualization, there were no Asian American males included in *People's* list.

The 1965 Immigration and Naturalization Act, which removed national origins quotas that discriminated against Asians, helped pave the way for the dramatic increase of Filipino immigration to the United States. Unlike their forebears prior to World War II, who were largely relegated to agricultural labor, fully two-thirds of recent Filipino immigrants are educated professionals or technical workers. Many have found employment in the health care professions. The chronic shortage of nurses in the United States has provided a key point of entry into the labor market for many Filipino health care workers. However, the entry of physicians, dentists, and pharmacists trained in the Philippines has been restricted by U.S. medical licensing procedures.

The clustering of Filipino American health care workers in inner-city hospitals was depicted in the program *E/R* (1984–85). A sitcom based on a play by the same title, *E/R* featured an ear-nose-and-throat specialist, Dr. Howard Sheinfeld (Elliott Gould), who supplemented his income by moonlighting at the Clark Street Hospital emergency room in Chicago. Filipina Maria Amardo (played by Japanese American actress Shuko Akune) was a no-nonsense individual who liked to read romance novels during lulls in activity, but leapt into action whenever an emergency case arrived at the hospital.[43]

In 1989, Public Broadcasting Service (PBS) affiliates aired *The United States and the Philippines: In Our Image*, a multipart series on the Philippines that provided a moderately critical assessment of the imperial relationship between the United States and its only overseas colony. Through its military, political, and economic control of the Philippines, the United States established the basis for subsequent ill-fated imperial adventures in Asia. The installment titled "Colonial Days" traces the origins of the American presence in this former Spanish possession.[44] What was officially known in the United States as the "Philippine insurrection" was in truth a nationalist revolt led by Emilio Aguinaldo in 1899 against American rule. As Thomas A. Edison filmed battlefield re-creations back home in New Jersey for exhibition to the moviegoing public, the nature and scope of U.S. imperial aggression in the Philippines was effectively hidden.

Foreshadowing the pattern of the U.S.-sponsored genocide practiced in Southeast Asia fifty years later, in "Colonial Days" a Filipina describes in graphic detail how American troops destroyed crops, imprisoned male civilians, and ordered the women to evacuate their homes during the Balangiga massacre of 1901. An estimated 200,000 Filipinos were killed, most of them civilians. Where outright terror and physical force were not enough, approximately 1,000 American schoolteachers were sent to the Philippines to help consolidate the pacification of the newly subdued colony by steeping its future leaders in the history and culture of the oppressor. Thereafter, Filipinos were to be members of an extended family headed by the United States. In the paternalistic phrase coined by the first civilian governor of the Philippines, William Howard Taft, Filipinos would be our "little brown brothers."

The American imperial mission was summarized nicely by General Douglas MacArthur, who justified the "Philippine Defense Act" as appropriate to the creation and preservation of a Christian democratic state modeled after the United States. In the words of MacArthur himself, the purpose of the Defense Act was "to preserve the only Christian state in the Far East. To perpetuate ideals of religious freedom, personal liberty, and republican government which have under American tutelage, flowered here into fruition." MacArthur's vision of a Far Eastern Christian outpost was dimmed after the Japanese invaded and occupied the Philippines while pursuing their own vision of creating a pan-Asian empire.

In the postwar era, the Philippines fell once more under the U.S. sphere of influence. The installment titled "Showcase of Democracy" features a film clip of the returning hero General MacArthur on July 4, 1946, Philippine Independence Day.[45] But it was independence in name only, for the newly amended Filipino Constitution contained a provision for the favored trade status of the United States in exchange for continued "aid." The amended document thus institutionalized the neocolonial relationship between the United States and the Philippines.

The American influence on the Philippines went beyond its political and economic institutions. In "Showcase of Democracy," noted film director Lino Brocka speaks glowingly of the American films he viewed as a youth, films that reflected the heroism and romance of American society and culture at its apex. And as the cultural shadows cast by American films taught Filipinos the superiority of U.S. life, the intelligence community was active in ensuring that attempts at Filipino independence were thwarted. None other than the infamous Colonel Edward Landsdale was sent by the CIA to subdue the communist Huk (Hukbalahap) insurgency against the regime of President Manuel Roxas, a former Japanese collaborator who had been hand-picked by General Douglas MacArthur to lead the country. Roxas, like his successors Ramón Magsaysay and then Ferdinand Marcos, was nothing more than an authoritarian despot who did the bidding of the United States in exchange for massive economic and military support.

Still in power at the time of an on-camera interview, Imelda Marcos explains how her courtly lifestyle confers international prestige to the country and the Filipino people. In speaking of her importation of world-class artists such as Pablo Casals and Rudolph Nureyev to serve as centerpieces at extravagant cultural events, the first lady of the Philippines seems utterly insensitive to plight of her countrymen, most of whom live in dire poverty. Thousands of young women from economically depressed areas such as the Visayas Islands, for example, have sought to assist their families financially by entering the prostitution industry that caters to U.S. military personnel. Home to the U.S. 7th Fleet, Olongapo at Subic Bay has a population of 200,000 who are dependent upon the sex in-

dustry. It is estimated that there are more than 300 R&R establishments in the Philippines that employ between 16,000 and 17,000
women.[46]

The thousands of Filipinos who apply for immigration to the
United States each year are fleeing a society where opportunities for
all but a select few are almost nonexistent. The depressed condition
of the economy, blocked opportunities for the educated middle class,
and political instability have made Filipinos the fastest-growing
Asian American group at present. But perhaps because of their
colonial preadaptation to American society and culture, Christian
and European heritage, Spanish surnames, and competence in the
English language, Filipinos have not yet appeared on television programs to any appreciable degree.

Aloha Spirit

The lives of Pacific American peoples are almost always romanticized on network television. In truth, the indigenous people of Hawai'i are forced to endure the legacy of U.S. colonialism and the ongoing depredations of militarism, nuclear testing, chemical waste
disposal, international tourism, and global capitalist investment patterns that have combined to affect adversely the environment, culture, and health of native Hawaiians. Ever since U.S. troops deposed
the legitimate government of Queen Liliuokalani in a 1893 coup, native Hawaiians have been denied the right of self-determination. In
1898, the annexation of Hawai'i by the United States was orchestrated through the combined efforts of *haole* (white) military, political, religious, and business leaders. A native Hawaiian sovereignty
movement is afoot, however, that seeks compensation for lands
wrongfully annexed by the United States.[47] "By a fragrant mix of
chicanery, legal hocus-pocus and political corruption, this land—
some of it of immense value—has never been distributed to its rightful heirs," writes Alexander Cockburn.[48]

Living in urban and rural slum areas, native Hawaiians occupy
the lower depths of a social order that heavily subsidizes the omnipresent U.S. military and encourages the investment of transnational capital in a one-dimensional tourist economy. As a matter of
survival, native Hawaiians are forced to "live in a hostage economy
where tourist industry employment means active participation in
their own degradation."[49] The "aloha spirit" of love, generosity, and
extended family happiness attributed to the Hawaiian people diverts
attention from the racism that undergirds life in this "island
paradise."

Pacific Americans from Samoa and Guam have also been brought into the global system of capitalism, which has irreparably altered traditional structures of political, economic, and cultural life. Having left their island homes in Guam and American Samoa because of poor economic conditions, Pacific Americans now living on the U.S. mainland face a host of problems associated with nonemployment or underemployment. The loss of status, poverty, questions of identity, and maladjustment to mainland society continue to plague the community of Pacific Islanders.

The lush ancestral lands that were once home to native Hawaiians have been put to service by Euro-American interlopers as a favorite backdrop for a number of television programs. Still running in syndication, *Hawaii Five-O* (1968–80) featured the heroics of Detective Steve McGarrett (Jack Lord), head of the elite state police unit in Honolulu. McGarrett's chief assistant was a younger white man, Detective Danny Williams (James MacArthur). Both were were aided by darker subordinates, most notably Detective Chin Ho Kelly (Kam Fong) and Detective Kono Kalakaua (Zulu).

The *kanakas* (native Hawaiians) and Asians in the cast — Chin Ho, Kono, Che Fong (Harry Endo), and Detective Ben Kokua (Al Harrington) — serve as a Greek chorus to the Euro-American heroes Danny Williams and Steve McGarrett. That is, they advance the dramatic action by posing rhetorical questions or serving as sounding boards to the principal characters. Their utterances give the show a bit of local color by being delivered in "pidgin" English, the language of the colonized. When discussing a large sum of embezzled money, for example, Zulu comments: "That's a lotta fish and *poi*, bruddah."[50] None of the Asian Pacific characters is permitted to make a move unless either McGarrett or his protégé Williams gives the okay. Even when the darker "bruddahs" have performed all the legwork, it is the white prince Williams who is given the honor of jailing the captured criminals, as heard in the stock phrase immortalized by McGarrett: "Book 'em, Danno."[51]

The infantilization of Asian Pacific Islanders on television can be attributed to their subordination within the white-dominated racial hierarchy. "Even those whites who opposed slavery were convinced Hawaiians were like children," write Paul Jacobs and Saul Landau in their documentary analysis of U.S. racial history, "unable to govern themselves or make sensible judgments."[52] In contrast to Pacific Americans, Asian Americans in Hawaii are more often represented as functioning with adult autonomy. In the episode "Killer Bee," for instance, a Chinese American psychiatrist by the name of Dr. Wong figures prominently in a story concerning a mentally disturbed Vietnam veteran on a kidnapping spree.[53] And of course, McGarrett's most formidable nemesis was the Asian criminal mastermind Wo Fat (Khigh Dhiegh).

Hawaii Five-O was replaced by *Magnum, P.I.* (1980–88) in the CBS lineup after a twelve-year run. The elaborate production facilities constructed for *Hawaii Five-O* were used in *Magnum, P.I.*, which "incorporated the rich landscape (both actual and symbolic) of the Hawaiian islands."[54] The lush, exotic backdrop was as much an integral part of the new program as it was for its predecessor. Unlike *Hawaii Five-O*, however, this paradisical setting was almost completely without a recurring nonwhite or indigenous presence such as represented by Chin Ho or Kono. As in *Hawaii Five-O*, the central character was a *haole*. Private investigator Thomas Sullivan Magnum (Tom Selleck) was a Vietnam veteran who had been traumatized by his wartime experiences. Magnum was assisted in his exploits by an African American buddy from the navy, T. C. (Roger E. Mosley). Apart from T. C., a Japanese American police officer, Lieutenant Tanaka (Kwan Hi Lim), would appear on occasion, but for the most part *Magnum, P.I.* marked off this tropical paradise as the exclusive preserve of Euro-Americans.

Big Hawaii (1977) was an ill-fated one-hour adventure program that centered upon a wealthy, autocratic landowner by the name of Barrett Fears (John Dehner). Fears and his children were served by a parallel family of friendly and sympathetic Hawaiian helpers named Kalahani, including "Big Lulu" (Elizabeth Smith), Oscar (Bill Lucking), Garfield (Moe Keale), and Kimo (Remi Abellira). Barrett Fear's rebellious son Mitch (Cliff Potts) often found refuge from his own family in the bosom of the Kalahanis. This mixed relationship echoed the popular theme of nonwhite adults providing a surrogate family for the white child until the time comes when he must assume the mantle of leadership.

In *The MacKenzies of Paradise Cove* (1979), the caretaker function of Pacific Islanders was performed by Big Ben Kalikini (Moe Keale) and his wife Mrs. Kalikini (Leinaala Heine). Along with fishing-boat operator Cuda Weber (Clu Gulager), the Kalikinis were the unofficial guardians of five orphaned white children whose parents died in a sailing accident. Little Ben Kalikini (Sean Tyler Hall) was a friend of the MacKenzie children, at least until they reached adulthood, whereupon they presumably would go their separate ways in conformity with their respective racially determined destinies.

No more successful than *Big Hawaii* were two one-season wonders, *Aloha Paradise* (1981) and *Hawaiian Heat* (1984).[55] A toney Hawaiian resort was the setting for *Aloha Paradise*, where Evelyn Pahinui (Mokihana) tended bar for the exclusively *haole* clientele. The premise of *Hawaiian Heat* devolved upon the culture shock experienced by two transplanted Chicago policemen – Polish American Andy Senkowski (Jeff McCracken) and Irish American Mac Riley (Robert Ginty) – carrying out undercover detective work in the the surf-and-sun setting of Honolulu. Their commanding officer, Major Taro Oshira, played by veteran Japanese American actor Mako, prevented the two cops from overly enjoying their work by keeping a lid on their libidinous tropic appetites.

By the time the medical drama *Island Son* (1989–90) appeared, the paternalistic racism of the white interloper formula had become too obviously outworn. Instead, Richard Chamberlain starred as a medical doctor who left a successful practice on the mainland so that he could be with his adoptive Hawaiian parents and minister to the needs of the natives at Kamehameha Medical Center in Honolulu. Although still the focus of the program, Dr. Daniel Kulani (Chamberlain) worked with an Asian American chief surgeon, Dr. Kenji Fushida (Clyde Kusatsu).

The white man's fascination with the South Pacific perhaps found its most complete expression in the program *Adventures in Paradise* (1959–62). Like many Euro-American males who gained direct experience of U.S. colonial possessions in the Pacific as GIs, Adam Troy (Gardner McKay) was a Korean War veteran who had discovered his personal paradise. He captained his schooner the *Tiki* on chartered trips. At one point in the program, Troy had a Chinese American partner named Oliver Lee (Weaver Levy), but it was Asian Pacific women such as Sondi (Sondi Sodsai, also Miss Thailand of 1960) and Kelly (Lani Kai) who saw to the needs of their white master. *Adventures in Paradise* was created by the bard of Asian Pacific exoticism himself, author James A. Michener.

Warner Bros. Television had a hit in its detective drama *77 Sunset Strip* (1958–64) and applied the formula to *Hawaiian Eye* (1959–63), only this time using Honolulu instead of West Hollywood as the glamorous setting for the show. The program featured two detectives – Tom Lopaka (Robert Conrad) and Tracy Steele (Anthony Eisley) – as partners at a detective agency they operated out of a plush hotel. The popular Hawaiian entertainer Poncie Ponce played a happy-go-lucky taxi cab driver named Kazuo Kim, who would often lend his good-natured assistance to the detectives. Poncie Ponce's pidgin English, a material reminder of colonial subjectivity, was a continual source of amusement to his social superiors.

In late 1991, a national audience received unexpected exposure to the grievances of Pacific Americans during a special ninety-minute edition of *ABC News Nightline* (1980–present). Broadcast on the eve of the fiftieth anniversary of the Japanese attack on Pearl Harbor, a "trans-Pacific town meeting" is opened by host Ted Koppel with the stated intention of bringing "together people who are worlds apart."[56] Reporting from the NHK Studio Broadcast Center in Tokyo, Japan, Koppel observes how the open hostility of Americans against their former World War II foe has been interpreted by the Japanese as "an unfair, unreasonable, even racist reaction." Koppel asks rhetorically whether Japan also might be accused of being a "racist nation" itself, in light of unflattering commments made about African Americans and Hispanics by Japanese officials.

But in one of those rare "television moments" that sometimes slip through the network *cordon sanitaire* during live broadcasts, native Hawaiian activist Haunani-Kay Trask gets right to the heart of the matter. Via a satellite link with Hawaii, Trask questions a panel of Japanese public relations flak-catchers about the displacement of native Hawaiians by the international tourist industry led by Japan. Because Trask's statement is so at odds with network standards of "objectivity," it bears quoting at length:

> Given that Japan is now an economic superpower in the Pacific Islands and that your effort to colonize the Pacific Islands through golf courses and through resorts is now dispossessing the native peoples of the Pacific Islands—and I refer of course to my own people, native Hawaiians, but also to Chamorros, and to Fijians, and to Tahitians . . . what is your moral responsibility to the native people on the Pacific Islands that you are evicting from their lands, their farmlands, when you come here to put up golf courses and resorts?

Once they recover from the initial shock of the blunt forcefulness of the question, the panelists agree that business decisions made by Japanese corporations should be made in consultation with local governments with an eye toward avoiding such problems. Koji Watanabe, deputy minister for foreign affairs, is quick to invoke the standard argument that business investment "creates employment" in the local economy. But the stock answers given by the Japanese panelists skirt the fundamental problem: they do nothing to acknowledge that the ruination of indigenous Hawaiian culture and society has been accelerated by the patterns of Japanese corporate investment.

"Deep Kim Chee"

In 1950, under the pretext of containing the spread of communism throughout Asia, the United States committed itself to war in Korea. A National Security Council document designated NSC-68 inadvertently released in 1975 revealed that the expansion of the military was calculated to revitalize a flagging postwar economy. According to former CIA operative Philip Agee, during the five-year period following the end of World War II, the gross national product of the United States had declined 20 percent and employment had risen to 4.7 million, up from 700,000.[57] There was serious concern among the corporate and government elite that the economy would sink back to the level of the Depression years if drastic action was not taken.

The Korean conflict was manufactured by the Truman administration to convince Congress and the public of the necessity of a permanent war economy. The war, however, proved costly for those who were killed, wounded, orphaned, or displaced. By the time an armistice was negotiated in July 1953, 34,000 U.S. soldiers had been killed in action, and another 100,000 wounded. More than a million Koreans died in the war, and much of the civilian population of South Korea suffered severe dislocation. As seen in the PBS television documentary *Homes Apart: The Two Koreas* (1991), the Cold War division of the country has taken an enormous personal toll on those who have been separated from family members for decades.[58] Even today, 700,000 North Korean, 600,000 South Korean, and 45,000 U.S. troops are under arms. Rear Admiral Gene Larocque of the Center for Defense Information adds that the U.S. has a "sizable number" of nuclear weapons stockpiled in one of the most heavily fortified regions of the world.

In the aftermath of the Korean War, Christian missionaries representing a variety of denominations found the country ripe for religious conversion. Humanitarian relief efforts and the rescue of children orphaned by the war pitted Christianity against "godless communism." As a seemingly supraideological symbol, the Korean War Orphan became a useful means of filling the coffers of various Christian evangelical organizations by gaining the sympathy of childless couples and the larger public in the United States. For a time, various church and secular relief organizations did a brisk business in the Korean War orphan trade.

The U.S. military role in South Korea has played a decisive role in shaping Korean American life in other fundamental ways. Between 1962 and 1983, 85,000 Korean women emigrated to the United States, many of them as brides of American GIs. During the same period, 50,000 children—many of them "Amerasian"—were adopted by Americans. These subgroups helped form links in the the kin-based chain of migration between South Korea and the United States in the postwar period.[59] As a junior military and economic partner of the United States in East Asia, South Korea has been one of the chief contributors of Asian immigrants to the United States since 1965.

The Korean War was the backdrop for the popular series *M∗A∗S∗H* (1972–83). The Korean War lasted three years, but *M∗A∗S∗H* ran for a full eleven seasons, eight years longer than the conflict itself. Based on the film directed by Robert Altman (1970), the television version retained much of the cynical, black humor of its cinematic predecessor, owing to the combined talents of producers Gene Reynolds and Larry Gelbart.

Although set in wartime Korea, the film was implicitly understood as a condemnation of American military involvement in Vietnam. In the TV spin-off, however, the allusive connection to the war in Vietnam was so weak as to be almost absent. The program featured a crew of manic medical personnel locked in a valiant but losing battle to save human lives under less-than-ideal conditions. Brilliant writing boasting scintillating repartee, combined with an exceptionally talented ensemble of actors, elevated *M∗A∗S∗H* above most other network television programs of the time. But by universalizing war and reducing it to an abstraction, the program evaded the reality of Vietnam while salving the angst of the era with its darkly humorous comedic hijinks.

Although *M∗A∗S∗H* was set in Ouijonbu, South Korea, there were few Asians or Asian Americans in evidence. Apart from the occasional walk-on who served as a visual reminder that this was after all a war being fought in Asia, the only recurring Asian American character in the program was a nurse named Kellye (Kellye Nakahara) and even she played a minor role, window dressing really. During the first season only, a Korean national named Ho-Jon (Patrick Adiarte) worked as Hawkeye's (Alan Alda) well-spoken houseboy. Ho-Jon left for the United States after the ever-resourceful Hawkeye arranged for him to attend medical school with funds raised through a raffle.[60] The theme of the white patron serving as sponsor to a promising nonwhite subordinate is not uncommon in American popular culture. Similar story lines invoking this particular manifestation of white paternalist power relationships are found in more than a few programs surveyed in these pages.

Yet another episode of *M∗A∗S∗H* dramatizes the Asian penchant for pimping one of their *own kind*.[61] Hawkeye, again cast as the world-weary liberal humanist intercessor, wins a Korean "moose" (GI slang for female servant) in a poker game to gain her freedom from an exploitative, racist ("The gooks; they don't mind working") enlisted man, Sergeant Baker (Paul Jenkins).[62] The sergeant had bought the "moose" Young Hi (Virginia Lee) from her *own family* for $500. "Some of the locals sell their children for the money, Hawkeye," native informant Ho-Jon explains. "They have no other means." Once Young Hi has been freed, the "head of the household" comes to reclaim her. To everyone's surprise, the family head is Young Hi's hustling, tough-talking younger brother Benny (Craig Jue), who is not yet in his teens. After Hawkeye snatches a cigarette from the boy's mouth, Benny announces his intention to resell Young Hi for up to three times her original price because she has gained valuable experience since first being sold into servitude. But thanks to coaching by Hawkeye and Trapper John (Wayne Rogers) concerning the exercise of individual rights versus familial obligation, Young Hi tells her pimp/brother to "shove off." Young Hi then promptly fixes martinis for her Yankee liberators to toast her newly won independence. Having been freed from bondage, Young Hi later writes to Hawkeye to tell him that she is now attending a convent school in Seoul, training to work as a nurse's aide.

In the final season of M*A*S*H, Soon-Lee (Rosalind Chao) was written into the show as a love object for the ever-malingering Corporal Maxwell Klinger (Jamie Farr). Even the goldbricking corporal was entitled to the spoils of war in the person of a docile Asian bride. The love relationship between Klinger and Soon-Lee was spun-off into the pathetic sitcom *AfterMASH* (1983–84). The program focused on the postwar lives of Klinger, Dr. Sherman Potter (Harry Morgan), and Father Francis Mulcahy (William Christopher), all veterans of the 4077th Mobile Army Surgical Hospital and now working together at a Veterans Administration hospital. In addition to the problem of readjusting to civilian life, Klinger and his war bride Soon-Lee were faced with the omnipresent reality of racism American-style.

In the episode "Klinger vs. Klinger," a patient at the V.A. hospital named McGee spies Soon-Lee bringing her husband his lunch and remarks, "You really are an operator, Klinger. You even got a little gook waiting on you hand and foot."[63] After Soon-Lee runs away, holding back tears, a surprised McGee says, "Boy, are they touchy." Klinger angrily informs McGee that Soon-Lee is his wife and berates the insensitive patient. "You know what that kid has been through? You have any idea?" demands Klinger. "Did *you* give up your country, your family, your home, everything, to marry some guy who's got nothing to his name but the discharge paper it's written on?"

After their encounter with garden-variety racism, Klinger and Soon-Lee are brought even closer together as a couple. Prior to the exchange with McGee at the hospital, they had been arguing over Soon-Lee's wish to have her family join them in the United States. Klinger had also opposed her desire to get an outside job to help support the expanded household. Individual acts of anti-Asian racism notwithstanding, Soon-Lee remains convinced that the future of her family lies "in this wonderful country where even the clams are happy."

A celebratory dinner at the Potter home is the occasion for cross-cultural exchange and reconciliation in an episode of *AfterMASH* titled "Thanksgiving of '58."[64] As Mildred Potter (Barbara Townsend) and Soon-Lee prepare food for the feast, the two have a discussion that confirms the commonly held notion that Asians enjoy dog meat as a source of nutrition. Soon-Lee expresses her amazement at the sheer quantity of food at the table. "Back in Korea," says Soon-Lee, "sometimes we were lucky to have a little dog with our rice." Mildred is aghast at the very thought of eating a "pet." She asks her husband Sherman whether he himself had sampled the forbidden flesh. "The locals would have the occasional Rover ragout," the doctor replies, "but we never saw any." Then follows the carefully scripted humor that defuses the racist purport of the discussion: " 'Course if the U.S. Army served it, it would have been powdered dog." The Euro-American abhorrence of dog meat is set off against the resistance of Klinger's parents to their new Asian daughter-in-law. However, by the end of the episode the Klingers have dispensed with their prejudice against Soon-Lee, and the assembled guests sit at a common table to give thanks.

There are a number of operations taking place in this mercifully short-lived situation comedy that allow it to disparage Asian Americans even as it conveys seemingly generous liberal pieties. For one, by setting *AfterMASH* in the 1950s past, the writers are able to circumvent cunningly the problem of casting negative aspersions upon recent immigrant groups (usually identified as Cambodian or Vietnamese) who supposedly hunger for the taste of dog meat. During the early 1980s, in areas of Orange County, California, where there were high concentrations of newly arrived Southeast Asian refugees, bumper stickers urging whites to "Save a Dog, Shoot a Gook" were not an uncommon sight.

Second, Soon-Lee conforms to what has become by now a familiar social type: the Asian War Bride. The Asian War Bride is the ideal companion or wife to white American males who prefer "traditional" women untainted by such quaint notions as gender equality. In recent years, perhaps in response to conservative male backlash against the advances of the women's movement over the past twenty years, there have been any number of "dating" and marriage services that promise to deliver compliant overseas Asian women to men in search of alternatives to native-born Americans who might have been exposed to the virus of feminism.

Finally, although the writers attempt to salvage Soon-Lee's dignity in "Klinger vs. Klinger" by having McGee appear foolish and ignorant, they have simply replicated the controlling image of the Asian "mama-san" and pressed her into domestic service for the benefit of Maxwell Klinger, a loser to any potential spouse but an impoverished Korean immigrant woman. By the standards of the dominant WASP society, the Lebanese American former GI is just another swarthy ethnic only slightly more acceptable than a non-white individual. But by the standards of a desperate Korean war bride, Klinger is a heroic American savior.

In sum, *AfterMASH*, like its parent program $M*A*S*H$, exploits the historical experience of Asians (as in the case of Soon-Lee Klinger) caught in the vise of American militarism by implying that their lives actually have been bettered by the invasion, occupation, and destruction of their native countries. After all, so it might be rationalized, if it were not for the war Soon-Lee Klinger would still be back in Korea, foraging for a little dog meat to eat with her bowl of rice rather than enjoying the bounty of the American way of life.

America's Vietnam

It is estimated that one million ARVN (Army of the Republic of Vietnam) soldiers were killed during the war in Vietnam. An equal number of Viet Cong and North Vietnamese regulars were killed as well. The civilian death toll is thought to be as high as 3.5 million. In addition, millions of acres—much of it precious agricultural land—were rendered unusable as the result of an aggressive defoliation campaign carried out by the United States through its RANCH HAND program.[65] During the course of "technowar" waged against a peasant society, the United States dropped more bombs on Vietnam than it did on Europe during all of World War II.[66] In staging the largest air war in history, the United States destroyed the hundreds of towns, villages, roads, and bridges that formed the infrastructure of Vietnamese society. The devastation was so complete that since 1975, more than one million Southeast Asians have been forced to leave their homeland.[67]

The social chaos and desperately harsh living conditions caused by years of U.S. military adventurism in Southeast Asia precipitated the largest movement of refugees in recent history. The U.S. Bureau of the Census reported that by 1980, 245,025 Vietnamese, 52,887

Laotians (including Hmong), and 16,044 Cambodians had found their way to the United States. Within less than a decade the U.S. population of Vietnamese increased to 679,378; the number of Laotians reached 256,727, and Cambodians 210,724.[68]

In a poignant reminiscence that appeared in *The Nation* late in 1990, Vietnamese American journalist Andrew Lam made mention of an uncle who complains, "When Americans say Vietnam, they don't mean Vietnam." His uncle was pointing out the fact that for most Americans, Vietnam exists only as a metaphor for an array of indefinable social ills and cultural malaise. Its complex history, intertwined as it has been with that of the United States, is lost in the miasma of current problems, both domestic and foreign. The concrete, historical Vietnam as the lost homeland of refugees now living in the United States does not register in the minds of most Americans. In the popular memory, Vietnam is little more than the "damn little pissant country" (Lyndon Johnson) that brought the American colossus to its knees. Who can forget the media images of little yellow men and women in black "pajamas," wielding vintage World War II rifles, holding their physically imposing captured foes at gunpoint? But mostly, we prefer to suppress the memory of this nation's most protracted and costly war. "Vietnam, in effect," wrote Lam, "has become a vault filled with tragic metaphors for every American to use."[69]

But popular memory, aided and abetted by the distortions of mass-mediated revisionist history in the form of television news and entertainment, cannot deny that U.S. involvement in Vietnam transformed a formerly prosperous and self-sufficient agricultural region into an impoverished country that is no longer capable of supporting its population without outside assistance. To punish Vietnam for having won the war against imperialism, the United States until recently blocked actions that would allow the devastated country to rebuild. Not only has the United States enforced a trade embargo on Vietnam since 1978, American leaders have had a hand in ensuring that humanitarian aid, food, medicine, and agricultural equipment not find its way into the country. The United States has also wielded its influence to prevent the World Bank and the International Development Fund from extending loans that would allow for the reconstruction of Vietnam. Pressure applied to U.S. allies has "kept their financial aid at a minimum and in some cases eliminated it altogether."[70]

In an updating of the "model minority" thesis, refugees from Southeast Asia have been heralded as the latest immigrant success story. James M. Fallows, for example, lavishes praise upon the Asian

American entrepreneurial family by charting the economic rise of a Vietnamese immigrant, Nguyen Dong (a pseudonym).[71] After first working for minimum wage at an El Segundo, California, waterbed factory, within ten years Nguyen had improved the financial status of his large family to the point where they now own two homes, a furniture store, and a beauty salon located in chic Beverly Hills.

Such selectively flattering portrayals of successful Southeast Asian refugee families belie the truth that half of the Vietnamese who live in California receive some form of public assistance.[72] Further, unlike other Asian American groups, Vietnamese Americans have a high percentage (14.2 percent) of households headed by women, with only 74.1 percent of Vietnamese children living with both parents.[73] And of course households headed by women (particularly those headed by nonwhite immigrant women with limited job training and communication skills) are more likely to be plagued by poverty.

Vietnamese American portrayals on network television have been slow in coming. Other than random appearances on various and sundry programs, only the Fox network's teen-oriented cop show *21 Jump Street* (1987–90) and the sitcom *Down Home* (1990–91) regularly featured Vietnamese American characters. Among a group of four young undercover cops in *21 Jump Street* was an Asian American named Harry Truman "H.T." Ioki (Dustin Nguyen). Interestingly, Ioki occupied a role substantially more than that of the traditional Asian American sidekick, the all-purpose helper to his white superiors. Even so, it was obvious that Officer Tom Hanson (Johnny Depp) was being positioned as the principal television teen idol. Johnny Depp's appeal for teenage American girls was such that he moved quickly into a movie career, starring in John Waters's *Cry-Baby* (1990) and Tim Burton's *Edward Scissorhands* (1990) in rapid succession.

A new cop named Dennis Booker (Richard Grieco) joined the young crime busters in the program's second season, and Grieco also became a teen idol in short time. Richard Grieco in turn moved into the *21 Jump Street* spin-off *Booker* (1989–90). H. T. Ioki eventually disappeared from the show, but not before revealing in one episode that he was not Japanese American but Vietnamese American! He had adopted the more acceptable Ioki identity to bury the painful memory of his past and begin life anew in the United States.

Vietnamese American actor Dustin Nguyen scored a coup of sorts in an ABC movie titled *Earth Angel* (1991).[74] In this made-for-television fantasy, a ghost from the high school class of '62 returns from the dead to help her mortal friends in matters of the heart. Peter Joy (Nguyen), a "geek" who works at a pet shop, wins the affection of the cute and popular Cindy Boyd (Rainbow Harvest). Cindy had been wooed by a macho jock named Mike (Brian Krause), but in the end asks Peter to attend the big prom with her. In a scene that violates the TV taboo against an Asian male having intimate physical contact with a white female, Peter Joy is shown kissing Cindy Boyd. As they dance cheek-to-cheek, Cindy's heavenly guardian Angela (Cathy Podewell) watches approvingly from the clouds above.

Perhaps because the movie is so obviously a fantasy, the interracial contact is deemed palatable. And because the nerdy Peter Joy is a "geek," he poses less of a sexual threat to white manhood, although his name hints otherwise. Indeed, it is a bashing that Peter receives at the hands of bully Mike that earns him the sympathy and loving affection of Cindy. In a television environment wherein only white males can choose freely among nonwhite females as sex partners, *Earth Angel* is noteworthy for its depiction of a romantic relationship between an Asian man and a Euro-American woman.

In *Down Home*, Tran Van Din (Gedde Watanabe) works as chief cook and bottle washer in a cafe on McCrorey's Landing, located on the Gulf Coast of Texas. Watanabe once more plays the dingy, madcap Asian, a role that he has virtually defined, beginning with the film *Sixteen Candles* (1984) and later in the sitcom *Gung Ho* (1986–87).[75] Kate McCrorey (Judith Ivey) is a former big-city executive who has returned home to help out with the family business, and it is she who serves as ringmaster for a three-ring circus of wisecracking layabouts. Tran functions as little more than a buffoon in this abysmally fatuous situation comedy. In one scene, Tran dresses in a grass skirt, cowboy boots, and a coconut-shell bra for a going-away party.[76]

A separate episode has Tran protecting his visiting sister Trini (Kimiko Gelman) from the amorous intentions of Drew McCrorey (Eric Allan Kramer).[77] Tran's overprotectiveness of his sister's virtue is generalized to include all men, who are assumed to be sexual predators. In an otherwise silly and uninspiring episode, Tran's latent prejudice against a white man dating his Asian sister supplies the serious subtext. It proves to be much ado about nothing, however. It is actually Drew whom Tran wants to protect, for the Vietnamese cook had mistakenly understood that his sister works in a "whorehouse" instead of a "warehouse."

In the episode described above, the specter of so-called reverse prejudice appears when it seems that Tran might be keeping his convent-educated sister Trini from Drew simply because he is white. This subtle twist of logic allows the majority fair-weather liberal viewer to indulge in the fantasy that minorities are equally guilty of racist attitudes and discriminatory behavior. But this exercise in liberal guilt relief has no basis in fact, given that immigrant Vietnamese fishermen, crabbers, and shrimpers working on the Gulf Coast of Texas have been met with vicious racial hostility. In certain instances, Vietnamese Americans have been subject to outright racist attacks. In 1979, for example, a well-known incident took place in Seadrift, Texas, that resulted in the shooting death of a white fisherman. In retaliation, three Vietnamese vessels were burned, a home firebombed, and the attempted bombing of a local packing plant forced most of its Vietnamese American employees to leave town. The Ku Klux Klan became involved after the Vietnamese American crabbers accused of the shooting were acquitted of the charge.[78]

In keeping with the inherent liberal pluralist ideology of most network TV programs, that the McCroreys would employ a Vietnamese immigrant at all implies that diverse groups have been admitted and settled into American society with little problem. But as the many documented clashes between Vietnamese Americans and whites reveal, a consistent pattern of racial hostility shatters the liberal mythology of a program such as *Down Home*. In creating the inane Tran Van Din character and placing him in a Texas Gulf Coast setting, the producers and writers of *Down Home* exploit actually existing racial violence, revise its implications, and deflect it into innocuous comedy. Thus the historically complete and accurate Euro-American (often violent) response to economic competition with Vietnamese immigrants is occluded through harmless entertainment.

Sweet and Sour Success

The historical record reveals that the dominant society and its institutions have exerted extraordinary destabilizing pressures against the diverse Asian Pacific American communities. Such chronic destabilization is often masked by an outward show of normalcy, adjustment, and adaptation among community members. Contrary to the myth of Asian American hypernormality and psychosocial adjustment, racial prejudice and social discrimination take a measurable toll on Asian and Pacific Americans.[79] History gives the lie to romanticized attempts by liberal and neoconservative commentators to herald the presumptive triumph of Asian Americans. Such revisionist tales do not square with the lived experience of Asian American peoples, who have confronted all manner of hostile challenges to their collective presence within U.S. society. Deracination and insecurity, not stability, characterize many Asian American communities.

Despite the best efforts of white supremacist institutions to stymie the social ascent of Asian Americans, the data show that a large percentage of this diverse population has attained middle-class status. A select few have even entered upper-level management within major U.S. corporations. Yet by other indices, such as wages and career advancement, Asian Americans lag behind their white counterparts with equivalent years of education and experience. As Margaret Fung of the Asian American Legal Defense and Education Fund observes, "We hear the same grievances again and again—that they come in at entry-level jobs, but the white employees hired at the same time have received promotions while they remain in technical or low managerial positions."[80]

Asian Americans, then, are both beneficiaries and "victims" of the system of abstract rewards, benefits, and opportunities that defines the United States as a democratic, pluralist, "open" society. It is the function of network television sociodrama to mediate symbolically the contradiction between the promise and the reality of American liberal democracy. Images of control are used as an iconic shorthand to explain, justify, and naturalize the subordination of Asian Americans within a society that espouses formal equality for all. Network television can never come close to representing the full depth and scope of Asian American life, because to do so would be to expose disturbing core truths about America itself.

Chapter 2

Asians in the American West

Eastward Ho

In the written history of the American republic, the often invoked phrase *the Westward movement* is fraught with deceptively benign meaning. It connotes a sense of historical inevitability, the realization of a higher destiny by the Euro-American executors of divine will. The phrase effectively masks the human and ecological depredation committed by "explorers," "adventurers," and "settlers," who, viewed through the eyes of the vanquished, might less sympathetically be considered brigands, pirates, and squatters.

The romantic concept of the Westward movement also obscures the central role played by Asian immigrants in the building of the American nation. In the parlance of the contemporary debate over university curricula, the very notion of the Westward movement is loaded with "Eurocentric" assumptions. Within recent years, scholarship in history and the social sciences has done much to correct the conventional assumption that the social wealth of the United States was the product of the special genius possessed by Euro-American forefathers. Rather, the explanatory focus has shifted to the crucial part played by the international recruitment of labor to core capitalist areas in the development of the U.S. economy.[1] Moreover, developments within the field of Asian American studies have stressed the centrality of immigration from Asia to the United States and its relationship to a capitalist world system whereby the "peasantry of less developed societies is encouraged, induced, or coerced to enter the orbit of the capitalist mode of production."[2]

It is estimated that 2.5 million Chinese left their homeland as part of the international migration of labor, a large-scale movement that constituted an "integral part of Western economic development and imperialist expansion."[3] The overwhelming majority of those immigrants who came to the United States were men. Unlike their Eu-

32

ropean immigrant counterparts, who formed an industrial-based proletariat, nineteenth-century Chinese laborers worked primarily in agriculture and mining. The imbalance in sex ratio was in part caused by Chinese tradition, which dictated that the female spouse remain behind in China with the main family. In addition, discriminatory labor practices, restrictive legislation, and immigration laws directed against Asians prevented the formation of "traditional" families. For example, the Page Law, passed by the U.S. Congress in 1875, severely restricted the number of female Chinese immigrants who could enter the country.[4] In 1882, the Chinese Exclusion Law imposed a comprehensive ban, which further impeded the process of family formation. It was this imbalance in sex ratio favoring male immigrants that gave rise to the "bachelor society" of early Chinese laborers in the United States.

Liberal Bonanza

The television Western enjoyed enormous popularity from the mid-1950s to mid-1960s. Among the many television "adult Westerns," as historian J. Fred MacDonald has described them, *Bonanza* (1959–73) rated highly among viewers who had outgrown the simplistic heroics of the genre in its earlier stage of development. MacDonald observes that the bedrock humanistic values of the show were enshrined in a domestic, family setting. "If in concept the family was the primary social unit of mutual support and shared love," writes MacDonald, "*Bonanza* accentuated the fact that even in times of great challenge, humane interests were critical to lasting, effective social values."[5] More specifically, the "effective social values" found in *Bonanza* were of the prevailing liberal democratic sort.

During the broadcast seasons spanning 1961 through 1970, *Bonanza* was among the five top-rated programs, according to Nielsen surveys. For three years straight, from 1964 through 1966, *Bonanza* was rated as the number-one program. It is no small coincidence that the years of the program's popularity reflected the political idealism and sense of expansive possibility associated with the Kennedy-Johnson years, for the social values that MacDonald alludes to were, specifically, those of Great Society liberalism. In this vision of frontier community, the stern but fair patriarch of the Ponderosa, Ben Cartwright (Lorne Greene), presided over an all-male household save for Hop Sing (Victor Sen Yung). The Chinese bachelor houseboy fulfilled certain female/domestic functions such as cooking and cleaning for Adam (Pernell Roberts), Hoss (Dan Blocker), and the baby of the family, Little Joe (Michael Landon). As in the Great Society, Hop Sing inhabited the same social space as his benefactors by being allowed to live under the same roof as the Cartwrights, but never was he permitted to sit at their table.

As stated above, *Bonanza* was in step with the values of Great Society liberalism. Virginia City was the archetypal liberal pluralist society transported back in time, a society that celebrated ethnic and racial diversity while being condemnatory of bigotry. It was an imperfect society, to be sure, but one that could be made better by piecemeal reform rather than through radical transformation. As liberals acting in good faith, the Cartwrights assumed collective responsibility for helping maintain an orderly world that accepted all those who wished to make a positive contribution to society, whether one was Asian, Mexican, Indian, or white. The Cartwrights would sympathize with the doomed Yaqui Indian named Amigo (Henry Darrow) who said, before succumbing to the laws of white civilization, that every man has the "right to live, be free, respected."[6] After failing to save the outlaw Amigo from self-destruction, Ben Cartwright offered a Great Society eulogy to the dead Indian in that voice-of-God baritone for which actor Lorne Greene was noted: "A man can do an awful lot of good with his life . . . if he has an even chance. Amigo never had the chance."

Brothers under the Skin

The principle of ethnic pluralism as a model of intergroup relations within American society is well illustrated in an episode of *Bonanza* titled "A Christmas Story."[7] The episode features Wayne Newton as Andy Walker, a young singer who has returned home to Virginia City for a visit after having attained success in the world of entertainment. In one particularly telling scene, Newton sings at a Christmas party held for a group of orphaned children. As Newton croons in that oddly androgynous voice that later made him a top-grossing marquee attraction in Las Vegas, the children—Mexican, Native American, Asian, and white—are shown basking in the warm glow of fellow feeling commonly associated with the Christmas holidays. So that the viewer does not miss the point, each child represents his or her respective group by being clothed in ethnically specific attire. There is no hint of how the diverse children became orphans in the first place. And with the exception of Hop Sing, who is seen waddling about serving hors d'oeuvres to guests, the adults in attendance do not reflect the ethnic diversity of the assembled children. Perhaps even in the Great Society presided over by the benevolent Cartwright (Kennedy?) clan, an implicit white paternalism was the order of the day.

The Cartwrights' abiding commitment to Great Society liberalism is also seen in the episode "The Fear Merchants."[8] Unlike most television Westerns, where minorities usually occupy subordinate or peripheral roles, this episode delves somewhat deeply into the lives of Hop Sing and his extended family. The Chinese American characters are shown as being ambivalent about their place in the unique social experiment that is America. Hop Sing's uncle, Lee Chang (Philip Ahn), expresses gratitude for witnessing the difficult birth of a new nation, but his nephew is not so sanguine. "Not many men are so privileged as we are," enthuses Lee Chang, "to see a new civilization born before our own eyes." But Hop Sing witholds praise, stating, "There are times in the streets of Virginia City when I question the use of the word *civilization*." But Lee Chang, the voice of liberal accommodationism, counters by saying, "It is always that way with the new, Hop Sing. A diamond, before it is polished, seems no more than a clod of dirt."

Hop Sing's reservations regarding American civilization are borne out when he is jumped by thugs almost immediately after his visit with Lee Chang. It is soon discovered that the assailants are henchmen for an attorney named Andrew Fulmer (Gene Evans), who is running for mayor of Virginia City on a nativist, anti-Chinese campaign platform. "Virginia City for Virginia City," reads one of Fulmer's campaign signs.

Ben Cartwright is justifiably upset by Hop Sing's beating, but Hoss asks whether the assault might be linked to their servant's possible involvement in "one of those *tongs* we've been hearing about." But Ben patiently explains to his simpleminded son that a *tong* (literally, "hall" or "gathering place") is no more than a "protective association," as he describes it. Hoss is the physical, impulsive, childlike member of the Cartwright household, and he immediately wants revenge for Hop Sing's beating. But Adam, the eldest Cartwright son and the voice of reason and liberal moderation, warns against retribution. Retaliation would mean only more problems for the Chinese of Virginia City.

When Ben travels into town to confront Fulmer about Hop Sing's bashing, the mayoral candidate rails against "outsiders" who are threatening the livelihood of white men. Ben asks Fulmer what he means by his targeting "outsiders." "It means our town's being overrun by foreigners who are willing to work for nothing," responds Fulmer. "And they're taking the bread and butter out of the mouth of folks like us who built this country." But Ben is not satisfied with Fulmer's mealymouthed response and challenges the barely concealed anti-Chinese racism of the attorney's campaign. "By 'foreigner' Andy," he asks, "who do you mean? The Irish? The Welsh? Or . . . the Chinese?"

The specter of racial fear in its worst possible form rears its ugly head when Lee Chang's son Jimmy is falsely accused of raping and murdering a white woman, Sally Hammond. His accuser and father of the victim, Cyrus Hammond, had earlier refused to sell Lee Chang eighteen miniature American flags that were to be placed on his son's birthday cake. Lee Chang had hoped to give his assimilated, college-bound son an "American birthday party" complete with a cake adorned with the stars and stripes. But Hammond, a key supporter of Fulmer's anti-Chinese crusade, would not permit Lee Chang the privilege of paying homage to Old Glory on the day Jimmy attained his majority.

As Jimmy Chang sits in the jail cell where the sheriff has locked him up "for his own protection," Lee Chang asks a Chinese elder to have the *tong* come to the young man's defense. But the elder denies the father's request, asserting that Jimmy had forsaken the Chinese American community by adopting the dress and customs of the dominant society. Lee Chang, however, remains committed to his vision of a "great society" that will one day include even Chinese Americans. "He is ambitious," says Lee Chang in defense of his son. "He desires to educate himself in this new land. He knows that one day, the Chinese will take their place alongside other people who have come from many other places to make this a great country." The elder remains unmoved, however. He is unwilling to sacrifice the welfare of the entire Chinese American community for the sake of one who has strayed too far from traditional ways.

The murder of a white woman by a man of color touches a raw nerve among the people of Virginia City, who are driven into a frenzy of racial hatred. Andrew Fulmer tries to capitalize on the incident and then incites a group of merchants to vigilantism by exclaiming, "We let that Chinaman get away with killing that white girl, it's just the same as saying we don't even care what happens to our own wives and daughters."

Fortunately for Jimmy Chang, the Cartwrights are able to protect him from a lynch mob until his innocence is established. In a kinky psychosexual complication, the murdered woman's younger sister Amanda reveals that it was actually Cyrus Hammond who had shot and killed Sally. The moralistic shopkeeper had murdered Sally out of shame for her past sexual indiscretions and placed the blame on the innocent Jimmy Chang. At this revelation, the townspeople are seen turning away from the racist demagoguery of Andrew Fulmer.

Although this episode of *Bonanza* explicitly repudiates racism, it nevertheless dramatizes a central fact of Asian American life: so long as the Asian American remains subordinated and infantilized, he is tolerated by the dominant society. Once he becomes a direct economic competitor, however, the Asian American is liable to be targeted for racist hate and persecution. In the matter of Jimmy Chang, no sooner does the ambitious young man reach adulthood than he is falsely accused of both murder and a sex crime against white womanhood, for the dread of Asian American male sexuality is linked to unequal power relations in society. Just as he is poised to fulfill his father's vision of a grandly pluralist American future, Jimmy Chang's ascent is blocked by the white-dominated political order that uses racial identity as a means of enforcing inequality in capitalist society.

Mutilated Family

In contrast to the virulent anti-Chinese sentiment dramatized in "The Fear Merchants," historian George M. Blackburn and sociologist Sherman L. Ricards depict a much more hospitable environment in an article on the Chinese residents of the real 1870s Virginia City, Nevada.[9] Indeed, the authors are struck by the "comparative lack of violence and the absence of strident calls for expulsion."[10] For Blackburn and Ricards, the relative lack of hostility against the Chinese of Virginia City could be accounted for by the small size of the community in comparison to the total population and their concentration in menial but necessary occupations.

At the same time, after sifting through extensive census records and personal accounts, Blackburn and Ricards report that the Chinese of Virginia City were predominantly male, segregated residentially, barred from better-paying mining jobs by labor union edict, and relegated to performing poorly compensated "women's work." In choosing to emphasize the relative tolerance toward the Chinese residents of Virginia City on the part of the dominant society, the authors incorrectly allow for the interpretation that a certain level of social oppression was livable. They review demographic data concerning the imbalance in the sex ratio, but they utterly ignore the importance of racism in the creation and perpetuation of what Morrison G. Wong has termed "mutilated" or "split households."

In contrast to the generous argument advanced by Blackburn and Ricards, Wong observes that one of the direct consequences of the imbalance in sex ratio was the "formation of the 'mutilated,' or 'split household,' family structure and the subsequent perpetuation of this Chinese family type by various racist and exclusionist immigration laws."[11] To be sure, the prevalence of the split household among

Chinese immigrants – whereby wives and children remained in China while men labored abroad – was in part a result of long-standing cultural convention. Nevertheless, it is clear that the system of exclusion, both formal and informal, ensured that family formation among Chinese American immigrants was held in abeyance for many decades subsequent to their first arrival. Characters in television Westerns such as Hop Sing are material reminders of Chinese "bachelor society."

In the jargon of the contemporary "recovery" movement, which offers therapeutic approaches to the ingrained problems of capitalist society, the Chinese American family in its early form might be considered "dysfunctional." Examples of early Chinese American families constituted along neolocal lines are rare indeed. Yet there is scant mention of these shallow roots of the Chinese American family when contemporary liberal apologists point to that selfsame institution as the key to the "success" of this group in more recent times.

The Chinese American family is very much a product of concrete historical and sociopolitical forces. If the income and educational profile of the contemporary Chinese Americans tends to be higher that of Euro-Americans, then reasons other than putative "family values" must be adduced. For one, more individual members within the typical Chinese American family contribute to the household economy than do white families, suggesting a higher per capita income enjoyed by Euro-Americans. Second, while average years of education might be higher among Chinese Americans when compared to whites, it is more often the case that their Euro-American counterparts hold better paying positions with an equivalent educational background. With the exception of wealthy recent immigrants from Hong Kong, Singapore, and Taiwan, Chinese Americans remain at a disadvantage in key areas when compared to Euro-American groups.

Bonanza invokes white-yellow conflict as a dramatic premise only, offering not much more than moralistic arguments against the entrenched racism of U.S. society. In the refusal of the *tong* leadership to assist Jimmy Chang, the Chinese American community of Virginia City is held at fault for its unwillingness to assimilate fully into mainstream Euro-American society. If, therefore, certain Chinese residents are sometimes victimized by isolated acts of racist violence, then they have only themselves to blame for not wanting to become fully American. Yet Euro-American society, as represented by the Cartwright clan, maintains its purchase on compassion, benevolence, and tolerance toward the less fortunate orders through its spirited defense, protection, and rescue of beleaguered nonwhite groups such as Asians.

Mongrelized America

One strategy of isolating Asian Americans from mainstream society has been to erect artificial and arbitrary barriers to marriage based upon specious racial criteria. In addition to cautionary messages against the "mongrelization" of the white race, formal restrictions imposed by antimiscegenation laws gave legal weight to popular injunctions against "race mixing." Antimiscegenation laws, which were in force until the late 1940s in certain western states, barred marriage between Asian Americans and Euro-Americans. It was not until the late 1960s that such discriminatory laws were rendered null and void at the federal level.

It should be obvious that the very notion of "miscegenation" is a socially constructed feature of a racist society. The prohibition of miscegenation stems perhaps from a desire for control on the part of the dominant Euro-American society, to prevent nonwhite peoples from laying claim to social resources on the basis of kinship and common descent. Once a nondominant member of society marries out of his or her color-caste, the principle of exclusion has been violated. This then allows the offspring of interracial marriage to claim legitimately the rights, prerogatives, and perquisites enjoyed exclusively by Euro-American members of the dominant society.

Where miscegenation does occur, it is a forgivable offense if the liaison is between a white male and a nonwhite female. A combination of sexism and racism makes this form of miscegenation more acceptable. However, intermarriage between a nonwhite male and a white female remains taboo. White men are allowed to marry nonwhite women and have children by them, but the system of racial exclusion prevents nonwhite men from freely marrying white females. Such an occurrence would upset not only racial taboos, but those that attend patriarchal authority as well. Although various state statutes banning miscegenation were rendered invalid by 1967, the network television programs that have addressed the theme imply that in actual practice, interracial relationships remain problematic.

Turning Chinese

An episode of *Gunsmoke* (1955–75), "Gunfighter, R.I.P.," provides an excellent example of how the deep-running theme of miscegenation or interracial marriage is typically treated in television drama.[12] The travails of a laundryman named Ching Fa (H. T. Tsiang) and his daughter Ching Lee (France Nuyen) are set in Dodge City, Kansas, during the late nineteenth century. As the episode opens, Ching Fa and Ching Lee are being harassed by three white ruffians. One of them grabs a stack of laundry from the laundryman and flings it onto the muddy street. Ching Fa is badly beaten while trying to resist humiliation at the hands of his antagonists, and he dies from the injuries inflicted upon him.

A stranger in town, Joe Bascome (Darren McGavin), happens upon the scene during the altercation and has mud splashed on his freshly laundered trousers. When Bascome hits one of the toughs, a gun battle ensues in which all three of the attackers are shot dead. Bascome, however, is seriously wounded. Out of a twisted sense of gratitude (it is clear that Bascome killed the men not because they were brutalizing the Chings, but because they had not shown proper remorse at having sullied his clothes), Ching Lee takes Bascome into her home to nurse him back to health.

As Ching Lee tends to her patient's wounds and prays devotedly at a Buddhist shrine, Bascome slowly regains his health. Ching Lee goes so far as to serve Bascome her dead father's precious rice wine, but he finds the wine undrinkable. She teaches her patient a Chinese toast that translates into "health and happiness," but Bascome cannot pronounce the foreign phrase.

As might be predicted, Bascome's affection for Ching Lee grows as he observes her hard at work, carrying out the daily tasks required by the business. During a tender moment that signals the onset of their budding romance, Bascome tells Ching Lee that she has a "nice laugh." "It's the sound of laughter that's nice," answers Ching Lee demurely. Their communion is complete when the lovers once more toast each other, but only after Bascome has asked specifically for the rice wine that had once repulsed him. As he has for the beautiful Ching Lee, with whom he has fallen in love, Bascome has acquired the taste for exotic drink. When they raise their cups this time, Bascome utters the phrase "health and happiness" in flawless Chinese. They gaze at each other in adoration. And in a stock melodramatic gesture, Bascome lightly lifts Ching Lee's chin with a single forefinger and draws her face to his for a passionate kiss.

The very next scene finds tough guy Joe Bascome whistling happily, carrying a neat bundle of laundry as if he were the new proprietor of the Ching Fa Wet Wash. But before Bascome fully settles into domestic bliss, two brothers by the name of Douglas visit Bascome at the laundry to remind the gunman of his contractual obligation to kill Marshal Matt Dillon (James Arness). Before leaving, the

Douglas brothers tease the hired gun about his role as a newly domesticated laundryman.

Joe Bascome decides to complete his part of the bargain with Paul Douglas (Michael Conrad) and his brother Mark (Stefan Gierasch). But in doing so, he shields Ching Lee from the truth by pretending to reject her. Bascome tells Ching Lee that he did not fight the three gunmen to save her father, as he cared nothing for either of them. Claiming that he had been using Ching Lee as a mere "convenience" all along, the reactivated assassin slaps $20 into his shocked mistress's hand in payment for "her services." She weeps uncontrollably as Bascome abandons her. Once outside the door, Bascome pauses, halted by a twinge of remorse at hearing Ching Lee's sobs.

Bascome and the two Douglas brothers meet in Dodge City to plan the killing of Marshal Dillon. "Did you bring that little laundry lady with you?" Paul Douglas asks Bascome. His lascivious question implies Ching Lee's availability for sex after having been disposed of by Bascome. Bascome, however, had secretly left Ching Lee a packet containing $500, half payment for the contract to murder Matt Dillon. Once Ching Lee receives the money she understands that Bascome had been trying to spare her from the truth.

Her faith in Bascome restored, Ching Lee seeks him out at the scene of the planned ambush. She sacrifices herself by diving out of a second-story hotel window to distract the Douglas brothers long enough for Dillon and Bascome to shoot the two gunmen lying in wait. By the end of the episode it is left unclear whether Ching Lee will live or die. Bascome is seen at her side, implying perhaps that this time it will be he who nurses Ching Lee back to health.

Apart from the more obvious theme of miscegenation dramatized in the episode, there is the secondary theme of the dominant white male displacing the weak yellow male, Ching Fa. Ching Fa's cremated Buddhist ashes have hardly cooled before Ching Lee takes up housekeeping with Joe Bascome and welcomes him into the family business. Yet there is a curious twist to the story that has, if only for a short time, the aggressive (gunfighter) white male (Bascome) adopt the identity of the passive (laundryman) yellow male (Ching Fa). Bascome even shows signs of partially assimilating into Asian culture, as seen by the taste he develops for rice wine, his mastery of Chinese expressions, and his sexual relations with a yellow woman.

Still, this selective, partial assimilation remains the prerogative of the white male only. That is, for Ching Fa to have had an affair with the demimonde Miss Kitty (Amanda Blake) would be unthinkable. Finally, the notion of the yellow woman as the white man's sexual property is voiced when Paul Douglas asks Joe Bascome about

Ching Lee's "availability." Miss Kitty worked for twenty-five years in a saloon, a setting not particularly known for its moral probity, yet would Ching Fa ever have dared ask about her "availability"? He would probably have been lynched like Emmett Till or any other nonwhite male suspected of coveting white womanhood.

Winning the West

How the West Was Won (1978–79), produced by MGM Television, was based upon the 1963 Cinerama epic directed by John Ford, Henry Hathaway, and George Marshall. John Mantley, who produced *Gunsmoke* during its twenty-year run, served as executive producer of this short-lived television series. The program reunited Mantley with actor James Arness. In *How the West Was Won,* Arness played Zeb Macahan, the head of a large Irish American extended family forging a new life for themselves in Wyoming. This high-budget series never quite caught on with viewers, however. Despite its lush outdoor cinematography, superior production values, excellent cast, and intelligent writing, *How the West Was Won* was a ratings failure.

Because individual installments of *How the West Was Won* ranged from one to two hours, the program was able to explore a number of complex themes with a degree of sensitivity all too rare on network television. Television genres that are only thirty minutes in duration, such as the situation comedy, must rely heavily upon stereotypes, stylized acting, punched-up writing, and contemporary settings to telegraph the minimum information required to elicit calculated responses over a short span of time. Feature-length television programs are better able to probe individual psychology, motivation, and intragroup dynamics. These characteristics of feature-length television drama also make it more difficult to deny the humanity of even the most peripheral characters in a given show.

Just as it is often difficult to cite examples of programs that treat complex issues with an appreciable degree of sensitivity, it is even rarer for a given program to convey an awareness and understanding of history. Yet *How the West Was Won* succeeds in bringing a better than usual historical sensibility, flawed though it may be, to the episode "China Girl."[13] That the episode dramatizes select aspects of early Chinese American history while preserving entertainment values makes it all the more exceptional. The episode is not without its weaknesses, however. Certain distortions of the historical record embedded within the dramatic presentation leave the viewer with an incomplete understanding of nineteenth-century Chinese immigration to the United States.

"China Girl" recounts the struggles of Leong Chung Hua (Keye Luke), his wife An Kam (Beulah Quo), son Chuk (Robert Ito), and daughter Li Sin (Rosalind Chao), who leave Kwangtung province for the United States in the year 1869. Although the portrayal of Chinese immigrant life is rich in historical detail, the very premise of the episode is questionable, given that so few sojourners arrived with families intact. Despite this dubious portrayal of the early Chinese America family, "China Girl" makes a few larger points concerning the history of Asian exclusion, labor exploitation, and social discrimination experienced by immigrants. The underlying intention of the program, however, is to celebrate the success of contemporary American social democracy. During the opening sequence, the epic struggle and triumph of liberal democracy is made abundantly clear by an omniscient narrator, who intones:

> Of all the immigrants for whom America eventually became a permanent home, perhaps none were so manipulated, or suffered as many indignities, as the Chinese. Though 12,000 of them built the western half of the transcontinental railroad, they were not permitted to become citizens of this country, and they had no rights whatsoever. They could not even testify against a white man in court. And seven years after the Emancipation Proclamation freed Black slaves, naked Chinese girls were being sold at auction to their own countrymen on the streets of San Francisco. But with famines sweeping China still they came at their thousands seeking food for their bellies and hope for the future. In the beginning, they often labored sixteen hours a day for as little as twenty cents. But they somehow survived these hardships to become a vital part of a growing America as one of the finest and proudest chronicles in the history of the West.

The episode takes great care in showing the multiple forms of oppression endured by Chinese immigrants. In one scene, a gathering of white children is seen taunting and throwing stones at the new arrivals. In another, three African American men encounter a group of Chinese on the sidewalk. The men are obviously common laborers, but two of them wear top hats and affect the airs of the highborn. "John Chinaman," says one of them, "You see gentlemen, you steps aside." Finally, gender oppression is depicted in separate scenes where Chinese women are being sold at a slave auction and held in bondage as prostitutes.

Demon Seed

"China Girl" would be little more than another tale of immigrant success were it not for the theme of Asian female sexual degradation that informs the larger narrative. As the young and beautiful Li Sin boards the ship that will transport her family to the United States, she is waylaid by the white captain of the vessel and locked into a cabin below deck for his sexual pleasure. Li Sin had been betrothed to a young man named Kee (Soon Teck Oh), who was to have joined her later in the United States. Much of the episode is devoted to resolving the dilemma of the pregnancy resulting from Li Sin's shipboard rape.

Once she learns of her pregnancy, Li Sin becomes positively enamored of the idea that she will bear the spawn of the Yankee sea captain, for although the child will be a mixed-race bastard, at least it will be born an American. Li Sin receives an informal lesson in American immigration law when she secretly visits an herbalist to purchase pregnancy medication. The herbalist informs her that the child will have U.S. citizenship by virtue of being born on American soil. "My son will be an American citizen?" Li Sin asks, as if she cannot fully believe her good fortune. As the mouthpiece of liberal democracy, the herbalist rejoices that this accident of birth will give the American-born child the franchise, allowing him to have a "voice in affair [*sic*] of this land." "He could be a very important man," adds the herbalist. Li Sin's industrious and entrepreneurial-minded brother Chuk is not in favor of her bearing the child. Nevertheless, Chuk gives his sister money to pay for her prenatal medical care.

The family patriarch, Leong, is none too happy about the blessed event once he learns the news. In a demonstration of the reputed Asian disregard for human life, Leong says matter-of-factly, "Of course, the child must die." Leong instructs his wife Ah Kam to care for Li Sin during the final stages of her pregnancy but demands that the baby be turned over to him upon its birth. Ah Kam resists her husband's instructions, but as Leong explains, "This is the seed of the White Devils who spit at us. Would you allow the blood of Leong to be tainted?"

Li Sin is forced to flee for the safety of her unborn child and is taken in by Irish matriarch Molly Culhane (Fionnula Flanagan). Molly insists that her brother-in-law Zeb Macahan (Arness) intercede on Li Sin's behalf. Although Zeb initially had been reluctant to confront Leong, he visits the Chinese patriarch and argues passionately against the infanticide. "Maybe you need a little instruction, on the value of human life," says Zeb. In response, Leong scoffs at the hypocrisy of Macahan's moralistic stance:

> Value of life? No, you do not condemn me. In this country I work
> for half the wages of the whites. Black slaves are free. But Chinese

are sold like cattle in the cities. If a white man should shoot me to see if I bleed, do I have rights and protection and law? Value of life! Life is cheap here for the Chinese. Cheaper than in China!

Li Sin gives birth at the Macahan ranch as a Chinese thug watches from a distance, presumably to snatch the infant at the earliest opportunity. Molly is overjoyed by the birth of the child, saying, "Even though he isn't a Macahan, I'm going to write his name in the family Bible anyway."

A complication arises when the baby is kidnapped. Molly travels to the Chinese mining camp to retrieve the baby, but no one is willing to provide information on its whereabouts. But as it happens, contrary to her husband Leong's orders, Ah Kam has spirited the child away and given it to a couple for safekeeping. Ah Kam's actions were spurred by the painful memory of having to kill her firstborn son to avert starvation for the rest of the family.

The conflict between Leong and the rest of his family, who by now have aligned themselves against him, is resolved when Li Sin's Chinese fiancé Kee finally tracks her down in Wyoming and assumes parental responsibility for the bastard child. Kee takes the child from a silent Leong and proudly states, "We have a child. The child will be written into the book of rites of the Kee family." At long last, three generations of the Leong family are reunited after much hardship and personal tragedy.

The liberal pluralist drift of "China Girl" is made more explicit at the end of the program. It closes with the implication that the hardships of the Leong family are on par with those of European immigrants. In the concluding scene, Kee and Leong stop by the Macahan ranch to say goodbye before moving their families to Montana. Molly gives them her blessing by saying, "Aye, they'll be taking their chances. But *all* of us did. That's a part of it." Molly's generous observation implies that as a nation of immigrants, the United States has afforded every entering group a fair and equal chance at finding their place in the sun. However, this has never been the case for nonwhite peoples such as Asians. Color has always been a barrier to the assimilation of Asian immigrant groups. Indeed, during the late nineteenth century, Irish American workers were militant anti-Chinese agitators and invoked a common white racial identity to escape the forms of discrimination practiced against nonwhite groups such as Asians, Mexicans, and Blacks. The almost total structural assimilation of Irish Americans in the present illustrates the crucial role played by race in social mobility and the distribution of power in American society.

Like most television drama, *How the West Was Won* embodies elements of both progressive and regressive social ideologies. That is, while "China Girl" sheds diffused light on select aspects of the Chinese American experience, it is also guilty of rewriting history in a manner that conforms to the dominant liberal pluralist model of society, whereby ethnic minority groups enjoy formal rights in the abstract but are denied the same in a substantive fashion. In effect, this bifurcation in liberal thought and practice minimizes the pervasive influence of racism in the maintenance of structured social inequality.

Male Prerogatives

In both *Gunsmoke* and *How the West Was Won*, the theme of Asian female sexual possession by the white male Westerner was clearly articulated. This motif in American popular culture has it that white males maintain the prerogative to cross racial boundaries when it is in their interest to do so. Whether for purposes of sexual gratification, as in the instance of "Gunfighter, R.I.P.," or to exert power and assert authority, as seen in the rape of Li Sin by the ship's captain in "China Girl," white males are afforded such license as part of their social endowment as the master race. So strong is this thematic imperative that even as recently as 1992, PBS's *American Playhouse* (1982–present) featured an independent film titled *Thousand Pieces of Gold* (1989) that reproduced the dominant white man-yellow woman power relationship.[14]

Within a system of racial oppression, the domination or sexual possession of nonwhite females by the white males of the master race becomes an additional means of enforcing unequal power relations. For the nonwhite male, the inability to provide for and protect female family members from men of the master race sometimes reduces him to impotence, self-loathing, and resignation.[15] But even within such a system of racial oppression, isolated acts of heroism and ongoing resistance against Euro-American society by nonwhite subordinates is the norm and not the exception.

There is an additional dimension to the sexual possession of Asian women, specifically, the oppression of women within patriarchal Asian society. The episode "China Girl" refers more than once to the institution of female slavery and prostitution as features of Chinese immigrant society. Recall that the episode's prologue tells of "naked Chinese girls" who were "being sold at auction to their own countrymen." Later in the program, there is a scene in which the prodigal son Chuk Leong encounters a Chinese prostitute who offers him "happy time" even as she is dying from venereal disease.

The existence of Chinese prostitution in nineteenth-century America reflects the multiple forms of oppression endured by Asian women within the larger capitalist system. Not only were Asian prostitutes bound by the patriarchal structure of traditional Chinese society, but they served the needs of both immigrant entrepreneurs and American capitalists. In a comprehensive essay that reveals the ideological underpinnings and historical basis of Chinese prostitution, Lucie Cheng observes that the institution arose out of the "need for cheap labor in California and the economic underdevelopment of China; and [out of] white racism and Chinese patriarchy."[16] Cheng also establishes that prostitution had the effect of preventing male immigrants from forming families, which in turn helped to perpetuate the exploitation of Chinese labor. Further, impoverished families in China were provided additional means of support through the repatriated earnings of prostitutes working in the United States. Prostitution also filled the void created by the unavailability of Chinese females and thereby helped prevent intermarriage with non-Chinese women.

In sum, prostitution as a social institution was fully functional and complementary to the requirements of nineteenth-century U.S. capitalism. Its long-term effects helped shape Chinese American "bachelor society" for close to eighty years. Exclusionist legislation, the avarice of *tongs* and other Chinese intermediaries, the shortage of women in the American West, the economic underdevelopment of China, the male supremacist complex, and prevailing racist attitudes all conspired to deny immigrants the bourgeois ideal of the nuclear family. In many a Chinatown, nonmarried men submitted to a "total institutional framework," where they were consigned to live in "lonely isolation" for all their days.[17]

Ties That Blind

Perhaps few other events in the history of the West have captured the popular imagination as much as the driving of the final spike at Promontory Point, Utah, on May 10, 1869. The linkage of the Union Pacific and Central Pacific railroads symbolized the final geographic integration of the American republic. An act of Congress in 1862 chartered the two companies for the purpose of developing the Great Plains region and the Far West. The driving of the golden spike nine years later "marked the climax of the transportation revolution that had begun early in the 19th century."[18] The network of transcontinental rail lines was intended to promote the agricultural settlement of the West. The railroad would stimulate economic growth by making it less costly to transport crops to distant markets.

This signal technological feat was accomplished largely through the efforts of immigrant Chinese laborers, who by 1867 numbered 12,000, or 90 percent of all workers employed by the Central Pacific Railroad. Chronicler of Asian American social history Ronald Takaki goes so far as to assert that the "construction of the Central Pacific Railroad was a Chinese achievement."[19] In the historic photograph that recorded this revolutionary engineering feat, however, there is not a yellow face to be seen among the assembled men. Chinese laborers were not invited to the ceremony.

An episode of the TV Western *Yancy Derringer* (1958–59) titled "Two Tickets to Promontory" foregrounds the mythic aspects of the building of the transcontinental rail line, but in doing so exposes its ideological underpinnings.[20] Yancy Derringer (Jock Mahoney) is the owner of a riverboat in New Orleans whose other business interests involve him in all manner of intrigue. One such adventure finds Derringer trying to obtain scarce train tickets that would take him to Promontory Point so he can witness the "wedding of the rails." Derringer wins a pair of tickets from a cardsharp named Wayland Farr (John Larch), but later discovers that they are good only for passage in the baggage car with his Indian sidekick Pahoo (X Brands). While riding there, Derringer uncovers a plot by Farr to dynamite the Jupiter rail car that is transporting dignitaries to the dedication site. Among those in the car is Central Pacific president (later, governor of California) Leland Stanford. Farr is the owner of a competing rail line that will be put out of business upon completion of the transcontinental rail system.

After a few complications and reversals, Derringer foils the plot to sabotage the rail car. Once having dispensed with Farr, the dapper riverboat gambler Yancey Derringer leads a group of his fellow travelers in a toast to the democratic vistas made possible by the transcontinental railway: "To the wedding of the rails. Which means that any man with an itchy foot can travel almost anywhere in this wonderful country." Derringer turns to Pahoo, who communicates only through sign language, and together they salute the greatness of American empire represented by the new transportation technology.

There are more than a few jarringly revealing contradictions that expose the ethnic/racial pluralist politics of most TV Western sociodrama, where even vanquished and exploited peoples are granted a dubious equality. Early in the episode, for instance, a Chinese man is shown freely socializing with white passengers in the train coach. Unless the man was a visiting dignitary from China, it seems unlikely that he would be found in such an exclusive setting. It is equally far-fetched that the native American Pahoo would be allowed on the train, although he rode in the baggage car in the company of a propertied white gentleman. Beyond such examples of artistic license, the duplicity of "Two Tickets to Promontory" lies in its mythologized depiction of racial equality and harmony, when in truth both interethnic strife and intense conflict between Chinese labor and capital attended the construction of the transcontinental railroad every step of the way.

Untrue West

One of the tendencies of popular art is for its creators to apply liberally a revisionist gloss on events drawn from the historical past. Nowhere is this more evident than in the art of the television Western. In this once tremendously popular film and television genre, American social history is appropriated and then reinterpreted to depict a world that is visited by sporadic, rather than plagued by sustained, conflict. Strife is only temporary or aberrant, never ongoing and systemic. The normative social order is restored through main force by either military (cavalry) or police power (sheriff/marshal). On occasion, lone heroic individuals substitute for state power.

Like all sociodrama, the television Western embodies a set of well-articulated rationalizations and justifications for the persistence of underlying social conflicts. Racial antagonism, for example, is the result of cross-cultural misunderstanding, irrational fears, or perhaps unfamiliarity with "foreign" modes of dress and speech. That racism is woven into the very fabric of the American republic is never hinted at, let alone admitted, in the television "horse opera."

When there are occasional outbreaks of "irrational" violence in society, it is invariably the white male authority figure who rides to the rescue. It is the lawman's sworn duty to maintain order within his bailiwick and to uphold the law of the land, the U.S. Constitution. Liberal pluralist guarantees of equality and freedom even extend to those most often victimized by violence and hatred: people of color. Indeed, the television Western has thrived on stories that perpetuate the myth of equal protection under the law, as seen in the following descriptions of episodes from *Gunsmoke* and *Cowboy G-Men*.

Gunsmoke (1955–75) began as a radio series in 1952, featuring William Conrad as Marshal Matt Dillon. As an interesting sidelight, a young writer named Sam Peckinpah adapted a radio version of "The Queue" for the tenth episode of the program's first year on television. Peckinpah, of course, went on to achieve notoriety as the director of such "anti-Westerns" as *Ride the High Country* (1962), *The Wild Bunch* (1969), and *Pat Garrett and Billy the Kid* (1973).

"The Queue" concerns the problems faced by a Chinese cook who hopes to make Dodge City his new home.[21] Chen Lan Wong (Keye Luke) no sooner steps off the stagecoach than he is greeted by a welcoming committee of two, Howard (Devlin McCarthy) and Rabb (Robert Gist). They pick up Chen and throw him back into the stagecoach and instruct the driver to leave town, but Marshal Matt Dillon (James Arness) happens by and puts an immediate halt to the proceedings. Howard Braden appeals to Dillon's sense of white loyalty by telling the marshal, "There's too many Chinese in this country already." When Dillon asks Chen to identify himself, he modulates into his obsequious Chinaman routine. Chen describes himself as "me good boy" who "all the time, workum hard."

Dillon informs Chen that he is welcome to stay in Dodge and offers the Chinese cook protection from the white toughs. Rabb and Howard are incensed by Dillon's decree, arguing that more of his kind will follow if the Chinaman is allowed to settle in town. Dillon is unmoved by their overheated sense of alarm and order the men to go on their way. A grateful Chen tries to convince the lawman of his harmlessness by saying, "Me velly sad. No likee bring trouble." Like most television Chinamen, Chen suffers from the linguistic affliction peculiar to TV Asians known as lambdacism, or the inability to differentiate the *r* and *l* sounds present in the English language. For Asians, lambdacism in speech functions as a shibboleth, a social marker that aurally reaffirms their status as aliens forever consigned to the margins of the dominant society.

Howard and Rabb bring a beer-swilling God-fearing man named Bailey (Sebastian Cabot) into the plot to rid Dodge of the yellow menace. The two convince Bailey that the humble cook is in truth quite wealthy because, like all Chinese, Chen lives frugally and therefore has saved a good deal of money that he has stashed in a "treasure box." Bailey agrees to join in the intrigue, but demands that no violence befall the man from the celestial kingdom. But Howard responds with a sentiment first applied to Native Americans: "Killin' Chinamen ain't really the same as killin' people."

During a visit to Doc (Milburn Stone) to have a tooth extracted, Chen inadvertently exposes a side of himself that he conceals from white society. As Dillon sits nearby, Chen hands Doc a dollar and utters in perfectly inflected English, "Very good." This utterance surprises the usually unflappable Dillon, who asks, "What happened to all that 'Velly good Chinese boy, all time workee' talk, Chen?" Chen explains to Dillon that he affects such speech because this is what white people require of him. "Most men resent a Chinaman who doesn't talk the way they expect him to," Chen says. "I wish to avoid trouble. But trouble comes, regardless."

Dillon observes that Chen has had his queue cut off, and when he asks Chen about it, the immigrant confesses that Howard and Rabb were responsible for the shearing. Chen explains to Dillon that he had been trying only to earn enough money to send for his wife so she could join him in the United States. But because he has been dishonored, Chen insists that now he cannot return to China before exacting revenge upon his assailants. Dillon, however, warns Chen against seeking retribution.

Chen's desire for vengeance is tested after he suffers a vicious beating at the hands of Bailey, who had come to his shack in search of the treasure box. Before Bailey is able to kill his victim, Dillon arrives on the scene and shoots the Bible thumper dead. Chen, now armed with a gun, turns it against Howard and Rabb, threatening them with death unless they return the queue. Dillon tries to talk Chen out of killing the bullies, but Chen insists, "Marshal, I will not lose my honor as a Chinese." Dillon responds with a short speech, which proves to be the underlying moral of the story:

> Your "honor as a Chinese"? Chen, you said you wanted to bring your wife here, to make your home in this country. Well, if you do that, you've got to live as an American, not as a Chinese. If you have to kill two men over a pigtail, you don't belong in Dodge or anyplace else in this country.

The lawman's plea has its intended effect. Chen relinquishes the pistol and Dillon orders Howard to return the queue. The "treasure box" proves to contain nothing more than $9.27 and a Chinese marriage certificate. Howard says nothing as he walks away from the scene, but his hangdog expression implies contrition. Chen sheds his Chinese identity by presenting Dillon with the queue as a "souvenir." In doing so, the immigrant signals his willingness to enter into a new social contract whereby the concept of maintaining "honor as a Chinese" is rendered meaningless.

In "The Queue," what begins as a tale of racial intolerance ends with Marshal Dillon demanding that Chen remove all vestiges of his Chinese ethnic indentity. This shift of emphasis turns attention from the deplorable actions of white racists to the reluctance of an immigrant to renounce his origins. By insisting that a mere "pigtail" is not worth killing for, Dillon displays his ignorance about what it signifies. In China, the wearing of the queue was imposed upon social subordinates and served as a mark of their collective inferiority, but its wearers inverted the intended meaning and instead wore the queue as a symbol of resistance to Manchu dynastic rule. In the United States, however, the queue functioned as a visible social marker that suggested a refusal to assimilate into the dominant society. For Marshal Dillon, that Chen wanted to defend his besmirched honor signaled a refusal to "live as an American." The explicit theme of anti-Asian racial oppression is neutralized and instead becomes an object lesson in American citizenship for those who are unwilling to conform.

Great White Father

Lawmen and authority figures in the television Western typically embody what might be dubbed the Great White Father syndrome. The principal feature of the syndrome is that the white male authority is made to serve as guardian and protector of the nonwhite subjects under his dominion. The syndrome stems from the larger liberal democratic mythology that presupposes equal protection under the law, to include nonwhite peoples such as Asians, Blacks, Indians, and Mexicans. So compelling is the Great White Father syndrome that never has there been a single instance in the television Western where discrimination or racism has been condoned by going unpunished by the authorities. Rather, the general tenor and specific themes of TV Westerns have been consistent in their opposition to expressions of racial intolerance.

That the television Western is so thoroughly steeped in the Great White Father syndrome implies a denial of the subterranean currents that course through actual American history. In keeping with the mythmaking function of popular art, the television Western supresses the legacy of genocide, legal and extralegal oppression on the basis of race, and attempts at the outright exclusion or repatriation of nonwhite Americans. In the TV Western, racism often wears the mask of liberal benevolence.

Sustained and systematic violence against Asians in the American West is an indisputable part of the historical record. In 1871, an attack on the Chinese community in Los Angeles resulted in the lynching of fifteen residents. In 1877, anti-Chinese violence resurfaced in Chico, California, and led to the destruction of property and homes of targeted individuals. Four Chinese were set afire and killed by members of a white supremacist labor organization. Perhaps one of the better-known instances of racially motivated murder was the 1886 massacre of twenty-eight Chinese miners in Rock Springs, Wyoming. "Although there is no accurate record of all the Chinese miners who were injured and killed," writes Sucheng Chan, "in 1862 a committee of the California State Legislature stated that it had received a list of 88 Chinese known to have been murdered by Euro-Americans, eleven of them by collectors of the Foreign Miners' Tax."[22]

The so-called Foreign Miners' Tax—first imposed in 1850—was a form of legal extortion whereby tax collectors received a percentage of the proceeds. In some instances, nonpayment of the extortionate tax was used as a pretext to remove Chinese miners from their claims. Curiously, this discriminatory taxation practice (which was enforced primarily against Chinese miners) forms the subtext of an episode of a short-lived syndicated TV program, *Cowboy G-Men* (1952).[23]

Like many early television Westerns, *Cowboy G-Men* opens with the quaint stentorian bombast typical of its cinema precursor, with the narrator introducing "hard-riding, fast-shooting government secret service men of the old West" who are "courageous, resourceful fighters for law and order." The setting is California in the year 1872. The gold rush has already come and gone, but resourceful Chinese miners have persevered. Some have managed to eke out a modest living. The "Orientals" are even given a measure of respect by the narrator, who observes that "no one could rework old claims or slag heaps better than the unoffending, pigtailed Chinese." The narrator even speaks of the resentment harbored by "less energetic white miners" who "envied" the "success" of their Chinese competitors, who were handicapped by discriminatory laws and taxes that "aided outlaws preying on the Orientals."

As the narrator speaks, outlaws are seen beating a Chinese miner and robbing him of gold. After repeatedly being subjected to such abuse, one of the miners sends a letter to the federal government in Washington, D.C., with an appeal for help and protection. It is in response to this anonymous letter that cowboy G-men Pat Gallagher (Russell Hayden) and Stoney Crockett (Jackie Coogan) arrive in the town of Volcano, California, to investigate.

Stoney Crockett goes undercover as a Chinese "coolie" to gather information on the case. However, because his function in this tale is to provide comic relief, Crockett spends most of his time trying to extricate himself from the clutches of an amorous young woman named Lotus Leaf (Judy Dan), who is forced on him by the leader of the Chinese community, Ling Yee (Robert Bice).

Pat Gallagher masquerades as Mr. Gilman, a mining engineer and geologist who claims to have developed a new hydraulic mining process that can extract gold ore from what once were exhausted mines. Gallagher/Gilman informs District Mining Commissioner Evans (John Vosper) that there is money to be made by everyone involved if the corrupt official will help identify the most promising mining sites. Evans readily agrees, observing, "The Chinese are about the best at smelling out a claim that can still be worked." But Gallagher/Gilman is skeptical that the Chinese would want to sell a paying claim. Evans, however, reassures the secret agent that the state of California has "some convenient laws for just such circumstances."

Later, Gallagher/Gilman pays a visit to the tax collector, Roberts (Fred Libby), who is working in cahoots with Evans and others. As fellow members of a white supremacist group that calls itself the White Dragon, they have been secretly terrorizing the Chinese miners. Roberts unveils a plan whereby the partners will use a combination of raw physical intimidation and legal machinations to drive Chinese miners from their claims. Roberts tells his visitor simply to "pick out the claims you want." But the cowboy G-man is skeptical. What if the Chinese resist and sue him, he asks? Roberts and his deputy share a belly laugh and explain that in California, a Chinese man cannot testify against a white man in court.

Evans is soon exposed as the leader of the White Dragon and Ling Yee (a white actor in "yellowface") is identified as the person who had made the anonymous appeal to the federal authorities for assistance. The cowboy G-men once more prove themselves worthy of their mandate from the federal government to restore law and order in even the most remote outposts of the white republic. To the undying gratitude of the Chinese miners, the cowboy G-men forcefully demonstrate that the supreme law of the land is meant to protect whites and nonwhites alike.

The Great White Father syndrome as dramatized by the television Western reflects a power nexus that theorists on race and ethnicity commonly refer to as paternalism.[24] In a paternalist social order, contact between groups is one of institutionalized inequality. This is amply illustrated by the relationship between the Chinese and the Euro-Americans in the episodes of *Gunsmoke* and *Cowboy G-Men* discussed above. The individual heroic acts of Marshal Matt Dillon and secret agent Pat Gallagher on behalf of Chinese immigrant workers overshadow the determining role that race plays in the near-total control of their Asian wards by the Euro-American master group. Thus, in a disarmingly subtle fashion, the seemingly enlightened liberalism of the TV Western reinscribes the legacy of a white paternalist social system onto the contemporary system of intergroup power relations.

White Maternalism

Among many feminists, the structure of male supremacy described loosely as "patriarchy" has been freely attributed to all groups in society, including, presumably, nonwhite minorities. If one is a male in American society, runs the argument, then one is necessarily the beneficiary of a patriarchal system designed to maintain the unequal relationship that exits between men and women. Not only is gender oppression reflected in almost all social institutions, but such inequality is an integral part of human psychology or "subjectivity." Drawing from her reading of Lacanian psychology, in a classic essay film theorist Laura Mulvey goes so far as to assert that the male supremacist complex is embodied in the "visual pleasure" taken by the "bearer of the look" (men) as focused on the passive, objectified "sexual object" (women).[25]

Jane Gaines has subsequently provided an important corrective to the sweeping inclusion of all males—regardless of color—into the white feminist critique of sexist power relations as it concerns patriarchal "looking positions." In introducing the often neglected variable of race into the contemporary discussion of gender relations, Gaines observes that the "notion of patriarchy is most obtuse when it disregards the position white women occupy over Black men as well as Black women."[26] What Gaines refers to as "white privilege" can be extended to all people of color, including Asian Americans.

In lending historical specificity to the argument articulated by Gaines, it should be noted that throughout much of American history an adult African American male could be lynched for so much as fixing his "male gaze" on a white woman. In 1955 the body of fourteen-year-old Emmett Till was fished out of the Tallahatchie River in Mississippi. He had been the victim of a lynching. His crime? Emmett Till had supposedly leered at and called out "Bye, baby" to a young white female clerk in a candy store as he was leaving. An all-white male jury later acquitted the alledged murderers of Emmett Till. More recently, a Chinese American engineer named Vincent Chin was brutally beaten to death with a baseball bat by two white auto workers outside the topless bar they had been patronizing in Detroit. According to one of the dancers who witnessed the initial altercation in the Fancy Pants bar, Ronald Ebens objected to the yellow man's spirited blandishments directed at the female performers.

Contrary to the assertions of not a few feminists, the "male gaze" is the sole prerogative of white males. Critic bell hooks notes that this nonrecognition of two radically different modes of "spectatorship" rests upon the fact that film theory itself "has been and con-

tinues to be influenced by and reflective of white racial domination."
Further, much current feminist film criticism contains the residue
of white supremacy because of its roots in the so-called women's
movement. "Since feminist film criticism was initially rooted in a
women's liberation movement informed by racist practices," writes
hooks, "it did not open up the discursive terrain and make it more
inclusive."[27]

As in the case of African Americans, for Asian Americans the system of racial oppression takes precedence over that of gender oppression fetishized by left-liberal feminists. In her multigenerational
study of Japanese American women, for example, Evelyn Nakano
Glenn makes the compelling argument that "conflict over inequities
within the family may be muted by the countervailing pressure on
the family to unite against assualts from outside institutions."[28] Such
"outside institutions" have sanctioned behavior and laws directed
specifically against Asian Americans ranging from mild social discrimination to verbal and physical attacks. Under such circumstances, male oppression—however problematic—is of secondary
importance within the Asian community.

Within a system of racial oppression, the white liberal/radical
feminist critique of patriarchy falls short of speaking to the vast
majority of social subjects who do not fit the profile of the educated,
Euro-American, middle-class professional. To the degree that Euro-
American women indirectly benefit from the white supremacist
complex, they share complicity in maintaining a social system that
subordinates both men and women of color. Historically, while their
bourgeois male counterparts have maintained a monopoly on key positions within central social institutions such as government, the
military, and major corporations, the bourgeois Euro-American female has exercised influence and power through the mechanism of
white maternalism.

As Jane Hunter documents in her study of American female missionaries in China, the ideology of maternalism was a crucial component in extending the influence of "imperial evangelism." Missionaries taught female Chinese Christian converts the value of a
home-centered life, where they would be responsible for "education,
culture, and public morality" and serve as a "stabilizing force" in society.[29] At the same of time, a sense of Anglo-Saxon racial superiority in combination with the privileges of class and American nationality gave the missionaries a "sense of power" that they would
not otherwise have enjoyed in the United States.[30] Foreign missionary work provided educated middle-class white women a protected
job market within a male supremacist social order. The spirituliza-

tion of Chinese social oppression, white supremacy, American nationalism, and matriarchal values were part of the ideological repertoire of female Christian missionaries. Whatever gender inequality they suffered was muted by the benefits that accrued to them as white middle-class members of an expansionist nation in its ascendancy, imperial America at the turn of the century.

An episode of *Annie Oakley* (1953–56) – the first television Western to feature a woman in the lead role – exemplifies white liberal maternalism as it extends to downtrodden groups who require special care and protection.[31] In the following example, it is a Chinese American who is the object of maternalistic concern. In "Annie and the Chinese Curse," Li Wong (Keye Luke) is being harassed by Nick (Craig Woods) and Clint Scanlon (William Tanney), two brothers who have a history of antagonizing the Chinese laundryman. A businessman named Mr. Rand (Lawrence Ryle), on the other hand, appears to treat Li Wong as an equal. Rand is eager to buy a piece of property owned by Wong, but the shrewd laundryman refuses the offer, choosing instead to wait for his real estate holdings to appreciate in value.

As Rand attempts to persuade Wong that he should sell before a predicted depression hits, a rock crashes through the window. A message attached to the projectile reads: "We don't want Chinamen in Diablo. Go back to China where you belong. If you don't leave town we'll run you out." The message was signed by the "Property Owners of Diablo." Rather than express anger at the latest in a series of attacks, Wong is only saddened by the experience. "Money will fix broken window," says Wong. "But money will not fix Li Wong's broken feelings." As Nick Scanlon flees on horseback after throwing the rock, Annie Oakley (Gail Davis) and Deputy Sheriff Lofty Craig (Brad Johnson) give chase. Lofty captures Scanlon by roping him, but Scanlon denies having done anything wrong, unless "disliking Chinamen" is considered a crime.

Later that evening, as Annie is tucking her kid brother Tagg (Jimmy Hawkins) into bed, he asks why some people do not like Li Wong. Tagg has been secretly learning how to work leather from Li Wong at night so he can surprise his sister with a handmade bridle for her birthday. Tagg has grown to love the laundryman and his family. As she lovingly says good night to her young brother, Annie attributes anti-Asian hostility to a problem that only "some people" have regarding people who are simply different. "Well, there's some people, Tagg, that have silly fears about other people that don't live exactly as they do," Annie explains. "I don't know why they don't just take the trouble to understand them."

According to this explanation, the only problem the Chinese laundryman faces is a lack of understanding. This suggests an all-too-easy remedy that ignores the institutional basis of racism. This liberal humanist explanation of Li Wong's plight denies the history of anti-Asian persecution throughout the West and other regions of the United States. Indeed, the very premise of this episode—that of a Chinaman owning real property—is fundamentally flawed, given that alien land laws in the state of California prohibited Asians from making such acquisitions.

Mr. Rand, it is revealed, has been using the Scanlon brothers to intimidate Li Wong into selling out. But when Wong continues to refuse, Rand murders one of the Scanlon brothers to cast suspicion on his Asian business rival. After Li Wong is jailed, Rand offers to obtain the best legal representation for him if only he will sign over the property as "security." It is his young admirer Tagg who saves Li Wong from wrongful prosecution, for Tagg had witnessed the murder of Nick Scanlon while leaving Li Wong's home late at night. The actual perpetrator having been identified, Li Wong is let go by the mob that had gathered to lynch him. In the closing scene, Lofty joyfully tells of Li Wong's good fortune: the humble Chinese laundryman has just closed a deal to sell his property to the railroad for the sum of $22,000. Such is the "Chinese curse."

As in many television shows, this episode of *Annie Oakley* hinges upon the fact of racial difference and the persistence of ideological racism in U.S. society. Yet racism as such is never alluded to in the program. Were *Annie Oakley* to be aired today, liberal humanist bromides such as "lack of understanding" or "cross-cultural differences," or even "multicultural diversity," would be deployed to account for persistent patterns of inequality based upon race. In this, liberal humanist explanations of racial discrimination are intellectually dishonest, politically regressive, and ultimately supportive of a status quo that offers only ameliorative gestures instead of substantive change. The television Western is a genre that is constituted at its core by racial conflict: white settlers versus Indian marauders, for example, or white Christians versus the "heathen Chinee." That the Western invariably suppresses the fact of racism suggests that racial oppression remains the dark secret of American society.

Half-Caste Will Travel

It is not uncommon for African American leaders of rebellions or social movements to be celebrated, however begrudgingly, in the popular arts. Nat Turner, Martin Luther King, Jr., and Malcolm X are select historical figures whose lives have been treated in literature, cinema, or television. Mexican American "social bandits" who have engaged in acts of resistence against Anglo society enjoy similar status within the popular culture. "Primitive rebels" Joaquin Murrieta, Gregorio Cortez, and Pancho Villa are all part of American national lore.[32] And there is even admiration for Native American warriors, such as Crazy Horse and Sitting Bull, who fought to repulse white invaders. But, unlike their nonwhite brethren, Asian Americans are bereft of a tradition—real or imagined—of "badness." Recognizing this absence, author Maxine Hong Kingston has posed the telling set of questions, "Where's our jazz? Where's our blues? Where's our ain't taking-no-shit-from nobody street-strutting language?"[33] While Hong Kingston's mythologized "woman warrior" figure might satisfy those content with fantasies of liberal feminist empowerment, it remains that network television has exerted overwhelming power in molding the popular consciousness with its endless representations of Asian Americans exhibiting weakness, dependency, subvervience, and vulnerability.

The houseboy Hey Boy (Kam Tong)—later replaced by Hey Girl (Lisa Lu)—in *Have Gun Will Travel* (1957–63) was indicative of Asian American servility as constructed by the television Western. At the beginning of most episodes, the nattily attired, cultivated, gunslinging mercenary Paladin (Richard Boone) would receive messages from prospective clients delivered by his Asian servant. Paladin's taste for Continental cuisine, rare wine, and expensive cigars, his refined speech, easy manner, and impeccably tailored clothes stood in stark contrast to Hey Boy's inelegant Chinese peasant's garb and tendency to break into incomprehensible Cantonese chatter when faced with a crisis that only his white master could resolve. Once Hey Boy was sufficiently calmed by the imperturbable Paladin, he was able to communicate passably in English.[34]

The standard portrayal of the Asian American male as a non-heroic victim was modified ever so slightly with the appearance of the program *Kung Fu* (1972–75). For the first time, an Asian American male was seen physically confronting prejudice and racially motivated attacks without fear. Although his training as a Shaolin priest restrained him from engaging in gratuitous acts of aggression, Kwai Chang Caine (David Carradine) neither ran from trouble nor allowed himself to be brutalized.

Kwai Chang Caine never failed to win his self-defensive fights against white attackers. Slight in build, he was usually set upon by more than one person at a time, each of whom was physically imposing, sometimes even brandishing a weapon against the empty-handed Caine. Each encounter was shown in slow motion, displaying the balletic poetry of Caine's supreme art, honed during years of rigorous martial arts training under the tutelage of Shaolin masters. These were not the brawls typical of the formula TV Western. They verged on being metaphysical contests that pitted a wildly violent frontier society against an Asian civilization whose vast achievements predated those of Europe by millennia.

For those members of the television audience who might not tolerate the idea of an Asian beating up white manhood, Kwai Chang Caine was made to be a half-caste, born of an American father and a Chinese mother. Only by virtue of his racially mixed heritage and, secondarily, his dual nationality was Caine's heroic status permitted. As a half-caste, Kwai Chang Caine was condemned to wander aimlessly between two worlds, neither of which fully accepted him. Because of his ambiguous identity, Caine was an Asian American version of the stock "tragic mulatto" figure. Caine found refuge among fellow acolytes and priests at the Shaolin temple, but even so, he initially experienced difficulty in gaining admittance because of his mixed parentage. "In the Shaolin temple we have never accepted anyone other than full Chinese birth," said Master Kan (Philip Ahn) sternly. Softening, the smiling Shaolin priest acknowledged, "There is a first for everything."

In his autobiography *Giant Steps*, Kareem Abdul-Jabbar writes admiringly of the man who orignally was to have starred in *Kung Fu*, Bruce Lee. Early in his career, Lee had caught the attention of a television producer and won the Asian sidekick role of Kato in *The Green Hornet* (1966–67), an adaptation of the 1930s radio program created by George W. Trendle. Subsequent to *The Green Hornet*, Lee made a memorable appearance on the detective drama *Longstreet* (1971–72) in the episode "The Way of the Fist." Lee played the role of martial arts tutor to the blind insurance investigator Mike Longstreet (James Franciscus).

According to Abdul-Jabbar, who studied with the Bruce Lee for five years and claimed him as a good friend, the man who later became an international film star was denied the lead role in *Kung Fu* because of the ingrained racism of network television. Writes Abdul-Jabbar:

> Bruce was an amazing martial artist, but I responded to him for several other reasons as well. He had been hurt by racism and said so. After having played Kato on *The Green Hornet*, he worked with the people who developed the *Kung Fu* character and was supposed to star in the television series. He would have been perfect, a master working his art before the national audience, but whoever it was

that decided such things made it clear to Bruce that they didn't think a Chinese man could be a hero in America. They passed over Bruce and gave the part, and the stardom, to David Carradine.[35]

Abdul-Jabbar, a student of non-Western philosophy and religion, first became interested in Asian martial arts after seeing a *Zatoichi* film, one of a series of Japanese action-adventure films that feature Shintaro Katsu as a blind masseuse and master swordsman who possesses preternatural skill in both capacities. Abdul-Jabbar was later to appear in a classic fight sequence paired against his mentor in *Game of Death* (1979), a film that included sequences from the classic *Enter the Dragon* (1973), released three weeks after Lee's death at the age of thirty-two.

The lack of film and television roles for Asian Americans frustrated Lee, who was born in San Francisco and studied at the University of Washington before embarking on his professional career as a martial artist and actor. Lee, who enjoyed early renown as a child actor, returned to the flourishing Hong Kong film industry to make the pathbreaking films that elevated him to international stardom. Upon losing the coveted role in *Kung Fu* to David Carradine, Lee was reported to have joked, "I guess they weren't ready for a Hopalong Wong."[36] Thirty years after his death, however, the legend of Bruce Lee continues to grow. In 1993, the biopic *Dragon: The Bruce Lee Story* opened to a wildly enthusiastic moviegoing audience. The film, according to *Los Angeles Times* reviewer Peter Rainer, exploits a racial subtext in some of its best fight scenes. "Bruce is like a one-man rescue mission for Asian manhood; he gleefully overthrows the bucktoothed wimp caricature," writes Rainer.[37] For most Asian Americans, Bruce Lee struck a blow against white racism with each high-velocity punch he delivered.

Fight the Power

Television drama tends to portray a world relatively free of ethnic, racial, gender, and class conflict. As the public relations arm of corporate America, network television is wont to minimize if not discount the positive results of sustained popular opposition to racism, economic exploitation, and sexism. But because television drama requires at least some degree of social realism, popular resistance and revolt sometimes filter through. The pilot episode of *Kung Fu* illustrates this contradiction perfectly.[38]

The wandering Caine's problems begin when the blind Master Po (Keye Luke) is gunned down by the imperial nephew for having inadvertently gotten in the way of an official procession. Although he has been taught to follow the path of nonviolence, Caine brings immediate justice to the government official by killing him with a spear. To avoid arrest, Caine is forced to flee China for America. Soon after his arrival, Caine faces down a white ruffian who verbally abuses an elderly Chinese man named Han Fei (Benson Fong). As Han Fei pokes his head through a saloon door, Raif (Albert Salmi) says, "Hey, you with the funny hat. You know I don't like any slant-eyes in a white man's saloon." Raif tells the men around the poker table, "You know, I got a nose for Chinamen." Turning to Caine, Raif tells him, "You smell a little yellow to me." Caine says nothing in response. But when Raif tries to remove him physically from the saloon, the wandering Shaolin priest subdues the bully with a mild application of *kung fu*.

A grateful Han Fei offers Caine a job as a laborer in railroad construction. At the work site, Caine's fellow workers are drawn to him when they happen to see marks on his forearms that reveal he is a Shaolin priest. Recognizing that membership in a Shaolin temple is in itself a form of political resistance against the state, the workers turn to Caine for leadership after an activist construction crew member named Fong (Robert Ito) is shot dead by company goons. Fong was killed for his protest against unsafe working conditions. From then on, the taciturn fugitive from imperial China stands alongside his yellow comrades to oppose their abuse and exploitation.

By the end of the episode, not only has Caine vanquished an assassin sent by the emperor to kill the outlaw priest, but he brings sadistic railroad foreman Dillon (Barry Sullivan) to justice. In a final act of defiance, Caine strikes a blow against frontier capitalism by setting fire to a railroad trestle built by the workers. After overcoming resistance to his entry into the Shaolin priesthood on the basis of his mixed racial heritage, Caine attains heroic stature by single-handedly punishing abuses of state power in imperial China, combatting individual acts of anti-Asian racism, and fighting the exploitation of Chinese labor under capitalism.

As a unique Western antihero, Kwai Chang Caine represents a radical departure from the traditional heroic figure, whom Alexander Saxton identifies as the "Jacksonian Indian killer," for in addition to eschewing violence, Caine is a "half-breed," non-European, and anticapitalist. Caine's training and subsequent entry into the Shaolin priesthood make him a member of an elite subculture, yet his sympathy and support of the common folk he encounters during his wanderings mark him as a populist. And as the child of white and Asian parents, Caine is the living repudiation of the "*Herrenvolk* democracy" enjoyed by the master race, an ideology that denies "class division within its own ranks by projecting hostility against racial enemies outside."[39] Beyond the dazzling displays of martial arts prowess and the gems of ersatz "Oriental" wisdom that occasionally break the profound silence kept by the rootless Kwai Chang Caine, the compelling drama of *Kung Fu* stems from Caine's syncretic racial identity as Asian "other" and Anglo-Saxon "self" in the form of one bad-ass individual.[40]

Chapter 3

War against Japanese America

Alien Subnation

The publication of *The Negro Family* in 1965 engendered a great deal of controversy among policy intellectuals, government officials, academics, and the educated public. In the "Moynihan Report" the ongoing economic plight of African Americans was attributed to the absence of a family structure that conformed to the bourgeois standard.[1] Shortly after the publication of *The Negro Family*, Professor William Petersen was asked by the editor of the *New York Times Magazine* to write an article on a distinct racial group that also had suffered past discrimination yet did not seem to be troubled by a breakdown in family life. The group happened to be Japanese Americans. Petersen himself admitted that he had little personal and absolutely no professional experience that qualified him to expound upon the subject matter, but he undertook the assignment nonetheless.

In retrospect, it is safe to infer that liberal policy intellectuals of the day were desperately in need of a "success story" that would demonstrate that group oppression does not necessarily result in the so-called social pathology exhibited by other racial minorities, for if *all* nonwhite ethnic groups were doomed to failure in a pluralist social system, then what would this imply about the "Great Society"? The liberal pluralist myth of "equal opportunity" would be exposed for what it is, leaving an explanatory gap wide enough to admit troubling opposing analyses that point to color as an important—if not primary—determinant of group mobility in American society. As Daniels and Kitano argue in their standard treatise on the nature of prejudice, color lies at the heart of structured racial inequality in that it serves as a visible marker used in "boundary maintenance," establishing the line of demarcation that separates the dominant group *64* from their subordinates in society.[2]

In undertaking his study, Petersen proposed to investigate "why in the case of *this* colored minority past oppression had led to phenomenal economic and social success, contradicting the generalizations derived from the experience of Negroes, American Indians, Mexican Americans, and others."[3] The intent, then, was not only to highlight the relative success of Japanese Americans, but to imply that other nonwhite ethnic groups might be responsible for their own victimization.

Petersen argued that the Japanese American family played an important part in instilling certain values and ethical norms that were instrumental in achieving group success. Unlike other liberal apologists, however, Petersen did not place total explanatory weight on the institution of the family to account for the relatively high educational and income status of Japanese Americans. Instead, he offered the dubious concept of "subnation" to explain the "anomaly" of Japanese American success. Petersen argued that Japanese Americans, "by working within a context of accord," placed their primary allegiance with the larger community for the purpose of maintaining "the Japanese image."[4]

Petersen's use of "subnation" as an explanatory concept, which he adopted wholesale from liberal ethnicity theorists, was rife with question-begging ambiguities that are impossible to invalidate because they are not amenable to empirical tests. At bottom, the argument Petersen advanced to explain Japanese American "success" was but a variation on liberal consensus theory. As the dominant model of American social scientific inquiry, liberal consensus theory assumes that political inequality can be ameliorated via piecemeal reforms and that race plays only a secondary role in determining what Weber terms the "life-chances" of nonwhite people.

Historical experience, which encompasses broad-based social movements and political mobilization against social oppression, is the best refutation of liberal ethnicity theory. Contrary to the view of society as a self-correcting, harmonious whole, as presented by liberal ethnicity theory, the American republic since its very founding has been plagued by structurally ingrained problems of race, class, and gender. Further, liberal ethnicity theory such as articulated by William Petersen fails to appreciate the often high degree of tension, intragroup struggle, and internal dissension that characterizes life within the ethnic group.

Because both ethnicity and individual identity are determined by a multiplicity of social, historical, cultural, and political forces, Asian American groups such as Japanese Americans are "internally differentiated" rather than a homogeneous "community" as described by Petersen.[5] Only superficially does the Japanese American community resemble what Petersen referred to as a subnation. Petersen's larger aim was to lend social scientific support to a conservative political agenda that places the individual, the family, and the "whole ethnic community" at the center of a minimalist definition of the social good that emphasizes self-help over state-supported welfarism.[6]

Farewell to Japanese Americans

The Japanese American experience during World War II demonstrated just how an actually existing "internally differentiated" ethnic community functions on a day-to-day basis, rather than as an idealized projection of liberal social scientists with no specialized training in Asian American studies. Not only were the tragic consequences of decades-old anti-Asian agitation made manifest with the coming of World War II, but the forced removal of Japanese Americans to concentration camps exposed fundamental cleavages and conflicts within the community.

Thirty years after America's concentration camps were emptied of their last remaining internees, a dramatic re-creation of a community torn asunder appeared on network television. Based upon the memoirs of Jeanne Wakatsuki Houston and cowritten by her husband, the television movie *Farewell to Manzanar* was broadcast March 11, 1976, on NBC.[7] *Farewell to Manzanar* remains one of the few television programs to have dramatized the daily life of an Asian American community in all its richness. It is ironic that the first full-length treatment of an Asian American group is set in a concentration camp rather than in freedom.

The narrative takes as its focal point an average working-class Japanese American family living in Santa Monica, California, before the outbreak of World War II. As the story begins, family and friends are celebrating the silver wedding anniversary of Ko Wakatsuki (Yuki Shimoda) and his wife Misa (Nobu McCarthy). The dining table is richly set with Japanese food amidst American favorites. At the piano, the children sing the popular songs of both countries. Those in the racially mixed group of guests, which includes whites, are seen helping themselves to the communal feast.

This peaceful tableau is shattered when the family learns of the Japanese attack on Pearl Harbor. Ko Wakatsuki, a fisherman, burns precious photographs along with a Japanese flag that his aunt had given him before he left for the United States. After destroying personal items that might be considered incriminating if found in his possession, Wakatsuki is soon arrested by FBI agents. Automatically suspected of disloyalty to the United States, the family patriarch is sent to Bismark, North Dakota, as his family remains behind to await the formal mass removal of Japanese Americans from their homes.

Richard Wakatsuki (James Saito), a young man who plans to study law, asks why German Americans and Italian Americans have not been similarly rounded up. In response to her embittered son, Mrs. Wakatsuki alludes to the underlying anti-Asian racism that helped justify the government's actions: "Look in the mirror, Richie. We can change our names, but we can never change our faces." The irreducible fact of race meant that the Wakatsukis and their coethnics would be deprived of their liberty for the duration of the war.

Not all of the newly defined suspected enemies of the state go along quietly. As a group of prisoners are driven to their new home in Manzanar, California, Joe Takahashi (Seth Sakai)—a veteran of World War I outfitted in full U.S. Navy regalia—upbraids his fellow passengers for their acquiescence and protests loudly against the injustice inflicted upon him by his own government. Takahashi later has a hand in organizing Manzanar inmates against abuses by the camp administration and spearheads the campaign against signing a loyalty oath administered by the War Relocation Authority (WRA).

Family and community pull together and "make life livable at Manzanar," says the narrator, Jeanne Wakatsuki.[8] "We organized block councils, kitchen crews, sanitation practices, volunteer police, and fire departments." All the while, Ko Wakatsuki continues to be harassed by military officials who accuse him of supplying oil to Japanese submarines supposedly anchored off the coast of California. After rejoining his family at Manzanar a defeated man, Wakatsuki begins drinking bootleg *sake* and slips into a deep depression.

A political dissident, Sam Fukimoto (Mako), rallies the camp population against those among them suspected of acting in complicity with the administration. Joe Takahashi emerges as the leader of the militant faction, and Frank Nishi (Frank Abe) is accused of heading the collaborationist contingent among the internees. Fukimoto summarizes the position of the dissidents when he states, "They have used Pearl Harbor as an excuse to take our land, our home, and then they put us here in prison as if we were the thieves."

Tension among camp inmates builds as living conditions worsen. First Frank Nishi is beaten and hospitalized, then Joe Takahashi is jailed as a suspect in the attack, which in turn causes Sam Fukimoto to call for a general strike. A mob attacks the camp hospital, calling for the camp administration to surrender Nishi to them for punishment. But the protestors are turned back when prison guards fire on the crowd.

Another crisis follows when the WRA demands a loyalty oath from all males over seventeen years of age. One of the purposes of the "Application for Leave Clearance" questionnaire was to identify and remove those internees suspected of disloyalty to the United States. The WRA was especially interested in isolating those who openly protested their unjust incarceration. "Loyal" *Nisei* who were deemed acceptable security risks were given clearance by the WRA, "enabling them to leave the concentration camps and resettle in the Midwest, mainly in and around the city of Chicago."[9] Those who refused to sign were often segregated from the main camp population and held under tight security.

The loyalty registration issue poses a dilemma for Ko Wakatsuki. He is filled with barely repressed anger for having suffered the indignities of anti-Asian racism all his adult life. "You know it gives me a strange sort of feeling to be suddenly sought after by the same government who denied me citizenship for thirty-five years," says Wakatsuki. Yet at the same time, Ko is grateful for the opportunities his adopted country has afforded the Wakatsuki family. The die-hard Joe Takahashi insists that Wakatsuki not sign the loyalty oath. "You know what this is?" asks Takahashi. "The final insult. They pen us up like cattle and then ask us to declare our loyalty."

Soon after Richard and Teddy Wakatsuki enlist in the U.S. Army, Ko Wakatsuki decides to sign the loyalty oath. Rather than becoming a "No-No Boy" like many of the camp militants, Wakatsuki addresses an assembled group of internees and explains why he must answer "yes, yes" to questions 27 and 28 of the WRA questionnaire, which asked internees whether they were willing to serve in the U.S. military and forced them to pledge their loyalty to the United States of America.[10] "I must say 'yes, yes,' " Wakatsuki says to the assembly, "because the life I have had here in American is *still* better than the life I would have had in Japan." In the end, Ko Wakatsuki—despite being denied the basic rights that attend U.S. citizenship—becomes a "good" Japanese American by answering the loaded questions with the proper responses. With Wakatsuki's decision, the ideological purport of *Farewell to Manzanar* is made all too clear: even though a grave injustice was done, being held prisoner in the democratic United States is still better than living under a military dictatorship in Japan. The program thus serves to excuse one of the worst abuses of constitutional rights in U.S. history by having Ko Wakatsuki's self-rationalization stand as the sentiment of the internees as a whole. The camp militants are seen as impetuous hotheads eager to score only philosophical points against their concentration camp keepers.

Richard Wakatsuki goes off to war, leaving behind Lois (Gretchen Corbett), a white nurse with whom he had an affair while in camp. Unlike most relationships between Asian men and white women represented on network television, this one is thoroughly sexualized, although the prohibition against touching is scrupulously observed. His brother Teddy is also seen kissing passionately his pregnant wife Chiyoko (Akemi Kikumura) as he leaves Manzanar to join the Army's famed 442nd Regimental Combat Team composed of *Nisei* GIs. Both of these scenes are noteworthy for their violation of the unwritten rule that the Asian male presence in media must be desexualized. However, the forbidden love between Richard and Lois proves to be ill-fated, for Richard soon meets his death on the field of battle.

The entry of the Wakatsuki brothers into military service leads to the end of their family's imprisonment. Only after Ko and his sons have demonstrated unswerving loyalty to the United States is the family given its freedom. Narrator Jeanne Wakatsuki Houston observes that the transition was not without pain, as she tells of internees who were afraid to leave the camp out of fear of the racist violence awaiting them once they returned home. "One family had been hung by a vigilante group," she says. "Others had been shot at or beaten on the streets."

The scene shifts to the present, as an adult Jeanne Wakatsuki Houston and her family visit the wind-blown site where Manzanar once stood. They duck under a barbed-wire fence and amble amidst the half-buried ruins, the desert slowly reclaiming all traces of the concentration camp in the face of fading historical memory. Wakatsuki Houston speaks of the way her life has been "scarred by a sense of guilt over a crime I never committed." In the years following her family's release from Manzanar, Wakatsuki Houston suppressed her memories of the experience. She went to college, married, and raised a family of her own, but in all that time, Wakatsuki Houston confesses, she "kept my years in camp from them, just as I kept them from myself."

Instead of recalling the climate of anti-Asian fervor and official acts of racism that forced families like the Wakatsukis into a concentration camp located in a desert wasteland, the producers of *Farewell to Manzanar* opt for a more forgiving final accounting. A flashback leaves the viewer with a riotous concluding scene of Ko Wakatsuki driving his family in a jalopy as they make their final departure. Ko Wakatsuki steers the automobile over a "Manzanar" sign, and with that, it is implied that past injustices have been set right. By the end of the program, the viewer is left with a depoliticized memoir of a dutiful daughter while the reality of concentration camp life blurs into soft-focus irrelevance.

Manzanar Revisited

Shortly after *Farewell to Manzanar* was broadcast in 1976, a scathing critique of the film was written by Raymond Okamura.[11] Okamura's evaluation reflected his personal and professional interests as a San Francisco-based political activist. Along with Edison Uno, Okamura was cochairman of the Japanese American Citizens League (JACL) National Committee to Repeal the Emergency Detention Act. The objective of the campaign was to place pressure on the U.S. Congress to repeal Title II of the 1950 Emergency Detention (McCarran) Act.

Okamura claimed that *Farewell to Manzanar* distorted the history of Japanese Americans by focusing on an atypical family. Moreover, the program did not fully confront the issue of white racism in American society. *Farewell to Manzanar* not only deprived Japanese Americans of their humanity, contended Okamura, it also had the effect of stifling organized protest in the present by encouraging submissiveness and perpetuated the myth of egalitarianism, all of which left the structure of white domination untouched.[12] In his essay, Okamura made some very astute observations about the white-yellow love affair between Lois the nurse and Richie Wakatsuki. He further pointed out that the incarceration of Asian Americans was fully consistent with the course of American history and not simply an aberration, as is often asserted. And, Okamura noted, the program tended to favor the political stance of the stoic (some would say collaborationist) JACL faction over camp dissidents.

In all fairness, however, the producers of *Farewell to Manzanar* engaged both Edison Uno and Karl Yoneda as technical advisers to bring interpretative balance to the program. As community activists who were intensely involved with Japanese American political issues, such as the redress and reparations campaign, Uno and Yoneda both possessed the necessary experience and credentials to offer the production as complete and accurate an account of concentration camp life as could be hoped for within the limitations imposed by network television practice.[13]

But for Okamura, *Farewell to Manzanar* can be understood only as a nostalgic distortion of American history. There is, however, an oppositional, ironic reading of *Farewell to Manzanar* that might complement the one-dimensional interpretation offered by Okamura.

That is, *Farewell to Manzanar*—maybe in spite of itself—does show the extent to which the Japanese American community has been assaulted in a systematic, sustained fashion by a legal and political system controlled by Euro-American elites who periodically resort to racially based social discrimination in times of crisis. The viewer, however, is placed in the position of reading against the grain of the text and reinvesting it with history in order to arrive at an oppositional interpretation of *Farewell to Manzanar*. This is a difficult task for two reasons. First, popular social struggles as dramatized on network television are almost always reduced to melodrama. Second, network television drama engages the audience on an emotional and visceral level, while the meaning of its intellectual component is largely left to sociocultural critics who may themselves suffer from historical and political blind spots. It is the political responsibility of the sociocultural critic to tease out the implications of history and aesthetics as found in television drama, especially because fundamental questions of power are at the last instance always shunted aside or deferred indefinitely beyond an ever-retreating horizon.

Although *Farewell to Manzanar* is hardly instructive concerning the official explanations advanced for the relocation of Japanese Americans during World War II, it nonetheless draws heavily from actual incidents and real-life persons to re-create the tensions and conflicts that typified life in a concentration camp. For one, there was indeed a major riot in Manzanar that took place on December 6, 1942. The previous day, a JACL officer named Fred Tayama had been attacked. The character of Frank Nishi in *Farewell to Manzanar* is probably modeled after Tayama. In addition, Harry Y. Ueno, a *Kibei* (American-born Japanese, educated in Japan) who had tried to organize kitchen workers at Manzanar and a major opponent of what his faction viewed as JACL collaboration with the camp administration, is most likely represented by the Sam Fukimoto character. Finally, Joe Takahashi is probably the fictional analogue of Joe Kurihara, a Hawaiian-born *Nisei* who relentlessly contested the unjust actions of the government he had defended during World War I.

The major themes in *Farewell to Manzanar* remain consistent with the liberal ideological underpinnings of almost all network television drama. Its most misleading feature is the implication that the forced relocation and imprisonment of Japanese Americans can be viewed in retrospect as simply a historical accident that attended the general hysteria of life during wartime. Also misleading is the willingness of Teddy and Richie Wakatsuki to die for their country, implying that this was the only way they could prove themselves to be "true" Americans.

Family Matters

Despite its limitions, *Farewell to Manzanar* rendered a relatively complex portrait of the Japanese American community such as had never before been seen on network television. For the first time, Japanese Americans were portrayed as more than cutout figures. They were seen harboring fundamental doubts about the meaning of their lives in the United States. They were shown fighting among themselves over vital political issues while struggling against an all-imposing power structure that deprived them of basic freedoms. *Farewell to Manzanar* was the first network television drama that gave expression to Asian American resistance to racial oppression and social inequality. The program celebrated the resilience of an Asian American community and its ability to repel the periodic racially motivated attacks upon it. Never before had Asian American characters on network television been given more latitude in expressing the full scope of their humanity.

If viewed ironically, a program such as *Farewell to Manzanar* exposes conservative/liberal evasions of the present that point to the stability of the Asian American family as the foundation of Asian Americans' integration into the larger society. For neoconservatives and the New Right in particular, the use of the master signifier "the family" is a means of explaining away the differential success or failure of various racial and ethnic minority groups, including Asian Americans. Thomas Sowell of the Hoover Institution, for instance, showcases Asian Americans as a shining example of traditional self-help (i.e., they supposedly stay off welfare and do not make heavy demands on government services), whereas the adaptive family forms of other nonwhite groups are blamed for high levels of unemployment, welfare dependency, and poverty.[14]

Rather than acknowledge the historical and political-economic causes of unemployment and poverty, conservative critiques of the family blame the victims for their collective plight. This line of argument not only relieves the state of responsibility for providing the bare minimum in social welfare services and benefits, it also places the burden of poverty squarely on the institution that has been most ravaged by the ill effects of the current fiscal crisis of capitalism: the family.

The family, then, has become a convenient conceptual foil in the ongoing contestation of power in society. At the dawn of the Reagan administration, Burton Yale Pines (formerly vice president of the Heritage Foundation and currently chairman of the National Center for Public Policy Research, a conservative think tank) wrote of a new "traditionalism" that was supposedly "sweeping grass-roots America." A key feature of this return to the conservative past (in rejection of "New Class" liberalism) was the renewed dedication to the so-called traditional American family.[15] Jerry Falwell's Moral Majority, the Eagle Forum, FLAG (Family Life America God), and the Conservative Caucus were among the organizations cited by Pines as joining with such public figures as Phyllis Schlafly, Senator Paul Laxalt, and Senator Jesse Helms in the crusade to restore America to greatness by harkening back to a fictive past when the individual, the family, and the community stood as models of self-sufficiency.

In this war of ideological position, conservative commentators have often offered the Asian American family as an example to other ethnic minorities of how a formerly disadvantaged group can overcome hardship through self-reliance, personal discipline, and mutual assistance, all within the opportunity structure afforded by a liberal democracy. This is a myth, of course. But such myths continue to have deep cultural resonance as they are retold through the omnipresent media of communications, such as network television. All told, the myth of the model Asian American family helps lend legitimacy to a crisis-ridden social democratic social order in an age of economic decline.

"Goodbye Mr. Moto"

The removal and imprisonment of more than 110,000 Japanese Americans during World War II was but one incident in the history of racism in the United States. On the basis of meticulous archival research, historian Richard Drinnon concludes that the anti-Japanese sentiment of the war years was linked historically with America's hatred of nonwhite people, Native Americans in particular. According to Drinnon, the removal of many thousands of Native Americans from East to West and their detention on government-maintained concentration camps set a woeful precedent for the forced removal of Japanese Americans.[16] Less than two decades later in Vietnam, the implementation of the "strategic hamlet" program once more revealed the way in which nonwhite threats to the American republic have been dealt with: under the pretext of providing protection, entire populations have been removed from their homes, deprived of their livelihoods, and then blamed for the squalor that inevitably results.

The systematic subjugation of nonwhite peoples is personified by the professional career of Dillon S. Myer, the WRA "Keeper of Concentration Camps," as Drinnon brands him, a well-intentioned middle-American innocent who presided over the "relocation" of his Japanese American wards. Not only did Myer work at different times for the WRA, but he had been employed by the Bureau of Indian Affairs as well. Dillon Myer later directed the Cuban Refugee Program on the behalf of the Agency for International Development and served as a consultant to the Organization of American States. The common tie among these agencies is that they are arms of a government that has created the conditions – domestically and internationally – whereby massive numbers of subjugated peoples have been dislocated, removed, and subsequently relocated.

As a man of his time, Myer shared the assumptions of liberals who pushed for the "Americanization," assimilation, and integration of nonwhite groups along the lines of Anglo-Saxon conformity. Political "progressives" such as Theodore Roosevelt bequeathed their racist prejudices to New Deal policy intellectuals who felt duty bound to reform a society that would nonetheless remain under the control and leadership of an Anglo-Saxon male plutocracy. As a logical extension of this racist logic, Americans of Japanese descent supposedly would benefit by living under the direct control of a white paternalist regime in concentration camps located, appropriately enough, on lands where Native Americans had been confined.

Carey McWilliams, who today has become a virtual demigod among those who share a commitment to left-liberal politics, perhaps best summed up the prevailing view of the "Japanese problem" around the time of their mass incarceration. In an essay titled "Goodbye Mr. Moto," McWilliams applauded the uprooting of those who had resisted assimilation by isolating themselves in "these in-grown Japanese communities." He took sarcastic delight in speculating that once Japanese Americans were taken away, "Beverly Hills matrons will have to get someone to replace Mr. Moto, the indefatigable and highly reliable gardener."[17] McWilliams, like not a few of his liberal counterparts in the American Civil Liberties Union, was glad to see the breakup of Japanese American ghettos on the West Coast. Scattering Japanese Americans to the four winds would speed their entry into the dominant society and ensure their integration and eventual absorption into white America. Of course, McWilliams said nothing of the inhospitable social conditions that served to isolate Japanese Americans in ethnic enclaves to begin with.

Against unfavorable odds, Mr. Moto and family survived the material losses and emotional indignities inflicted upon them during World War II. Returned to civilian life, Americans of Japanese descent began a long, slow rebuilding process. Homes and small businesses were gradually reestablished. Professional and educational pursuits that had been forcibly interrupted were resumed. But the vibrant economic and cultural life of Japanese American communities such as had existed in Los Angeles were never quite restored to their prewar level. The expansion of neighboring African American and Hispanic communities, the removal of restrictive covenants that had previously barred Asians from purchasing homes in certain areas of the city, economic growth, and commercial development were all factors in the wider dispersion of Japanese Americans throughout Los Angeles County.[18]

Life behind barbed wire had important consequences for the Japanese American family. First, the traditional patriarchal family structure was partially eroded by communal living and eating arrangements. In addition, the unassailable role that the male head of household occupies in the traditional Japanese family proved to be inoperative under conditions where he was deprived of both a livelihood and the ability to make basic decisions governing the family. Second, the relocation helped effect the transfer of leadership from first-generation Japanese Americans, or *Issei*, to the more assimilated *Nisei*, or second generation.

If historian Roger Daniels is correct in asserting that the so-called relocation "remains *the* central event of Japanese American history," then it is understandable why its effects lingered long after the last concentration camp was closed.[19] Not only did the relocation experience expose the significant divisions and factions that existed within the Japanese American community, it also forced the recognition that many individuals had been warped by the insidious effects of racism, effects that sometimes led to self-loathing, superachievement, and the desperate desire to "blend in" at all costs.

No-No Boy (1957), a novel of resistance written by John Okada, raised basic issues over the community's varied responses to the anti-Asian racism that motivated the government's decision to relocate the Japanese American population. At the time of its publication, however, most of the Japanese American community was not yet ready for such intense self-scrutiny. The community roundly rejected the book when it was first published.[20] Only when *Sansei* political activists reclaimed the novel as their own during the 1970s did the Japanese American community finally begin to confront the reality of white supremacy and the far-reaching shadow it had cast over the U.S. republic at its founding.

Remembering Pearl Harbor

A national poll conducted between January 31 and February 3, 1992, by the *Los Angeles Times* revealed that almost one-third of all respondents considered Japan to be a "very serious threat" to the United States, with another 39 percent considering the "threat" to be "fairly serious." Thus, combining these percentages, fully 70 percent of those polled viewed Japan as somehow imperiling the lives of Americans.[21] An earlier poll taken by Yankelovich Clancy Shulman, contracted by the advertising firm Saatchi & Saatchi, "indicated a hardening of attitudes toward the Japanese among American leaders in business, government and the media."[22] Perhaps the most alarming sentiment uncovered by the poll was that 72 percent of the 800 respondents – 200 of whom were government and business leaders –were convinced that Japan seeks to dominate the world economy.

In reviving the fear of the contemporary yellow peril, the news media has given extensive coverage to certain disparaging remarks made by prominent Japanese political and business leaders in reference to the dismal state of American society. Journalists have gone so far as to identify a new strain of thinking among some Japanese known as *kenbei*, a neologism that connotes a visceral hatred of things American. Journalist Leslie Helm notes how novelist Akiyuki Nosaka refers to the United States as a nation of "refugees, a nouveau riche country," and how one professor describes the United States as a "vegetating nation."[23] With a sense of alarm, Helm writes of certain Japanese opinion leaders who have become fed up with the patronizing attitude of a nation they view as being plunged into ruin by poverty, crime, drugs, illiteracy, and the disintegration of the family.

The fiftieth anniversary of the attack on Pearl Harbor served as an occasion for many Americans to vent their hostility against Japan, now the chief economic rival of the United States. And, as in the case of Japanese Americans caught in the web of xenophobia, racism, and wartime hysteria fifty years ago, the current anti-Japanese mood once more threatens those who bear the stigmata of racial difference. In an intensifying climate of racial hatred exemplified by the electoral appeal of the former Nazi and Ku Klux Klan leader David Duke and the popular resurgence of white separatist siege groups such as those led by Tom Metzger in California, the Japanese American once more has become a convenient scapegoat for those frustrated by the decline of the U.S. economy.[24]

A *Los Angeles Times* article by Sonni Efron published on the eve of the Pearl Harbor anniversary provided a semblance of balance to the anti-Japanese media campaign.[25] Efron examined the negative implications of the Pearl Harbor anniversary for Japanese Americans, who often have borne the brunt of racist hostility. She cited the example of a Japanese American community center in Norwalk,

California, that had been vandalized for the fourth time in recent years. In November 1991, the walls of the community center were defaced by slogans such as "Nip, go back to Asia." In nearby Gardena, a professional apologist for the Japanese American internment by the name of Lillian Baker cultivates a loyal cadre of followers with mean-spirited writings that deny the reality of the concentration camp experience. "It's the same kind of stuff that's put out by people who deny the Holocaust happened," observes historian Peter Irons in reference to Baker's dogged propaganda campaign.[26] No mere garden-variety racist, Lillian Baker probably reflects the views of that 30 percent who, in response to a recent poll, agreed that the internment of Japanese Americans during World War II was fully justified.

Economic Pearl Harbor

In the midst of this climate of fear and hostility, ABC News devoted two consecutive broadcasts on its *Nightline* program to a special report titled "Pearl Harbor + 50."[27] The ABC special was only one of many programs produced by competing broadcast and cable networks to mark the occasion. Among other commemorative offerings were *Pearl Harbor: Attack* (Discovery Channel, December 7), *Pearl Harbor: Fifty Years After* (CNN, December 8), *Secret Subs of Pearl Harbor* (TBS, December 8), *World War II: A Personal Journey* (Disney Channel, December 7–10), *Victory at Sea* (Arts & Entertainment, December 7), and *Remembering Pearl Harbor* (KCAL-TV Los Angeles, December 7), hosted by Edward "The Equalizer" Woodward. In addition, NBC aired a rerun of its miniseries *Pearl* (1978) December 3–7.

CBS News had planned a coproduction with the Tokyo Broadcasting System, to be cohosted by the media hero of Operation Desert Storm retired General H. Norman Schwartzkopf and news correspondent Charles Kuralt. The Japanese executive producer for the program, Norio Tokumitsu, however, withdrew from the project after criticizing the double standard held by his U.S. counterpart. Tokumitsu expressed his worry that American leaders might exploit the broadcast to exacerbate an already intense anti-Japanese mood in the United States. "There is a rising tide of anti-Japanese sentiment in this country because of bad economic times and the U.S.-Japan trade imbalance," observed Professor Doris Graber of the University of Illinois. "If you're an auto worker in Detroit who's just been laid off and is predisposed to disliking the Japanese, seeing the programs about Pearl Harbor could give you additional reason for not liking them."[28]

Ostensibly, the purpose of ABC's "Pearl Harbor + 50" is to study the differing perceptions of the surprise attack held by the Japanese and Americans, respectively. But *Nightline* host Ted Koppel quickly links the attack on Pearl Harbor with the question of Japanese economic mastery over the United States. Koppel frames his intentions in prefatory remarks that describe Japan as a "functioning democracy with a thriving economy" modeled after the United States, an economy that has "thrived beyond our wildest expectations." Although tensions between the two countries are not the same as they were in 1941, "once again, Japan and the United States are talking past one another, getting on one another's nerves."

Part 1 of the special opens with World War II-vintage combat footage showing the devastation wreaked upon the fleet of U.S. Navy vessels anchored in Pearl Harbor, Hawaii. A Japanese audience is seen viewing the joint ABC-NHK production detailing the attack that began the hostilities between the two nations. A brief discussion ensues between host Ted Koppel and audience members about Japanese perceptions of the war. An older man states that for the Japanese, the nuclear holocaust at Hiroshima was more significant than the attack on Pearl Harbor.

At this point, Ted Koppel abruptly shifts the discussion to economic issues. Koppel asks the group what U.S. products they like to purchase. There is an embarrassed silence. A young woman pipes up that she very much likes American T-shirts and an older man speaks fondly of a reliable garbage disposal he bought many years ago, but otherwise the group sits bewildered by Koppel's question. Koppel is quick to note, however, that the quality of life in Japan lags behind that of the United States. A young woman who had once visited the United States says wistfully that were it possible to be reborn, she would want to be reborn as an American. Koppel concludes this prelude to the main body of the program by reaffirming the conventional wisdom that Japan is indeed a "nation of workaholics."

The next segment takes place at the NHK Studio Broadcast Center in Tokyo. Sitting with Ted Koppel are three guests who represent the Japanese point of view on the current relationship between the two economic superpowers. Both Koji Watanabe (deputy minister for foreign affairs) and Kazuo Nukazawa (managing director of Keidanren, or Federation of Economic Organizations) have become familiar fixtures on American television as official "explainers" of Japanese business and political policy. For most viewers, the unflappable, debonair Watanabe and the twitchy, gruff Nukazawa have become the public face of corporate Japan and the Japanese government. Completing the panel is Watako Hironaka, a member of Parliament and, as a member of the Komeito party, an opponent of the ruling Liberal Democratic party.

The theme of economic "competitiveness"—not the attack on Pearl Harbor—dominates the remainder of the program. When questioned, Watanabe attributes Japan's superior economic competitiveness to solid work habits, high levels of saving, and an emphasis on education. Hironaka observes that the disintegration of the family, the loss of the "Puritan work ethic," and the poor quality of public education help explain the decline of U.S. competitiveness. Nukazawa also offers a culturalist explanation by noting that American society is "permissive" and makes the larger point that since the Cold War has ended, the United States is now shifting its attention to the "economic arena."

By the end of the thirty-minute program, no real understanding of the current friction between the United States and Japan has been gained. The war between the two countries is interpreted by Koppel as a "failure to communicate" rather than as an epochal struggle between two capitalist superpowers seeking to outperform each other in the global economic arena. The cumulative effect of this special report is to relate the current economic conflict to the war in the Pacific, a dangerously flawed logical leap that in the past has had a devastating impact on Americans of Japanese ancestry.

Economic Warfare

The connection between the sorry state of the U.S. economy and World War II is made ever more explicit in a *Frontline* episode that aired about two weeks prior to the Pearl Harbor anniversary. *Losing the War with Japan*—the title itself is revealing—surveys the domestic economic terrain fifty years after the U.S. military defeat of Japan.[29] Among the experts interviewed are Professor Chalmers Johnson of the University of California, San Diego; Lee Iacocca, chairman of the Chrysler Corporation; Clyde Prestowitz, Jr., former Commerce Department official and author of *Trading Places: How We Are Giving Our Future to Japan and How to Reclaim It* (1988); Dutch journalist Karel van Wolferen, who wrote *The Enigma of Japanese Power: People and Politics in a Stateless Nation* (1990); and Pat Choate, author of *Agents of Influence: How Japan Manipulates America's Political and Economic System* (1991).[30] Choate first burst upon the national media scene in an interview more than a year earlier on the top-rated television newsmagazine *60 Minutes*, where he warned against Japanese lobbying efforts in Washington.[31] Completing the survey are comments and observations made by various government officials and private businessmen who have been on the receiving end of "unfair" Japanese competition.

Reporter Martin Koughan situates the current economic struggle between the United States and Japan by observing how the American high-tech victory in the Persian Gulf with Operation Desert Storm obscures a different type of "war" that currently is being waged. Professor Chalmers Johnson snidely remarks how the Gulf War was an exercise in "showing off our smart bombs in order to disguise our dumb VCRs." Johnson pronounces the Cold War over, with Japan having emerged the victor.

Chrysler chairman Lee Iacocca, one of the more highly compensated chief executive officers in American industry, despite the lackluster performance of the firm he heads, complains about the lack of U.S. access to Japanese markets. He utters a few platitudes about being a believer in "open markets" and so-called free trade, arguing that the United States and Japan are not competing on a level playing field. "We're getting clobbered," says Iacocca. Even Japanese patterns of investment in the United States are held suspect by the former Ford executive. According to Iacocca, Japanese automobile manufacturers who build plants in the United States are cynically taking advantage of U.S. labor. "They go into a corn field, they don't go in there in the ghettos," Iacocca charges. By hiring "farm boys," the Japanese automakers escape the high health care costs that Chrysler generously provides to its employees. "I got a workforce in downtown Detroit," says Chairman Iacocca, "I'm putting a billion dollars in that. The Japanese would never do that." Iacocca professes a sense of responsibility to American society that is lacking in the Japanese.

The benevolent outrage of Lee Iacocca masterfully manipulates interregional competition and racial politics by denouncing the reluctance of Japanese manufacturers to locate auto plants in the "ghettos" (Black) or "downtown Detroit" (northern urban), choosing instead to build in a "corn field" (southern rural) staffed by healthy "farm boys" (white). This is a coded method of alluding to the condescending attitudes toward African Americans that have been voiced by some Japanese leaders. By this self-serving declamation, Iacocca offers himself as the advocate of organized labor, protector of nonwhite minorities, and savior of decaying American cities in one fell swoop. Apparently, Iacocca's "buy American" campaign has won the backing of Benjamin J. Hooks, executive director of the NAACP. Hooks recently called upon African Americans to boycott Japanese-built cars. "This is not Japanese bashing," said Hooks. "We don't hate anybody. But we want to take care of our own."[32] In total, the Big Three automakers employ 143,000 African American laborers.

Further perpetuating the image of the Japanese as ruthless economic predators is Pat Choate, who caused a minor uproar when his book on the "Japan lobby" appeared in 1991.[33] According to Choate, the "Japan lobby is literally able to dominate politically virtually any issue that it chooses to take on." Choate denounces the legions of U.S. government officials, trade negotiators, legal experts, and regulatory specialists who acquire expertise and cultivate crucial contacts on the job only to switch sides and sell their services to Japan as "foreign agents."

A third theme is hammered home in an exchange among Karel van Wolferen, Chalmers Johnson, and businessman Richard Frick, whose company, American Video Entertainment, is having difficulty establishing a foothold in the highly competitive multibillion-dollar video game industry dominated by Nintendo, which controls 90 percent of the market.[34] Frick, along with van Wolferen and Johnson, comes close to charging Japanese rival Nintendo with abridging the constitutional freedoms of American consumers by their monopolistic practices.

"It's a matter of the American public having a choice as to what they can and can't do," says Frick in criticism of Nintendo's proprietary technology. Beyond video games, van Wolferen argues that the Japanese stranglehold can also negatively affect the American film, television, and publishing industries. "It begins to affect what's seen, what's done, what's shown," says Johnson. "That is to say, if you don't think ownership matters, you're not playing capitalism any longer." In response to an interviewer who asks Johnson whether he is suggesting that "Japanese ownership could abridge free speech in this country," the professor replies in the affirmative. "No question about it. I mean, that is to say, money does talk."

The highly charged themes raised by Iacocca (Japanese racism directed toward Blacks), Choate (alien infiltration), and Johnson (loss of individual freedom) all contribute to the overall impression that the "war" being waged by Japan against the United States goes beyond simple economic competition, that the battle is over the very destiny of the American people. The themes and tropes that find their way into this piece of reportage are alarmingly reminiscent of the kind of inflammatory rhetoric that precedes all-out military conflict.

By way of example, Senator Ernest F. Hollings (D-S.C.), while campaigning for reelection in March 1992, visited the Roller Bearing Company of America, located in Hartsville, South Carolina.

Hollings jokingly told a gathering of 90 workers that they should draw an atomic "mushroom" cloud on their product with the inscription, "Made in America by lazy and illiterate Americans and tested in Japan." Hollings's remarks came in response to Japanese Parliáment Speaker Yoshio Sakurauchi, who in January 1992 referred to U.S. workers as lazy, unproductive, and illiterate. Only two weeks previously, Prime Minister Kiichi Miyazawa had suggested that Americans lack the proper work ethic to keep the United States economically competitive. In response to such incautious remarks, a spokesman for Hitachi Chemical Research Center in Irvine, California, observed, "Certainly, negative statements from Tokyo hurt us and it causes a lot of tension in the workplace and it makes our situation here difficult."[35]

Not all Japanese have been content to accept passively the barrage of criticism from American politicians and corporate chieftains. In the sensational *The Japan That Can Say No*, writer and politician Shintaro Ishihara fires a volley of complaints and counteraccusations at such "Japan bashers" as Clyde Prestowitz and Lee Iacocca. Using the bombing of Hiroshima and Nagasaki with nuclear weapons as an example, Ishihara accuses Euro-Americans of an anti-Asian racism that has carried over into their military and business dealings with Japan. Addressing a Japanese audience, Ishihara urges his readers to "never forget" the race prejudice behind the decision to use the atomic bomb against them, and that the "same virulent racism underlies trade friction with the United States."[36]

For all the indelicate comments made by certain Japanese political and business leaders, it is Asian Americans who must bear the brunt of hatred and ever-increasing acts of violence committed by those responding to the thinly veiled racial rhetoric of U.S. union leaders, corporate chieftains, elected officials, and even heads of major civil rights organizations. A report issued by the U.S. Commission on Civil Rights, *Civil Rights Issues Facing Asian Americans in the 1990s*, states explicitly that remarks critical of Japan made by political leaders foment bigotry and often precipitate acts of violence against Asian Americans.[37] The national director of the Japanese American Citizens League, Dennis Hayashi, applauded the findings of the commission for establishing a clear connection between inflammatory political rhetoric and hate crimes committed against Asian Americans. "That's something we've been saying for some months now," said Hayashi. "In particular, we feel this 'Buy American' campaign that's spreading across the nation is the cutting edge of anti-Asian prejudice that leads to anti-Asian violence."[38]

The voting citizens of Los Angeles turned a deaf ear to the dire warnings of the Civil Rights Commission by casting their ballots in favor of Charter Amendment G (the "Buy American" amendment) in the June 1992 election. According to Kevin Starr, a social historian who has written extensively on California politics, the charter amendment "gives new expression to a streak of xenophobia that runs deep in the L.A. psyche."[39] Starr relates the "Buy American" charter to earlier Alien Land Laws (1913, 1920, 1923, 1927) that prohibited Japanese immigrants from owning property in California, which were intended to preserve and protect the interests of the "Anglo-Saxon oligarchy." This time around, rather than erecting transparently discriminatory barriers, the charter amendment would simply prohibit municipal government from engaging in business with nonlocal (i.e., Japanese) companies. The institutionalization of xenophobia in the Los Angeles city charter testifies to the tenacity of anti-Asian racism, even in 1992.

The retaliatory measure enacted by the city of Los Angeles came on the heels of a municipal brouhaha created when the Sumitomo Corporation of Japan was awarded a $121.7 million contract in late 1991 to build an automated train for the Metro Green Line. The announcement was met by the hue and cry of a public who did not protest when Sumitomo earlier was awarded a contract to build the Metro Blue Line, which became operational in 1990. The Los Angeles Transportation Commission quickly reversed its decision after California Assemblyman Richard Katz (D-Sylmar) and Los Angeles City Councilmen Zev Yaroslavsky, Nate Holden, and Joel Wachs orchestrated a campaign to stir public opposition to the contract. Many callers to Councilman Wachs's telephone hot line left "overtly racist messages with references to Pearl Harbor and World War II."[40] Councilman Yaroslavsky, who was considering running for mayor of Los Angeles, resurrected the memory of both the attack on Pearl Harbor and the Jewish Holocaust by shouting "Never again! Never again!" to a crowd of unemployed workers.

To his credit, Deputy Mayor Mark Fabiani accused Katz, Yaroslavsky, Holden, and Wachs of "whipping up xenophoic sentiments all over Southern California. . . . There is certainly no shortage of demagogues on the City Council who are eager to exploit anti-Japanese sentiments."[41] A Japanese American spokesman for the firm of Kindel & Anderson had the unenviable task of defending his firm's role in representing Japanese business interests on a local news discussion program, *Life and Times*, aired on the Los Angeles PBS affiliate, KCET-TV.[42]

On the program, cohost Patt Morrison warns guest Robert A. Takeuchi against invoking the "easy reaction of Japan bashing" to explain the reversal of the Metro Green Line decision. But Takeuchi nevertheless states his belief that "Japan bashing" indeed might have been responsible for the popular uprising against the Sumitomo Corporation. "The trade imbalance should not be an issue," says Takeuchi, whose firm has represented various Japanese business interests in the city of Los Angeles for more than thirty years.

Opportunistic political and business leaders, however, made it an issue. The anti-Japanese frenzy allowed Sumitomo competitor Morrison-Knudsen to mount an ultimately successful letter-writing campaign directed at California members of Congress and the California State Assembly. William Agee, president of Morrison-Knudsen, denied that his firm had anything to do with turning public sentiment against Sumitomo but all the same declared the contract cancellation "a great victory for all the people of the United States."[43]

In a PBS *Frontline* documentary titled *Coming from Japan,* writer and longtime America watcher Shuichi Kato observes that the Japanese community has become increasingly vulnerable over the past few years, especially in Los Angeles.[44] "As our numbers here grow, we begin to make an enclosed community," Kato observes, "an easy target for American resentment." In the ten visits he has made to the United States over the past thirty years, Kato has seen Japan emerge from the devastation of World War II eventually to eclipse the United States as the wealthiest country in the world. He suggests it is America's need for external enemies that has made it possible for Japan to overshadow its former benefactor. "You find energy and purpose when you have an enemy," says Kato. "And today, some Americans would like Japan to fill that role."

So long as the former Soviet Union maintained its status as the "evil empire," as President Ronald Reagan once branded it, Japan in the postwar era stood as an important military ally to the United States in East Asia. As economist John Kenneth Galbraith remarks in the documentary *Power in the Pacific,* the Japanese economic power of the present is the "stepchild of American policy."[45] That is, the architects of the U.S. postwar world order decided early on that Japanese industry should be induced to become the "workshop of Asia" to keep communism from taking root throughout the region. The special procurement programs of the U.S. military during the Korean War helped to transfer the necessary technology and sophisticated mass-production techniques that soon would become the envy of the world. "By 1970," says narrator Sab Shimono, "the United States had transferred to Japan $10 billion in aid and trade." Ironically, then, it is the U.S. permanent war economy that is largely responsible for the international success of Japanese corporations such as Sumitomo.

Homeless on the Range

In addition to the panicky themes of Asian infiltration, racist condescension, abridgment of freedoms, there is another emotion-charged issue that recently has been highlighted by the television news media: the "buying up" of America by the Japanese. A teaser for a segment on the ABC newsmagazine *20/20* (1978–present) aired in October 1990 promises a scoop on "Japanese cowboys" who are buying "huge spreads" in the heartland of America. Celebrity journalist Barbara Walters introduces the segment "A Yen for Beef" by gaily announcing, "Instead of 'Happy Trails' it's '*sayonara* cowboy.' "[46]

Reporter Lynn Sherr heads to the "big sky country" of Montana to file a story on the Zenchiku Company, a Japanese corporation that deals in land, livestock, and ranching on a massive scale. Zenchiku's Lazy 8 Ranch is home to 3,000 head of cattle, which represent an investment of $12.6 million. Sherr personalizes the piece by focusing on two Zenchiku managers, Kazuhiro Soma and Tommy Fukutomi, "greenhorns" who are being trained in the business and art of ranching American-style. The reason given for Zenchiku's entry into the cattle-ranching business is the $1 billion worth of U.S. beef sold in Japan each year. An even higher volume of sales to Japan is expected with the impending removal of protectionist trade barriers that restrict the importation of U.S. beef.

The report details how since 1987 Japan has been buying cattle ranches, feed lots, and packinghouses in five western states. But to put this accelerated pattern of investment into proper perspective, it is stated that Japan's cattle ranch holdings represent less than 1 percent of the total in the United States. Great Britain, Canada, France, and Switzerland are correctly mentioned as having far more investments in cattle ranches in the West than does Japan. Apparently, for the producers of *20/20*, the sight of English, Canadian, French, or Swiss "cowboys" is not quite so amusing as that of Japanese wranglers.

Sherr imparts a lighthearted, humorous spin to her report as she records a friendly farewell party organized by Lazy 8 ranch hands held in honor of Tommy Fukutomi. Fukutomi is given a pair of spurs by his newly acquired American friends as junior fiddlers serenade the Japan-bound manager. But an outburst of nativist anger mars this otherwise perfect portrait in cross-cultural business exchange. While the party is in full swing, an irate local man old enough to have firsthand memories of World War II drives up in a pickup truck and says that American boys fought for this land and that they would never surrender it to the Japanese. To the Canadians, the British, the French, and the Swiss, perhaps, but never to the Japanese.

After quotas on U.S. beef imports were lifted by Japan in April 1991, resident *Los Angeles Times* Japan watcher John Balzer turned his sights on the Zenchiku operation in an article that described how the Japanese company leases 41,000 acres of "U.S. taxpayer-subsidized federal rangeland."[47] A sense of national violation, both of the land and of American destiny, is conveyed by Balzer's poetic evocation of the leased rangeland located "100 miles from Yellowstone in a sage and scrub-tree valley explored by Lewis and Clark in 1804." And now, the virgin land will be overrun by cattle just so that the rapacious appetites of Japanese diners can be satisfied.

Balzer also reported on another sensitive U.S.-Japan business transaction that, if consummated, would have struck at the heart of American national identity.[48] In late January 1992, Nintendo of America, based in Redmond, Washington, was offered a 60 percent controlling interest in the financially strapped Seattle Mariners Major League Baseball franchise. Because Japan is the state's number-one trading partner, many Washingtonians, such as Governor Booth Gardner, were in favor of the proposed deal. Others in the Pacific Northwest were not at all pleased. In Anchorage, Alaska (where the Mariners are considered a "home" team), a Chrysler-Dodge dealer expressed his displeasure by running a red, white, and blue newspaper ad that linked the proposed purchase with the Japanese attack on Pearl Harbor and World War II.

Major League Baseball Commissioner Fay Vincent at first vehemently opposed the Nintendo offer, but then took a more diplomatic approach, stating that "we are in fact flattered by their attention and their willingness to invest." A lead editorial in the *Seattle Times* suggested that opposition to the change in ownership might have been rooted in racism. Despite the accusation, Vincent restated his "strong preference in favor of local ownership."[49] By "local ownership," Vincent apparently meant white North Americans only, given that Major League Baseball includes two Canadian franchises, the Toronto Blue Jays and the Montreal Expos. The official explanation for the rejection of the Nintendo offer was that American and Canadian owners were fearful that the entry of Japanese corporate interests into Major League Baseball might bid up the price of player talent. But there seemed to be little doubt in the minds of many observers that the current anti-Japanese mood in the United States had more than a little to do with the position taken by baseball officials.

Six months later, however, jingoism bowed to commerce when Commissioner Fay Vincent acceded to the wishes of Major League Baseball team owners, who voted to allow the purchase of the Seattle Mariners by Nintendo. The president of Nintendo, Hiroshi Yamaguchi, offered to front $75 million of the $125 million purchase price in exchange for less than 50 percent of the voting stock. Yamaguchi was quoted as saying that his partial purchase of the Mariners was "a form of community service."[50] To restrict Japanese control of the Mariners, Vincent approved the deal only after ensuring that John Ellis, CEO of Puget Sound Power & Light, stood at the helm of the organization.

Alien Invasion

The widespread perception of Japan "buying up" America is but the latest manifestation of yellow peril panics that have periodically gripped American society over the past 150 years. This latest wave of fear was set in motion by heavy Japanese investment during the 1980s in Hawaiian real estate, the purchase of several "trophy" properties such as Rockefeller Center, and the acquisition of large media companies such as MCA by Matsushita ($6.59 billion) and Columbia Pictures Entertainment by Sony ($3.4 billion).

The theme of Japanese invasion makes its way, albeit in a wry fashion, into the quirky program *Northern Exposure* (1990–present) when two Japanese investors visit the Alaskan town of Cicely with the idea of building a thirty-six-hole golf course. As Mr. Vincent Chiba (Lenny Imamura), Mr. Matsuto (Michael Paul Chan), and Dr. Joel Fleischman (Rob Morrow) test their skill on a synthetic putting green, the strains of Kyu Sakamoto's number-one hit single "Sukiyaki" (1963) bring the scene to a close.[51]

Japanese tourism later becomes big business when busloads of young couples flock to town for the opportunity to copulate under the northern lights, for according to Japanese folk legend, marriages consummated beneath the radiant glow of the aurora borealis will produce a gifted child.[52] Maurice Minnifield (Barry Corbin), a pompous former NASA astronaut and hero to the Japanese tourists, gives them a lecture on economic protectionism during a visit to his home: "I would like to take this opportunity to tell you that I admire the Japanese people. You have a very strong sense of culture and a very distinguished military tradition. But, I do think it's time that you opened your markets to foreign trade."

Not content with seizing strategic control of America's material legacy, Japan is currently being depicted as having launched a sneak attack on the very spirit and soul of the nation. During ratings "sweeps week" in late February 1992, the half-hour newsmagazine *Inside Edition* (1988–present) sent host Bill O'Reilly on location to Japan. His mission: to gain insight into the mind of America's arch-rival in Asia. Along with other tabloid news programs that have proliferated on the "fringe" of prime time, such as *A Current Affair* (1987–present), *Hard Copy* (1989–present), and *Now It Can Be Told* (1991–92), *Inside Edition* is prone to sensationalizing its often pedestrian reports.

The teaser clip introduces Daisaku Ikeda, the leader of the religious organization Soka Gakkai (referred to as a "cult" throughout the program).[53] Ikeda is described as a "billionaire cult leader, whose next goal might be buying up America." As affable host Bill O'Reilly explains before launching the series, "We have come to Japan to give you an inside look at the country that most affects America." Promising to shed light on certain "controversies" that affect the U.S.-Japan relationship, O'Reilly introduces the Ikeda report (two years in the making) by describing him as a cult leader with "thousands of American followers." Ominously, O'Reilly warns that "some say he's on a mission to take over Japan and buy up America."

Inside Edition reporter Janet Tamaro interviews a number of individuals identified as "experts" who comment upon the nature and scope of Soka Gakkai under the leadership of Daisaku Ikeda. The segment opens with a shot of a typically American parade, but among its participants is a phalanx of Ikeda's U.S. shock troops, all carrying the stars and stripes. Such open displays of American patriotism disguise a more insidious purpose, according to Steve Hassle, described as a "cult expert." Says Hassle, "They're going around waving the American flag when in fact the organization is Japanese. You have an organization that has probably several hundred thousand members in the United States alone and nobody's heard of them."

George Jackson, a "former cult leader," describes Ikeda as a "combination of Jerry Falwell, Jimmy Bakker, and Jimmy Swaggert with a little more political punch than Jerry Falwell." The narrator of the piece states that 250,000 of his American devotees donate "millions of dollars a year" to the organization in the belief that the funds are being spent on efforts to achieve world peace. In fact, "Ikeda is using the money to advance his own political ambitions." The narrator claims that Ikeda, far from seeking world peace, seeks the return of Japanese militarism. As World War II footage of Japanese warplanes in flight fills the television screen, the viewer is told how Ikeda's "once pacifist party talks of rearming Japan."

As if Ikeda's absolute control and manipulation of his legions of followers were not enough, Soka Gakkai International reportedly has paid "double market value" to "secretly buy up" pristine ocean-front property in California, outbidding the National Park Service, which had wanted to convert the land into a "national monument." The organization established an educational institution called Soka University on the site. But, the reporter notes, the university is "unaccredited," grants no diplomas, and is attended by "eighty Japanese cult members" who are there to study English. Once again, as in the case of the leased federal rangeland in Montana, the Japanese have outsmarted and outspent the U.S. government in gaining control of America's precious heritage.

To conclude the segment, George Jackson sounds the alarm, warning against a new Japanese invasion of the U.S. mainland. He says that Ikeda plans to move Soka Gakkai International world head-quarters to the United States. According to Jackson, Ikeda has set his sights on the United States as a new target of opportunity because Soka Gakkai needs a "new frontier" to explore "as things deteriorate in Japan." That is, the planned move of Soka Gakkai onto American soil runs in parallel to the overseas expansionism of Japanese corporate interests.

The underlying motive for the negative report on Daisaku Ikeda and Soka Gakkai becomes more apparent in a later companion piece that sets out to determine what the average "man on the street" in Japan thinks about Americans. "Do they love us," O'Reilly asks rhetorically, "or hate us?" News footage of Americans destroying Japanese cars in response to comments about "lazy" U.S. workers follows O'Reilly's query. The omnipresent Kazuo Nukazawa (seen on *Nightline*, "Pearl Harbor +50," and many other programs) of the Japanese Federation of Economic Organizations says that if the United States is to regain world economic leadership, the country must return to the traditional values of hard work and creativity as taught by Benjamin Franklin.

The economic rivalry between the United States and Japan forms the subtext for the *Inside Edition* series. In his closing comments, O'Reilly observes that although the Japanese are "polite," they are the "toughest negotiators around and very simply, it is much easier for them to sell products in America than for us to sell products here." O'Reilly charges the Japanese with not being "fair" in trade matters. "Let's hope the playing field evens out a bit," says O'Reilly.

The closing plea by Bill O'Reilly makes it obvious that the piece on Daisaku Ikeda is intended to connect the religious activity of Soka Gakkai International with the larger insidious Japanese economic assault on the United States. The purpose of this "news" program and others like it is to create a sense of general alarm among the American public that a new yellow peril is threatening to overrun the United States.

Taken as a whole, this half hour of reportage on *Inside Edition* draws from a storehouse of accumulated clichés and controlling images to make its case against the new Japanese invasion. For one, the frightening idea of mystical "Oriental" brainwashing techniques is revived by self-proclaimed cult expert Steve Hassle when he asserts that followers of Ikeda are victims of "mind control," as if the Soka Gakkai leader were the incarnation of Dr. Fu Manchu himself. Bill O'Reilly characterizes the Japanese as "polite," but implied by this left-handed compliment is the notion that treachery and deceit lurk behind the deep bows, smiles, and politesse. The Japanese are the "toughest negotiators around" because Westerners find it impossible to penetrate the mask of Asian inscrutability. Their well-known secretiveness, cutthroat competitiveness, predisposition toward militarism and authoritarian mass movements, predatory economic behavior, and love/hate relationship with the United States ("Do they love us or hate us?") make the Japanese a formidable, unpredictable foe in the years ahead.

Unlike the conditions preceding World War II, the prospects of military conflict with Japan are remote. Rather, Japanese Americans and Asian Americans as a physically distinct racial minority will be interposed as targets of the deep-seated hostility fed by the superheated rhetoric of observers and demagogues ranging from the pronunciamentos of Chalmers Johnson, Karel van Wolferen, Pat Choate, Lee Iacocca, and Ernest Hollings to the racist hatemongering of David Duke and Tom Metzger. Controlling images of Asian Americans as a fifth-column enemy will act as a buffer to the growing global might of East Asian economic power.

A problem of grave consequences arises when the genteel anti-Asian rhetoric spouted by academics, journalists, corporate heads, and political leaders joins with an increasingly disaffected and resentful white working class led by figures such as Duke and Metzger. This volatile mixture of highly prejudicial expert opinion and working-class populist resentment is further fueled by the sensationalism of network and, to a lesser extent, public television programs that place undue emphasis on the Japanese threat to American society. As Japan continues to incur the wrath of working Americans suffering the effects of the worst economic depression since the 1930s, Canada and European countries (whose investments in the United States far exceed those of Japan) escape similar scrutiny by the television news media.

Color of Racism

The anti-Asian racial bias of commercial television programs such as *Inside Edition* has not gone unremarked. For the past twenty years, a generation of Asian Americans working in the independent media arts have devoted themselves to challenging the cultural and political authority of those institutions most responsible for the manufacture of racial meaning in society. Director and media activist Loni Ding, for example, came of age amidst the cultural and political ferment at the University of California during the 1960s. Ding went on to write, direct, and produce a number of films and television programs that give fuller expression to the lives of ordinary Asian Americans. Most of her work has been designed for television in the belief that the lives of Asian Americans should be represented before the larger mass audience. "Television is the contemporary, publicly accepted record of faces and voices," Ding writes. "To be absent in T.V. imagery is a special kind of 'nonexistence' or way of being 'non-American.' "[54]

The controlling images created by the dominant media of Japanese Americans as perpetual aliens, as long-suffering victims, or as a group "success" story are challenged by Loni Ding at every turn in *The Color of Honor*. First released in 1987, the film later was revised for broadcast by PBS affiliates.[55] In 1991, KCET-TV Los Angeles broadcast *The Color of Honor* as part of its monthlong "Asian Pacific Heritage" series. Subtitled *The Japanese American Soldier in WWII*, the ninety-minute documentary effectively challenges every cliché and controlling image imposed upon the Japanese American community by network television.

The Color of Honor begins its daunting task by combining a variety of media to evoke textures and memories that reach fifty years back into the past. In the opening sequence, still photographs and film clips dating from the World War II period are used to recapture a sense of time and place. The photographs are then joined by contemporary film sequences such as that of the actual courtroom where the historic *Korematsu* case was argued. This skillful blending of media is both artful and instructive, dramatizing as it does the continuity between past and present.

The body of the documentary is composed of interviews with primarily *Nisei* GIs who served in U.S. Army Military Intelligence units in the Pacific theater of operations and whose contributions to the war effort have purposely been kept from public knowledge. Interviewee Manny Goldberg claims that "*Nisei* boys" were not properly credited for the invaluable service performed for the U.S. military and that their contribution is largely missing from the chronicles of war. Spark Matsunaga, a U.S. senator from the state of Hawaii who saw duty as a first lieutenant in the 100th Battalion in Italy, explains that the work of the *Nisei* soldier "could not be recognized" because they were on a "secret mission."

The exemplary performance of the *Nisei* GI in battle is beyond dispute. Indeed, the 442nd Regimental Combat Team, which saw duty in Italy and France, is the most highly decorated unit in U.S. military history. But such patriotic sacrifice stands in ironic contrast to the mass removal and incarceration of Japanese Americans shortly after the United States declared war on Japan. The filmmaker establishes that the anti-Asian mood of the prewar period helped set the stage for the mass relocation and removal of Japanese Americans from the West Coast. Harry Fukuhara, a career military man, recounts how he was fired from his gardening job by the "lady of the house" once news of the Japanese attack on Pearl Harbor broke. A photo (1920) of a scowling white woman pointing to a sign that reads, "Japs Keep Moving, This Is a White Man's Neighborhood" illustrates the intense, long-standing racial animosity directed against Japanese Americans. Another photo features a sign that reflects the fear of economic competition on the part of whites: "Anti-Jap Laundry League, Patronize White Laundries Only." After having endured decades of vilification by nativist groups, the Japanese American population became an even more vulnerable target of racial hatred once the war began.

Young Rudy Tokiwa and his brother were kicked out of Salinas High School near San Jose, California, shortly after the war commenced. The principal called Tokiwa a "troublemaker" before tossing him out of school. But before Tokiwa left the school grounds, he vowed revenge. After returning from military service a disabled veteran, Tokiwa visited the grounds of his former high school and by chance caught the principal addressing the student body during a school assembly. In full view of those present, Tokiwa forced the educator to make a public apology by threatening to "wipe the stage" with him unless he complied.

The Color of Honor is noteworthy for its exploration of the complex issues and contradictory demands faced by an internally fragmented Japanese American community. The program demolishes the myth that concentration camp internees accepted their incarceration with willing gratitude. Rather, the interviewees tell of organized resistance to both camp authorities and the federal government. Among draft-age *Nisei* men, a dividing line was drawn between those who chose to "volunteer" for military service (even while their families remained in concentration camps) and those who refused to serve, the "No-No Boys."

One of the volunteers was John Aiso, a graduate of Brown University and Harvard Law School. Aiso served as "academic director" of the secret Military Intelligence Service Language School, U.S. Army, at the Presidio in San Francisco. Aiso later became a prominent judge in Los Angeles, California. Unlike Aiso, Barry Saiki refused military service out of principle. "I did not want to volunteer," says Saiki, "because my father was interned. How could I willingly join the United States Army when my father was classified as an enemy alien?"

The extent of organized resistance to the extraconstitutional actions of the U.S. government was seen in the prosecution of sixty-three "No-No Boys" who were incarcerated at the Heart Mountain, Wyoming, concentration camp. According to the narrator, "Theirs was the largest mass trial for draft resistance in the history of this country." Frank Emi, one of the principals in the Fair Play Committee at Heart Mountain, explains in an on-camera interview how the group was charged with "conspiracy to violate Selective Service laws." Members of the Heart Mountain dissident group were tried in Cheyenne, Wyoming, in 1944. Eighty-five internees were convicted and sentenced to serve terms in federal prison. In retrospect, veteran of the 442nd Regimental Combat Team William Kochiyama expresses a grudging respect for the Heart Mountain "No-No Boys." "They were right," says Kochiyama, "that's what they believed in. And they had every right to oppose the draft at that time."

In addition to the fundamental rift between volunteers and dissidents, the Japanese American community was further divided by those who were born and raised in the United States and the *kibei*, U.S. citizens by birth who were raised and educated primarily in Japan. Having grown up in Japanese society, free of the discriminatory treatment endured by their American cousins, the *kibei* were perhaps less accepting of their second-class citizenship. Because they had grown up in Japan, military authorities held the *kibei* enlistees under greater suspicion than the general *Nisei* population.

So distrusted were the *kibei* that a good number of them were assigned to "labor battalions" instead of being sent overseas like the *Nisei*. A group of twenty-eight *kibei* protesters known as the "Detention Barracks Boys" were court-martialed for insubordination after refusing to obey a routine work order. The "DB Boys" refused to continue combat training "unless they were given assurances about their imprisoned families and the rights of *all* Japanese Americans were restored." *Kibei* servicemen such as Masao Kataoka and Hakubun

Nozawa were court-martialed in 1944 and given lengthy sentences to be served at Leavenworth Penitentiary. In 1988, as a consequence of the redress and reparations campaign, the rights and privileges of the protesters were restored in full.

Service in the U.S. military did not win freedom for the families of the *Nisei* veterans. Ernest Uno recalls the bittersweet reunion with his family at the Amache, Colorado, concentration camp upon his return from service with the legendary 442nd Regimental Combat Team. Uno was allowed to see his family in a "visitor's cottage" under armed guard and for one hour only. Uno's sister recalls that they were not permitted to welcome the returning warrior in their "home," nor were they allowed to prepare him a meal. Uno vents the suppressed anger and bitterness of many Japanese Americans of his generation who remained "forever the loyal American" despite their betrayal. "This is something we had to take," offers Uno. "Part of the shit we *always* take."

Throughout the 1980s, a number of court battles challenging the constitutionality of U.S. government actions concerning the internment were won. The Korematsu, Hirabayashi, and Yasui convictions were overturned between 1983 and 1986 in the federal courts. Years of political struggle by *Sansei* and *Nisei* activists culminated in the passage of the Civil Liberties Act of 1988 by the U.S. Congress. The act called for both a formal apology and monetary reparations to be given to those Japanese Americans whose constitutional rights had been so egregiously violated.

The Color of Honor does much to undermine the controlling myth of Japanese American passivity and resignation at the hands of all-powerful white authority during the war. Like no other previous film or TV program, *The Color of Honor* documents the forms of opposition and resistance to racial oppression. From the apology exacted by expelled student Rudy Tokiwa from the white principal, to the organized refusal by the "No-No Boys," to the Supreme Court challenges mounted by Fred Korematsu, Minoru Yasui, and Gordon Hirabayashi, Japanese Americans aggressively fought the injustice done them.

Complementing the straightforward documentary style of *The Color of Honor*, the *Independent Eye* series on PBS aired a more poetic and evocative meditation on the Japanese American concentration camp experience titled *History and Memory*.[56] The film is an assemblage of various media that help illuminate the lived experience of the concentration camps, including contemporary voice-over interviews of camp survivors; still photographs; 8-mm home movies made with a camera smuggled into camp; contemporary film footage; clips from Hollywood films such as *Bad Day at Black Rock* (1954), *Teahouse of the August Moon* (1956), *From Here to Eternity* (1953), and *Come See the Paradise* (1990); superimposed historical information scrolled on the left part of the frame; and official U.S. government propaganda films.

The documentary stands as both a disquisition on the selective and synthetic nature of memory and more specifically as a historical account of the Japanese American internment during World War II. In undertaking this twin objective, the politics of interpretation and epistemology, history and memory, combine to produce a parallax view of the truth wherein even forgetting is part of the remembrance process. Director-writer Rea Tajiri's mother, for instance, claims she has absolutely no recollection of the internment. She tells the story of a beautiful woman who went mad while in camp for having dwelled too heavily upon the hopelessness of her plight. The suppression of memory, then, had become a strategy of survival for the elder Tajiri.

With clips from *Bad Day at Black Rock* recurring at various points throughout the documentary, Tajiri interprets the noncharacter "Kamoko" as an apt metaphor for Japanese American life. "Kamoko's disappearance from Black Rock was like our disappearance from history," says Tajiri. "His absence is his presence." For filmmaker Tajiri, the inexplicable removal of Kamoko from the historical stage is related to the "ever-absent image" of Asian Americans and the "desire to create an image where there are so few."

Perhaps the "ever-absent image" is related to the social voyeurism that afflicted Tajiri's sister. According to Tajiri, her sister had the odd habit of following and observing people at a distance. Nor was it mere happenstance that her favorite movie stars were white. Tajiri's sister, like many other Japanese Americans who suffered from this curious psychic affliction, were cast as scoptophilic outsiders, disenfranchised spectators. In this, perhaps all people of color in U.S. society indulge in varying degrees of social voyeurism, as cultural invisibility, political marginalization, and the media-induced fetishism of white supremacist social practices force the transfixion of their yearning gaze on Euro-American objects of desire.

Programs such as *The Color of Honor* and *History and Memory* demonstrate the absolute necessity for Asian Americans to represent their own historical experience free from the constraints imposed by market-driven network and independent for-profit television broadcasters. Unlike a network program such as the made-for-TV movie *Farewell to Manzanar*, discussed above, *The Color of Honor* and *History and Memory* are not constrained from placing the relocation of

Japanese Americans within the historical context of persistent anti-Asian racism. The boundaries set by the dominant liberal democratic ideology and the aesthetic limitations of TV melodrama preclude programs such as *Farewell to Manzanar* from addressing the root causes of the war against Japanese America. In contrast, *The Color of Honor* can more truthfully reveal the contradiction between the stated principles of democracy and the legacy of racism in the United States.

History and Memory cites an August 28, 1990, article appearing in the *New York Times* reporting the campaign of California State Assemblyman Gil Ferguson of Orange County to have "children taught that Japanese Americans were not interned in 'concentration camps,' but rather were held in 'relocation centers' justified by military necessity." The attempt to rewrite history by Ferguson and others of his ilk points to the absolute importance of ongoing efforts by Asian Pacific Americans to produce films and television programs that resist the antidemocratic forces of right-wing political reaction.

Chapter 4

Asian Americans and U.S. Empire

Defensive Perimeters

At the conclusion of World War II, approximately 44,000 Japanese Americans were still being held in concentration camps scattered throughout the western states. The U.S. government's goal of dispersing the Japanese American population had proven effective to a certain extent, but in time fully two-thirds of the Japanese American population returned to the West Coast after having been "relocated."[1] Many families who returned to their former communities were welcomed back with racially motivated violence. However, because Japan was no longer the hated enemy, hostile acts against Japanese Americans were made somewhat less acceptable.

Under the guidance of General Douglas MacArthur—supreme commander of the Allied Powers—Japan underwent its peacetime rehabilitation. The image of Japan as a nation of fanatical, bloodthirsty militarists transmuted into that of a thoroughly contrite country eager to absorb the lessons of American democracy while restructuring its economy along capitalist lines. The reduction in media-induced anti-Japanese hysteria meant that the Japanese American population was less often targeted for hate, as they could no longer be suspected of fifth-column activity. Thereafter, the Asian "enemy" within U.S. borders was displaced to the continent of Asia itself. In the mind of General MacArthur, the end of World War II meant that the "American strategic frontier had shifted from the West Coast to the Asian offshore island chain" and that long-term global security mandated the control of Southeast Asia by the United States.[2] U.S. hatred of its former enemy, Japan, was replaced by the fear of Asian communism, especially in its Chinese manifestation.

The consolidation of U.S. global hegemony by military means continued unabated after World War II. In Europe, the Truman Doctrine helped inaugurate the Cold War by enacting a policy of *97* containment intended to check what the U.S. national security establishment believed to be unbounded Soviet expansionism. The purposely exaggerated threat of the spreading Chinese communist menace meant an increased U.S. military presence in countries such as Korea and, soon after, in Vietnam. Through the creation of an external Asian enemy, U.S. political and corporate leaders hoped to justify the subsidization and maintenance of a thoroughly militarized social system to fuel economic growth.

Just as the coming of World War II had forever altered the lives of more than 110,000 Japanese Americans (77,000 of whom were born in the United States), U.S. military adventurism in Asia wrought widespread destruction upon the land and was responsible for the massive loss of life throughout the region. Less than five years after the end of World War II, the United States again found itself at war, this time on the Korean peninsula. When North Korean forces launched a surprise attack against South Korea in June 1950, President Truman ordered General Douglas MacArthur to initiate a "police action" that soon escalated into a full-blown war whose final death toll numbered 34,000 U.S. soldiers, with 100,000 wounded. Approximately 4 million Koreans were killed during the war.

The Korean War ended in a military and political stalemate three years later, with the United States having exhausted a total of $54 billion in military expenditures. With the Korean War, the United States extended the scope of its "strategic perimeter" throughout much of Asia, a process that had begun with the imperial acquisition of the Philippines at the turn of the century. After Korea, the United States moved into the vacuum created by the military abandonment of Indochina by France after almost a century of imperial rule. This in turn led to the military and political quagmire of the Vietnam War, which dragged on until the hasty American exit in 1975.

For the civilian victims of war, the psychic and material costs are not often tallied. Too often it seems that the suffering and loss of life they sustain is not deemed worthy of attention unless it serves a larger propagandistic purpose. This is particularly true in the case of the Asian wars that the United States has conducted during the past forty years, wars in which countless civilians have been killed, maimed, murdered, and orphaned.

Supposedly neutral countries in Southeast Asia were brought into the Vietnam War by the United States. The secret bombing of Cambodia and Laos is perhaps the best-known example of U.S. genocidal destruction visited upon Asian peoples. Between 1969 and 1974, Cambodia had more bombs dropped on it than all of Europe during World War II. The intense, unrelenting bombing attacks all but destroyed an agrarian peasant society. Moreover, the widespread devastation caused by U.S. bombing helped set the stage for the Cambodian holocaust. Between 1975 and 1979, the Khmer Rouge, led by Pol Pot, destroyed 1,200 villages, 5,857 schools, and 796 hospitals and clinics. It is estimated that in a country of approximately eight million people upwards of three million were killed or displaced during those four years. Cambodia, which is still officially listed as an enemy of the United States, is today a "land of widows and orphans."[3]

The PBS series *Vietnam: A Television History* (1983) documents the inhuman horrors the United States has inflicted upon Asian peoples on a routine basis. In the episode "Cambodia and Laos," the narrator states, "For eight years, Laos was the most bombed country in the world."[4] As a matter of course, B52s would drop bombs indiscriminately on civilian populations. In one such incident, 100 civilians were killed and several hundred more wounded. As punishment, a crew member was fined $700 and survivors of the bombing were each given $100 in compensation for lost family members. A land once graced by agricultural abundance, Cambodia was drawn into the regional war by the United States and was soon overcome by widespread famine and disease. The ravaged political and economic condition of contemporary Cambodia and Laos is directly linked to the American military presence in Southeast Asia.

In the years following the Vietnam War, various organizations have emerged to voice their sense of betrayal by the U.S. government. In the United States, veterans' groups have protested the injustice of their collective neglect in the aftermath of the war, and the government has demanded a full accounting of mythical American POWs/MIAs by the Democratic Republic of Vietnam (North Vietnam) as a precondition for the normalization of diplomatic and economic relations.[5] CBS contributed an MIA story in late 1992 on its newsmagazine *48 Hours* (1988-present), hosted by Dan Rather.[6] In the feature, it is suggested by reporter Phil Jones that Vietnamese authorities are deliberately withholding information on MIAs with hopes of collecting "ransom money." Jones also says that the Vietnamese government might be using the POWs as leverage in an attempt to end the U.S. trade embargo.

Dan Rather puts the MIA/POW issue into proper perspective by comparing the estimated 2,000 of their numbers with the 8,000 listed as missing in action during the Korean War and the 80,000 MIAs of World War II. But with all the concern for American MIAs/POWs, the Asian victims of U.S.-sponsored terror have been given scant attention. They have remained faceless on television with the exception of one stock character: the Asian War Orphan. Since the the Korean War, the Asian War Orphan has been used as an effective tool in the U.S. propaganda effort against the communist foe. The figure of the Asian orphan evokes liberal humanist compassion, depoliticizes the meaning of war, and, most important, confers a sense of moral superiority to the American saviors.

Little Orphan Asians

In its first decade, the new medium of television proved an effective weapon in creating the proper Cold War political mood. It was especially effective in vividly dramatizing the evils of "godless" Asian communism to the American people. According to historian J. Fred MacDonald, television "became the most important vehicle through which citizens learned the latest developments in a rivalry that, in simplified terms, matched good Democracy against evil Communism."[7] What better way to bring home the irredeemably corrupt nature of communism than to demonstrate via television how communist regimes mistreat *their own people*. What better way to justify U.S. interventionism on the behalf of freedom-loving peoples the world over.

In the postwar era, television has been of inestimable help in making U.S. foreign policy understandable and acceptable to the American public by producing programs with high propaganda content. The television portrayal of Asian war orphans is noteworthy in this regard. A virtual television subgenre has developed that exploits the humanitarian impulses of many well-meaning Americans. Such programs, however, do not discuss the extent to which the United States has been responsible for systematically creating the conditions that have given rise to Asian orphanage. The lack of such discussion absolves the United States of responsibility for spreading misery that attends war and instead places the blame exclusively on the ruling regimes of communist countries. Further, the authoritarian rule of U.S. client states in East Asia such as South Korea, the Philippines, Indonesia, and Thailand goes unmentioned.

Countless families have been displaced, split up, or snuffed out of existence as a result of U.S. military intervention throughout East Asia. Yet there is little concern expressed for such families other than the function they serve in mass-mediated television tales of humanitarian aid offered by caring, compassionate Americans. The orphaned Asian child often has been employed masterfully as a method of graphically dramatizing the evils of communism to good-hearted Americans.

A prime example of the double exploitation of the war orphan is

Korean Legacy (1964), a television documentary produced by Golden West Broadcasting.[8] The documentary is a virtual hagiography of a simple American farmer from Oregon by the name of Harry Holt, who is portrayed as a saintly rescuer of Korean war orphans. Billed as "a true story as told by Mr. Dana Andrews," the documentary promotes the Holt Adoption Agency, based in Cresswell, Oregon, which is in the business of supplying American couples with children orphaned by the Korean War.

As singing children are shown walking down a dirt road in Korea, narrator Dana Andrews explains that Holt operates an orphanage in Il San, South Korea. Il San is located about sixteen miles outside the South Korean capital of Seoul. Holt's wife Bertha, already mother to six children of her own, has nevertheless assumed the additional burden of caring for Korean foundlings while helping to place others like them with loving American parents back in the United States.

According to the script read by Andrews, 700 children are brought to the Il San orphanage each year, "many thousands over the span of years, 3,000 who have homes found for them in America." No less than the notorious Flying Tiger airlines itself is shown at the Los Angeles International Airport assisting in the transport of those involved with the humanitarian relief effort. (Flying Tiger is noted for having been one of the original "civilian" airlines established as CIA proprietaries employed in the U.S. government's covert war against communist regimes.)[9] As thirty-two Americans sit aboard the airplane flying them to Korea, a passenger mentions the book *Seed from the East* as having inspired her to adopt "a little Oriental" child.

The documentary film crew conveniently happens to be on the scene when it is learned that Harry Holt has died suddenly of a heart attack. As news of their savior's death spreads, the film crew captures the grief of the children and staff members. A baby is heard wailing in the background as a veil of mourning descends upon the orphanage. Bertha Holt will see to it that her deceased husband is buried in Korea, as was his wish, rather than in the United States. The Flying Tiger flight back to the United States is understandably subdued, save for the irrepressible joy of the newly adopted tykes. With their "little Oriental" children cradled in their arms, the adoptive American parents seem all the more grateful that Harry Holt succeeded in this, his final mission of mercy.

Decades after the airing of *Korean Legacy*, the theme of the fragmented Asian family remains strong in American popular culture. After all, the Holt Adoption Agency alone was responsible for placing 6,293 children in the United States between 1955 and 1966.[10]

An episode of *Sons and Daughters* that aired in early 1991 illustrates the persistence of this compelling theme.[11] In the episode, titled "Crime and Punishment," a Korean American real estate agent named Lillian Park (Patty Yasutake) tracks down the ten-year-old daughter she had given up for adoption. Her biological daughter Astrid Hammersmith (Michelle Wong) now lives with a wholesome young white professional couple in suburban Portland, Oregon. Astrid and her mother are allowed to become reacquainted, but when Lillian Park asks the Hammersmiths whether they would allow their adopted daughter to undergo a "DNA scan" to positively determine her genetic identity, she is sent packing, never to return. By being denied further visits to Astrid, Lillian Park is given proper "punishment" for the "crime" of surrendering her daughter for adoption by the white couple.

The baby trade between Asia and the United States has far from ceased. On the contrary, it is thriving. In 1989, Asian countries were still the largest suppliers of children per year (5,000), with Latin America a distant second (2,600).[12] As reflected by the above-noted episode of *Sons and Daughters*, decades after Harry Holt placed his last orphan child, South Korea remains the chief Asian source of babies for American couples unwilling to buy domestically bred spawn (especially if black or brown). A war that was ostensibly fought to stem the tide of communism in Asia has had the effect of transforming South Korea into a reliable source of cuddly human capital.

Good Morning, Vietnam

Harry Holt was not alone in his humanitarian crusade. Better known to the American public during the 1950s was Dr. Tom Dooley. Dooley was a former ship's doctor in the U.S. Navy whose self-appointed mission it was to resettle and medically assist Vietnamese refugees fleeing the communist scourge to the north. Dooley's popularity stemmed from a best-selling book he authored, *Deliver Us from Evil* (1956). The book told the story of how his organization provided medical care for 600,000 Vietnamese refugees during 1954–55. An installment of *This Is Your Life* (1952–61) broadcast during the summer of 1960 featured Dr. Dooley. In the episode he appears skittish and effeminate, hardly fitting the image of the hypermasculine Cold War crusader. But the program captures perfectly the Christian anticommunist mood of Cold War America.[13]

Under the pretext of viewing a film on India, Dr. Dooley is lured into the NBC studio. Instead, a filmed greeting from the minister of foreign affairs for the "Kingdom of Laos" appears on screen. After paying brief tribute to the American humanitarian, the official exclaims, "This is your life!" to an apparently surprised Dooley. Once the shock of the bizarre opening wears off, host Ralph Edwards displays a map of Vietnam and tells of Dr. Dooley's work in caring for refugees who were part of a mass "evacuation" following the battle of Dien Bien Phu. (The French defeat at Dien Bien Phu is commonly interpreted by historians as the fateful moment when the imperial torch was passed to the United States as it extended its overseas empire into Vietnam.) In hindsight, these circumstances make Dooley's appearance on *This Is Your Life* all the more fascinating historically.

As the testimonial continues, Dooley is credited for having established a refugee camp in Haiphong. Dooley's Christian anticommunist message is conveyed in graphic terms when he speaks of children who had "chopsticks" thrust into their ears by the communists for having committed the crime of reciting the Lord's Prayer. Consistent with the anticommunist rhetoric of the Cold War period, Ralph Edwards disparagingly refers to Vietnamese communists as "reds." A number of friends and colleagues of Dr. Dooley appear on camera after first reciting the off-stage tributes that are the trademark of the program. Among them are men who served in the military with Dooley, a Vietnamese young man who as a child had been the beneficiary of his care, and a certain Madame Ngai who operates an orphanage in Saigon.[14] At the conclusion of the program, Dooley's book and fund-raising lectures are mentioned in conjunction with Medico, an international medical relief organization founded by the doctor.

There was a certain poignancy captured by this installment of the popular program *This Is Your Life*, for even as Dr. Tom Dooley was being celebrated by Ralph Edwards, he was dying of the cancer that claimed his life in 1961 at age thirty-four. All sentiment aside, this particular program illustrates how the real suffering of Asian children and civilians has been exploited as an effective method of gaining public support and sympathy for the American anticommunist crusade. This is not to say that individuals such as Dr. Tom Dooley were motivated by selfish reasons alone. The larger point is that professional humanitarians such as Dooley have chosen to ignore the cynical political and military policies of the United States that have caused such widespread devastation and misery in the first place.

Sadly, the doctor was not all that he appeared to be. Late in 1991, a lengthy article by Diana Shaw appeared in the *Los Angeles Times Magazine* that definitively demolished the heroic image manufactured by Dr. Tom Dooley and his handlers within the U.S. military and the intelligence community. According to Shaw, Dooley had hopes of being appointed surgeon general of the U.S. Navy on the basis of his good works in the battle against Asian communism. All appeared to be going according to plan until the navy received detailed information that the good doctor was homosexual. The Office of Naval Intelligence prepared a 700-page report that documented his homosexuality, which effectively turned Dooley "into a frightened pawn of U.S. policy-makers who were laying the groundwork for U.S. military involvement in Vietnam."[15] Dooley, in sum, was coerced into becoming a propaganda tool for the U.S. government.

According to Shaw, none of the atrocities allegedly committed by Viet Minh soldiers against defenseless children and civilians were proven to be true. Neither was Dooley's appearance on *This Is Your Life* spontaneous and unrehearsed, as it was made to seem. Dooley's guest spots on various radio and television talk shows were all part of a larger propaganda campaign orchestrated by the military and the CIA. The success of this U.S. government propaganda was borne out by a 1961 Gallup poll that listed Dooley behind Dwight D. Eisenhower and Pope John XXIII as the man most admired by Americans.

In addition to his role as national hero, Dr. Dooley also assisted the CIA in transporting weapons into neutral Laos along with medical supplies to be used in his Vientiane clinic. The clinic itself was little more than the site where young Laotion men were administered physical exams prior to their induction into the military. Dr. Dooley acted in clandestine complicity with the CIA and the U.S. military in Southeast Asia long before the American people had an inkling of the government-sponsored terror overseas. By celebrating Cold War heroes such as Dr. Tom Dooley, programs hosted by trusted household television personalities such as Ralph Edwards, Arthur Godfrey, and Jack Paar helped to mobilize domestic consensus against the evils of Asian communism.

Even the affable (announcer Dennis James introduces him as "the nicest guy in show business") successor to popular radio host Major Bowes, Ted Mack of *The Original Amateur Hour* (1948–60), was enlisted in the ideological war against the red menace. In a special remote program sponsored by Pet Milk, Mack travels to South Korea, where he stages a talent contest featuring GIs.[16] Filmed at the "Seoul City Command Theatre" are an array of country singers, an African American mime, a harmonica stylist, assorted crooners, and a pair of vocal impressionists who re-create the singing styles of popular artists of the day, such as Frankie Laine and Nat "King" Cole.

Apart from showcasing the talents of GI amateur entertainers, the program is obviously intended to justify the U.S. military presence in Korea. As a letter from General Christenberry – chief of staff of the 8th Army – states, "We here in Korea feel that the airing of this show will do much to aid the American public to give proper emphasis to the Korean situation and what it stands for in the fight against Godless communism." Ted Mack keeps the motley acts moving along and reaffirms that the purpose of the American mission in South Korea is one of "combatting international communism, preserving the American way of life, and keeping up the dignity of the individual." Back in the States, Ted Mack expresses his gratitude to the servicemen who have fought to stop the communist menace in Korea.

Ports of Entry

The U.S. government had a direct hand in the Cold War propaganda campaign as seen on television. Not only were countless hours of anticommunist informational films produced by various government agencies for broadcast, but many television programs had direct ties to the military.[17] One such program was *Navy Log* (1955–58), whose stories were drawn "from official U.S. Navy files." Each episode of *Navy Log* personalized the U.S. mission in fighting global communism by focusing upon the role played by ordinary military men in containing its spread throughout the Asian continent.

The first order of business for the government/civilian propaganda apparatus was to help the untutored civilian audience distinguish Good Asians from Bad Asians. With the defeated nation of Japan squarely within the U.S. sphere of influence in the postwar world order, the symbolic rehabilitation of the formerly hated enemy needed to be negotiated. As junior partners of the United States in the Pacific and principal bulwark against Asian communism, the Japanese were now Good Asians. The defeat of Jiang Jie-shi (Chiang Kai-shek) and his nationalist forces by the communists led by Mao Zedong transformed a former ally during World War II into Bad Asians.

The *Navy Log* episode "A Guy Named Mickey" serves as an excellent example of the symbolic rehabilitation undergone by the former Japanese enemy.[18] The story concerns an American aviator, David Taylor (Charles R. Keane), who during World War II was shot down off the coast of Japan. After bailing out of his disabled fighter plane, the pilot was rescued and nursed back to health by a Japanese man and his son. Taylor's rescuer, however, was no ordinary Japanese citizen. Toyama (Teru Shimada) happened to be a judge on the Japanese Supreme Court who had been educated in the United States at the University of Michigan.

Opposing the military regime, Judge Toyama was later arrested by authorities and executed as a political dissident. In an earlier scene, Judge Toyama had given his son Mikio (Lane Nakano) an heirloom samurai sword. Now a symbol of peace rather than war, the sword had been welded in its scabbard to prevent the weapon from ever being drawn. In denouncing his country's militaristic rule, Toyama had told Mikio that the "true law," the "law of justice," is embodied in a constitutional system of government and not in the brute force represented by the sword. The scene is meant to underscore the distinction between Good Japanese Constitutionalists who resisted Bad Japanese Militarists during the war. Purged of their warlike tendencies, the Good Japanese are therefore deserving of U.S. economic assistance now that the outcome of the war has been decided.

Five years after the surrender by Japan, Taylor now finds himself serving in the Korean War as the commander of the ship U.S.S. *Philippine Sea*. Taylor hits upon the idea of sending a deserving Japanese person through college: Mikio. Lieutenant Taylor explains his plan to two seamen who sit on a committee called the Enlisted Men's Welfare and Recreation Fund. His plan stems from the wish not only to repay the Toyamas for their lifesaving kindness, but to educate the Japanese public about the benevolence of the American people. "If we educated Toyama in the United States," says Lieutenant Taylor, "he can go back to Japan and tell his people how we think and how we feel." As a "goodwill ambassador," Mikio will help ensure that his people "won't go starting another war someday."

Commander Taylor convinces his crew that putting "Mickey" Toyama through school would be a worthwhile "investment." After he locates the younger Toyama in Japan, Mikio expresses the desire to attend the University of Michigan, just as his father had before him. The crew members collect $5,000 for the fund and send the young man to law school. A few short years later, Mikio is shown dressed in cap and gown, law diploma in hand and ready to help further the cause of normalized U.S.-Japan relations. The propaganda value of "A Guy Named Mickey" becomes obvious when the final credits roll at the conclusion of the program: "This program was produced with the full cooperation of the Department of Defense and the Department of the Navy."

Many American opinion leaders viewed the retreat of Jiang Jie-shi from the Chinese mainland to the island of Formosa (Taiwan) in 1949 as tantamount to a U.S. defeat. Between 1945 and 1949 the United States contributed more than $2 billion to Chinese National government forces. The so-called China Lobby, led by Senators

Karl Mundt of South Dakota and William S. Knowland of California, blamed the State Department for the "loss of China." Henry R. Luce, the powerful publisher of *Time* and *Life* magazines (born in China of Christian missionary parents), circulated the notion that many of the East Asian experts in the State Department were "soft" on Chinese communism. Senator Joseph McCarthy served as point man in ridding the State Department of a number of senior-level personnel. The nationally televised purges fed the repressive Cold War political climate and further convinced the American public of the need to root out communist sympathizers both at home and abroad.

As in the episode discussed above, *Navy Log* helped rewrite the history of postwar Asia for popular consumption in "Incident at Formosa."[19] The time noted in the navy log is June 1950; the location, somewhere near the Korean peninsula. Actual newsreel footage of Mao Zedong addressing the masses jolts the viewer into acknowledging the reality of the yellow communist menace. The narrator (Robert Carson) solemnly states, "This is the Chinese dictator who said 'Formosa is ours and we will attack.' " The footage of Mao Zedong is immediately followed by the heroic image of the Nationalist leader, Jiang Jie-shi. States the narrator, "This is the man who said, 'We will stand and defend it.' "

Newsreel footage of President Harry S. Truman leaves no doubt as to the resolve of the U.S. military. Via the narrator, the leader of the free world declares his intention of defending Formosa by ordering the U.S. 7th Fleet to patrol the "Formosa Strait" and "guard against any attack from the Chinese mainland." The boundary between fact and fiction begins to blur as a "real" shot of Soviet Premier Joseph Stalin shifts to that of a Chinese communist general (Peter Chong) who plots a sneak attack on the island of Formosa. Like the Japanese attack on Pearl Harbor, the conquest of Formosa will commence on December 7, 1950.

As "Chinese communist ships" speed toward Formosa in inclement weather, the crew of a navy patrol bomber on a routine search for signs of enemy activity suddenly sights "hundreds" of ships heading for Formosa as if to invade. Fortunately for the Western democracies, the Chinese communist commanders call off the planned attack once they realize that the element of surprise has been lost. Once more, the eternal vigilance of ordinary citizens serving their country through military duty saves the peace-loving folks at home from foreign aggression.

From postwar occupied Japan to the Korean War to U.S. involvement in Vietnam, the fictional files of *Navy Log* brim with apocryphal accounts of Pax Americana in the Pacific empire. The mass evacuation of Vietnamese "refugees" from the north to the south provides the narrative armature for the episode "Bishop of the Bayfield."[20] The story centers on an irreligious, hard-drinking, gambling, brawling, womanizing sailor named Deacon Jones (Peter Whitney) who, along with his shipmates aboard the U.S.S. *Bayfield*, is en route from San Diego to "Haiphong, Indochina." Their mission is to help evacuate 2,000 "refugees" who are "fleeing the Vietminh reds." The code name for the operation is "Passage to Freedom."

After delousing the boarding refugees with DDT, Jones is mistaken for a priest by a young boy, Tay (Wellington Soo Hoo). The boy at first had been frightened by U.S. sailors because of communist propaganda that depicted them as evil. But because Tay had received training in a Christian missionary school, he takes an immediate liking to Jones. The word quickly spreads among the refugees that Jones is a religious leader, the "bishop of the *Bayfield*."

So as not to disappoint Tay and the refugees, Deacon Jones mends his errant ways and adopts an air of religiosity among the other sailors. In short order, Jones becomes a devout Christian and leads his Asian flock in church services. That Deacon Jones suddenly gets religion is all the more remarkable given that he had been punished earlier for having gotten into a fistfight with a civilian at an off-limits bar after making a pass at the man's date.

In truth, the battle between Christian civilization and the forces of atheistic Asian communism was not so simple as presented in this specific episode of *Navy Log*. Based upon earlier accounts by Bernard B. Fall and Robert Scheer, journalist Frances FitzGerald notes that the 860,000 predominantly Catholic "refugees" transported from the north formed the basis of political support for Ngo Dinh Diem, the Catholic anticommunist leader who was backed by the United States at the time. Diem's plea for assistance in the transport and resettlement of those who sought to flee the Viet Minh was of enormous propaganda and political value for the United States. "The request could not have been more politic from an American point of view," writes FitzGerald, "as it permitted U.S. military and civilian welfare services to take up the congenial cause of 'saving' Vietnamese from Communism and from starvation."[21]

After transporting the Vietnamese evacuees to the south, American advisers assembled the U.S.-backed government that in 1955 was to become the Republic of Vietnam (South Vietnam), with Ngo Dinh Diem as its first president. In 1963, the unpopular Diem was assassinated during a coup that was planned (according to a European edition of *Time* magazine) with the full knowledge of Dean

Rusk and Averill Harriman of the U.S. State Department along with Robert S. McNamara and Roswell Gilpatrick at the Defense Department. Even the deified television legend Edward R. Murrow, who became director of the U.S. Information Agency in 1961 during the Kennedy administration, was aware of the coup plot.[22]

Captain Cronkite

To the present day, the political Right has often blamed former *CBS Evening News* anchor and managing editor Walter Cronkite for turning public opinion against the Vietnam War. After returning from a fact-finding mission in South Vietnam, Cronkite voiced his doubts over the prospects for U.S. victory during a historic February 27, 1968, special report. President Lyndon Johnson was especially alarmed by the impact Cronkite's on-air crisis of faith would have on the "middle-of-the-road folks" who had loyally supported the war.[23]

To hold Cronkite responsible for influencing antiwar sentiment is both unfair and inaccurate. If anything, the opposite is true. Cronkite had always played the role of the indefatigable Cold Warrior/correspondent, since the beginning of his television career. Around the time of the Korean War, for example, Cronkite hosted a *CBS News Special* titled "The Face of Red China" (1950) that warned of the global threat posed by this newly developing nation populated by virtual automatons numbering in the hundreds of millions.[24]

The one-hour special makes use of footage shot by a German cameraman with commentary by Gerald Clark, a Canadian reporter for the *Montreal Star*. Clark describes the Chinese as "poor people by our standards," but says that this "human energy" is "ready to be turned in any direction that suits the state." The communal organization of life in the People's Republic of China is seen as inherently oppressive by Clark. "In return for the promise of security," Clark says, "the peasant is also surrendering his child to the state, for a massive experiment in indoctrination that makes the Soviet example seem amateurish by comparison." The communist state stands as the antithesis of the privatized existence of Western bourgeois family life, which values privacy and individuality, according to Clark. The "hoe and the gun," the "spiritual regimentation" of the masses, the abolition of the family, and the harnessing of vast "human energy" have led the communists to "believe they can defeat the capitalist countries through *economic* warfare." Like an Old Testament prophet, Cronkite warns America of the sleeping giant that might very well come to challenge the freedoms taken for granted by the Western world:

The Red revolution has been built over the graves of millions of its victims. Millions more have fled. In the country's vast reaches, millions more live as little more than serfs of the Marxist regime. But the picture we have just seen is an unprecedented look at a giant stirring; at a nation with the resources and manpower and the raw material to fundamentally alter the course of history; to change *our* future. Whether we like it or not, here is a matter we cannot ignore.

Dignified, stately, authoritative, and controlled, Walter Cronkite was loath to descend into the realm of strident advocacy as did many of his colleagues in print and television journalism. But by his seemingly dispassionate reportorial objectivity, Cronkite could be depended upon to represent the United States to itself as the protector of weaker nations struggling to be reborn as full-fledged democracies in a hostile international environment where lurked the enemies of liberty. In retelling the myth of American innocence each night, the dean of Cold War television news helped reassure his viewers that their duly elected leaders were doing their level best to contain the spread of the communist contagion. Caught in the spell cast by Cold War TV, the American public surrendered its virtue to a regime bent upon the despoilment of Asia under the pretext of its anticommunist crusade.

Yellow Reds

While the Japanese, former enemies, were being assiduously rehabilitated on many television programs throughout the 1950s, the Chinese were once again being demonized as a malevolent threat to the West. The Cold War demonization process was made slightly more complicated because China itself was split between the U.S.-backed Nationalist government and the communists (who were at the time situated within the Soviet camp). By contrast, all Chinese were viewed as uniformly evil during the high point of American Sinophobia from the late nineteenth through early twentieth centuries. As a consequence, 1950s television introduced a new twist to the long history of anti-Chinese representations in American popular culture: the Yellow Red.

Mike Waring (Charles McGraw), the hero of the Cold War drama *Adventures of the Falcon* (1955–56), specializes in ferreting out the yellow communist menace as part of his work with U.S. Army intelligence. In the episode "Backlash," Waring is dispatched to Macao, the "devil's playground" as he describes it, "the melting pot of the Orient. A Portuguese colony off the coast of China, where East meets West in illegal enterprise."[25] His assignment is to stanch the flow of U.S. currency into "Red China," as the People's Republic of China was always referred to in the days before diplomatic normalization. "With American dollars," says Waring, "the Reds can buy strategic material from any country in the world." It is Waring's job to prevent the Chinese reds from gaining nuclear weapons capability.

Mike Waring's investigation leads him to an acquaintance of his superior Thad Henderson (Douglas Kennedy), a sinister-appearing man named Li Sung (Ted Hecht). At the same time, a crime reporter for the *Macao Record*, Sandra Davis (Laura Mason), goes about gathering information about the case. Davis, however, is in truth the daughter of Li Sung, with whom she is in cahoots. Through this double-dealing identity switch (a plot technique often employed in programs featuring duplicitous "Orientals"), Sandra Davis has used her position as a newspaper reporter to keep her father from detection.

The kicker comes when Sandra Davis is forced to reveal her true identity to Mike Waring. Northern European in appearance, Davis taunts the intelligence agent by saying, "I thought you would have guessed. . . . I have *Chinese* blood." Although U.S.-born, Sandra Davis apparently feels the primordial bonds of blood strongly enough to betray her own country, the United States. Interestingly, this specious connection made between social race and consanguinity is assumed to invalidate any claim of primary loyalty to the United States on the basis of nationality. Alone among all nonwhite groups in the United States, only Asian Americans have been placed in this role of biological outcast. Sandra Davis is Anglo-Saxon in physical appearance, but the "drop-of-blood" criterion makes her irredeemably Asian and therefore doomed to disloyalty.

In keeping with the Cold War mood, the all-purpose Chinese evil genius Dr. Fu Manchu was revived in this period as the personification of the yellow menace. Based upon the character created by British author Sax Rohmer, *The Adventures of Fu Manchu* (1956), a syndicated half-hour program, fed public paranoia over the political and military might of postrevolutionary China. In the episode titled "The Prisoner of Dr. Fu Manchu," the theme of nuclear annihilation surfaces.[26] Sir Dennis Nayland-Smith (Lester Matthews) is a Scotland Yard detective who eventually foils the plan of Dr. Fu Manchu (Glen Gordon) to sabotage an international conference that had been convened to discuss the sharing of a U.S.-developed technology, the "Rutledge Radiation Shield."

Assisted by a white dwarf in Chinese costume and a buxom, scantily clad white woman named Karamaneh (Laurette Luez), Dr. Fu

Manchu stopped at nothing to achieve his nefarious goals. The Asian evil genius engaged in despicable acts of kidnapping, drugging, and mind control through hypnotism in his effort to subvert the proceedings at the "Conference of Nations." According to Nayland-Smith, as head of a "secret society" Fu Manchu sought to provoke nuclear war between East and West. Presumably, in the aftermath of a nuclear holocaust Dr. Fu Manchu would be free to rule the world as it suited him.

The character created by Sax Rohmer (Arthur Henry Ward) first appeared in the novel *The Mystery of Dr. Fu-Manchu* (1913). Throughout the 1920s and 1930s, Rohmer was one of the world's most successful authors of popular fiction. Rohmer's imagination had been gripped by the travel writing of Sir Richard Francis Burton, who made his reputation by traveling to the remote outposts of the British empire in Africa and the Near East. A bank clerk whose hopes to enter the civil service were dashed after he failed the entrance examination, Rohmer redirected his talents to the writing of popular fiction. Lurid newspaper reports of the Chinese population residing in the Limehouse district of London drew his attention. The Chinese of London's East End were commonly viewed as leading unspeakably squalid, criminally depraved lives. The market for a Chinese villain was ripe as well. "I wondered why it had never before occurred to me," Rohmer mused. Not only had news of the Boxer Rebellion "started off rumors of a Yellow Peril which had not yet died down," but the goings-on in Limehouse virtually invited the sensationalism of Rohmer's literary imagination.[27]

Metro-Goldwyn-Mayer adapted the short stories serialized in *Collier's* magazine into the film *The Mask of Fu Manchu*, starring Boris Karloff (1932). According to Rohmer's biographers, Cay Van Ash and Elizabeth Sax Rohmer, the MGM film drew protests from the Chinese embassy in Washington: "The Chinese diplomats took a humorless view of Fu Manchu, whom they considered damaging to their 'image.' "[28] But because China was needed as an East Asian ally against Japanese military expansionism, the official protest was taken seriously enough to stymie the production of subsequent Fu Manchu films. After the war, Rohmer repackaged the Fu Manchu character and tried to sell the concept in the United States as a Cold War Oriental villain but met with no success. As a matter of poetic justice, Sax Rohmer died of "Asiatic" flu on June 1, 1959.

Foreign Espionage

Like *Navy Log*, the military anthology *Behind Closed Doors* (1958–59) featured thirty-minute dramas whose claims to veracity hinged upon their having been based upon the "files and experiences of Rear Admiral Ellis M. Zacharias, U.S.N. (Ret.)." The program took its title from a book authored by the admiral in collaboration with an individual named Ladislas Farago. Surprisingly well researched and professionally written, at least on the surface, the book goes into some detail about international events that helped shape the early Cold War period.[29] Each episode opened with the viewer being led by the camera eye to a nondescript, unmarked door located somewhere in Washington, D.C., among top-level government security agencies that worked around the clock to protect the free world from communist subversion.

In "Mightier Than the Sword," Admiral Zacharias sits in a semi-darkened "situation" room facing an illuminated map of the world that pinpoints various international hot spots.[30] The admiral swivels his well-cushioned high-backed chair to face the camera as series regular Commander Matson (Bruce Gordon) walks onto the elaborate set to introduce the episode. After a brief introduction, Admiral Zacharias releases the file to his aide Commander Matson for safekeeping.

The episode itself is a rather pedestrian account of a naturalized American citizen named Douglas Kincaid (Simon Scott), who was born in Yalta, but who now works as a double agent for the United States. After helping bust "communist cells" in San Francisco that are thought to be assisting the People's Republic of China, Kincaid is shipped back to the place of his nativity to gather intelligence on the Soviets. It is there that he completes his assignment against the reds.

Agent Kincaid's raids on the Chinese American community are based upon a series of incidents drawn from actual history. In December 1955, Everett F. Drumwright, U.S. consul general in Hong Kong, tipped the State Department to a supposedly "fantastic system of passport and visa fraud."[31] Drumwright alleged that Chinese communists were sneaking into the United States through immigration fraud. Kincaid might very well have been the fictional analogue of Immigration and Naturalization Service agents who in March 1956 conducted sweeps in Chinatowns across the country in search of "illegal aliens."

An earlier episode of *Behind Closed Doors*, "The Quemoy Story," takes place in the Portuguese colony of Macao, a city depicted as a hotbed of vice and foreign intrigue.[32] A local detective, Lieutenant Mike Perrera (Paul Picerni) and a U.S. agent named Commander Bennett (Robert Richards) foil a plot by a certain "Red Chinese" Colonel Faitu (Robert A. Harris) to capture the Nationalist ("free

Chinese") island of Quemoy. Perrera and Bennett uncover Faitu's plan to replace Nationalist troops with "Red Chinese" troops in disguise after trying to rescue a kidnapped U.S. agent named Anna Sung (Roberta Haynes). Apart from its fictional connection to the U.S. "loss" of China, "The Quemoy Story" is of interest for its use of Euro-American actors in "yellowface," an execrable practice still in evidence on network television.[33]

In "The Gamble," the intrepid Cold Warriors go to the rescue of Prince Tallat (Peter Votrian) and his sister Princess Santha (Nyra Monsour), who are kidnapped by North Vietnamese communists seeking control of the country.[34] Introducing the episode, Admiral Zacharias explains that the prince and princess are "about to live through one of the most terrifying experiences ever encountered in the communist attempt for world domination." Zacharias, as is his wont, then turns the file on the story over to his aide, Commander Matson. A further "factual" introduction by the Commander Matson character eerily foreshadows the full-scale American military involvement in Vietnam, as he describes a conference of "top-level" statesmen who have gathered to discuss "blocking communist infiltration southward from North Vietnam."

Prince Tallat had been scheduled to make a speech at the conference to argue in favor of continued Western intervention, but the prince is forced by his captors to denounce American involvement in Asia. The prince's denunciation is induced through "narcosynthesis" and "posthypnotic suggestion," presumably "brainwashing" techniques that are commonly understood to be the unique property of such "Oriental" masters of mind control as Dr. Fu Manchu.

Philip Canning (Jeff Richards), posing as a troubleshooter for a utilities company but in truth a U.S. agent, succeeds in outwitting a duplicitous communist double agent in a push-up bra, Major Karen (Carol Thurston). Canning rescues the prince and princess and foils the plans of the Vietnamese communists who had sought to sabotage the conference. "Thanks to our agents like Canning and the freedom-loving peoples in Asia," sermonizes Admiral Zacharias in the epilogue, "we can continue to preserve that peace against all possible odds."

Standing at the Crossroads

The Cold War religious dramatic anthology *Crossroads* (1955–57) each week featured a Chevrolet-sponsored "true story based on the actual experiences of American clergymen." One particular episode dramatized the story of a courageous clergyman, Father Robert W. Greene (Arthur Franz), who organized and led the Legion of Mary in a Chinese village shortly after World War II.[35] The narrator describes the China of 1949 as having been utterly devastated by years of armed conflict. Foreign occupation had come to an end after World War II, but the country now was caught in the throes of the "new and deadlier terror of civil war." The Maryknoll mission led by Father Greene provides comfort to a people grown weary of war. Second in command is a Chinese convert, Ah Hiu (Philip Ahn), "Father Bob's cook and right arm in his ministry."

The remoteness of the Chinese village so far had spared Father Greene and the Legion of Mary from anti-Christian attacks by the communist forces. But in early December of 1949, the Red Army finds its way to the village and plunders the church. Father Greene is brought before a demoniacal Red Army officer. The military inquisitor (Richard Loo) accuses the clergyman and his church of subversion, of harboring "guerrillas, spies, saboteurs." Father Greene denies speaking out against the revolutionary regime, although he admits to having criticized its "communist, atheistic doctrine."

The military officer questions the priorities of a Christian Chinese nun by telling her how the people need an "educated woman" to lead them. "I am working for the good of all Chinese," the nun replies. Ah Hiu, Father Greene's acolyte, is subjected to the same treatment by the sinister inquisitor. "Why are you not working for the people's government," the Red Army officer demands, "instead of serving as a running dog for this priest? Helping to spread his imperialistic American propaganda?" Father Greene is placed under house arrest, and the Chinese Christian converts are summarily executed. Mastermind (Richard Reeves), a guard described as "imbecilic" by the narrator, stands guard over the persecuted priest.

The priest's prospects seem to improve when a certain Leang Fan (Keye Luke) visits him to obtain some form of personal identification so that the U.S. authorities can gain his release. Fan, however, turns out to be an agent who produces false documentation that "proves" Father Greene functions as both spy and *agent provocateur*. The military inquisitor induces other villagers who once worshipped with the priest to bear false witness against him. Among the betrayers is none other than Ah Hiu. In a private moment, Sister Teresa (Maryn Maro) explains to Father Greene that Ah Hiu's testimony was exacted through torture and that his wife and daughter were being held hostage.

With a portrait of Mao Zedong hanging conspicuously in the courtroom where Father Greene is being tried, the inquisitor pronounces the clergyman free: "You are to be an example of the mercy and kindness of our leader, Mao Zedong, who graciously permits you to live." Leang Fan informs Father Greene that his freedom is but a brief reprieve, because "in ten years, the communists shall have America." As Father Bob is handed over to American authorities, the narrator brings the tale to a merciful end by informing the viewer that in 1952 the priest "was ejected from behind the Bamboo Curtain."

Another episode of *Crossroads* inadvertently reveals the religious leadership represented in the program as little more than a cover for a white, paternalistic power structure wrapped in the veil of transcendental benevolence. As "Chinese Checkers" opens with a stock shot of the Statue of Liberty, the narrator describes how beleaguered masses of people from the "four corners of the globe" arrive as the "hopeful and frightened" wards of their adopted land. In this episode, a priest once again serves as protector and savior of the spiritually benighted breeds.[36] This time it is the Reverend Ira Langston (Richard Denning) who comes to the rescue of the prototypical Chinese laundryman Ling Chang (Philip Ahn). A numbers runner named Luther Harrington (Denver Pyle), called "Dial," has been operating his racket out of the laundry by threatening Chang with nondelivery of product. True to form, Ling does not want the Reverend Langston to inform the police. But as the voice of otherworldly salvation and mundane procedural justice, the Reverend Langston reassures the terrified Chinese: "Don't be afraid, Ling. In this country we have laws to protect us from men like Dial."

With the Cold War in full swing, the ever-popular American Protestant missionary-held-captive-in-"communist China" theme also served as the basis for a story anthologized in *TV Reader's Digest* (1955–56).[37] Taken from the pages of the bedrock conservative *Reader's Digest*, "The Brainwashing of John Hayes" concerns the unsuccessful attempt by officials of the Red Army to break the spirit and political will of the Reverend John Hayes (Vincent Price). The clergyman is accused of being an "impertinent spy" working for "Wall Street warmongers" by a Red Army officer played by the inimitable all-purpose TV Asian, Richard Loo.

In keeping with the belief that the Soviet Union was the true force behind Chinese communism, a certain Comrade Commissar Chernik (Steven Geray) oversees the show trial of John Hayes. A portrait of Joseph Stalin hangs conspicuously beside that of Mao Zedong. Despite repeated attempts at "brainwashing" the cleric, the truth of American democracy burns so strongly in his heart and soul that Hayes steadfastly denies working on behalf of the FBI and Jiang Jieshi's Nationalist government. When tribunal head Wang Tsu (Philip Ahn) expels Hayes from China after failing to exact a signed confession from the stalwart missionary, Comrade Chernik has the incompetent Chinese inquisitor arrested. As he is being led away, Wang Tsu curses his Soviet supervisor.

The underlying purport of this episode is to establish the duplicity of the Soviet Union as it goes about orchestrating a global communist movement. It is Stalin, not Mao, who is the great international villain. Indeed, in defending himself during his trial Hayes suggests that the People's Republic of China could serve as a "bridge" between the United States and other Asian nations who are treading the path toward democracy.

But the communists will have none of it. They banish the clergyman to Hong Kong pending his eventual return to the United States. A young boy (Warren Lee) and his mother (Beulah Kwoh) stop Hayes in the street to bid him farewell. The boy gives Hayes the "thumbs up" and tells him that America is still number one. With this final affirmation given by the young Chinese boy, the Reverend John Hayes can now return home with the knowledge that his personal sacrifice has not been in vain.

Cold War Thaw

Popular novels by Ian Fleming such as *Casino Royale* (1953), *Live and Let Die* (1954), *Diamonds Are Forever* (1956), and *On Her Majesty's Secret Service* (1963) were set against the backdrop of East-West conflict, but with a droll, understated sense of humor that slyly mocked Cold War power politics. Educated at Eton and Sandhurst, Fleming combined schoolboy fantasy and firsthand familiarity with the British intelligence community to spawn a James Bond craze on both sides of the Atlantic. Film adaptations of Fleming's work, including *Dr. No* (1962), *From Russia with Love* (1963), *Goldfinger* (1964), and *Thunderball* (1965), further fueled the mania for adolescent fantasies of international intrigue.

Network television responded with a slew of spy programs influenced by Fleming. These included *The Man from U.N.C.L.E.* (1964–68), *I Spy* (1965–68), *The Wild Wild West* (1965–70), *The Man Who Never Was* (1966–67), *Mission: Impossible* (1966–73, 1988–90), and British imports *Secret Agent* (1965–66) and *The Avengers* (1966–69). So strong was the influence of the James Bond films that the police/detective drama *Burke's Law* (1963–66) changed both its format and title in the fall of 1965 to become *Amos Burke—Secret Agent.*

Ian Fleming himself played an early role in the development of *The Man from U.N.C.L.E.* before assigning his financial interest in the program to its creator, Norman Felton, in 1963. The program featured a duo who represented a post-Cold War, U.S.-Soviet bipolar world order: Napoleon Solo (Robert Vaughn), an American, and Illya Kuryakin (David McCallum), a Russian. In teaming an American with a Russian, writer Sam Rolfe demonstrated his conception of U.N.C.L.E. as an "international organization that had no Cold War philosophical differences to contend with."[38] What Americans and Soviets shared, however, was a common Asian enemy.

Unlike almost all of the classic Cold War television programs of the 1950s featuring sexually seductive "Dragon Lady" types, only Asian males were cast as villains in *The Man from U.N.C.L.E.* "The Green Opal Affair" featured an Asian henchman named Chuke (Shuji J. Nozawa), "The Yellow Scarf Affair" concerned a band of Thuggees led by a maharajah (Murray Matheson), and "The Finny Foot Affair" found Solo battling a certain General Yokura (Leonard Strong) to find the source of a deadly chemical leak.

Conversely, the Asian women in *The Man from U.N.C.L.E.* reject their Asian male counterparts by assisting the forces of a white bipartite world order. In "The Cherry Blossom Affair," Cricket Okasada (France Nuyen) helps Solo and Kuryakin locate a secret device acquired by the rival organization, THRUSH. Miki Matsu (Victoria Young) fulfills a similar function in "The Her Master's Voice Affair." This common pattern, the female version of the Tonto syndrome, reflects objective power relations in American society by its reaffirmation of white male supremacy over the Asian male threat. In its more benign, liberal manifestation, the white male might act as protector of the weak and defenseless Asian male. In either case, the politicosexual favors of the Asian female accrue to the Euro-American male power figure.

In addition to her one-shot role as Cricket Okasada in *The Man from U.N.C.L.E.*, France Nuyen appeared in numerous TV programs requiring an Asian female presence. Nuyen might even be considered the premier Asian American actress on network television through the 1960s and 1970s. More recently, she held the role of surgeon Dr. Paulette Kiem on the medical drama *St. Elsewhere* (1982–88) from 1986 to 1988. Joining her real-life husband Robert Culp on an episode of *I Spy*, Nuyen appeared as Mei Lin, a Chinese empress living in San Francisco.[39] In "An American Empress," Kelly Robinson (Culp) and Alexander Scott (Bill Cosby) help Mei Lin elude Chinese communist agents who seek to abduct and then return her to "Red China." Cheng (Benson Fong), leader of the communist agents, explains to Scott that they extort gold from Chinese living in the United States to buy "H-bomb, missiles, scary things like that." Once Scott and Robinson free Mei Lin from the clutches of her pursuers, the former empress enters college and embarks upon a new life as an ordinary American.

The partial thaw in Cold War ideology was seen in *Get Smart* (1965–70), a zany spoof of the spy genre craze launched by the James Bond novels and films. Created by Mel Brooks with Buck Henry, the sitcom combined broad ethnic-based humor with a certain "camp" hipness that earned it the approval of the pop culture cognoscenti. The strains of the Jewish American comedic tradition were contributed by Brooks, who had honed his skills at resorts in the Catskills with such entertainers as Sid Caesar. The high-context, ironic, modernist sensibility came courtesy of Buck Henry, the son of a Wall Street executive. Educated at private schools and Dartmouth College, the genteel humorist gained his early professional experience in off-Broadway improvisational comedy and theater.[40]

Get Smart featured the stock array of villains who work for KAOS, an international crime organization pitted against Maxwell Smart and his outfit, CONTROL. Conrad Siegfried (Bernie Kopell), a crypto-Nazi spy, was accompanied by the usual complement of Asian fiends, including Dr. Yes, the Claw, and the Whip. Dr. Yes (Donald Davis) – a takeoff on Ian Fleming's Dr. No – resembled Dr. Fu Manchu and wore long fingernails that were wielded as lethal weapons. The only sympathetic Asian Pacific American character was the Hawaiian private detective Harry Hoo (Joey Forman), who was modeled after Charlie Chan even down to his yellowface make-up job.

In addition to the predictable cast of Asian heavies, Lum Fong worked out of his Chinese laundry as a cypher expert for CONTROL. But more often than not, Chinese laundries in *Get Smart* were exposed as fronts for criminal activity engaged in by KAOS. This is in keeping with the commonplace suspicion of Asian-owned businesses as places of mystery and hidden danger. (An episode of *Front Page Detective* [1951–52], for example, makes gratuitous use of a Chinatown "Oriental" curio shop simply to spice up an exceptionally dull story.)[41] *Get Smart* drew from decades of representations in the popular culture that have depicted Asian stores as fronts for such illicit pleasures as prostitution, gambling, and drug use. Murderous attacks on innocent customers or the kidnapping of nubile white females seemed likely to occur at any moment, no matter how innocent the place of business might appear on the face of it.[42]

Such revulsion stems from the potential competitive threat posed by the Asian entrepreneur working within an ethnic enclave economy. The subterranean fear of territorial invasion combined with the practice of socially sanctioned segregation finds a convenient target in the Chinese laundryman, the Japanese shopkeeper, and, more recently, the Korean grocer. Add to this the fear of ritual pollution through personal contact with social inferiors whose ever-widening sphere of activity threatens to expand into a well-ordered world dominated by a white oligarchy that jealously guards the sources of its power.

Through its parodic treatment of Cold War politics, *Get Smart* exposed the naked falsity of the anticommunist fervor that gripped the nation during the 1950s and into the subsequent decade. *Get Smart* was born of an ingenious premise and remained consistently funny during its entire run on television. So thoroughly did the program become part of the popular culture that some of its catch-phrases entered the everday language: "Sorry about that, Chief" and "Missed it by *that* much," for example. The enduring quality of *Get Smart* was such that it is still being aired in syndication throughout much of the country. But in satirizing the absurdities of the national security state, producers Leonard Stern and Jay Sandrich and the writers of *Get Smart* sacrificed the humanity of Asians and Asian Americans by setting them up as the butt of a grand ethnic joke that they were not let in on.

Commie Baby-Eaters

Almost twenty years later to the day, the very same Madame Ngai who appeared on *This Is Your Life* for Dr. Tom Dooley's in-studio testimonial resurfaced on television, this time in semifictionalized form. In an eerie turnabout, a Dr. Tom Dooley character appears briefly in a scene in this made-for-TV movie. Purportedly based on a series of events that took place during the fall of Saigon in April 1975, *The Children of An Lac* (1980) recounts the hurried evacuation of orphans from Vietnam by Madame Ngai (played by veteran actress Beulah Quo) and two American women, Betty Tisdale (Shirley Jones) and Ina Balin (as herself).[43]

The two-hour drama depicts the sometimes strained professional relationships among these three dedicated women who work tirelessly to keep orphaned Vietnamese children from the clutches of the North Vietnamese. Betty Tisdale and her husband had been involved with Madam Ngai's orphanage for fourteen years. Tisdale herself is the the mother of several adopted children, five of whom are Vietnamese girls of Asian and white parentage. Ina Balin is an actress who for presumably altruistic reasons seeks to adopt an Asian child. Madame Ngai is the somewhat intractable director of An Lac ("Happy Place") orphanage who has been placed on a "death list" by the authorities, who have accused her of being a "child stealer."

Of particular concern to Ina Balin is the plight of "mixed-blood" children. She fears that they will be harmed somehow by the "Viet Cong." Balin explains to a TV journalist while en route to Vietnam that "mixed-blood" children are "not treated very well by the *South* Vietnamese, you can imagine what the Viet *Cong* will do to them." It is implied that the children will be victimized by their *own people* because of their racial impurity. This makes American intervention all the more urgent.

Balin's fear for the welfare of mixed-race children in Vietnam seems a bit overdrawn given the harsh social sanctions that attend interracial liaisons in the United States. Considering the systematic pattern of human rights violations committed by ARVN and U.S. soldiers, Balin's sense of alarm makes sense only if its propaganda value is recognized. If anything, her concern about the abuse suffered by mixed-race children in Vietnam is probably more a projection of Balin's experience with American racism than the result of any firsthand knowledge of Viet Cong barbarism. In addition, there is no mention of the responsibility borne by American GIs who fathered thousands of children for whom they had no intention of providing. If mixed-race children are scorned in Vietnam, it is because the reciprocal rights and responsibilities that attend familial relations have been invalidated by the absence of the (American) father, not because the children are racially "impure."

Removing the children from their Saigon home proves to be more difficult than the trio of anticommunist heroines had anticipated. Government authorities argue that the young people will be instrumental in the rebuilding of their war-torn country. As a consequence, they block the exit of all children under the age of ten. Not to be deterred, the intrepid three succeed in cutting through the bureaucratic red tape that had delayed the evacuation of the children to the United States.

In a postscript to *The Children of An Lac,* it is noted that Madame Ngai escaped to the United States "just before Saigon fell to the Viet Cong." She died on April 23, 1978, at the Tisdale home in Columbus, Georgia, but not before fulfilling her earthly mission: the postscript states that "all the children brought to the United States have been adopted." But by far the biggest winner in this "true story" is Ina Balin. By capitalizing on the plight of helpless Vietnamese orphans, the former USO entertainer and aspiring actress finally made the limelight, costarring with Beulah Quo and Shirley Jones in a movie that Balin both conceived and coproduced.

Most of the location work in *The Children of An Lac* appears to have been done in the Philippines. The production credits acknowledge Clark Air Force Base, the government of the Philippines, and Philippine Airlines for their assistance in the making of the film. The use of the Philippines as the backdrop for the program seems only appropriate, given that the country has been the most important Asian client of the United States since the turn of the century. The U.S. military occupation of the Philippines also points to the legacy of American imperialism that has kept the country in a perpetual state of economic underdevelopment.[44] How appropriate that our "little brown brothers" (as colonial governor William Howard Taft paternalistically referred to his subjects) in the Philippines be enlisted in the task of manufacturing television reenactments of the U.S. imperialist sojourn in Vietnam.

Employing Filipino child actors in the movie provided an additional set of conveniences for the producers: the children already spoke English (itself evidence of U.S. imperial presence) and, to the undiscriminating eye of the white American audience, the Filipino children could easily pass for less cost-effective Vietnamese actors. By these seemingly minor details, *The Children of An Lac* exposes itself unwittingly as a false representation (despite its claim of being based on a "true" story) of the historical relationship between the United States and the countries of East Asia. History is denied by the failure to name the root cause—U.S. military and economic domination—of the suffering of Asian families, orphaned children, and the abandoned spawn of American GIs. That do-gooders like Ina Balin simplistically point to communist baby-eaters as responsible for the death, destruction, and deracinated state of the Vietnamese people makes a program such as *The Children of An Lac* all the more pernicious. Unfortunately, Ina Balin typifies the supraracist thinking of all too many Americans who think of themselves as the global humanitarian saviors of a nonwhite world left underdeveloped and destabilized by the capitalist superpowers.

The propaganda value of *The Children of An Lac* is made even more evident by the knowledge that "Operation Baby-Lift" took place during the fall of Saigon in 1975, whereby 2,000 Vietnamese children were taken from local orphanages and spirited away to the United States to elicit sympathy for the fallen South Vietnamese regime and its loyal American allies.[45] The operation was meant to confer a tragic nobility on the American rescuers. However, accounts of the public relations operation indicated that most of the children were not even orphans and that many were taken from their Vietnamese parents illegally. Scenes of a tearful President Gerald Ford greeting the "orphans" tugged at the heartstrings of the American public while the sight of Playboy Bunnies off-loading forty Vietnamese orphans from Hugh Hefner's private "Big Bunny" jet bordered on the pornographic.[46] Through television programs such as *The Children of An Lac* and "humanitarian" efforts such as "Operation Baby-Lift," the U.S. has attempted to absolve itself of all responsibility for the creation of countless Vietnamese orphans. Instead, it is the commie baby-eaters who are blamed for causing the suffering of their *own people.*

Christian (Tax-Exempt) Charity

"Children are a reflection of God's love for us," announces Stan Mooningham, the soft-spoken president of World Vision International, based in Pasadena, California. Founded in 1950 for the "stated original purpose of helping Korean War orphans," the organization currently operates "humanitarian projects in ninety countries."[47] World Vision International has occasionally bought commercial time to air television specials that combine light entertainment with emotional appeals directed at viewers who might be persuaded to donate money to the self-described "Christian humanitarian organization." One such special titled *One to One* (1975) even features the winsome Julie Andrews, with Jim Henson's Muppets in support.[48]

The program opens with a musical extravaganza featuring the thirty-member Korean Children's Choir, most of the members of which are orphans. The orphan choir is soon joined by Julie Andrews and the warm fuzzy feelings associated with *The Sound of Music* begin to overcome the viewer. Stan Mooningham himself makes an appearance to set the tone for the program, asserting that "this is a show about love, about caring, and about children." He flatters the audience in advance for its generosity in helping support "needy children" such as those in the Korean Children's Choir, "who have become what they are today because generous and loving people are willing to share one to one."

Julie Andrews sings "Getting to Know You" as the Korean orphans frolic around her, dressed in identical sneakers, jeans, and baseball jerseys with their names emblazoned on them as if they were a team of all-American kids. Sprightly musical arrangements of "Everything Is Beautiful," "He's Got the Whole World in His Hands," "Day by Day," and other uplifting feel-good popular songs round out the rest of the show. The cast even warbles "I'd Like to Teach the World to Sing," a song given wide exposure by a near-legendary soft drink commercial (1972). The tune even reached the Billboard Top 100 twice in the same year as delivered by the Hillside Singers and the New Seekers. The spectacularly effective commercial featured a large gathering of children from around the world singing "in perfect harmony," a paean to Coca-Cola imperialism.

Just as Julie Andrews conjures memories of an idealized childhood, the popular television host Art Linkletter is remembered for his special love of youngsters. He made a career of playing straight man to cute but disarmingly truthful children in segments of the daytime television program *Art Linkletter's House Party* (1952–68) and his earlier evening audience-participation show, *Life with Linkletter* (1950–52).[49] Thus it is hardly surprising when Linkletter appears on camera to describe the mission of World Vision International.

Beginning twenty-six years ago "in the heartbreak and despair of the Korean War," World Vision "gathered the sick, the orphaned, the forgotten, into the arms of love." World Vision, a "Christian humanitarian organization," has worked in thirty countries the world over, helping "hundreds of thousands" through "medical clinics, children's homes, community development, hospitals, trade schools, and emergency relief." The organization is motivated by, according to Linkletter, the "love and compassion of Christ."

Linkletter's pitch is accompanied by film footage of World Vision relief efforts. Later in the program, the appeal for money becomes more direct. As a film of the Korean Children's Choir is shown, Linkletter says that most of its members had been "rescued from poverty and hunger." Fourteen American dollars a month—that is all it takes for "sponsors" to provide orphaned Korean children with food, medicine, and a "Christian education." The Muppets add a touch of patriotism for good measure, singing "hooray for the red, white, and blue."

Filmed interviews with actual sponsors present decent, caring, middle Americans who contribute to the maintenance of children in underdeveloped countries. In what appears to be a home movie, Julie Andrews is seen playing with two "*Vietnamese* orphans," as Mooningham describes them, adopted by Andrews and husband Blake Edwards. Amy and Joanna, seventeen months and seven months old, respectively, appear to be enjoying themselves with their new American parents. As for the fate of their Vietnamese biological parents, we are never told.

The mood turns serious at the conclusion of *One to One*. Stan Mooningham describes without a trace of condescension how he has "walked down the crowded streets of Asian cities surrounded by a sea of little brown faces." In closing, he reminds us that "children are a reflection of God's love for us." Benign as this parting statement might be, its universalist thrust effectively denies the role of U.S.

history and politics in creating the deathly conditions that have ensured the fragmentation of countless Asian families. The World Vision International slogan, "Helping the World of Plenty Help the World of Need," is a clever formulation. More accurately, the organization represents the "World of U.S. Imperium Helping the World Underdeveloped by Capitalism."

The close relationship between the forces of right-wing political reaction and Christian televangelism is found in a program hosted by none other than Charlton Heston, an actor known for both his political conservatism and the epic biblical roles he has assumed in the cinema. In *When Will the Dying Stop?* Asian children are once more used as props for eliciting compassion and soliciting money for yet another religious organization.[50] In this instance it is World Relief, the "service arm of the National Association of Evangelicals," which claims to represent 900,000 churches and 20,000 Christian missionaries around the world. Conveniently enough, World Relief is also touted as a "registered voluntary agency by the Department of State," which demonstrates the complementary fit between the otherworldly orientation of Christianity and the earthly political-economic interests of U.S. empire.

Documentary film clips transport the viewer to the economically depressed countries of Thailand, the Philippines, India, and Bangladesh. It is stressed that World Relief is not in the business of giving handouts. Rather, the organization provides supplies, equipment, and livestock to impoverished people so that they might be able to sustain themselves on an independent basis. Once in business, the recipients of assistance repay World Relief, which then reinvests the proceeds in other human souls hoping to escape the karmic circle of poverty.

In Bangladesh, for example, a man is given ownership of a rickshaw so he will not have to rent one. Repayment in turn will allow for the purchase of a new vehicle for yet another operator. World Relief also supports vocational training in weaving, sewing, and light manufacture. But whether the organization helps build a fish pond for drought-stricken farming families, starts a "pig bank" in Northern Thailand, or constructs a rice mill in a remote village, World Relief believes in the gospel of self-help. "Not handouts," Heston emphasizes. "No, just people helping other people make their own futures."

Just in case the appeal is not strong enough, Heston—garbed in a neckerchief color coordinated with a tailored safari outfit—holds a limp child in his arms as a visual aid while reminding viewers of the Gospel of Jesus:

Two thousand years ago, Jesus came to bring good news to the poor, to people like this. Sick, oppressed, hungry. Now we can share that same message, that same good news. If you were here holding this child, I wouldn't have to say anything to you, you'd feel the same way I do. You can't help him, though, there's no time left for Raja. He's been sick too long. You can help others, though. The tens of thousands of other boys and girls who are sick too. Please help stop the dying.

Again, there is no hint of the political-economic forces that contribute to the impoverishment and squalor that World Relief hopes to allay by exporting its self-help programs to so-called Third World nations. Instead, World Relief offers a religious, supernatural, and personalistic response to a host of related problems that can be attributed directly to the insatiable appetite of Western capitalist societies for land, labor, and cash crops provided cheaply by former colonial possessions. Programs such as these reveal the function of universalist religions, which is to mystify the material causes of human overpopulation, overintensification of the land, and the exploitation of labor. By mystifying and spiritualizing the poverty of underdeveloped nations, the great world religions such as Christianity relieve the ruling classes of responsibility for providing the material resources needed to eliminate physical suffering caused by malnutrition and hunger.

Global Saviors

For decades, Cold War tensions served as a convenient pretext for religious leaders to both lead and shield their flocks against a common atheistic enemy. Bishop Fulton J. Sheen, host of *Life Is Worth Living* (1952–55) and *Mission to the World* (1955–57), served as the model for later televangelists who also tapped the unique properties of the new mass medium to spread the gospel among a geographically far-flung congregation bound together by the national television networks. According to the catechism of postwar America, the world was divided between communist nations that forbade religious freedom and countries such as the United States that defended this sacrosanct principle. If religious pluralism formed the very foundation of the American republic, then atheistic communism was viewed as an insidiously corrosive agent that would weaken the nation's basic institutions.

But with the lessening of Cold War tensions beginning in the latter part of the 1980s, the anticommunist rhetoric of the televangelists lost much of its righteous punch. For at least one enterprising televangelist, however, the thaw in U.S.-Soviet relations proved to be a boon for his ministry. In mid-1991, prior to the dissolution of the Soviet Union, televangelist George Vandeman struck a deal with Soviet National Television to broadcast *It Is Written*. First aired in 1956, *It Is Written* reaches approximately forty markets in the United States and is ranked among the top fifteen of all religious broadcasts. The potential market for the program in what was then the Soviet Union is estimated at forty million viewers.[51] Based in Thousand Oaks, California, *It Is Written* is identified as a "telecast ministry of the Seventh-Day Adventist Church."

While the contemporary anticommunist message has lost much of the stridency of 1950s religious TV programs, it is evident that contemporary media apostles such as the soft-spoken Vandeman are still concerned with the saving of heathen souls. The violent military response to the prodemocracy movement in the People's Republic of China provides Vandeman with the opportunity in one program to moralize on the relationship between political freedom and religious freedom.[52] A videotape of protesters gathered in Tiananmen Square during the spring of 1989 opens the program as strains of ominous music are heard in the background. Vandeman tells of the valiant protest directed against a repressive government that decided "to crush the revolt, whatever the cost." With the cruel suppression of democratic stirrings died any hope of religious freedom.

Vandeman interprets the modern prodemocracy movement as being consistent with the spiritual goals of nineteenth-century Christian missionaries in China. Chinese Christians first had to suffer the eviction of foreign missionaries after the communist victory, which was then followed by the cultural revolution in 1966, "when the Red Guards burned millions of bibles and shut down the churches and temples." Vandeman then describes how a "home church" movement among laypersons thrived despite official religious persecution. After signs that a new liberalism might permit Christianity to flourish once more in China, such hopes were dashed by the massacre at Tiananmen Square.

Vandeman interviews a Dr. Wilbur Nelson (actually a "doctor of public health") who operates a "flying doctor ministry" called "Wings of Health." Nelson describes how young people are forbidden to make independent decisions. "They're told where to go to school, what to think, what to study, where to work," says Nelson, the implication being that religious freedom is a precondition of individual liberty. But Nelson is not to be deterred. He senses a tremendous opportunity to win new souls for Christ. "You know, it seems almost as if we were back in the days of the apostles," the missionary exults. "One billion, 100 million people." Perhaps it was the possibility of losing such a vast market of potential customers that resulted in the muted response of the U.S. government to the Tiananmen Square massacre.

Errand unto the Asian Wilderness

The spirit of Dr. Wilbur Nelson's glowing numerical estimate of prospective converts awaiting the word of God in the People's Republic of China remains startlingly consistent with that of his Yankee trader forefathers who for more than 100 years have sought ways of tapping the vast wealth of Asia. Then as now, Christian religious institutions and their representatives have been used as the advance guard for the spread of American empire across the Pacific into the Asian continent. By offering comfort and relief to victims of the dislocation and social turmoil resulting from colonial contact, Christian soldiery fulfilled its dual mission of spiritual salvation and economic expansionism.

In his study of the "origins of American Anglo-Saxonism," liberal historian Reginald Horsman makes explicit the systemic relationship between what he euphemistically refers to as "commerce" (capitalism), "economic penetration" (imperialism), and the Christian religion. "Most enthusiasts for the penetration of the Pacific region," writes Horsman, "believed that commercial and technological progress would do just as much as Christianity to bring civilization and progress to backward regions."[53] Although he cannot quite bring himself to employ the language of leftist analysis, Horsman all but admits that the incursions of American commercial interests and religious institutions into Asia helped pave the way for its economic underdevelopment, the exploitation of its peoples, and the establishment of indigenous authoritarian regimes, many of which have had the full backing of the United States. Horsman cannot bring himself to acknowledge honestly that the "American Anglo-Saxonism" he critiques is but a coded means of describing the ideological underpinnings of U.S. imperialism.

At its inception, the evangelical "search for souls in China" has worked in concert with the "sentimental imperialists" whose primary mission in China was the quest for profits.[54] Further, the private Christian missionary movement served as the archetype for subsequent U.S. government programs such as the Peace Corps and "foreign aid" policies designed to bring capitalist-dominated underdeveloped Asian countries under ideological as well as military control. The notorious high-level CIA operative Colonel Edward Lansdale, for example, having spent his career overseeing various covert operations that led to the deaths of thousands, took a post with the seemingly humanitarian Food for Peace program after resigning from the military. In the select television programs surveyed above, cute, lovable Asian children were employed as a drawing card that humanized and personalized what otherwise would have been a battle between two ideological abstractions, capitalism versus communism.

Historically, white American women have also been the beneficiaries of the imperial relationship between the United States and China. As Christian missionaries doing the work of God in China, educated middle-class white women thrived in a "protected market" of sorts, free from male domination and competition. In China, missionary work afforded well-educated and ambitious Euro-American women the opportunity to use their relatively underused skills to win a measure of autonomy, power, and privilege outside the domestic sphere. "As early as 1890," writes Jane Hunter in her insightful history of American women missionaries in China, "women constituted 60 percent of missionary volunteers and proved to be particularly persuasive voices in the crusade for American influence in China."[55] Like their white male counterparts, female American missionaries shared the assumption of Anglo-Saxon racial superiority while enjoying the opportunity to exercise moral authority over their Asian charges.

Placed in a more pragmatic context, for more than a century Christian missionaries and capitalist adventurers alike have coveted China as a vast market ripe for development. In this, state-level religious institutions and capitalism follow a similar logic of expansion and growth. This is not to say that acts of caring and devotion as seen in such television programs as *Korean Legacy, Sons and Daughters, This Is Your Life, Navy Log, The Children of An Lac, One to One, When Will the Dying Stop?*, and *It Is Written* are entirely cynical and self-serving. Without a doubt, countless thousands of Asian children have been helped by Americans engaged in good works. However, each of the programs discussed above exploits the misery of Asians to sustain the belief that basic goodness and benevolence underlie the mythic American errand unto the wilderness.

Chapter 5

Southeast Asian America

Vietnam Syndrome

On April 30, 1975, the South Vietnamese capital city of Saigon fell to communist forces. After decades of armed struggle, the war of Vietnamese national liberation had been won at last. An advanced industrial society boasting the most powerful military machine ever assembled in the history of humankind had been vanquished by an agrarian peasant society with a total population of 18 million. On April 29, the eve of the American debacle, a fleet of Marine helicopters ferried close to 1,000 U.S. officials and almost 6,000 Vietnamese to waiting aircraft carriers stationed off the coast in the South China Sea. The sight of frenzied evacuees at the U.S. embassy desperately clamoring for space aboard overloaded choppers was indelibly impressed upon the minds of those who witnessed the fall of Saigon on network television.

The United States of America had cut and run, abandoning its professed commitment to contain the spread of communism in Asia through armed military might. Perhaps even more significantly, the United States had suffered the humiliation of not fulfilling its self-imposed mythic destiny, that of holding dominion over the darker peoples of the world who were assumed to crave American-style democracy. "From the time of the Philippine annexation and their initial appearance on the stages of world diplomacy in a major role," writes Lloyd Gardner, "American policymakers always believed they were specially endowed by their heritage of revolution against George III's England to undertake a similar mission to *give* Asians self-determination."[1] With the defeat in Vietnam, the U.S. imperial quest seemed to have reached its geographic terminus, forcing a reevaluation of the bedrock belief in American exceptionalism.

The war, however, was won at enormous cost to the Vietnamese people. In the South alone, thousands of villages or hamlets were destroyed along with 25 million acres of farmland, 12 million acres of forest, and 1.5 million farm animals. The U.S. military adventure in Vietnam was responsible for the creation of an estimated 200,000 prostitutes, 879,000 orphans, 181,000 disabled persons, and 1 million widows. Unexploded military ordnance and the 19 million gallons of herbicide sprayed indiscriminately across the countryside are also deathly legacies of the war.[2] In waging total race war, the U.S. military undertook a policy of "pacification," whereby regions held by the National Liberation Front (NLF) were emptied of civilian populations "not merely by firepower but also by defoliation, forced removals into strategic hamlets, and other means of separating peasants from their land."[3] The seemingly value-free term *pacification* was nothing more than Pentagon-speak manufactured to make more palatable the practice of traditional American genocide.

In the aftermath of the American defeat, the crisis of confidence known as the "Vietnam syndrome" was said to have paralyzed the political and military will of the United States. The nagging syndrome also was supposed to have caused a loss of stature for the United States in the eyes of the noncommunist world. The Vietnam syndrome, however, found a deceptively quick and easy antidote in the U.S. "victory" over Iraq in the Gulf War.[4] In the most extensive military attack since World War II, the full force of the U.S. high-tech war-making machinery was brought to bear upon a signficantly smaller nation with only modest means of defending itself. As in Vietnam, most of the news reportage issuing from Riyadh and Dhahran came via the corps of safely ensconced "hotel warriors." Unlike in Vietnam, where journalists routinely accompanied troops into battle and whose news dispatches were not formally censored, the Pentagon ensured that Operation Desert Storm would be covered in a manner similar to the U.S. invasion of Grenada, a "war without witnesses."[5]

The grievous effects of the war in Vietnam once more revealed the extent to which American empire has been sustained through state-sponsored terror and violence waged upon people of color. The punitive military expeditions against Native American sovereign nations, the international trade in African slaves, the mass removal and relocation of Japanese Americans during World War II, and the 1991 war against Iraq are select examples of the redemptive violence that marks the history of U.S. imperium.

Historian Richard Drinnon observes that over a span of 300 years, the Westward expansion of U.S. empire and attendant rise of nationalism were undergirded by the "metaphysics of Indian-hating." Such deathly metaphysics extended to the Asian continent as well, beginning with the mass slaughter of Filipinos, who U.S. soldiers referred to alternately as "niggers" and "Injuns." The outstanding ten-part series *The Pacific Century*, aired on PBS member stations, illustrated the discrepency between the official U.S. policy of "benevolent assimiliation" and the systematic killing of Filipinos as supervised by General Howlin' Jake Smith.[6] At each new frontier, the metaphysics of Indian hating was born anew among white settlers, according to Drinnon. "Rooted in fears and prejudices buried deep in the Western psyche," he writes, "their metaphysics became a time-tested doctrine, an ideology, and an integral component of U.S. nationalism."[7]

The idea of the frontier looms large in the Anglo-American imagination. It is the psychic terrain where dark savagery and white civilization come into contact, followed inevitably by conflict. As an ideological construct, the metaphysics of Indian hating not only informs basic political, social, and economic institutions in the United States but is embedded in cultural practices and artistic expression as well. The Anglo-American fantasy of an unsettled, hostile world populated by treacherous natives perpetually on the verge of rebellion against white colonial settlers remains a barely repressed fear in the popular consciousness.

The metaphysics of Indian hating that underlies American racism and xenophobia manifests itself in a kinder, gentler guise that masks its malevolent intent. The myth of American innocence, of white America as the "innocent victim" of dusky, predatory forces, lies at the heart of what historian Patricia Nelson Limerick describes as the "legacy of conquest."[8] In donning the mantle of the innocent, aggrieved victim, the metaphysics of Indian hating is absorbed, albeit incompletely, into the dominant "myth structures of benevolence," as Edward S. Herman phrases it. As it pertained to the war in Vietnam, the "benevolent role" of the United States in Southeast Asia "rested on our claim of devotion to self-determination and democracy, as well as the importance of resisting aggression."[9]

It is the myth of American benevolence that allows contemporary liberals and conservatives alike to argue that the role of the United States in Vietnam, although well-intentioned, was simply misguided in the belief that democratic institutions and practices could be transplanted to unreceptive foreign soil. Walter H. Capps, for example, has stated unapologetically that a "great nation, even when it means well, can do more harm than good when it does not understand precisely what it is doing."[10] Combined with the enormous war-making capability of the United States, the disingenuous myth of American benevolence becomes all the more lethal as the search and destruction of new "Injuns" is conducted across global frontiers.

Vietnam Revisited

In renegotiating the meaning of U.S. military involvement in Vietnam, a counterhistory has been manufactured by popular films starring figures such as Sylvester Stallone, Chuck Norris, and other would-be heirs to the right-wing militarist legacy of John Wayne. To an equal extent, network television has been implicated in the process of historical revisionism. The Vietnam War counterhistory as seen on television attempts to reconcile the contradiction between the metaphysics of Indian hating and the myth of American benevolence. This forced reconciliation has been attempted through two related strategies: (1) personalizing the war experience and (2) recasting it in the form of television melodrama.

So far as the first strategy is concerned, dramatizing the Vietnam War through the lens of individual action and personal heroism represses the concrete political and military decisions that stemmed from the imperatives of empire building. Further, the pivotal relationship between white supremacist state power and the conduct of a race war against Asian peoples remains unacknowledged. In remaking the war into a series of individual heroic struggles, a program such as *Tour of Duty* (1987–90), according to one critic, "denies history and politics, and redefines the war and warriors in traditional, glorifying ways."[11] The American defeat in Vietnam is elevated to the status of myth through the retelling of tales of personal triumph over adversity, with the war serving as merely a convenient set piece for the dramatization of "universal" human truths.

Concerning the second strategy, in structuring a program such as *China Beach* (1988–91) as television melodrama, it has been argued, an already "passive" audience "moves closer to a feminized position, and an otherwise problematic representation is made consumable and, ultimately, unquestionable."[12] The reality of the widespread death and destruction wrought by the U.S. technowar machine is in a sense doubly domesticated and the historical meaning of the Vietnam War is therefore contained by television melodrama. In sum, the Vietnam War for a detachment of U.S. Army medical and recreational personnel stationed at China Beach becomes little more than a concatenation of intense emotional encounters only incidentally related to the larger structure of power that placed them on foreign soil to look after American interests. The "feminized" role of the television spectator gives precedence to feeling and affectivity over political analysis and an understanding of the historical forces responsible for the war. The specific, concrete experience of the Vietnam War and its aftermath is reduced to simple melodrama. "I come at my stories from the emotional end—then I fit my action in," said Carol Mendelsohn, writer and coproducer of *Tour of Duty*. "I don't really care about guns. I don't care about the military moves per se, and I don't care to write 47 minutes of action."[13]

Within four years after the U.S. evacuation of Saigon, CBS was ready to take on the Vietnam War as the subject of television drama. In 1979, the network offered to bankroll a program created by Gary David Goldberg called *Bureau*, to be produced by MTM. But for both political and (mostly) commercial reasons, the show never got off the ground.[14] It was the rival NBC network that earned the distinction of airing the first Vietnam War-themed program, the short-lived situation comedy *6:00 Follies* (1980). In both *Bureau* and *6:00 Follies*, battlefield truths were filtered and sifted through an assortment of rear-echelon journalists, photographers, and broadcasters reporting on the war. The hardships of the average American "grunt," let alone those of the Vietnamese, were only incidentally touched upon. "It is TV seeing itself covering Vietnam and being covered by the war," according to one commentator.[15]

In an autobiographical account of his experiences covering the Vietnam War for CBS news, Morley Safer roundly criticizes *China Beach*, and its cocreator William Broyles, Jr., for its titillating sensationalism. Safer expresses mock incredulity that Broyles could be the same person who authored *Brothers in Arms* (1986), a memoir written after a return trip to Vietnam in 1984. Broyles had served in the U.S. Marine Corps during 1969–70. As Safer assesses it, the program "reduces the nurses to randy Barbie dolls or pretentious schoolmarms and the marines to shambling fools or psychopaths."[16] But Safer breathlessly agrees with Broyles that China Beach was one of the few places in Vietnam where GIs could see real-live "round-eyed" women who worked as nurses or as Red Cross volunteers known as "Donut Dollies."[17] Although "Vietnamese women were there for the asking," writes Broyles, "without the difficult demands of American women," it was the sight of Euro-American nurses and Donut Dollies that drew the "hungry stares of thousands of lonely men."[18] Safer and Broyles were both equally struck by the racial and psychosexual dimensions of the Vietnam War that leak into the subtext of the program *China Beach*.

The ABC pilot for *China Beach* aired on April 26, 1988.[19] In a touch of historical irony, nurse Colleen McMurphy (Dana Delany) is seen reading Graham Greene's prescient novel of the Cold War, *The Quiet American* (1955), during the opening credits sequence.

Nurse McMurphy of the 510th Evac. unit is stationed at an American recreational facility known as China Beach, located just south of Da Nang, and is at the end of her two-year tour of duty in the year 1969. Because of the horrors she has witnessed as a military nurse, McMurphy has become hardened, desensitized, and detached from her immediate surroundings. She is described as having "gone robot" by one of her compatriots. McMurphy has become inured to the death and suffering of the once-vital young American men brought in from the battlefield for emergency medical treatment.

Colleen McMurphy begins to regain her humanity by befriending a naive nineteen-year-old Donut Dollie appropriately named Cherry White (Nan Woods), who is in Vietnam to find a lost brother whose last known whereabouts were the remote outpost of Khe Sanh near the 17th Parallel.[20] Cherry's first encounter with the flesh-and-blood reality of Vietnam comes when a young (also nineteen) but battle-hardened soldier fresh from the field blankly tells her, "You have round eyes. I haven't seen a round-eyed woman in a long time." Cherry is taken aback by the soldier's observation, but accepts the remark as a compliment paid by a young man made old by his battlefield encounters with death. In the eyes of the common grunt who is unable to distinguish between Asian friend and foe, Cherry White is the embodiment of Euro-American womanhood: sister, wife, and mother all in one.

But the perceived racial difference between Asian and Euro-American women goes far beyond simple physical characteristics. In the social construction of race, such physical differences possess a meaning inseparable from male aggression and the routine conduct of war. Evelyn Yoshimura has observed that, during the Vietnam War, the U.S. military exploited the presumptive physical differences between Asian women and white women as a means of perpetuating a dehumanizing racism within the ranks. "The image of a people with slanted eyes and slanted vaginas enhances the feeling that Asians are other than human," she wrote, "and therefore much easier to kill."[21] And, as with Cherry (virgin) White (Euro-American), such socially constructed somatic differences place Anglo women on a racial pedestal.

With almost lascivious glee, Morley Safer writes that China Beach was known as one of the few places in Vietnam where a "restless GI" could view white American women. Otherwise "abusive and presumptuous with Vietnamese women," GIs were "reduced to awkward adolescents" by the nurses of China Beach. The "round-eyed" women, pants Safer, "were viewed as part mother figure, part inaccessible movie goddess.[22] According to Yoshimura, GIs would pay a "round-eyed chick" (a Red Cross Donut Dollie) the premium rate of $65 for sex rather than the standard $10 for the services of a Vietnamese prostitute.

Presumed racial difference is reinforced by alien cultural practice, as when the lead singer for a USO troupe, Laurette Barber (Chloe Webb), visits a local Vietnamese marketplace to absorb a bit of local color. Laurette spies a cute dog at a stand and buys it from an elderly Vietnamese woman. As the woman disappears to prepare the animal for purchase, Laurette excitedly tells her companion that the pet will be named "Sugar Pie Honey Bunch" (after the first line in "I Can't Help Myself" by the Four Tops). The old woman returns with the dog in a shopping bag, butchered. "It's very good for stew," she suggests helpfully.

Thereafter, Laurette becomes nauseated whenever the USO revue launches into its Motown medley. Because the revue needs a substitute, Cherry White prevails upon McMurphy to stand in for the ailing entertainer. Once McMurphy dons a silver lamé minidress, white go-go boots, and a magnificently teased wig to entertain her fellow enlistees, she begins to pull out of her deep funk. In adopting a new identity McMurphy recovers her lost humanity. It just so happens that McMurphy's rehabilitation comes courtesy of the Vietnamese appetite for dog flesh, for had not Laurette been made ill by the butchered dog, McMurphy never would have been pressed into service as an entertainer in the first place. Thus it is the alien horror of the Vietnam experience, epitomized by the eating of dog flesh, that is both the cause and the cure of McMurphy's short-timer's malaise.

Therapeutic Readjustment

In its final few episodes, aired after the network canceled the program, *China Beach* shifted its emphasis slightly by focusing on the therapeutic readjustment of Vietnam-era veterans. One of the last episodes of the critically acclaimed series in fact has McMurphy undergoing both group therapy at a veteran's center and individual counseling when her long-repressed memories of the war resurface as flashbacks.[23] In the episode, McMurphy joins an all-male "rap" group in which veterans struggle to find meaning in their wartime experiences. As in the program at large, rarely are the lives of the Vietnamese people even acknowledged except as faceless victims, purveyors of such culinary abominations as dog-meat stew, or self-sacrificing servants to the American occupiers.

Asian self-sacrifice and devotion to the American cause becomes a central theme in the last few episodes of *China Beach*. The illegitimate daughter of the head China Beach camp follower, K. C. Koloski (Marg Helgenberger), for example, had been raised by an *amah* or nursemaid, a female Asian figure appearing in the literature of European colonialism. In Vietnamese society, a woman domestic helper is known as a *chi ba*.[24] In *China Beach*, the prominent Vietnamese actress Kieu Chinh was enlisted to fill this dramatic role.[25]

As part of a college class project, K. C.'s adult daughter Karen Lanier (Christine Elise) conducts a videotaped interview with her Vietnamese substitute mother Trieu Au (Kieu Chinh), who now works as a hairdresser in the United States.[26] Trieu Au describes herself as a "jealous old *ma ba*" who resented K. C. for the freedom and independence she enjoyed as part of her birthright as an American. While K. C. was off earning substantial sums of money as a highly sought prostitute and proprietor of night spots patronized by Europeans and North Americans, the Vietnamese *chi ba* had raised Karen with all the devotion of a biological parent before the eight-year-old child was spirited away to the United States during the fall of Saigon.

In the episode "The Always Goodbye," Trieu Au scolds K. C. for not meeting her responsibilities as a mother.[27] K. C., however, refuses to sacrifice her thriving business for the welfare of her own flesh and blood. K. C. responds by telling Trieu Au that she should be grateful for being employed as her daughter's nursemaid. "If you don't like it," says K. C. to Trieu Au, "we'll send you back to Vietnam." But K. C.'s toughness, it is implied, does not reach to the core of her being. She later confides to McMurphy (who is visiting on R&R) that she feels guilty because her daughter Karen is being raised by "two mothers, one to get her dressed at night and one to hang out in bars with."

Despite K. C.'s vague remorse, it is Trieu Au who is left with the principal child-rearing burden. True to the Asian *amah* social type, Trieu Au is the model of self-sacrifice when it comes to her white masters. As Saigon falls in the spring of 1975, Trieu Au even submits to a beating at the hands of Citizen's Committee members who come to her house in search of the Americans K. C. and the young Karen (Shay Astar).[28] After witnessing the Vietnamese *amah* being beaten, the otherwise hard-bitten and cynical K. C. softens her previous skepticism of Trieu's altruism. K. C. had believed that the former diva was looking only for a one-way ticket out of Vietnam at her expense.

In the two-hour final episode of *China Beach*, the veterans of the "five and dime," or 510 Evac. unit, gather for a reunion after the passage of many years.[29] Much to the disappointment of her daughter

Karen, Jr., K. C. – who now heads a large international corporation – does not attend the reunion. After the reunion, Dodger (Jeff Kober), Major Lila Garreau (Concetta Tomei), Sergeant Pepper (Troy Evans), Boonie Lanier (Brian Wimmer), and other principal characters join Colleen McMurphy and her family at the Vietnam Veterans Memorial in an emotional tribute to their fallen comrades. Back at the hotel, as group members depart for their separate destinations, a stretch limousine pulls up and a darkly tinted window lowers to reveal the smilingly unrepentant face of none other than hooker-turned-business executive K. C. Koloski. After a twelve-year absence, K. C. has finally arrived for a mother and child reunion.

Trieu Au, of course, by this time is nowhere to be seen. Having raised K. C.'s bastard child to age ten, the jealousy of the Vietnamese *chi ba* seemed to have been well-founded after all, exceeding the ordinary resentment of a woman who in her own words was just "learning to bitch." After all, although limited by her gender in a patriarchal society, at least K. C. has the privilege of white skin, a privilege she was able to capitalize upon in marketing her services as a prostitute to her male "oppressors." Further, her status as a rich (relative to the Vietnamese) American allowed K. C. to farm out the work of mothering to nonwhite women or *amahs* at the expense of their own families.

Angels of Mercy

As a nurse, Colleen McMurphy embodied all that is selfless and caring in a war-torn world where such sentiments were a liability. Nursing was an extension of her woman's role as caregiver and nurturer. In tending to the wounded and giving comfort to the dying, McMurphy and her fellow nurses were the lone representatives of humanitarianism amidst the brutalizing reality of war. The revisionist television version, however, does not square with the raw racial hatred harbored by many female nurses in Vietnam.

In his oral history of Vietnam veterans, Al Santoli records the thoughts of Gayle Smith, a nurse with the 3rd Surgical Hospital in Binh Thuy. Smith tells of the animus she had developed for the Vietnamese to the point where she had fantasies about "putting a .45 to someone's head and see it blow away." She had even sworn to herself that "if the Vietnamese ever came to this country I'd kill them" and that only the law prevented her from acting upon such all-consuming rage.[30]

Official estimates set the number of women who served in Vietnam at about 7,500. Among them was Anne Simon Auger of the 91st Evac. Hospital in Chu Lai. She freely speaks of her visceral hatred for the Vietnamese POWs who were brought in for treatment. After trying to resume a normal civilian life, Auger suffered from severe depression, experienced nightmares, and became suicidal. Many of her nightmares "were centered around gooks" and it reached a point where she "couldn't see a slant-eye without getting upset."[31] Similarly, Karen "Kay" Johnson Burnette of the 24th Evac. Hospital in Long Binh speaks of the bitterness, frustration, and anger she vented upon Vietnamese patients. "It took me several years to realize that we've kind of been indoctrinated into that," Johnson Burnette says, "but that was something kind of hard to live with, the fact that I could be prejudiced."[32]

The resentment and anger against Vietnamese victims was common within the nursing corps. An unofficial form of triage was practiced, for example, that ensured the American wounded were tended to before the Vietnamese. Vietnamese patients—men, women, and children alike—were assumed to be enemy agents or soldiers and therefore could be justifiably left untreated. The "no front line" argument made all Vietnamese suspect in a war where women, children, and the elderly alike might be enemy saboteurs. As one nurse expressed it, "It was easy to imagine the Vietnamese, especially the men, as enemies because they were of a different race, a different culture."[33]

Even the most morally upstanding of military nurses drew a color line around their compassion when it came to the treatment of "gooks." Lynda Van Devanter, a nurse raised in a Catholic household who describes herself as an "All-American Girl," shamefully recalls how she lapsed into hatred of the Asian enemy. "If you're such a gook lover, why don't you scrub on the case?" she told a superior who had ordered her to prepare an enemy casualty for emergency treatment. In retaliation, Devanter scrubbed for the operation by spitting on her hands. "If he died of an infection," she thought, "fuck him."[34]

First-person accounts by military nurses graphically expose the thoroughgoing anti-Asian racism of the American crusade in Vietnam. Even angels of mercy were not immune to the venom of racial hatred that spewed forth during the routine conduct of their duties. Many nurses returned home bearing their categorical dislike of Asian people. Despite their social subordination within a patriarchal system of power, white female nurses could at least share in the metaphysics of Asian hating on an equal basis with their male counterparts in the military. Contrary to the ideas of "difference feminism" given currency by academic feminists such as Carol Gilligan and Nancy Chodorow, firsthand accounts of women in the military cast serious doubt on the implied claim to female moral super-iority.[35]

Platoon System

China Beach was canceled after three seasons on ABC. Although hailed by critics, *China Beach* never cracked the list of the twenty top-rated TV shows, even after a promising start. The networks and the viewing public preferred to stick with a familiar diet of situation comedies such as *Cheers* (1982–93), *The Cosby Show* (1984–92), *The Golden Girls* (which became *Golden Palace* in its final season, 1985–93), *Roseanne* (1988–present), and *The Cosby Show* spin-off *A Different World* (1987–93).

Despite its shortcomings, *China Beach* seemed to have had a radicalizing effect on its star, thirty-five-year-old Dana Delany. Delany, who won an Emmy (1989) in the category of outstanding lead actress in a drama series, criticized ABC for canceling *China Beach* while introducing a new program *Homefront* (1991–93) that was set nostalgically in the years immediately following the end of World War II. The actress was especially bitter about the U.S. "victory" in the Gulf War that had supposedly cured the Vietnam syndrome. "It's absurd to think that the Gulf War has erased the failure of Vietnam," said Delany. "I just laugh when I read people saying that. Now that we've won the Gulf War, people are eager to brush aside Vietnam."[36]

Given the low ratings of television programs with manifest Vietnam-era settings or themes, it seems that the American public was less than willing to subject itself to even the barest hint of self-censure. As Delany's remarks imply, that the overwhelming major-ity of citizens supported the U.S. military attack on Iraq suggests that the genocidal metaphysics of Indian hating remains very much a part of the American character. The real tragedy of the Vietnam War is that Americans, believing themselves to be martyrs in a holy crusade, would thereafter dare not initiate a war unless it could be won at minimal cost. After Vietnam, so-called low-intensity conflict would come to replace outright invasion and occupation.

Preceding *China Beach* by one season, the hour-long CBS drama *Tour of Duty* appeared in the fall of 1987 shortly after the theatrical release of *Platoon* (1986), directed by Oliver Stone. *Platoon* earned an Academy Award for Best Picture and Stone won top directorial honors in 1987. Along with *Platoon*, the release of such stark, non-romanticized films as Stanley Kubrick's long-awaited feature *Full Metal Jacket* (1987) and Brian De Palma's *Casualties of War* (1989) hinted at a certain degree of acceptance by many Americans of the

U.S. role in Vietnam. At the same time, films such as *First Blood* (1982), *Missing in Action* (1984), and *Rambo: First Blood Part II* (1985) represented a powerful countertendency: denial and retribution.

Like its more politically progressive cinematic counterparts, *Tour of Duty* did little to glorify the war in that there were few overt example of heroics or patriotic gore. Few of the men of the multiethnic Bravo Company appeared to be motivated by anything other than group survival. *Tour of Duty*, unlike earlier military action-adventure programs such as *The Gallant Men* (1962–63), *Combat* (1962–67), *Twelve O'Clock High* (1964–67), *The Rat Patrol* (1966–68), *Baa Baa Black Sheep/Black Sheep Squadron* (1976–77/1977–78), depicted war with a greater degree of complexity and realism.[37] Not a few of the lead characters, for example, were killed in combat during the run of the program, precluding close audience identification with the principal protagonists. Breaking with network television convention, Private Randy "Doc" Matsuda (Steve Akahoshi), the only regularly appearing Asian American character, and Captain Rusty Wallace (Kevin Conroy) were "killed" during the first season. But perhaps Doc Matsuda's being of Asian ancestry made his "loss" easier to bear.

Despite its praiseworthy improvements over earlier mindlessly patriotic and nationalistic action-adventure military dramas, *Tour of Duty* nevertheless rehearsed a litany of contemporary conservative bromides that have been invoked to explain away the U.S. defeat in Vietnam. Yet the program also introduced a number of progressive elements, such as better numerical representation of minority soldiers (who saw combat in disproportional numbers) and extended probes into the inner lives of Black and Latino characters. The Asian characters, however, were no more multidimensional than those "beasts in the jungle" featured in World War II propaganda films.[38] A close reading of a specific *Tour of Duty* episode illustrates the above observations.

In "I Wish It Would Rain," an FNG ("fucking new guy") who was a schoolteacher as a civilian is cut in two by the lethal spring-loaded mine known as a "Bouncing Betty."[39] Outraged, his partner, Taft (John Shepard), goes berserk and crosses the border into Cambodia to seek revenge against the stealthy Asian enemy. Taft catches up with the enemy soldiers, who appear to be in good cheer after having inflicted lethal injury upon the Americans. In an extreme close-up, the laughing face of a Vietnamese soldier fills the entire frame. Once the viewer's hate for the Asian soldier has been built to a fever pitch, Taft knifes the enemy after catching him alone, urinating by a tree.

A couple of grenades tossed into their camp dispose of more "Viet Cong" soldiers.[40] When a survivor of the one-man revenge squad begs for mercy, Taft shoots him dead without hesitation.

After a brief search, Taft is located and brought back to the Ton Son Nhut airbase near Saigon. At the base, Lieutenant Myron Goldman (Stephen Caffrey) voices a now-familiar complaint to Alex Devlin (Kim Delaney), a reporter for a wire service. "I think the policy's insane," Goldman says. "They keep sending us into combat with our hands tied and we're losing." To reward themselves for having survived the search-and-destroy mission, a few of the men go into town to do some drinking and whoring. There is lascivious talk about going to "mama san's." Corporal Danny Percell (Tony Becker) and Private Marcus Taylor (Miguel A. Nunez, Jr.) accompany an officer to a whorehouse, but they are told by a shadowy Asian businessman and pimp named Mr. Tsung (Raymond Ma) to come back later.

The scene then shifts to the Golden Dragon, where a Vietnamese bikini dancer moves suggestively to Wilson Pickett's "In the Midnight Hour," much to the delight of hooting GIs. It is in this setting that a French journalist named Jacques Fournier (Andrew Masset) engages Percell and Taylor in a philosophical discussion concerning U.S. involvement in the war. "You know, we could win this war if they'd let us fight it," says Percell in a familiar postwar refrain. Fournier says that public opinion in the United States has turned against the war, with "even Walter Cronkite" having modified his formerly hawkish position as anchor of the *CBS Evening News*.

Fournier turns to Taylor, who is African American, and tests his loyalty by bringing the issue of race and racism into the discussion. The journalist says that Black soldiers are deserting because they realize that they are "being used to fight a white man's war." "Even your boxing champion Muhammad Ali refused the draft," says Fournier. "No one's deserting," Taylor answers. "We're still here." To provide proof, Fournier leads Percell and Taylor on a tour of Cholon, the predominantly ethnic Chinese suburb of Saigon known for Viet Cong terrorist attacks on American soldiers. To the disbelieving GIs, Fournier claims that a number of Black American deserters are living in Cholon and have severed all ties with their parent country. Taylor does indeed encounter a Black deserter shortly after arriving in Cholon, but is rebuffed when the ex-soldier says he will have nothing to do with "his kind" anymore.

While looking for other GIs who have gone over the hill, Taylor and Percell are captured by the Viet Cong. Like the VC soldier earlier knifed by Taft, the most notable trait of these enemies is their utter sadism. One Viet Cong soldier in particular (Michael Paul

Chan) beats Percell mercilessly, laughing all the while. He calls Percell "honkie," a term of derision probably picked up from the Black deserters.

As for the African American Taylor, the VC soldier exploits the problem of U.S. race relations by suggesting that he stay in Cholon with his "soul brothers." Taylor, however, does not rise to the bait. Instead, he reaffirms his loyalty to the United States by arguing that white racism is only partly behind the desertion of the "brothers." Equally as important to Taylor is the fact that "they can't fight to win over here." Taylor has nothing but contempt for the Black deserters who must "live like rats in a hole." "Least I got *some* chance at home," says Taylor to his fellow captive Percell before they make good their escape.

Within the action and adventure matrix formed by this *Tour of Duty* episode, two related issues are introduced that aid in rewriting the contemporary historical record on the Vietnam War. In both cases, Asian characters are used as dramaturgic devices to achieve this delicate ideological operation. For one, the notion that the U.S. government did not fully support its troops by giving them the wherewithal to achieve total victory is very much in evidence here. The Viet Cong are seen as ruthless in the conduct of guerrilla warfare, darting back and forth across the porous borders of "neutral" countries such as Cambodia to evade their pursuers. All the while, U.S. troops are forced to fight by Marquis of Queensbury rules that place them at an unfair disadvantage. Never mind that the covert Asian wars conducted by the United States since the end of World War II neither respected national boundaries nor placed a very high premium on fighting "fair."

The enemy Victor Charles relied upon stealth, torture, and instruments of terror such as booby traps to attain victory. The VC even sacrificed the lives of their *own kind*—men, women, children, entire families—to achieve its goal of totalitarian communist rule. That the United States unleashed the most massive campaign of destruction against a civilian population the world has ever witnessed is never alluded to. On a smaller scale, the Phoenix Program, developed in 1967 by the Central Intelligence Agency, specifically targeted civilians to be "neutralized" as an integral part of its counterterror campaign against the Vietcong "infrastructure" (VCI). Suspected members of the VCI were "brutally murdered along with their families or neighbors as a means of terrorizing the neighboring population into a state of submission."[41] Atrocities committed against civilians often were attributed to the enemy for propaganda purposes.

The second, more subtle, implication of this episode is that life in the United States, even with its well-documented history of white racism, still beats existing in Vietnam "like rats in a hole." At least American society affords people of color an opportunity to overcome social disadvantages, whereas no such possibility exists for those living in Vietnam. Taylor's VC captor snidely offers him the chance to cast his lot with other American Blacks by living among the Vietnamese in Third World racial solidarity, but Taylor chooses life in "the World" among the white master race instead of siding with the African American defectors and the yellow people they have been sent to destroy. Taylor's decision therefore signals the triumph of an abstraction, American nationalism, over the concrete politics of race as temptingly articulated by Black nationalists such as Muhammad Ali, the African American defectors, and the "Third World" as represented by the Viet Cong. That Taylor is somewhat jaded and cynical excuses him from being written off as a classic "Uncle Tom." But this subtle and nuanced characterization makes Taylor's reaffirmation of Americanism all the more compelling. Through Taylor's embrace of an admittedly imperfect American society, the audience is made to accept the revisionist truths about Vietnam planted in the narrative like a claymore mine.

Viet Movie of the Week

By far, apart from network-produced documentaries and the evening news, the largest number of programs treating the war in Vietnam have been made-for-television movies. Although the genre might not share the advantage of the larger canvas enjoyed by the cinema, made-for-television movies have grappled with themes of equal magnitude from time to time. Elayne Rapping has stated that even though the worst of made-for-television movies might be "reactionary" in content, the better ones can be "very progressive and worthwhile, more so than the most popular theatrical films today."[42] Certainly the range of issues and problems addressed by television movies is as diverse as that of most commercially produced feature films. And their politics are not any more appreciably muted than the majority of theatrical films produced, distributed, and marketed by transnational corporations.

Whether reactionary or progressive, made-for-television movies must abide by a set of aesthetic, commercial, and ideological constraints dictated by industry practice and political considerations. But even when they are patently "bad," made-for-television movies are a window to the collective consciousness of the ideal audience as envisaged by the institutional complex comprising producers, writers, directors, advertisers, and executives. That is, the products of these creative minds betray latent sociocultural information in the form of entertainment. The two-hour television movie *Shooter* (1988), for example, is indicative of the manner in which contemporary Asian American women are "framed" by the relatively homogeneous group that staffs the dominant media institutions.

In a war not otherwise noted for acts of individual heroism, journalists and news reporters came closest to embodying the sense of romance, sacrifice, nobility, and national purpose that the people back home expect from their foreign military adventures. In a diffuse regional conflict, it was members of the press corps who constructed the first-draft, middle-range narratives that allowed a larger comprehensible history to be shaped out of the confusion, chaos, and turbulence that attended the war in Vietnam. One such journalistic "hero" to emerge was David Hume Kennerly, who won a Pulitzer Prize for his Vietnam War photography. His experiences as a combat photographer form the basis of the made-for-television movie *Shooter*, for which he served as both executive producer and cowriter.[43]

The movie opens with a montage of Vietnam War photographs, presumably taken by Kennerly himself. His fictional alter ego is Matt Thompson (Jeffrey Nordling), a U.S. military photographer shooting battle scenes in March 1967. Thompson is ambitious professionally. He admires the famed Hungarian war photographer Robert Capa (who died in Vietnam at age forty) and aspires to a job working for *Life* magazine, for Capa had covered the European theater of action for *Life* during World War II. Thompson, however, is not so single-minded in his pursuit of taking the perfect photograph that it keeps him from sexual dalliance, illicit or otherwise. While Thompson is in Saigon, three streetwalkers in succession call out to him as he rides in an open-air cab with a former paramour: "Hi, Mr. Matt"; "Mr. Matt, you numbuh one!"; "Careful Mr. Matt. You butterfly too much."

Although the whores of Saigon hold special appeal for the shooter, Thompson is sexually interested in a somewhat independent and aloof American-educated Vietnamese woman. Lan (Rosalind Chao) is a coworker of Thompson's at the news bureau; he has been pursuing her for some time, but to no avail. Although almost thoroughly Americanized, Lan wears an *ao dai*, the traditional Vietnamese long-sleeved, high-necked silk garment with knee-length front and rear panels that drape over black or white pants. Lan's Asian attire is meant to connote her alien being vis-à-vis the American Thompson.

Lan finally succumbs to Thompson's entreaties, but with her own — not his — sexual desires foremost in mind. "Everyone in the bureau has asked you out, and you've refused," Thompson says, mystified. "Why me? Why last night?" "You wanted me," Lan responds flatly, "I wanted a man." Thompson pays Lan a whore's compliment when he tells her, "I love Vietnamese women. You really know how to make a guy feel special."

The "shooter" is astounded at Lan's uninhibited lustfulness, an attribute apparently not often found among the ordinary Vietnamese women that the U.S. military presence had not already turned into prostitutes. Matt Thompson expresses awe at his sex partner's uncharacteristic (i.e., non-Vietnamese) erotic demonstrativeness. "You certainly know what you want," he says. "Is that something you picked up in the States?" "I studied political science, Matt," Lan responds dryly. "I didn't have to go to Berkeley to learn how to be a woman."

Although Thompson and Lan are coworkers, their erotically charged repartee exposes Mr. Matt's not entirely successful attempt to exercise control over the meaning of White male–Asian Asian female sexual relations. It is evident that Thompson perceives the Vietnamese American woman as a whore first and foremost ("I love Vietnamese women"), not as a coequal professionally. He assumes that Lan's stay in the United States was dedicated to the refinement of sexual technique and gratification ("You certainly know what you want") rather than the pursuit of knowledge through her studies in political science at Berkeley. In the racist eyes of Matt Thompson, Lan's social existence is subsumed by her sexual being.

Matt Thompson's "love" of Vietnamese women might be interpreted as a form of condescension, but he is portrayed as a kind and sincere Yankee nonetheless. When Sister Marie (Grace Zabriskie) needs money to assist Montagnard families displaced by the war, Thompson donates his freelance photo earnings to her refugee center under a pseudonym to escape detection by his superiors. Thompson even comforts his young dying friend Minh (Rummel Mor), who has been shot by the police while carrying out a bomb attack. Minh had worked as a street vendor and, like Thompson, was a fan of the New York Mets. Minh, however, repaid Thompson's kindness and friendship with "terrorist" bombings. Even so, Matt Thompson forgivingly holds Minh in his arms as the life of the enemy operative slips away. This concluding tableau implies that even the worst acts of betrayal committed against America are repaid by unconditional love.

Memorializing the War

After viewing Michael Cimino's film *The Deer Hunter* in 1979, a federal employee and Vietnam veteran named Jan Scruggs was inspired to mount the hard-fought campaign that would eventually result in the construction of the national monument that honors the memory of Americans who died in the war. After years of chronic funding problems, bureaucratic delays, and an acrimonious battle with Texas multimillionaire H. Ross Perot, the Vietnam Veterans Memorial was formally dedicated in Washington, D.C., on Veterans Day, November 1982. Few had anticipated the intensely visceral impact that "the Wall" would have upon the millions of visitors each year who come to stand before the polished black granite surfaces of the twin walls that rise out of the earth listing the names of 57,939 American dead. "The Memorial's ambiguous stance generates a shifting symbolic ground," according to one interpreter, "a fluctuating, constantly renegotiated field in which veterans and other *enact* Vietnam's meaning."[44]

The Vietnam Veterans Memorial stands as a stark testament to the longest, most costly war in the history of the United States. Like the bitter controversies that attended the planning and design of the memorial, the battle over the meaning of the Vietnam War is far from over. It is a battle that has been conducted, among other places, on the airwaves via television movies. Soon after the American defeat in 1975, ABC produced *Green Eyes* (1976), a made-for-TV movie that dramatized the plight of a Black American veteran (Paul Winfield) who returns to Saigon in 1973 to find the son he had sired with a Vietnamese "bar girl." Carol Burnett gave a stellar performance as a middle-American woman who tries to make sense of her soldier son's accidental death in *Friendly Fire* (1979). The following year, two fact-based television movies appeared on the networks, *The Children of An Lac* (1980) and *A Rumor of War* (1980). In addition, *Fly Away Home* (1981), a television pilot that failed to materialize as a network series, featured the exploits of a photojournalist in search of exciting stories in Vietnam around the time of the Tet offensive.

More recently, the CBS docudrama *Vestige of Honor* (1990) recounted the heroic efforts of a Vietnam veteran named Don Scott, who rescued Montagnards (employed by the CIA as anticommunist mercenaries) from a Thai refugee camp and then resettled more than 200 of them in North Carolina. NBC's *The Girl Who Came Between Them* (1991) starred former Charlie's Angel Cheryl Ladd as the wife of a veteran (Anthony John Denison) who brings his Amerasian love child (Melissa Chang) to the United States, and NBC's *Last Flight Out* (1990) dramatized the plight of the final 500 evacuees who fled Saigon on that fateful day of April 24, 1975. *Last Flight Out* was a "fact-based" television movie that told the story of Pan Am pilot Dan

Hood (Richard Crenna), who saved an "Amerasian" boy during the evacuation and later adopted him. "We have a tendency to forget that there are civilians in combat zones," said Crenna in an interview. "We forget because it's been a long time since a war was fought on our own land, and it's been a long time since we've had to deal with invading armies. We don't understand the legacy those armies leave behind."[45] Beyond their superficial differences, the made-for-television movies mentioned above have one feature in common: the Vietnamese characters are used simply as props that allow acts of American benevolence, self-sacrifice, and suffering to be staged realistically.

The politics of remembrance found further expression in the television movie *To Heal a Nation* (1988), which dramatized the considerable wrangling that occurred over the issue of how the Vietnam War would be memorialized.[46] Jan Scruggs (Eric Roberts) is the Vietnam veteran and Purple Heart recipient who spearheads the war memorial project. After first jumping through numerous financial and bureaucratic hoops to begin the project, Scruggs encounters the imposing H. Ross Perot (Conrad Bachmann) while in search of funding. Perot offers to donate a large sum of money to underwrite the cost of the monument's design, which will in turn attract the funds needed to complete the project. Little does Scruggs know that he has struck a deal with the devil. Perot pledges $160,000 in seed money, but warns Scruggs that he will "hear about it" if the design does not satisfy Perot's personal tastes.

A national competition for a suitable design is launched, and it attracts 1,421 entries coming from almost all regions of the country. Ironically, it is an Asian American woman – an undergraduate student of architecture at Yale named Maya Ying Lin – who wins the contest with the unanimous agreement of the jury. It is at this crucial juncture that the racial, more specifically anti-Asian, subtext creeps into an otherwise pedestrian television movie.

Maya Ying Lin (Tamlyn Tomita) appears at a press conference to discuss her winning design. Articulate and self-possessed, Lin explains the concept behind the design for the memorial. "I wanted to describe a journey," says Lin. "A journey that would make you experience death." This is certainly not the approach favored by H. Ross Perot and his ilk, who fancy a realistic, representational rendering that would serve as a reflection of American patriotism in its finest hour. Unhappy with the design, Perot threatens to withdraw his support of the project. Neither are many members of the Vietnam Veterans Memorial Fund committee entirely comfortable with the forthright style of the Asian American woman whose perceived "defensiveness" might hinder the fund-raising effort.

In the end, H. Ross Perot and Secretary of the Interior James Watt (David Wells) are overruled by the tens of thousands of veterans who support the design as it is. The American Legion, with its 2.9 million members, had already shown its support by donating $1.25 million to the monument project. Actual documentary footage of the memorial undergoing construction—the off-loading of the raw granite, the grinding and polishing of the stone, the inscribing of the names of the dead—rescues *To Heal a Nation* from mere bathos. A stonecutter is seen breaking down after chancing upon the name of her dead brother as she works. Similarly, the documentary footage of the completed memorial being officially dedicated on Veterans Day is profoundly affecting. Extended scenes of the large crowd that gathered on the mall to hear the names of the war dead as they were read aloud underscores the elemental power of the Vietnam Veterans Memorial.

It is one of the supreme ironies of the Vietnam War that the 58,000 Americans who lost their lives in a race war would be memorialized by the work of an Asian American woman. *To Heal a Nation* only fleetingly alludes to the problem posed by the Asian ethnicity of Maya Ying Lin, but immediately after the identity of the design competition was announced there were rumblings of discontent. In certain quarters, Lin's design was met with outright hostility. H. Ross Perot even threatened to overturn the decision of the expert judges by calling for a "national referendum."[47] When that tactic failed, Perot hired the notorious attorney Roy Cohn to impugn the integrity of those who administered the Vietnam Veterans Memorial Fund by demanding to inspect their financial records. A compromise was struck when it was agreed that a statue of three GIs—two white and one Black—would be placed near the memorial. The sculptor of "The Three Servicemen," Frederick E. Hart, was one of the more vocal critics of the Lin design. The creator of what one observer has described as "an out-size depiction of three Ramboesque soldiers" reportedly received a commission fee of more than ten times the $20,000 prize awarded to Maya Ying Lin.[48] Maya Ying Lin strenuously objected to the addition of the statue, likening it to drawing a mustache on a piece of art.

At first, the veterans associated with the memorial project were delighted at the idea of a young, female, "Oriental," nonprofessional having won the competition. Maya Lin, however, soon came into conflict with the vets, whom she felt treated her like a child. It seems that the veterans were not pleased that an Asian American woman would dare assert the right to protect her artistic vision. According to Jan Scruggs, the veterans thought Lin "too cold and cynical," approaching her work with an emotionless, clinical detachment.[49] Maya Lin thought that the memorial should, in her words, be "honest about the reality of war and be for the people who gave their lives." Her architectural masterwork stemmed from "an impulse to cut open the earth" in an act of "initial violence that in time would heal." "It was as if the black-brown earth were polished and made into an interface between the sunny world and the quiet world beyond, that we can't enter," said Lin. "The names would become the memorial. There was no need to embellish."[50] Over the objections of the architectural community, the Hart statue was installed near the Vietnam Veterans Memorial two years after its official dedication. Maya Lin went on to enjoy a successful career as a sculptor and architect, her most notable recent project being the Civil Rights Memorial in Montgomery, Alabama.

Unlike the granite walls upon which thousands of American names are etched, there are no monuments to the Vietnamese war dead, save perhaps for Chris Burden's mordant art piece "The Other Vietnam Memorial" (1992). In film and television, the Vietnamese have been memorialized, but only as an indirect means of paying tribute to the essential goodness of the American people who tried their best to prevent their Asian wards from falling victim to communist rule. Helpless Vietnamese orphans, "Amerasian" children, the "boat people" – these are the heartrending images that have been put to good use on network television. Such representations are effective in reinforcing the myth of American benevolence while suppressing the truth of U.S. genocidal activity throughout Southeast Asia.

Amerasian Love Children

Though not nearly as newsworthy as the MIA/POW mythology that has been kept alive by right-wing ideologues, television programs have begun to address the problem of so-called Amerasian children with growing frequency. Both fact-based and fiction programs have exploited the plight of Amerasians through mass-mediated rituals of public compassion that expiate guilt while denying responsibility for creating the conditions under which the abandoned children were sired. In a report on one man's mission to reunite Amerasian children with their American parents, host of the newsmagazine *Inside Edition* Bill O'Reilly states that there are an "estimated 10,000 Amerasians in Vietnam whose American fathers, usually veterans, left them behind."[51] The segment opens with amateur video footage of Amerasian children in Vietnam. Pathetically, the children sing "We Are the World" in broken English.

The audience is then introduced to John H. Rogers, Jr., an African American veteran who has been reunited with his Vietnamese daughter, Gloria. Rogers, we are told by the narrator of the segment, has "dedicated his life" to resettling Amerasian children in the United States. Having spent five years in Vietnam, Rogers fathered his daughter in 1970 and later founded an agency called Faces to assist others who seek to recover children they left behind. Now married to a second Vietnamese woman and living in Hawaii, Rogers was granted permission to enter Vietnam in 1988 to search for his daughter. He was lucky enough to locate her on the first day of his trip. Gloria Parker now lives in Milwaukee with Rogers's sister and is enrolled in a trade school. Rogers has been able to parlay his expertise into a thriving cottage industry; he has returned to Vietnam twenty-five times to assist other Americans hoping to reclaim their war babies.

The subject of Amerasian children takes an unusual twist in a program geared toward a youth audience, *K*I*D*S*.[52] Produced under contract to the U.S. Department of Education, the episode "Tien's Story" is a remarkably mature and sensitive account of an Amerasian teenager in search of her identity. After visiting an "I Remember Vietnam" photographic exhibit, Tien Do (Tien Tran) becomes curious about the father she has never known. Her mother, Mai Tran (Kieu Chinh), at first denies any knowledge of the GI who fathered Tien, but then speculates that the man—Robert Lee—might still be alive.

Tien succeeds in tracing Robert Lee to San Francisco, where he operates a photography studio. When she calls his home, a child answers. Tien is upset to learn that Robert Lee has begun a new family. Unable to bear the pain any longer, Tien confronts her mother at their family-run restaurant. Mai confesses that although her GI lover abandoned her, he had no knowledge of her pregnancy before leaving. Tien, however, cannot forgive her mother for concealing the truth.

Mai contacts her wartime lover and invites him to visit her and Tien at the family restaurant. In a bizarre twist, Robert Lee (James Ishida) happens to be *Chinese* American! Bobby Lee is far from the cold and heartless man Mai has described to Tien. On the contrary, Lee is the picture of contrition, remorse, and fatherly concern. The former GI explains that after having seen "all of my buddies" being killed, he wanted to forget his wartime experiences altogether. But Bobby Lee ends his visit with Tien and Mai on good terms. He states his intention to remain in close touch with Tien by issuing her a standing invitation to visit his family in San Francisco.

In an otherwise expertly realized drama, the Asian ethnicity of Robert Lee stands out as a glaring inconsistency. Given the relatively small numbers of Asian Americans who saw military service in Vietnam, it seems improbable that the father of Tien would be an Asian American. He would far more likely have been white, Black, or Hispanic. The question then arises as to why an Asian American was cast in the role of derelict father. It could be that because the target audience of *K∗I∗D∗S* comprises preteens and younger teenagers, the theme of miscegenation would have only added more moral confusion to an already muddled set of circumstances that includes illegitimacy, child abandonment, and bigamy. It could also be that, whereas all other sins can be forgiven, the "crime" of miscegnation simply cannot be countenanced.

In the Heat of Passion

The search for the lost American father is also the theme of a Christmas holiday episode of *In the Heat of the Night* (1988–present). Unlike in the 1967 film on which the television show is based, the relationship between African American detective Virgil Tibbs (Howard Rollins) and white Chief of Police Bill Gillespie (Carroll O'Connor) is largely free of black versus white racial tension. In the Sparta, Mississippi, of the post-civil rights era, race is no longer the dividing line between Gillespie and Tibbs. Instead, they work closely together in solving an array of big-city crimes in a small-town setting. In the more than twenty years that have elapsed between the original film and its television rendition, the Sparta Police Department has become both racially integrated and balanced in gender. This is not to say that the small southern town of Sparta is devoid of racism. In an episode that originally aired on Christmas Eve, it is seen that the animus once reserved exclusively for African Americans is now extended to Asian newcomers.[53]

A young Vietnamese boat person arrives in Sparta after having spent time in various Asian refugee camps before escaping to the United States. The refugee, "Hank" (Barry K. Bernal), seeks out Chief Gillespie for help. The young man's father, Henry Boyer, who was killed in action, once was both a coworker and close friend of Gillespie. In the United States illegally and with no surviving family members to rely upon, Hank has sought out Gillespie for help. Although Chief Gillespie receives Hank with open arms, his deputy, Parker Williams (David Hart), has had wartime experiences that have left him with a deep and abiding hatred for yellow people.

When Hank first arrives at the police station, for example, Williams snidely remarks about the Asian man's supposed taste for "eels and rice." Williams then mutters that "the only good use for his kind is fertilizing the rice paddies."

Hank runs into trouble when he is falsely accused by a young white man of having shot a clerk during a holdup attempt. Hank's problems are compounded when Deputy Williams finds a packet of suspicious letters in the refugee's backpack that casts doubt on the veracity of his story. Virgil Tibbs tells Williams that he is "saying the kid is lying simply because he's Vietnamese." Williams admits as much, but offers an explanation for his inherent distrust of the Vietnamese:

> When people say they're gonna treat you fair as a prisoner and then they take you out and they beat you and they kick you in your privates and they break your arm and they bust your fingers, and then they urinate in your face, I find it kinda hard to believe *those* people after *that*.

Once the chief confronts Hank about the incriminating letters, he confesses that he found them in an "army bunker near Da Nang." Hank, however, argues that although his father was not Henry Boyer, his father was nonetheless an American. "This is my country," says Hank.

After Hank is cleared of the shooting, Chief Gillespie directs his energies to getting at the root of Williams's anti-Asian hostility. Gillespie makes a somewhat far-fetched psychoanalytic leap by speculating that Williams is directing anger at Hank simply because he might be feeling guilty about having had sexual relations with numbers of Vietnamese women and therefore fears that the young Asian man might be his illegitmate child. "How many Vietnamese women did you go fornicating with over there?" Chief Gillespie demands. "You are mad because you're guilty . . . because you have a feeling that maybe *you* left a little fellow there without a father."

Chief Gillespie says that he will not forget Parker Williams's behavior toward Hank until he can learn to behave "like a decent, Christian, soldierly man." Having been chastised through a combination of secular (psychoanalytic) and religious (Christian) invective, Williams is later seen treating Hank in an almost a fatherly fashion. In the tag scene, Chief Gillespie and Hank are partaking in a Christmas Eve dinner at a cafe. Gillespie shares with Hank a scheme he has devised to keep the Vietnamese refugee in the United States legally. The chief hints conspiratorially that he will have Deputy Parker Williams himself claim Hank as his very own flesh and blood.

Following a common pattern seen in various television episodes, Vietnamese refugees such as Hank might encounter a bit of residual hostility on the part of select individuals such as Deputy Williams. But overall, the program implies, the tolerance and caring of a Bill Gillespie are more representative of American society. A desperately trusting refugee like Hank can be thankful that the chief will even bend the rules so that he can remain in the United States. Through the skillful use of the good cop/bad cop technique, almost all traces of the racism that undergirds the story have been erased. More important, the underlying anti-Asian racism that motivated the U.S. mission in Vietnam has been made to disappear as well.[54]

Divine Intervention

Highway to Heaven (1984–89) was the last series Michael Landon starred in before he died of cancer in 1991. The premise of the program bore no resemblance to the long-running *Little House on the Prairie* (1974–83), but both shared the same mawkish sensibility that Landon seemed to favor over the course of his television career. In *Highway to Heaven*, Jonathan Smith (Landon), assisted by his partner in a detective agency, Mark Gordon (Victor French), was an angel who had been sent to earth so he could bring a little bit of sunshine into the lives of everyday people.

In an episode constructed around the ever-popular Asian orphan theme, a Vietnamese couple engage Smith and Gordon to help find the children they had given up for adoption before being sent to prison for almost two years by the North Vietnamese.[55] After escaping to Singapore as "boat people," Dr. Truong Vann Diep (Haing S. Ngor) and his wife Truong Lan Minh (Lang Yun) remained there for ten years, all the while waiting for the time when they could reclaim their sons. Dinh, or "Dinny," is eighteen years old and has just been admitted to a university; he has ambitions of studying medicine, as his father had done. "Champ" is Dinny's eleven-year-old brother, who has little memory of his natural parents. The boys live with a kindly white couple, Howard (Arthur Rosenberg) and Barbara Hopkins (Michele Marsh).

After locating the Hopkins family, Jonathan and Mark arrange a meeting with the Truongs. After exchanging pleasantries, the Truongs announce that they will be taking the boys back to Singapore to live. Barbara Hopkins asks them, "What right have you to come here and ask for them back?" "We are their parents," answers Truong Vann Diep. "Not anymore you're not," says Howard Hopkins. The Truongs will have to take the Hopkinses to court if they want to gain custody of the boys, says Howard. The older boy, Dinh, however, explains to his adoptive parents that he made a solemn vow to his father that the two boys would rejoin their Vietnamese family if they somehow happened to reunite.

Dinh visits his Vietnamese parents at their hotel and asks to be released from his vow. He and Champ, Dinh explains, have made a new life in the United States and do not want to leave. "It's a life with a good future," says Dinh. But Truong is very much a traditionalist and wants to reconstitute the family. "You will be with your own family again," says Truong. "You will be Vietnamese and you will be called by your rightful name, Dinh." Dinh will have none of it, however, claiming his "rightful name" to be Hopkins. "I am an American," Dinh says defiantly. When Dinh criticizes his father's traditional patriarchal rigidity, Truong Lan Minh recounts the privations and suffering the couple endured to make the reunion with their children possible. As a dutiful Vietnamese son, Dinh reluctantly informs his American father that he will return to Singapore with the Truongs.

At this point, the divine emissary from heaven Jonathan Smith asks the Truongs to reconsider their position. Jonathan is so disturbed by the turn of events that he refuses to accept payment from Truong for having found the boys. Jonathan will take no reward for his part in having "torn apart" a family. Later, while the Truongs are at the airport awaiting their departure for Singapore, Truong Vann Diep spies a father and son being reunited. He has a sudden change of heart and allows Dinh to stay with the Hopkins family. Once more, Jonathan Smith has accomplished the good works needed to keep him an angel in good standing.

It is curious that Truong Vann Diep is blamed for breaking up a happy household, that it is he who is made to feel guilty for trying to restore his fragmented family. After all, it was a U.S.-sponsored war that caused the massive destruction and dislocation of Vietnamese families such as the Truongs. Dr. Truong and, to a lesser extent, his wife are portrayed as being overbearingly selfish in their single-minded pursuit of the Vietnamese family ideal. However, if there is one aspect of the episode that strikes at the heart of truth, it is that the program raises doubts over the liberal notion of the normative Asian American family. Despite their largely ahistorical and distorted depictions of Asian Pacific American life, television programs must admit a certain minimal quotient of social truths in order to create the necessary conflict and tension that underlie all drama, even drama that hopes to evade historical unpleasantries.

The truth remains that the United States did indeed wage a war in Vietnam that produced legions of refugees who were forced to leave their homeland or face death if they stayed behind. But this truth is supressed in favor of sustaining the larger myth of benevolence personified by Dinny's and Champ's American adoptive parents. Thus moral capital accrues to the Hopkinses and, by extension, to all sympathetic Americans who choose to remain willfully ignorant of the earthly misery the United States has visited upon the Vietnamese people. Accusing Truong Vann Diep of breaking up the Hopkins family is like holding Vietnamese refugees responsible for their statelessness, a classic case of blaming the victim.

Mere Gook Rule

As part of the one-sided memorialization process, the Vietnamese victims of the war are expected to "forget" their traumatic past, whereas Americans are allowed to indulge themselves in all manner of ritualized selective memory. After all, Asian victimage does not exist on the same moral and ethical plane as that of the superior Euro-American race. The Asian enemy does not feel pain, emotional or physical, to the same degree as the invading army of Americans. And most horrific of all, the dehumanized Asians—"dinks," "gooks," and "slopes"—place a low premium on life itself. Life is cheap in Asia, but not so in the West. So commonplace was this assumption in Vietnam that GIs coined a phrase to describe it: the Mere Gook Rule. From minor irritation at their strange eating habits and odd folkways to routine atrocities committed against civilians, the Mere Gook Rule allowed Americans to view Asians as less than human and therefore all the more legitimate as targets to be mocked, exploited, and perhaps murdered.

In the production of foreign enemies, the separate and distinct concepts of race and species become falsely conflated, with the lesser breeds occupying a lower position along the Great Chain of Being, thus making it that much easier to rationalize their mass killing. The Mere Gook Rule was so thoroughly entrenched in the attitudes and behaviors of the American fighting man that Robert Jay Lifton devoted an entire chapter to the phenomenon in *Home from the War: Learning from Vietnam Veterans*.[56] Although his analysis of "victimage" is limited by its strict reliance upon psychoanalytic categories at the expense of social and political critique, Lifton observes that the "Gook syndrome" or systematic dehumanization of Asians paved the way for what he describes as an "atrocity-producing situation" wherein GIs found themselves engaging in unspeakable acts of evil such as the My Lai massacre.

A My Lai-style massacre provides the underlying theme for an installment of the hour-long program *Midnight Caller* (1988–91).

Memory and forgetting, vengeance and justice are the dual polarities that propel the story. A Vietnamese American man whose family had been slaughtered in Vietnam by American soldiers when he was nine years old identifies one of the killers at the San Francisco restaurant where he works. The killer is a recently retired San Francisco cop named Stan Jessick (Robin Thomas). The twenty-nine-year-old man, Le Minh (Yuji Okumoto), confronts Jessick, but the veteran (who spent two tours of duty in Vietnam) denies having killed anyone. Jessick's friend Jack Killian (Gary Cole), a former cop turned late-night radio talk-show host known as "the Nighthawk," warns him of the danger posed by Le Minh.

Minh first attempts to go through formal channels, visiting a government official to report Jessick, but he is brushed off in bureaucratic fashion. The offical rebuff does not deter Minh from seeking justice, however. Rather, it strengthens his resolve. Minh's wife counsels caution, advising him, "You can't live in the past." Minh counters, "If you forget the past, you forget who you are." He further argues that there is no danger in challenging government authorities in the United States. "This isn't Vietnam," Minh says, "this is America." His wife responds by pointing out that "we're not Americans . . . not to them." To this point, Minh remains steadfast in his belief that the abstract principles of procedural justice will protect him as they protect any other American.

Le Minh's accusation against Stan Jessick is made public via an investigative article written by *Dispatch* reporter Deacon Bridges (Mykel T. Williamson). In researching the story, Bridges has confirmed that Sergeant Stan Jessick was at the site of a village that was "torched" while he was in command. Minh's story checks out in every detail, Bridges informs a disbelieving Killian, even though the military never filed a formal report of the atrocity.[57] During his radio program, Killian receives a number of calls concerning the Le Minh story. One such call comes from a ranting racist named Al who says that the "only time he [Le Minh] should be allowed to open his mouth is when he gets down to kiss the ground he walks on." In response to Killian's indignation at this statement, the call-in racist argues that the newcomers are "laughing at us." "One minute we're at war," he says, "the next minute we're giving them small business loans to buy the neighborhood grocery store."

Killian tries unsuccessfully to explain that the Vietnamese now living in the United States "were on *our* side," but the caller counters by arguing, "We couldn't tell then, how can we tell now?" In keeping with the prevalent notion that anti-Asian racism had little or nothing to do with the conduct of the Vietnam War, Killian offers a familiar denial: "The issue is war, not race," he says. "If you get the two confused, you forget what you're fighting for." Killian's attempt to separate analytically U.S. wars in Asia from white racism is a common rhetorical tactic employed by the liberal/conservative media. Unfortunately, the "trail of tears" left by wars waged against nonwhite peoples domestically and abroad empirically invalidates Killian's assertion.

It seems as though the entire city of San Francisco is transfixed by the Nighthawk's coverage of the Le Minh story. Jessick's wife Mary (Ayn Ruymen) even coaxes her husband to call in and set the record straight over the air. Le Minh himself calls to voice his accusation live, before thousands of late-night listeners. By the standards of network television, Minh's speech is filled with extraordinary rage and is exceptionally graphic in its description of his parents' murder by Jessick. "When I was nine years old," says Minh, "I watched an American soldier slit my mother's throat and gut my father like a pig." Minh had tried to avenge the killing of his parents "through the system," but to no avail. He issues a threat that "whatever has to be done . . . I'll do myself."

Minh makes one last appeal before two military men, but gives up all hope of obtaining justice when they claim that nothing can be done now that Jessick is a civilian. One of the high-ranking officers tells Minh not to give up hope. "Well, I never had hope," Minh responds bitterly. He even suggests that there is a racially motivated double standard in force that prevents Jessick's being brought to justice: "I know where I was born. And I can see the color of my skin." Minh's disillusionment is complete by the time he announces, "When you get right down to it, the Great America is no better than my country."

As the controversy threatens to overwhelm the city, Jack Killian has Stan Jessick on his radio program to defend himself. Jessick's denial builds in emotional intensity as flashbacks become interspersed with his account. Jessick claims that the young Le Minh could not have remembered the attack and once more denies the charges of murder lodged against him. As Killian and Jessick leave the radio station, they are accosted by three armed Asian males, including Le Minh himself. Jack is let go, but Jessick is whisked away to an unknown location by the kidnappers.

Minh later calls Killian at the station to announce that he and his coethnics will place Jessick on trial, given that "we can't get justice in your system." Minh then demands that Killian carry the "trial" live on the air. Killian agrees only on the condition that the listening audience serve as the "jury." Minh balks at the idea, believing that the jury will not be impartial because it is made up of "Americans." In response, Killian reminds Minh that "this is a country of minorities, a nation of immigrants." Exasperated, Killian asks his Asian American engineer Billy Po (Dennis Dun) what he thinks of Minh's crusade. Po is sympathetic to Minh, but in no way condones his actions. Says Po: "What do you want me to say? He's a victim of a racist society? I know where he's coming from. But that doesn't mean I agree with what he's doing."

Jack Killian stages a live remote broadcast from the warehouse where Stan Jessick is being held for trial. Minh speaks of his life in Phu Loc as the city of San Francisco listens. He tells of American troops invading his village in pursuit of the elusive Viet Cong. Out of frustration, the GIs killed civilians at random. Minh again accuses Jessick of bayonetting his father and slashing his mother's throat. Jessick defends himself in a fairly convincing manner until callers begin to side with Minh. A Vietnamese American man claims that incidents described by Minh happened all the time, and says that he therefore considers Minh's story to be credible. But when a former member of the platoon in question calls to demand that the "sarge" confess his crime, Jessick snaps. After a complete breakdown, Jessick begins to rant about the "eyes" that had haunted him after he killed Minh's parents.

An Asian American cop who has been disguised as a radio technician jumps out of the remote broadcast van and prevents Minh from shooting Jessick on the spot. The cop and kidnappers are caught in a standoff, but Jack Killian talks Minh out of executing Jessick, arguing that his parents have been avenged now that a confession has been exacted from the killer. "The war's over," says Killian. Minh relents and puts his pistol down on a table. Unfortunately, the weapon is within Jessick's reach and when no one is looking, the retired policeman puts the gun to his head and squeezes the trigger.

Upon Jessick's self-inflicted punishment, order is restored to the hermetic moral universe of television drama. Jack Killian as the reasoned voice of liberal tolerance amidst the chatter of the alienated, confused, and angry masses provides much-needed balance to a social order always threatening to spin out of control when confronted with destabilizing forces such as those set in motion by Le Minh. In his able handling of the Le Minh case, talk-show host Jack Killian fulfills his social role as moderator in the literal sense of the word by having regulated and controlled the meaning and memory of the Vietnam War for both the fictional listeners of the Nighthawk and the actually existing audience for the TV program *Midnight Caller*.

The primary inference that viewers might draw from this episode is that although innocent victims of war such as Le Minh are justified in their anger and thirst for vengeance, any attempt they make to seek justice for past wrongs will come to no good end. "The war's over," Killian informs Minh. More truthfully stated, in the minds of most Americans the Vietnam War is over only for the Asian dead and those who seek to keep their memory alive. For Americans, the revised historical memory of the Vietnam War has already transformed an aggressor nation into one victimized by its own good intentions, which were squandered on a less-than-worthy race of people.

The producers of the program *Midnight Caller* can be applauded for attempting to represent the Vietnam War from the perspective of its Asian victims for a change. The material role that racism plays in American society is also unflinchingly discussed, which is highly unusual for network television fare. But in the final analysis, even *Midnight Caller* must hew to the limits established by the dominant revisionist post-Vietnam War mythology. As perverse as it may seem, that Stan Jessick dies by his own hand after a complete psychotic break moves him into the category of the sick or pathological. This makes his crime seem less like cold-blooded murder and more like an act of temporary insanity. Yet the opposite is true; upstanding, moral, sane, and sober individuals such as Stan Jessick killed Vietnamese civilians on a routine basis. Further, such acts of murder were condoned by the military. A *Frontline* (PBS) broadcast of a British-produced documentary on the My Lai massacre offers honest and probing insights into the routinization of atrocity in Vietnam.

Double Veteran

The Yorkshire Television Ltd. documentary *Remember My Lai* (1989) is a riveting depiction of a particularly horrific example of U.S. atrocities committed against the Vietnamese people.[58] The documentary is composed of interviews with both former GIs attached to Charlie Company and Vietnamese witnesses to the massacre that took place in March 1968. It was the men of Charlie Company who were responsible for the systematic murder of 400 to 500 Vietnamese civilians in My Lai, a hamlet located within the larger village of Song My. A U.S. Army coverup delayed public knowledge of the My Lai massacre by approximately twenty months. Disclosure of the atrocities was greeted with general outrage and only further mobilized public opinion against the war. Two decades after the massacre, *Remember My Lai* serves as a much-needed reminder of the horrors inflicted upon the Vietnamese people by the United States.

Survivor Truong Thi Li is interviewed in front of a simple stone marker that stands as a memorial to the Vietnamese dead. She breaks into tears at the memory of her children and mother, who were killed in the attack. Su Thi Qui describes seeing the body of a woman ("a virgin") who had "her vagina slit open" by members of Charlie Company. A woman identified as Mrs. Thieu tells how her sister was raped as she watched. After the rape, the American soldier put the woman's clothes back on her and then shot her dead. Mrs. Thieu then saw her house burned to the ground by U.S. soldiers, leaving the charred remains of her brothers, sisters, and mother. "My loved ones were burned to death," she says.

Varnado Simpson, Jr., sits on a couch in a modestly furnished living room surrounded by the several bottles of assorted prescription drugs he requires to numb his guilt-induced pain. Simpson claims that he killed between twenty and twenty-five Vietnamese villagers. He slit throats, scalped heads, severed hands, and cut out the tongues of the people he personally slayed. Others in his unit committed such acts as well, according to Simpson. "My whole mind just went," explains the veteran. "Just put the M-16 on automatic."

The Vietnamese dead have been memorialized in photographs and newspaper clippings that Simpson has kept in a scrapbook. When Simpson's own young son was shot in the head and fell dead outside their home, he interpreted the boy's passing as divine "punishment" for his murder of Vietnamese children. As Simpson looked upon his dying son, the faces of the Vietnamese children he had murdered came back to him. A framed photographic portrait of Simpson's deceased son sits nearby. There is a crack in the glass running diagonally across his smiling face. Simpson explains that the crack appeared one day, but he never bothered to replace the frame. Apart from remaining heavily medicated and utterly incapacitated, Simpson has attempted suicide on three occasions. He says there is no guarantee that there will not be a fourth attempt.

Not all the GIs at the scene participated in the carnage at My Lai. U.S. Army photographer Roit Haeberle captured the expressions of sheer terror on the faces of the villagers on film just moments before they were gunned down. A helicopter crew chief named Hugh Thompson was so revolted by the indiscriminate killing that he evacuated villagers at great personal risk. He ordered his door gunner, Lawrence Colburn, to fire upon any Americans who shot at the Vietnamese they were trying to evacuate. Other GIs, such as Harry Stanley, refused to shoot civilians in defiance of the orders given by Lieutenant William Calley. Even so, by lunchtime the men of

Charlie Company had killed close to 500 women, children, and elderly male residents of the village GIs referred to as "Pinkville."

Although a member of Charlie Company named Ron Ridenour, now a journalist, wrote a letter to military authorities that described the genocidal acts committed at My Lai, it was not until November of 1969 that the news finally broke in the United States. Out of the forty-six soldiers investigated, it was Lieutenant William Calley the army decided to hold principally responsible for the massacre. The testimony offered by Calley at his trial was reminiscent of the Nuremberg defense invoked by Nazi war criminals who claimed that they were just following orders in commiting atrocities. After his trial, Calley was sentenced to life in prison, but he spent only three days in the stockade before being released by order of President Richard Nixon. Three years later, William Calley was paroled. Today Calley lives in Columbus, Georgia, where he operates a jewelry store.

That the heinous crimes committed by William Calley and the men under his command were a matter of routine was publicly revealed during the 1971 "Winter Soldier Investigation" organized by the Vietnam Veterans Against the War (VVAW). More than a hundred veterans gathered to describe their wartime experiences from January 31 to February 2 in Detroit, Michigan. Al Hubbard, executive secretary of the VVAW, wrote that the hearings were intended to demonstrate that the My Lai massacre was not an uncommon occurrence in Vietnam, but rather "only a minor step beyond the standard official policy in Indochina."[59] Participants in the investigation told of witnessing countless incidents of rape, torture, and murder of civilian noncombatants. They cited the pervasive anti-Asian racism among military personnel and the dehumanization of the Vietnamese as preconditions for the routine commission of atrocities.

Vietnamese women in particular were targeted for special abuse, with rape-murder being common enough to merit a perverse appelation for perpetrators: double veteran. For not a few GIs, the rape-murder of Asian women had a chillingly racial and psychosexual allure. In *Nam: The Vietnam War in the Words of the Soldiers Who Fought There*, journalist Mark Baker records the musings of one such unidentified American soldier:

> You take a group of men and put them in a place where there are no round-eyed women. They are in an all-male environment. Let's face it. Nature is nature. There are women available. Those women are of another culture, another color, another society. You don't want a prostitute. You've got an M-16. What do you need to pay a

lady for? You go down to the village and take what you want. I saw guys who I believe had never had any kind of sex with a woman before in that kind of scene. They'd come back a double veteran.

These were not men who would normally commit rape. They had not had psychological problems. Being in that kind of environment, you give a guy a gun and strange things happen.[60]

According to this informant, the very act of wielding a weapon is the ultimate expression of male power and sexuality, an experience he likens to maintaining a permanent erection. "It was a pure sexual trip every time you got to pull the trigger," says the GI.[61]

Nor were atrocities the sole prerogative of white invaders. Under battlefield conditions, the interracial tensions back home were temporarily put aside as Blacks and whites alike worked in concert for the sake of sheer survival. In *Bloods: An Oral History of the Vietnam War by Black Veterans*, a former member of a long-range reconnaissance patrol (LRRP) recounts situations where his fellow soldiers shared in the spoils of war through the rape and murder of Vietnamese women. In one incident, after his squad kidnapped a pregnant woman and raped her, she was murdered for fear of giving away their position to the enemy. "But I don't think we murdered her out of malice," recalls the soldier. "I think we murdered her because we didn't want to be captured."[62] But in America's first racially integrated war, Asian American soldiers also found themselves engaging the Vietnamese enemy in the field. Asian American LRRPs (pronounced "lurps") "were highly sought after because of their oriental appearance." Their physical resemblance to the enemy gave them precious seconds of battlefield advantage. "Some LRRP teams even dressed Asian-Americans in captured enemy uniforms and even had them carry AK-47s to provide an added edge," writes a Vietnam combat veteran who has chronicled their exploits.[63]

For the GI combatants, the violence, aggression, racism, and sexism that were part of almost every aspect of the Vietnam War were accepted facts of military life. It was as if the worst features of U.S. culture and society had been transplanted to Asia, magnified many times over, and given free rein. The shock and horror induced by *Remember My Lai* stand in stark contrast to pop culture appropriations of the Vietnam War as seen on network television, which have been masterfully effective in naturalizing the evil that has sustained U.S. global hegemony in the postwar era. A television documentary such as *Remember My Lai* serves as a vivid reminder that the military involvement of the United States in Southeast Asia was not merely a "tragic mistake." Rather, the wars in Southeast Asia were very much in the American grain, consistent with an ignoble national history characterized by military invasion and conquest, imperial annexation, and political-economic exploitation. The controlling images of Asians and Asian Americans to be found on much of contemporary network television are rooted in this same historical legacy.

Chapter 6

Contemporary Asian America

Reinvented Asian Americans

On January 17, 1989, a Vietnam veteran named Patrick Purdy toted his Chinese-made AK-47 to Cleveland Elementary School in Stockton, California, and proceeded to shoot and kill five Asian American children. Four of the dead children were refugees from Cambodia: Ram Chun, Sokhim An, Rathanar Or, and Oeun Lim. The fifth child, Tran Thanh Thuy, was Vietnamese. Of the twenty-nine other children wounded in the attack, most were refugees from Vietnam, Cambodia, and Laos. Although not officially listed as a hate crime, telltale scrawlings found on the rifle and Purdy's known white supremacist beliefs strongly suggest a racial motivation in the mass killing. Consider the pain inflicted upon the families of the dead children: after having survived the horrors of American technowar, they were then uprooted from their homes and evacuated to an indifferent society eager to bury the memory of the war. Now living as Americans, their children were murdered by a white man made mad by the mere presence of yellow faces in his town. Characteristically, TV news reports blamed the mass murder on the workings of an irrational mind and discounted the racist dimension of Purdy's crime.

In June 1982, two Detroit autoworkers attacked a Chinese American man named Vincent Chin and killed him by smashing his skull with a baseball bat. The perpetrators of the crime—Ronald Ebens and Richard Nitz—were fined $3,780 each and granted probation. Lily Chin, a widowed immigrant who married a Chinese American GI who had served in the U.S. military during World War II, embarked upon a personal campaign to win justice for her dead son. The documentary *Who Killed Vincent Chin?* (1988), broadcast by PBS affiliates, captures the outrage experienced by Asian Americans who organized themselves to protest the light sentences meted out to the cold-blooded killers by the justice system.[1] The structure of the documentary itself, however, is consciously restrained and free of direct editorial intrusion by filmmakers Christine Choy and Renee Tajima. Such restraint "does not function as an obedient bow to the canons of good journalism but as a powerful rhetorical strategy."[2] By employing the synoptic epistemological strategy of Kurosawa's *Rashomon* (1951), the filmmakers force the viewer to grapple with highly nuanced questions that reach far beyond the simple determination of the guilt or innocence of the accused.

In July 1991, a group of fifteen to twenty white supremacist skinheads jumped a Chinese American high school student and beat him with merciless fury because of his race. This was but one of dozens of hate crimes that have been committed with increasing frequency in Orange County, California. City of Fullerton mayor Chris Norby registered the surprise typical of government leaders who for public relations purposes prefer to play down the existence of racial hate crimes: "I know they're out there, I know they're punks," said Norby, "but I'm surprised they're operating in these great numbers."[3]

By all appearances, a twenty-five-year-old ethnic Chinese born in Vietnam named Thanh Lam was on the path to success American-style. Along with his family, in 1979 Lam fled Vietnam and arrived in the United States after spending a year in a Malaysian refugee camp. The family of twelve surmounted many obstacles and eventually opened a small market in Compton, California, which was looted and torched shortly after the "not guilty" verdicts were announced in the Rodney G. King beating case. The following day, while on his way to clean up the wreckage, Thanh Lam was shot to death by at least two gunmen while stopped at an intersection in his truck. Both the Compton Police Department and the FBI approached the killing as a "hate crime." Witnesses stated that they heard one of the gunmen shouting a racial epithet before the attack. At the funeral of the slain young man, his father, Ha Lam, was told that Thanh's death on April 30 coincided with the fall of Saigon seventeen years before. "The first time, I lost my home," said Ha Lam. "And now I lost my son."[4]

In Fort Lauderdale, Florida, eighteen-year-old Bradley Mills was convicted of second-degree murder for participating in the beating death of Luyen Phan Nguyen. When nineteen-year-old Nguyen objected to racial slurs being hurled at him at a party in nearby Coral Springs, Mills and at least six others fell upon the Vietnamese American student and beat him to death. Witnesses say that a frenzied mob chased down Nguyen like "a wounded deer," shouting "Viet Cong" at him as onlookers refused to intervene.[5] Circuit Judge Richard D. Eade sentenced Mills to fifty years in prison because of the "savagery" of the crime.[6] But if the gross miscarriage of justice in the Vincent Chin case is any indication, it remains to be seen whether Mills and the others will actually serve prison time appropriate to the severity of their crime.

In January 1993, an eighteen-year-old football player for San Clemente High School in south Orange County, California, led an attack on an Asian man who was beaten so severely that investigators initially had difficulty in establishing his race.[7] Because the incident took place near a bar frequented by homosexuals in Laguna Beach, the attack was viewed as a "gay bashing" by community members and law enforcement officials. Jeff Michael Raines—6-foot-1 and 200 pounds—was arrested on suspicion of attempted murder, and police have asked that he be charged with having committed a hate crime against Loc Minh Truong, 5-foot-6, 125 pounds, and 55 years of age. Absent from news accounts, however, was the important dimension of the victim's Asian ethnicity, owing in part to the social myopia of the largely white Laguna Beach gay community.

Hate crimes are usually explained away by government officials as acts committed by misguided individuals rather than as being symptomatic of deep racial divisions that have been exacerbated over the past decade by the undeclared war against the ethnic underclass, the phony battle against Black and Hispanic "drug lords," Japan bashing by certain politicians and high-profile corporate executives such as Chrysler CEO Lino "Lee" Iacocca, and the manifest anti-Arab racism of the Persian Gulf War. These are all signals to a dispossessed, alienated white working class and a large segment of the financially faltering middle class that it is open season on people of color.

The incidents cited above are reminders of the simmering hostility and frequent violence against Asian Americans even after a 150-year perilous presence in the United States. These incidents, though dramatic, do not represent aberrations from the larger system of racial oppression. Rather, they are simply glaring examples of the daily terror to which many Asian Americans are subjected. In an article pertaining to the Vincent Chin case, Michael Moore states that the U.S. Justice Department reported a 62 percent rise in hate crimes directed against Asian Americans during 1986.[8] There are indications that the problem will only worsen in the coming years.

Short of overt violence, Asian Americans continue to suffer the effects of racism in subtler ways: educational opportunities blocked by discriminatory admissions policies maintained by certain elite universities, restriction to secondary labor market participation within the economic system, and lack of occupational mobility for those holding professional positions.[9] Regarding restricted occupational mobility, a report issued by the U.S. Commission on Civil Rights states that although Asian American males on average enjoy high occupational status, they "may be denied access to high rungs of the corporate ladder," which might result in their exclusion from "spheres of power and influence."[10] Despite their high qualifications, educational credentials, and demonstrated merit, Asian Americans often find their professional rise halted by the "glass ceiling" of institutional racism.

The problem of traditional anti-Asian racism has been aggravated by the increased flow of immigrants to the United States since 1965. The passage of the 1965 Immigration Act removed discriminatory racial barriers that had restricted the entry of immigrants from Asia in favor of those from Europe. As a result, Asian Americans have become the fastest-growing ethnic group in recent history. It is projected that their numbers will continue to increase and that by the year 2000, Asian Americans will constitute 4 percent of the total U.S. population.

More recent Asian immigrants such as Vietnamese, Laotians, and Cambodians differ from earlier groups in that they are refugees from Southeast Asian wars conducted by the United States. They are not so neatly cast from the "model minority" mold favored by many liberal social scientists and journalists. Rather, newly arrived Southeast Asian refugees resemble other groups composing the ethnic underclass in that they are young, noneducated, and poor. "More than a third of all Vietnamese families were below the poverty line," writes Roger Daniels, "and more than a quarter of all Vietnamese families received some form of public assistance."[11] In short, Southeast Asian refugees do not conform strictly to the idealized portrayals of America's latest immigrant success story such as found in James Fallows's exercise in wishful thinking, *More Like Us: Making America Great Again.*[12]

The "reinvented" life of Nguyen Dong's extended family in the United States as described in *More Like Us* must be understood in the context of a larger social agenda that Fallows hopes will attract the attention of Washington policy makers. Fallows seeks to exploit the desperation of Asian immigrant families whose lives have been disrupted by the effects of U.S. technowar waged against their home countries. Without apology, Fallows frames his argument for increased immigration in the dispassionate rhetoric of pragmatic cost-benefit analysis: "Immigrants are disproportionately entrepreneurial, determined, and adaptable, and through history they have strengthened the economy of whatever society they join."[13] Along with Fallows, American Enterprise Institute pundit Ben Wattenberg has weighed in with his celebration of the "first universal nation" by extolling the virtues of a multiethnic society in a PBS program, *Trends in the Nineties*.[14] In addition to roundtable discussions with ethnic spokespersons such as Linda Chavez (identified as "Scholar, Manhattan Institute") and author Bette Bao Lord, Wattenberg speaks to a number of nonexperts representing a variety of white and nonwhite minorities. He even visits the home of a seemingly well assimilated middle-class Vietnamese American family to illustrate the beauty of liberal democracy.

Other commentators within conservative and liberal political circles are not so ready to embrace the notion that increased immigration will help restore the United States to economic health. In a review of Fallows's book, Peter Skerry, a scholar affiliated with the UCLA Center for American Politics and Public Policy, resists the tendency for both conservatives and liberals alike to "focus on Asian successes, while ignoring problems evident not only among Hispanics, but also among Asians—such as gang activity and welfare dependency among Vietnamese in California."[15] Skerry's purpose is not necessarily to correct certain misconceptions regarding Asian immigrants. Rather, he is more intent on issuing a mainline conservative caveat that would force the question of whether American society can adequately absorb the influx of new immigrants without bringing about undesirable changes in both the dominant Euro-American culture and political institutions under white control. Cutting through Skerry's thinly veiled reactionary rhetoric, one can see that a twofold fear is being expressed: fear of concerted challenges to WASP cultural hegemony and fear of potential demands made upon the capitalist welfare state by politically mobilized claimant groups such as Asian Americans.

Neoassimilationist Fables

The theme of "reinvented lives" for newly arrived immigrants to the United States did not originate with James Fallows. The theme dates back to assimilationist theories of immigration such as that advanced by Robert E. Park in the 1920s. The assimilation model is not without its flaws, however. For one, it is assumed that assimilation will take place only along the lines established by the dominant Euro-American society. That is, "acceptable" nonwhite minority groups are those that conform to the dominant, primarily English, American culture and institutions. Further, contemporary proponents of the neoassimilationist argument disregard the fact that currently "acceptable" Asian American groups were once targets of intense white hostility during the same historical period when theories of assimilation were being formulated by establishment social scientists.

Because of its inherent order-based conservatism, neoassimilationist representations of Asian American groups can be found in a wide range of recent television programs. In a special report by KNBC-TV News (Los Angeles), reporter Jack Perkins tells the story of several Vietnamese refugees whom the NBC network helped resettle after the fall of Saigon in 1975.[16] All of the refugees, whose lives presumably would have been in danger had they remained in Vietnam, were employed by NBC. As the strains of the "Star Spangled Banner" are conjoined by an image of the American flag, Perkins speaks of the special friendship between the refugees and the network. "Twenty years ago they had welcomed us to their country," says Perkins, "ten years ago it was our turn to reciprocate."

The program features interviews with Vietnamese refugees resettled in the United States interspersed with film footage of the American evacuation of Saigon. Koi Ding Nguyen, now living in Burbank (also the home of KNBC-TV), had been an NBC driver in Saigon, and Dong Buh Fong worked as a cameraman. NBC executive Sid Grau helped orchestrate the evacuation of his Vietnamese employees. Grau also authorized the disbursement of three months' salary to the faithful NBC employees who had helped bring the "television war" to the American public each evening.

All told, about 300 Vietnamese were resettled by NBC, aided also by a local church. The productivity of the new Americans and their adjustment to their adopted homeland is praised by Perkins. "Today, virtually all are American citizens, are working, in school, or both," Perkins says admiringly. "We know of not one on welfare or needing it." The reported ease with which the NBC-assisted refugees adapted to life in the United States probably can be attributed to their better-than-average English-speaking ability, preexisting employment contacts, and job skills that could be transferred readily to a new setting. Unlike the select group assisted by NBC, subsequent Southeast Asian refugees have not necessarily arrived with the same set of advantages, and as a consequence have not weathered the transition with similar ease.

Along with its network parent NBC, Los Angeles affiliate KNBC-TV coproduced a short-lived series titled *The American Promise* (1987) that examined topical issues of general interest. One edition, "Wanting It All," takes as its subject the current Asian immigration and discusses its implications for the future of American society.[17] As the program opens, none other than the venerable NBC network anchor John Chancellor is seen sitting before a huge backdrop of Old

Glory as he raises the conflicting issues concerning contemporary immigration:

> Today in America, things are changing so quickly the ideas we had as children about our country are being challenged every day. And those changes are most apparent in the makeup of the American population. The immigrants flowing into the United States are shaping a new country, full of promise for some and peril for others. It's a situation which is not totally in our control. Troubles in other parts of the world produce new Americans, legal or illegal.

KNBC reporter David Garcia narrates a series of vignettes once Chancellor has set the tone for the program. First comes the story of a marriage between an Anglo-American man, Tim Morris, and his Japanese American bride, Dianne Kawashima. Garcia alludes to the antimiscegenation laws of thirty years ago that would have precluded such a union.

In a separate interview, Professor Harry Kitano of UCLA offers an analysis of intermarriage patterns for Japanese Americans such as Dianne Kawashima. It is an argument that, if true, portends the dissolution of Japanese Americans as a distinctively Asian ethnic group. Professor Kitano strongly suggests that the last stage of assimilation – amalgamation – might well be in the offing for Japanese Americans, who with each succeeding generation are "becoming more Americanized." Kitano places the contemporary incidence of outmarriage for Japanese Americans at 60 percent, although parents state a strong preference (90 percent) for their children to marry within the group. "I think one can almost predict that by the year 2000," says Kitano, "there might not really be a significant *visible* Japanese American community."

Professor Kitano places great store in the notion that romantic "love" plays a preponderant role in interracial marriages. Contrary to this dubious explanation, it is conceivable that the high rate of outmarriage (particularly for females) is indicative of the favorable opportunity cost it represents for the Japanese American spouse who is marrying "up" (and therefore "out of") the racial/gender hierarchy, where white males occupy a superordinate position. Dianne Kawashima might indeed be marrying Tim Morris out of "love," but that very concept is historically constructed. What three decades ago was considered to be "forbidden love" is now viewed as acceptable because Asian women, with their favorable exposure in the media, have become more "in vogue" as partners for white males.[18] In addition, the persistent desexualization of the Asian male might also help contribute to the flight of Asian females, who do not perceive their ethnic counterparts as desirable partners in romance or marriage. Viewed in this light, the high rate of outmarriage for Japanese Americans might well be interpreted as the material outcome of an interlocking system of sexism and racism rather than a matter of interracial couples "voting with their hearts," as Kitano argues.

In keeping with its neoassimilationist drift, "Wanting It All" concludes with a fable of mixed success. A photographic portrait of a Vietnamese American family is seen as Garcia sermonizes, "What immigrant parents pass on to their children can sometimes be measured in spirit and determination." This next vignette centers on the great expectations of a young man named Linh Dan Nguyen, a straight-A student and valedictorian of his graduating high school class. He and his family were evacuated from Vietnam in 1975, after the fall of Saigon. Linh Dan Nguyen's father had been a government official in Vietnam, but now works as an electrician. By all appearances, Linh Dan Nguyen might be simply one of the many Asian American overachievers who have "inexorably surpassed" their less ambitious, "softening" white suburban counterparts.[19] But Nguyen's mother is quick to remind him of his subordinate status within the racial hierarchy: "I always tell them, your own way is the Vietnamese. You are a U.S. citizen, but you cannot change your blood. . . . You cannot change your skin. You cannot change your nose. You cannot change your eyes."

This simple but profound statement, uttered in the broken English of the refugee, conveys precisely the dilemma faced by Asian American "success stories" such as that of the Nguyen family. Uprooted by an inhuman war of attrition, they must still grapple with the basic problem of racial difference in a society that waged a race war against the Vietnamese people. No matter how Linh Dan Nguyen manages to distinguish himself academically or otherwise, the socially constructed stigmata of his race—his "yellow" skin, "flat" nose, and "slanted" eyes—will stand as a barrier against his full assimilation into the dominant Euro-American society.

Multiculturalist Impasse

Also produced by KNBC was a documentary written and narrated by journalist Tritia Toyota, *Asian America* (1989).[20] Unlike the program featuring Jack Perkins, this documentary is quick to address the substantial problems that historically have confronted the Asian American community. In introducing *Asian America*, Toyota does not skirt the issue of racism. She begins by directly acknowledging the "severe racism" encountered by early Asian immigrants to the United States and even asserts that neither racism nor discrimination has disappeared in contemporary American society. Toyota recounts recent acts of violence against Asian Americans: the murder of Vincent Chin, attacks on Vietnamese American fishermen on the Gulf Coast of Texas, and an incident in which a woman was pushed in front of a train in a New York subway by a person who claimed Asians frightened him. Appearing on camera, California State Assembly Speaker Willie Brown offers his fatalistic assessment of the current climate of anti-Asian hostility: "As the Asian community is symbolically viewed as economic competitors, or economic peers, and sometimes superiors, that kind of negative reaction will be forthcoming."

Underlying the fear of Asian American economic competition is the demographic reality that as early as 1980 approximately 500,000 Asian Pacifics lived in Los Angeles County alone, a figure that represented 6 percent of the total population.[21] According to Toyota, foreign-born Asian Pacifics outnumber those born in the United States by two to one in the state of California. These demographic pressures have led to racial tensions and overt conflict even in affluent communities such as the suburb of San Marino. Interethnic strife, for example, has arisen at San Marino High School as Asian students become an ever-increasing segment of the general population.

In a matter of only a few years the city of Monterey Park has become the first U.S. city with a majority Asian population, many of them immigrants from Taiwan or Hong Kong. Once an all-white suburb of Los Angeles, Monterey Park is experiencing simmering tensions between Anglo and Chinese residents that have boiled over on occasion. In one instance, Lily Chen, the city's Chinese American mayor, raised the ire of some residents by daring to publish a bilingual city newsletter. In a social climate where state and national "English-only" campaigns have been mounted in response to growing populations of non-English-speaking immigrants from Asian and Latin American countries, Mayor Chen's attempt to communicate with her constituency in their principal language was a decidedly risky political move. Historically in the United States, attempts to impose English-language competence and usage upon non-Anglophone speakers have been used as a means of social, political, and cultural control.[22]

Asian America also discusses the proliferation in recent years of small-scale Asian-owned businesses in Los Angeles's Koreatown. Beneath the apparent industry and dynamism of this new ethnic entrepreneurial community there exists a certain resentment among its denizens over the marginalization and disparagement they suffer at the hands of the larger dominant society. Community activist Dr. Matthew Ahn, for example, voices his frustration over the cavalier treatment of Koreans in the media. In particular, Ahn criticizes 20th Century Fox for employing non-Korean Asian actors who mangle the Korean language on the long-running TV program *M*A*S*H*. Ahn complains that he has even seen episodes of the program in which the South Korean flag was shown hanging upside down.

Tritia Toyota gains a fairly broad perspective by interviewing a cross section of prominent Asian Americans in her report, including Yori Wada, a member of the University of California Board of Regents; Harry Kitano, professor at the UCLA School of Social Welfare; John Tateishi, with the National Committee on Redress and Reparations; and Dan Kuramoto, the leader of the Asian American jazz fusion group Hiroshima. She concludes her survey by issuing a plea for a "multicultural" society as a means of ameliorating the persistent problems faced by the Asian American community.

Toyota's closing plea, however, raises the question of whether genuine multiculturalism or cultural pluralism can exist within a society whose very foundations rest upon a tacit acceptance of racial difference and white supremacy. Although the notion of multiculturalism represents the rejection of dubious assimilationist models of intergroup relations, it nonetheless helps to reproduce structured social inequality along ethnic and racial lines. By assuming that all ethnic and racial groups stand on equal footing, multicultural or cultural pluralist theories overlook the history of past discrimination and its crippling effects on people of color in the present. As a means of ensuring that a plural society remains unequally plural, the notion of "multiculturalism" is prescribed too freely as a painless panacea that both liberals and conservatives can enjoy without guilt and at little expense to themselves.

Black versus Yellow

On June 17, 1991, President George H. Bush addressed a crowd of an estimated 40,000 Asian Americans at Mile Square Park in Fountain Valley, California. The event was billed by the White House as the first presidential speech ever delivered specifically to an Asian American audience. Over the past several years, the GOP has sought to strengthen its ideological ties to the growing Asian American community, which now constitutes 10 percent of the total population in politically conservative Orange County, California. The Southeast Asian community in particular embraces such Republican verities as "free enterprise," entrepreneurialism, self-help, and a minimalist definition of government. In addition, many if not most Southeast

Asian immigrants are attracted to the "anti-communist rhetoric of some Republican leaders" in combination with the "pro-business attitude of the party."[23]

As part of the concerted attack on the welfare state, the forces of conservative reaction point to recent Asian immigrant families as exemplars of the new entrepreneurial ideal that eschews federal support in favor of a self-sufficient "localism." It is not uncommon for newspaper accounts to mention "Asian newcomers" who have "provided a fresh injection of economic investment and ingenuity for their new communities."[24] Vietnamese and Korean merchants are effusively praised for their "revitalization" of areas in Orange County that were formerly in economic decline.

There is, however, a downside to the modest success enjoyed by select Asian American immigrant families. Setting up shop in urban core areas written off by large corporate supermarket chains, Asian American merchants operating family-run stores sometimes have been met with hostility by residents of the surrounding communities. There have been numerous reported instances of Korean American merchants coming into conflict with African Americans. In Brooklyn, New York, the "Family Red Apple" grocery store operated by Bong Jae Jang was boycotted for sixteen months by protesters after it was claimed that store employees beat a customer they had accused of stealing.[25]

For a medium often derided for its lack of social realism, contemporary network television drama has provided more than a few stories that explore the hidden costs of the much-ballyhooed Asian American entrepreneurial success story. Some programs at times have handled complex social issues with a laudable degree of sensitivity and insight. As an example, an episode of the ABC legal drama *Equal Justice* (1990–91) was inspired by the March 16, 1991, shooting death in Los Angeles of fifteen-year-old Latasha Harlins by Korean American store owner Soon Ja Du.[26]

The story opens with a scene of demonstrators picketing a Korean-owned store and calling for the arrest of one Don Min Sung (Chi-Muoi Lo), who is accused of shooting to death an African American customer in the store owned by his father Young Ti Sung (Bill Cho Lee). In a scene made familiar by countless television news reports, a demonstrator carries a sign that reads "Koreans must go." Jameel Kimble (John Cothram, Jr.), a self-styled community activist leading the protest, collars a representative of the district attorney's office, Mike James (Joe Morton), as he is about the enter the store. Kimble in no uncertain terms tells James—who is chief prosecutor for the Pittsburgh district attorney's office and also an African

American – that the victim, William Devereaux, was shot "because he was Black."

Once in the store, Mike James meets Una Yung (Kim Miyori), the attorney representing the Sungs. Yung's cool reaction to the African American James conveys skepticism that her Asian American client will be treated fairly by the office of the district attorney. Yung expresses her anger at the demonstrators for trying to close the store and, like her counterpart Jameel Kimble, claims that the incident is about "racial hatred." "That's for the grand jury to determine," replies James. Over Yung's objections, Don Min Sung is placed under arrest and taken to jail. A forensic report, however, later confirms Sung's claim that the killing was in self-defense. Despite the new findings, Sung is kept in jail because James's superior Arnold Bach (George DiCenzo) does not want to alienate his African American constituency.

As an African American who has worked his way into a position of high importance in the district attorney's office, Mike James finds himself trying to resolve a personal and professional dilemma. Jameel Kimble plays on James's sense of guilt by taking him to task for forsaking the interests of the African American community. He implies that James is an "Uncle Tom." "Any white boy from Princeton could be doing what you're doing here," says Kimble.

James lays bare his mixed feelings during a dinner conversation with his friend Maggie. He tells Maggie how "Koreans won't even take welfare"; that they "work a sixteen-hour day, sacrificing an entire generation to make it better for the next one." At one point, James goes so far as to imply that African Americans might be responsible for their own plight. "I feel guilty for thinking it and I feel even more guilty for saying it," says James, "but I just don't think that we're trying hard enough, Maggie." African Americans might be "angry because the Koreans have moved in and made something of themselves," but why, asks James, does this preclude Blacks from doing the same?

Maggie bristles at James's assessment of the African American inability to engage in entrepreneurial activity like the Koreans. She counters that African Americans are discriminated against by lending institutions. "The Koreans can't get a loan either," James argues, "they band together." This is enough to set Maggie off on a tirade. "Yes, they have twenty people in a room," says Maggie. "You cannot ask African American people to live like immigrants who just got off the boat." For 400 years, "we've sacrificed, we've paid our dues, and still, still, we're not members of the club."

Maggie's protestations notwithstanding, James makes a final argument for African American economic self-sufficiency. "In the final analysis," says James, "no one is going to change anything for us, but us. And until African Americans in that neighborhood understand that, they're not going to own their own stores." This final statement by James places him firmly within the school of liberal thought that assumes the commensurability of all ethnic and racial minorities without regard to past discrimination. As the activist Kimble had implied earlier, James's primary loyalty is to the class of petit bourgeois professionals who represent transcendental state power. His existential identity as an African American is subordinated to his overriding sense of legal-juridical professionalism.

The heated discussion between James and Maggie shifts the focus of the story ever so slightly. What originally began as a question of establishing the guilt or innocence of a Korean American storekeeper is transposed into the theme of African American economic self-sufficiency. James's observations can be interpreted to mean that African Americans have themselves to blame for their plight. If only they were hardworking and resourceful, like Korean families, then African Americans would be patronizing Black-owned stores. It is almost anticlimactic when Don Min Sung's innocence in the shooting of William Devereaux is confirmed by an eyewitness who had been lying all along.

If the "message" of this program was to lay the problem of interethnic strife at the feet of the African American community, this certainly was not the intention of *Equal Justice* executive producer Thomas Carter. In an article that appeared shortly before the airing of the episode, Carter (himself an African American) said that he was disturbed by "minority groups fighting among themselves when neither of these groups have any real economic or political power."[27] He interpreted the current conflict between Asian Americans and African Americans as the outcome of economic inequality.

Unfortunately, Carter's unusually incisive critique of late capitalism never quite finds its way into the actual program. This is hardly surprising; television drama never fails to reduce the contradictions of capitalism to the level of personal problems that have no definitive political or economic solution. Instead, the viewer is left with the idea that the beliefs, values, and behavior of individuals and groups in society are utterly disconnected from larger historical and political economic forces. If Korean merchants enjoy a modicum of success, then it must be simply because they are hardworking and thrifty and have solid families. If African Americans have not been able to lift themselves up by their own bootstraps by now, then it must be because they are welfare dependent, profligate, and burdened by broken families. In both cases, purely culturist pseudoexplanations are offered for what is at bottom a matter of the structured social inequality that forms the very basis of capitalism. As Earl Ofari Hutchinson has noted, "African-Americans and Koreans both carry the twin burdens of economic and racial oppression."[28]

Immigrant Hustlers

Within a week of the *Equal Justice* broadcast, an NBC program took up the theme of Korean American family entrepreneurialism. In an episode of *Shannon's Deal* (1990–91), the Korean proprietor of Courteous Jewelry and Loan is shot by two undercover policemen while trying to stop a robbery in progress.[29] The episode is not concerned with the slain pawnshop owner so much as with a fast-talking, ambitious young immigrant who wants attorney Jack Shannon (Jamey Sheridan) to file a wrongful death suit against the police department on behalf of the shopkeeper's widow, Mrs. Oh (June Kyoko Lu). Shannon, an attorney who had left a lucrative corporate practice to work solo on the behalf of everyday people, is irritated by the (literal) ambulance chasing of the self-described "legal facilitator" Kee Sung, played by Tony Award winner B. D. Wong.

Kee Sung explains to Shannon that although he has failed the bar examination twice in the United States, he was once a "fast-track" attorney in Seoul, rather like Jack Shannon himself. Since he cannot legally practice law in the United States, Sung has been "forced to do what other immigrants do; I create my own profession." Sung wants Shannon to file the lawsuit and then Sung will collect a finder's fee for himself as "legal facilitator." Sung cynically tells Shannon that were he to claim police "overreaction" and "race prejudice" this might prove effective in persuading a jury that the police acted improperly in the killing.

Shannon rejects Sung's opportunistic blandishments until a series of incidents partially convinces him that police wrongdoing might indeed have been responsible for the pawnbroker's death. It turns out that the pawnbroker, Mr. Oh (Ralph Ahn), was killed by three crooked policemen who belonged to a secret crime suppression unit whose purpose was to assassinate criminals who police authorities felt were let off too easily by the court system. The undercover cops had staked out the pawn shop with the intention of first killing a known holdup artist named George Kim (Chi-Muoi Lo) and then taking the stolen goods and money for themselves. Unfortunately for the renegade cops, they were later identified by Shannon's assistant Lucy (Elizabeth Peña), who happened to witness the robbery as a customer.

Created by writer and independent film director John Sayles, *Shannon's Deal* also boasts music written by the outspoken guardian of the African American jazz tradition, Wynton Marsalis. Listed as legal consultant is Harvard law professor Alan Dershowitz, noted gadfly, defender of the wealthy (Claus von Bulow, Leona Helmsley, Michael Milken, Mike Tyson), and relentless self-promoter. With such a pool of superior talent involved in various aspects of production, a liberal-progressive sensibility might be expected to inform the program. But this episode does little to advance an understanding of Asian American immigrants other than to portray them as passive victims (Mr. and Mrs. Oh), criminal "germs" (George Kim), or hustling opportunists (Kee Sung). Perhaps the only redeeming feature of this episode is that it partially debunks the myth of the successful entrepreneurial Asian immigrant family. In contrast to frequent journalistic accounts and media portrayals of self-starting, profitable, independent businesses, it is more the case that long hours, financial insecurity, and dangerous working conditions characterize the lot of the Asian immigrant family. Incidents such as the May 1991 murder of two Korean immigrants employed at a liquor store have become all too frequent. Shortly before robbing K&W Liquor in South-Central Los Angeles, the convicted killer, Victor Beltran, had stated that he intended to "smoke the Buddaheads."[30]

An *In Living Color* (1990–present) skit spoofs the controlling image of the single-minded Korean American economic hustler portrayed in many television programs and films.[31] Two Black students are making a purchase at a Korean-owned store when regular cast member Steve Park recognizes them as classmates who copy from his schoolwork. The two refer to Park as "Fresh Fish" (as in Fresh Prince) and "L. L. Cool Sushi" (as in L. L. Cool J) in an attempt to humiliate him. In response, Park doffs his apron, dons a pair of locs, and becomes transformed into rap artist "Rice Cube" (as in Ice Cube). He rhymes to the Naughty by Nature track "O.P.P.," but instead calls it "Down Wit' MSG" (monosodium glutamate, a seasoning often used in Asian cooking and believed to cause headaches). Rice Cube speaks to a number of commonly held perceptions of Asian Americans, such as that they cannot drive well, have no rhythm and cannot dance, are computer nerds, are asexual, and are interchangeable with other Asian groups, and that Asian men are "built like a grain of rice." Rice Cube ends his rap by going into a break dance. The skit ends with an MTV-like video ID:

Rice Cube
"Down Wit' MSG"

We Own the World
Kim Chee Records

Steve Park was added to the supporting cast of *In Living Color* after its inaugural season as an obvious gesture of goodwill toward the Korean American community. But by mid-June of 1992, the producers announced that Park would be leaving the program by mutual agreement. During his short tenure with the program, Park received scant exposure and was given little opportunity to display his talents along with the predominantly African American cast. Park's departure leaves dancer Carrie Ann Inaba—one of choreographer Rosie Perez's "Fly Girls"—as the sole remaining Asian American on the show.

Yellow Germs

Criminalizing the behavior of certain social groups, such as Asian Americans, has been an effective means of enforcing their subordination. During the late nineteenth century, for example, the immigration of female Asian immigrants to the state of California was made difficult by the official assumption that they were being brought in for purposes of prostitution. In 1875, the U.S. Congress passed the so-called Page Law to prevent women of "disreputable character" from entering the country.[32] Drug use, especially the smoking of opium, was later criminalized, despite the success the British enjoyed in spreading it throughout much of China. In 1881, the California State Legislature passed a statute that prohibited the sale and consumption of opium.[33] These and other repressive measures governing "morals" were meant to exercise social control over the Asian immigrant population.

Currently, under the guise of fighting a "drug war," law enforcement agencies have been given license to control the largely Hispanic and African American populations residing in core urban areas through tactics of intimidation, fear, and physical abuse. Internationally, the demonization of Latin American drug lords provides the United States with the pretext for violating the sovereignty of foreign states through direct military intervention. Such was the case with the December 1989 invasion of Panama followed by the capture and show trial of President Manuel Noriega, who the U.S. government had accused of trafficking in drugs. As Noam Chomsky observes, the war on drugs—both foreign and domestic—has replaced the Cold War as a method of "population control."[34] In addition, the current war on foreign "narcotraffickers" and their domestic connections helps maintain the requisite level of social paranoia central to the normal functioning of a garrison state.

Asian Americans are not immune from this new regime of state terror. Even as they are being applauded for their high level of academic achievement and industry, certain sectors of the Asian American immigrant community have been identified as threats to the larger social order. "Triads," for example, are claimed to be engaged in international and domestic criminal activity on a scale that boggles the imagination. "The same ingenuity and dedication of purpose that allowed the Chinese to develop a culture before the pharoahs and to make Hong Kong a commercial paradise," writes Gerald L. Posner, "are some of the same traits that have been applied by Chinese criminals, through the secret societies, to create massive underworld empires."[35]

This media-assisted criminalization process is very much in evidence on network television. Some programs merely have given a new twist to stock themes, such as the purported prevalence of "tongs" in the life of the Chinese American community. "Tongs," an episode of *Gideon Oliver* (1989), dramatizes the inner world of Chinese American society by showing an African American professor of anthropology at Columbia University, Gideon Oliver (Louis Gossett, Jr.), as being sympathetic to the ideals of the secret societies while condemning their unlawful activities.[36]

The Asian connection in international crime was given extended treatment in a special hosted by Geraldo Rivera, *The New Godfathers* (1993).[37] The media-savvy Rivera rode the publicity surrounding the capture of Mafia don Salvatore "Toto" Riina by conducting the broadcast "live" from Palermo, Italy, surrounded by gun-toting carabinieri. In introducing the program, Rivera describes the "global wave of terror" and the "multinational attack on the United States" taking place in New York, San Francisco, Los Angeles, Miami, and even Sacramento, California. Especially fearsome are the Hong Kong-based triads, whose estimated 60,000 to 80,000 members are looking to establish a base in the United States before the British crown colony reverts to Chinese rule in 1997.

Geraldo also devotes a segment to the Japanese *yakuza* influence in the United States. With all the prurient indignation he can muster—a trademark of his reportorial style—Geraldo reveals how young, innocent, blonde-haired white women are promised lucrative jobs as entertainers in Japan but are instead forced into pornography and prostitution against their will. Geraldo uses his patented reporter verité method, confronting a suspected procurer for the "white slavery rings" that are supposedly operating in Southern

California. Geraldo's career has been based on his ability to bait his surprised subjects into spontaneous, often physical responses,[38] but this time Geraldo fails to get a rise out of the imperturbable, well-spoken white man, even though the reporter refers to him as a "pimp" on camera.

Other programs advance the notion that Asian criminality is a qualitatively new phenomenon that must be controlled at all costs, perhaps even at the expense of civil rights. Representing this tendency is a recent documentary produced by a small independent television station in Southern California, KDOC-TV. As part of the Golden Orange Broadcasting Co., Inc., the Anaheim-based station is partly owned by erstwhile white teen idol and entertainer Pat Boone. The station is also home to the program *Hot Seat*, hosted by the provocative right-wing talk-show personality Wally George since 1983.[39] Much of the programming for KDOC-TV consists of sitcom and drama reruns as well as old feature films. The station provides little in the way of news, information, or community service programming, even by the lax standards of the present "deregulated" broadcast environment. Perhaps the occasional sensationalistic investigative reports produced by KDOC are token attempts to compensate for the relative lack of original community-based programming.

Asian Gangs: Terror in the Streets (1992) depicts politically conservative Orange County as being overrun by heavily armed, cold-blooded killers who come from "violent backgrounds."[40] Reporter Beth Bingham cites experts who estimate that seventy different "gangs," boasting "several hundred members," roam Orange County. The so-called gangs specialize in blackmailing individuals or engaging in the extortion of Asian-owned businesses located primarily in the "Little Saigon" section of Garden Grove and Westminster, an area with a high concentration of Southeast Asian residents. In addition to blackmail, extortion, auto theft, and protection rackets, a unique crime attributed to Southeast Asian gangs is the "home invasion" robbery. As part of their *modus operandi*, the well-armed criminal perpetrators first target their victims and then burst into the victims' houses, demanding cash (Vietnamese are said to be distrustful of banks, and thus have large amounts of cash at home), jewelry, and other valuables. Sometimes victims are pistol-whipped or otherwise roughed up during the commission of the crime.

In *Asian Gangs*, Thaddeus Pham, a real estate broker, tells of gangs trying to exact "protection" money from him. The theme of yellow on yellow crime, that Asian gangs prey on their *own kind*, underlies the program. A supplemental theme is that of the white law enforcement establishment that must intercede to protect Asians from other Asians. The white intercession of the police force is thus presented as a gesture motivated by goodwill and justice rather than as the imposition of state power upon the ascendant Southeast Asian community. Routinely, police agencies representing different jurisdictions have cooperated in conducting "sweeps" of suspected gang members. A number of police departments have even formed "gang suppression units" dedicated exclusively to Asians. Even the federal government has become a player in the repression business through the Bureau of Alcohol, Tobacco and Firearms.

A number of white law enforcement personnel are interviewed to lend insight into the problem of Asian gang violence. Detective Marcus Frank of the Westminster Police Department is articulate, thoughtful, and able to analyze the problems of gangs from a broader perspective than most other street cops. But he exaggerates the difficulty of his job by stating, "Of all the street gangs out there, there is no question in my mind that the Indochinese street gangs are by far the most criminally sophisticated element we have ever seen in this country." Asian criminal activity supposedly has been observed in major cities across the country, including Los Angeles, San Francisco, Seattle, Boston, New York, and New Orleans. Reporter Bingham goes so far as to claim that Asian gangs from other parts of the country are sending their members to Orange County for "training in criminal activity," as if Little Saigon has become a Mecca for lawless hordes.

At the close of the documentary, Detective Frank would have the viewer believe that the problem of Southeast Asian gangs is qualitatively different from that of other ethnic groups. Frank explains that many of the gang members have been exposed to criminal behavior while still in Vietnam, that many come from "violent backgrounds," some having left "refugee camps that resemble concentration camps." Detective Frank implies that the new breed of Asian criminal is one made up of individuals who are not bound by the conventions of civilized behavior because of the debased conditions under which they have been raised. As a consequence, Asian gang members have no fear of punishment if they are caught breaking the law.

Reporter Beth Bingham employs the "Chinatown" strategy to conclude the investigative report. That is, she appeals to the Vietnamese community at large to break the wall of silence that makes it difficult for police authorities to offer protection. The police are in need of information and "witnesses" who will voluntarily come forward whenever a crime is committed, Bingham asserts. By portraying the Vietnamese American community as an impenetrable fortress of secretiveness, the "Chinatown" strategy provides police agencies with the excuse they need to attack a problem that has been exaggerated to begin with. Further, even if Asian community members continue to be victimized by their own, police agencies are absolved of responsibility as they enjoy the funding of special gang suppression units. All the while, police repression of the Southeast Asian American community through such routine activity as gang "sweeps" is legitimated under the guise of law enforcement.

With the exception of a lone "suspected" member of the "Santa Ana Boys" named Lan, whose back is turned to the camera as he answers questions in monosyllabic bursts, the *Asian Gangs* narrative is controlled by reporter Beth Bingham and law enforcement personnel. The only other Asian person interviewed, however briefly, is well-to-do businessman Thaddeus Pham, who stands squarely on the side of law and order. The documentary, in short, is not so much about "Asian gangs" as it is about the generalized fear and terror among whites of the large Southeast Asian American population that has sunk roots in the very heart of Orange County, California.

In a review of the news special, critic Randy Lewis poses the question whether such programs as *Asian Gangs: Terror in the Streets* fuel current anti-Asian sentiment: "With anti-Japanese rhetoric increasing in the United States, do law-abiding Asian-Americans fear increased racism against their community because of the actions of a small percentage of Asian youths?"[41] Today, as has been the case in the past, the control and repression of Asian American communities is justified by the criminalization of a segment of the population through media sensationalism.

A more balanced exploration of Asian American gang life is found in a sixty-minute documentary by Renee Tajima. Produced for Lifetime Television and hosted by Susan Dey, *Jennifer's in Jail* (1992) devotes a segment to the development of female Asian American gangs in Orange County, California.[42] Unlike *Asian Gangs: Terror in the Streets*, the Lifetime documentary does not depend exclusively on the insights of white law enforcement personnel. Fred Wong of the "L.A. Asian Gang Unit" is consulted on the problem, as are members of Little Saigon's "South Side Scissor Girls," who are allowed to explain the scope and purpose of gang life from their own perspective. The documentary even captures a spontaneous altercation between the Scissor Girls and a rival "Asian girl gang," IBK, or "Innocent Bitch Killers," at a Little Saigon shopping mall.

Faced with academic failure, alienation, racism, "status incongruity," parental problems, and limited job opportunities in a consumerist society, disaffected youth who become involved in gangs may be making a predictable adaptive response to their marginalization.[43] Gangsterism – Asian or otherwise – is a response to organized elites in society who, like gangs themselves, jealously guard their privilege and "turf" in key social, cultural, and economic institutions to the exclusion of all others.

Euro-American Intercession

The flip side of Asian American criminalization is found in the heroics of the Euro-American intercessor. This television type might be a police officer, detective, private investigator, lawyer, or any professional who is connected in some way to the criminal justice system. In the television programs of the past, the Euro-American intercessor was almost exclusively an Anglo-Saxon Protestant male. In the era of multicultural "diversity," however, other ethnic groups and even women have been brought into the fold to reproduce the dominant social order. Although he or she might be brown, black, or even yellow, the "Euro-American" intercessor works on behalf of the white male power structure by policing minority communities such as Asian Americans. This fundamental loyalty to the dominant power structure is played down by casting the "Euro-American" intercessor as an "outsider" within a bureaucratic institution such as a police agency or office of the public defender. The intercessor's outsider status is pivotal to this ritual of legitimation because it allows him to mediate the inherent conflict between two distinct but overlapping social orders, each struggling for supremacy or, at the very least, autonomy.

The connection between the Euro-American intercessor and the structures of power and dominance is most often occluded by a common diversionary stratagem that finds its way into the television text. That is, the Euro-American intercessor assumes the moral high ground by offering protection and assistance to nonwhite groups victimized by their *own kind*. The intercessor must first overcome the resistance of the nondominant group, which is seen as distrustful of formal authority and wary of involving outsiders with the internal affairs of the ethnic community. Once the trust of the nondominant group is won, the Euro-American intercessor proves the sincerity of his intentions by bringing a given offender to justice in a manner deemed satisfactory by all involved. At bottom, the legal-juridical system and larger social order are the beneficiaries of the Euro-American intercessor's success in patrolling the otherwise hidden lives of nondominant groups.

A recent episode of the cop show *Tequila and Bonetti* (1992) provides a good example of the ritual of legitimation outlined above.[44] In "Language of the Heart," Detective Nico Bonetti (Jack Scalia) seeks to identify and arrest the murderer of a Chicano gang member. Bonetti is a "gold shield detective" from Brooklyn on a visiting assignment at a trendy Los Angeles beachside precinct. While on duty, the detective had mistakenly shot and killed a twelve-year-old child. In the aftermath of the accidental killing, Bonetti moved temporarily to La La Land, in part to overcome his grief.

As might be expected, the charm of the program lies in the contrast between the supposedly laid-back idyllic "lifestyle" of Southern California and that of the mean streets of Brooklyn. In addition, Bonetti plays up his white ethnic heritage by punctuating his conversation with Italian words and phrases for emphasis. As a member of a white ethnic minority that was once criminalized by the dominant society, Bonetti now stands on the side of law and order, but without having abandoned the street smarts and toughness that are part of his Italian American upbringing. In sum, Bonetti is the personification of the Euro-American intercessor in the era of multiculturalism.

Teamed with Bonetti is Angela Garcia (Mariska Hargitay), an attractive Mexican American rookie, which injects gender-related issues and sexual tension into the program along with that of ethnicity. Garcia uses her thoroughgoing familiarity with the Chicano community to assist in the investigation, much to the chagrin of the somewhat macho and self-prepossessing Bonetti. As friendly rivals who also show signs of mutual sexual interest, Bonetti and Garcia round up the members of two opposing gangs, a Chicano gang known as the Coyotes and an Asian American gang with an equally unlikely name, the Vipers. The Vipers are suspected of murdering Jesus Montoya of the Coyotes in a dispute over previously neutral turf.

In the sweeping arrests of gang members, Garcia arrests the putative leader of the Vipers, Gilbert Kwan (François Chau). "You can handle me, baby," Kwan says to Garcia as he is being locked up. The gallant Bonetti immediately rushes to defend her honor. Bonetti tells Kwan to "watch your mouth" and threatens to feed him "like sushi" to his canine sidekick, a "talking" French mastiff named Tequila (voice by Brad Sanders). The yellow man's predatory sexual aggression is thus blunted by the threat of punishment by being fed "like sushi" to a dog.

The Vipers, as it turns out, had nothing to do with the murder. Jesus Montoya had been killed by his *own brother* Miguel in a fraternal power struggle. After subduing Miguel Montoya in an old-fashioned knife fight before the assembled members of both the

Vipers and the Coyotes, Bonetti moves to cart the offender off to jail. One of the Chicano gangsters, brandishing a Mac-10 machine pistol, indicates to Bonetti, "We'll take care of him," intending to dispense the gang's own brand of justice to the traitor. "No you're not," says Bonetti, "not on my turf." The surly detective, only one step removed from gangsterism himself, instructs his partner Garcia to arrest the suspect, who will be prosecuted by the legally constituted criminal justice system.

Of course, the premise of gang warfare between a Chicano gang and an Asian gang is far-fetched to say the least. The larger lesson in this liberal morality play lies in the intercession of the white ethnic good guy, Bonetti, who has one foot in "the system" and the other in "the street." Moreover, the Bonetti-Garcia investigatory team reasserts the power of the Foucauldian "panoptic regime," which— in a perverse twist on affirmative action and multiculturalism—has enlisted Euro-American surrogates and non-Anglo coethnics to police, punish, and discipline prepolitical urban rebels organized as street "gangs."

An episode of *MacGyver* (1985–92) further illustrates the use of Euro-American surrogates in dispensing justice to other nonwhite minorities such as Asian Americans.[45] In "The Coltons," the members of a family of African American bounty hunters are approached by District Attorney Johnny Denmark (also Black) to help him find an Amerasian woman named Medusa (Akiko Morrison). The "number-one lady" of the godfather of Chinatown, she had witnessed the gangster's slaying at a restaurant by a pretender to the throne, Mr. Chi (Francois Chau). Denmark engages brothers Frank (Cleavon Little) and Jesse Colton (Richard Lawson) to first locate and then protect Medusa from being silenced by Mr. Chi's assassins.

Mr. Chi's principal business consists of smuggling Chinese workers into the United States and holding them captive in a warehouse to unpack heroin concealed in cheap toys imported from Hong Kong. Heavily armed Chinese thugs monitor the activity closely and threaten their coethnics with death should they attempt to escape. It is at the warehouse where the Colton brothers eventually rescue Medusa and expose the heroin importation business overseen by Mr. Chi.

Within the formulaic conventions of the Chinatown murder mystery, this episode of *MacGyver* offers the general viewer a wealth of updated social information on the supposed influence of a new breed of Asian criminal. Like his nineteenth-century progenitors, the contemporary Chinese American criminal exploits his own countrymen under conditions of slavery, keeps women like Medusa in sexual bondage, and seeks to undermine the moral fabric of the country by addicting its citizens with drugs. But rather than have the conventional Euro-American intercessor halt the baneful influence of Chinese criminality, African Americans are given equal employment opportunity to act on behalf of their masters.

To reinforce further the liberal pluralist notion that good guys and bad guys come in all colors, District Attorney Johnny Denmark proves to be as crooked as the Coltons are upstanding. Denmark had used the Coltons to locate Medusa so that Chi's men could kill the only witness to the crime. Mama Colton (Della Reese), by contrast, is the hardworking matriarch of the clan who is interested only in ensuring that the youngest of her sons, Billy (Cuba Gooding, Jr.), makes it into college before joining the family bounty-hunting business.

Affirmative Police Action

Tequila and Bonetti features an Italian American detective, and *MacGyver* devoted an entire episode to an African American family of bounty hunters. An episode of the police drama *The Commish* (1991–present) completes the circuit of power connecting Anglo police authority with ethnic collaborators. Tony Scali (Michael Chiklis) seems more like a social worker than police commissioner of a suburban precinct far removed from his native Brooklyn. He is attentive to his wife Rachel (Theresa Saldana) and even spends quality time with his preteen son David (Kaj-Erik Eriksen).

The Commish and his assistant Lucille (Kimberly Scott) inadvertently wander into the netherworld of Asian-style extortion when they have lunch at a Vietnamese restaurant. In an earlier scene, three young Asian men have been shown trying to leave the Pho Duong Restaurant without paying. They then demand protection money from the proprietor, Mr. Duong (Haing S. Ngor), who tells them, "I don't pay." Seconds later, masked members of the "Charlie Don't Surf" (after the memorable phrase uttered by Colonel Kilgore in *Apocalypse Now*) gang return and fire their weapons randomly into the restaurant, terrorizing its patrons.

The Commish intercedes in the internal affairs of the Vietnamese community when he visits the restaurant for lunch and spies bullet holes in the wall, looks further, and finds a 9-mm slug. He asks Duong what happened, but, true to form, Duong denies any knowledge of extortion attempts. Later, the Commish obtains a report from the office of the district attorney that says Charlie Don't Surf served as the "muscle" for a "Chinese triad" before being expelled because they were "too violent." The Commish is faced with the dual

problem of overcoming Duong's reticence in allowing outside inter-
ference and putting the renegade Asian gang out of action.

Most of the episode is devoted to tracing the Commish's efforts
in winning the trust of the intimidated Vietnamese restaurateur.
The Commish muses about the *"goombata"* who used to extort
money from his grandfather Arturo. An otherwise strong and proud
man, his grandfather would be absolutely cowed when shaken down
by the local wise guys. The Commish compares his firsthand experience with Italian American gangsters with that of recent Vietnamese immigrants who are also being victimized by coethnic
criminals.

To penetrate the closed world of the Vietnamese American community, the Commish enlists the aid of Detective Robert Heu
(Dustin Nguyen), a self-described "first-generation American" who
resents being typed as a *Vietnamese* cop. In assuming a fully American identity, the detective has gone so far as to change his name from
Heu Tran. Heu is described as the first and only Vietnamese American to have graduated from the department's police academy, and he
says that his parents were ashamed that he chose to become a policeman, for in Vietnam, police work is considered a disreputable profession. Heu is intent upon distinguishing himself as a police officer
without regard to his Asian ethnicity.

Wanting to assimilate into mainstream American society on his
own terms, Heu resists being cast into the role of *Asian* intercessor
and at first is unwilling to help the Commish. "You don't need me,"
he says to the Commish. "You need my face, the color of my skin."
The Commish abandons the ethnic approach and instead plays upon
Heu's sense of professionalism. "Okay, let's forget that you're
Asian. . . . Let's forget *they're* Asian," says the Commish. "There
are people being abused. Their rights are being violated. As a police
officer you have to respond to that." Heu still refuses. "I'm a cop, sir.
I don't want to be a Vietnamese cop. Thanks for the offer but it's not
my, uh . . . bowl of rice." Detective Heu soon has a change of
heart, however, and decides to work the case after a fellow officer he
had been dating, Carmela Pagan (Gina Belafonte), is wounded by
the gangsters in a drive-by shooting.

The Commish finally convinces Mr. Duong to cooperate with the
police. Duong had been hesitant to involve the authorities, because
in Vietnam the police are corrupt and ineffectual. It is at this juncture that the "moral" of liberal benevolence is allowed to seep
through the text. The Commish recites a touching speech: "Mr.
Duong, you're a brave man. Because it took a lot of courage to fight
your way out of the country and immigrate to what you dreamed was

a better place. But you have to continue to fight to keep that dream alive. Only this time I'm going to help you to fight."

As Heu, Duong, and the Commish sit together enjoying a meal of fraternal conciliation, masked members of Charlie Don't Surf enter the restaurant intending to rob it. The gang leader, Tuan (Michael Andaluz), moves to shoot Heu for being a cop and having betrayed his "own people." No, Duong counters, it is they who are guilty of betrayal by preying upon coethnic businesspeople. When the Commish distracts one of the gunmen, Heu joins him in disarming the gangsters and placing them under arrest. This final criminal act forces the Commish and Officer Heu to act together as a biracial law enforcement team.

The credits for this episode of *The Commish* list an Asian American (James Wong) as cowriter, which would presumably lend the program some semblance of "balance" and added credibility. Regardless, an undercurrent of liberal assimilationist ideology runs strongly throughout the episode. For one, there is the assumption voiced by the Commish that the experience of Italian immigrants like his grandfather is commensurate with that of Mr. Duong. This false analogy completely collapses two historically unique circumstances into one larger American Immigrant Saga. Second, Mr. Duong is not, strictly speaking, an "immigrant," but a refugee. Mr. Duong and other Vietnamese like him did not emigrate voluntarily. Rather, they were forced to flee Vietnam in the aftermath of the U.S. military pullout in 1975 and relocated to a society that did not necessarily want them. Although there are superficial similarities of experience shared by all ethnic groups new to the United States, the substantial differences that exist are too easily glossed over in a manner typical of television melodrama.

More revealing of the liberal assimilationist drift of the episode is the character of Detective Robert Heu. By becoming a police officer, Heu has consciously distanced himself from the ethnic community to the point of incurring the disapproval of his parents. But it is this very distancing that allows Heu eventually to prevent his "own people" from preying upon one another. It is the character Heu who delivers the inner world of the Vietnamese American community to transcendental White Police Authority. Through Heu and other ethnic enforcers, the state is able to cast its already extensive net of control over diverse ethnic communities such as Vietnamese Americans.

Overnight Succession

The immigrant analogy as applied to Mr. Duong in the above-described episode of *The Commish* is consistent with the principle of "ethnic succession." The principle of ethnic succession has it that each and every immigrant group that has entered U.S. society starts at the bottom of the socioeconomic ladder and works its way up by dint of hard effort. According to the model, arriving without any appreciable skills and lacking basic English language competence, the immigrant generation must hold backbreaking jobs, working long hours under dangerous conditions, in the struggle to survive. There is, however, a supposed payoff for such hard work and dedication. The assumption is that the sacrifices of the immigrant generation will enable their children to gain a formal education, enter high-paying professions, and eventually ascend to the middle class. This questionable assumption has been most recently echoed by Andrew Hacker, who writes, "As Asians find their place in the economy, they are allowed to move upward on social and occupational ladders."[46]

The principle of ethnic succession as applied to recent Asian immigrants underlies an episode of *Wiseguy* (1987–90) that explores the seamy underside of the garment industry in New York.[47] Vinnie Terranova (Ken Wahl) works undercover for the FBI's "Organized Crime Task Force" investigating sophisticated criminal activity. In "All or Nothing," Terranova poses as a "security" consultant employed by Eli Sternberg (Jerry Lewis), the hard-driving owner of a garment manufacturing concern, Elrose Fashions. Terranova is intent on busting a mobster, Rick Pinzolo (Stanley Tucci), who has targeted Elrose for extortion.

Sternberg's son David (Ron Silver) lands a huge manufacturing contract, but must work "local and cheap" because of an upcoming "Buy American" campaign. Elrose turns to Hong (Ed Hong-Louie), a reliable subcontractor located in Chinatown, who makes assurances that he can contain manufacturing costs in his nonunion shop. Hong operates a modern-day sweatshop. Infants cry in the background as children run amidst ill-maintained equipment, exposed electrical wiring, and even rats. Entire families are seen working in unsafe conditions under a union sign boasting of its "American Made" clothing.

Outside in the street, community activist Maxine Tzu (Joan Chen) stands with a megaphone trying to organize apathetic Chinatown garment workers against "Seventh Avenue manufacturers." A fire later breaks out at the sweatshop, killing two employees. Back at the FBI headquarters of the Organized Crime Task Force, a parallel is drawn between the Chinatown fire and the historic Triangle Shirtwaist Co. disaster. That 1911 fire drew considerable public outrage over the poor working conditions endured by the largely Eastern European immigrant laborers and helped pave the way for unionization.

Eli Sternberg and Terranova arrive at Hong's factory accompanied by an Old World pattern cutter named Moe (Harry Goz), only to find Maxine Tzu leading a picket line and blocking the entrance. Sternberg is angered by the demonstration, but Moe has mixed feelings. Earlier, Sternberg had voiced displeasure at the union's role in compounding his costs, whereas Moe had expressed views that were strongly prolabor. Moe went so far as to scold his boss for having managed to "forget where you came from." Representing first-generation Jewish American immigrant garment workers, Moe experiences a good deal of guilt ("I never crossed a picket line in my life!") over the dispute. "Don't give me that commie pinko crap!" Sternberg replies.

Sternberg then turns his wrath on Tzu: "You got your wires crossed, honey. We're *all* losing money here. That fire wasn't in my shop." "You worried about your big mortgage payments, Mr. Manufacturer?" Tzu answers. "C'mon, honey, work is work. This is certainly better than picking weeds out of rice fields," Sternberg replies. Tzu then asks the picketers, "How many of you want to sell your souls for a new shiny Cadillac?" In a fit of anger, Sternberg hurls the ultimate insult at the organizer, calling her an "anti-Semitic commie witch!"

Terranova is given instructions to visit Tzu and "set her straight." At her apartment, Terranova tries to convince Tzu that she is wrong for placing political ideology before the welfare of the Chinatown workers. He accuses Tzu of being just an ideologue who is sacrificing jobs simply to score philosophical points. Tzu, however, explains that in Beijing her father went insane after being tortured by the authorities for his political beliefs. Her mother, who had been a poet, had a finger broken by thugs to prevent her from writing. As a consequence, Tzu battles the evils of "the system," whatever form it may take.

Moved by this personal account, Terranova cradles Tzu's head in his hands and apologizes. "I don't want to see you hurt," he says. He then kisses her forehead lightly before their lips meet in passion. A story line that seemed more akin to the film *Save the Tiger* (1973) abruptly modulates into a scene out of Nagisa Oshima's *In the Realm of the Senses* (1976) when Tzu leaves the room only to return with a tray holding a shaving brush, soap, and a straight razor. Tzu sets the tray down, slides Terranova's jacket off his shoulders, allowing it to crumple onto the floor, loosens his necktie, and pushes him backward onto her bed. She viciously rips his shirt open, sending the popped buttons flying across the room, scattering over the hardwood floor. The labor leader turned Oriental Vixen lathers up her prey with cream as the undercover cop leans back on the bed and offers his exposed neck for a deathly shave with Asian sensuality.

"Do you trust me?" asks Tzu in a round of terse sadomasochistic pillow talk. "No. You gonna hurt me?" "Only if you want me to," says Dragon Lady. Terranova slips the band of gold from his hand as Tzu gingerly removes the eyeglasses from his face. The yellow dominatrix straddles the supine agent of the federal government and mounts him, legs astride, riding straight into the collective sexual fantasies of the white male producers of *Wiseguy*.

The sudden transformation of Maxine Tzu from fiery union organizer into kinky Asian female sex pot is a discursive strategy worth noting. This maneuver functions as a radical negation of Tzu's oppositional social role and casts her into a position more consistent with white male expectations. Tzu might indeed be politically committed, the implied narrator seems to say, but deep down, all Yellow Woman truly desires is to have sexual relations with White Man. The eroticized shaving tableau is jarring in its utter inappropriateness, even though the viewer fully expects that Terranova and Tzu will share sexual intimacies from the moment they meet. The perversely nonsensical plot twist reduces labor organizer and political activist Maxine Tzu to the role of Asian American Jezebel. At bottom, beyond ideology, she desires only orgasmic—not social—equality.

Beneath the interracial psychosexual dynamics of the encounter between Vinnie Terranova and Maxine Tzu is the subtext of Asian American immigrant succession patterned along the lines of Jewish Americans. Within three generations, American Jews to a large degree have become structurally assimilated into the cultural, social, and economic mainstream. Moe is a living reminder of the Jewish American immigrant generation that helped found the U.S. garment industry and acts as Eli Sternberg's conscience in his dealings with the new Asian industrial proletariat. But, as Maxine Tzu implies in her hostile encounter with Eli Sternberg, Jewish Americans are now the owners and it is they who currently exploit immigrant Asian workers under conditions as bad as or worse than those that existed during the early 1900s. But at least it is "better than picking weeds out of rice fields," according to Sternberg.

The principle of ethnic succession implied in *Wiseguy* does not necessarily hold true for the tens of thousands of legal and undocumented Latino, Caribbean, and Asian immigrants who perform piecework at less than minimum wage with few or no benefits in substandard sweatshops across the United States.[48] In Southern California alone, an estimated 111,000 are employed in the manufacture of apparel, an industry that generates revenues of $7 billion per year.[49] In an article that provided a glimpse into the Southern California garment industry, a partner in a highly successful Los Angeles firm known as Chorus Line commented on questionable business practices that have attracted the scrutiny of both state and federal authorities. Mark Steinman, president and partner in Chorus Line, was unapologetic about the exploitative conditions endured by garment workers. Such work is a simple fact of life in capitalist America, according to Steinman. When his grandparents emigrated to the United States earlier in the century, they too had to take jobs at the bottom rung of the economic ladder. "The world is what the world is," said Steinman.[50] In 1987, Steinman and his two partners sold an interest in Chorus Line to Merrill Lynch & Co. and another institutional investor for $30 million.

To suggest that the new industrial proletariat occupies a position analogous to that of earlier immigrant groups such as Jewish Americans is disingenuous at best. In his belletristic meditation on contemporary Los Angeles, David Rieff writes somewhat disapprovingly of Westside liberals who accept the analogy that Hispanics are like the Italians of an earlier era, just as Asians, "with their access to capital, their reverence for study, and their entrepreneurial zest, [are] the latter-day Jews."[51] Rieff's reading of history, however, does not allow him such facile generalizations. He senses a larger, epochal, techtonic shift that makes the current immigration qualitatively different from that of previous generations.

Stephen Steinberg, in his critical interrogation of what he refers to as the "Jewish Horatio Alger Story," explains that despite their poverty, Eastern European Jewish immigrants were "concentrated in economically advanced sectors" in the countries from which they emigrated and "therefore had industrial experience and concrete occupational skills that would serve them well in America's expanding industrial economy."[52] Steinberg also notes that the majority of non-Jewish immigrants who arrived in the United States during the same period were peasants or agricultural workers. Non-Jewish immigrants, then, were less able to transfer their skills and social preparation to the burgeoning U.S. industrial economy. Therefore, the "Jewish Horatio Alger Story" was to a large degree a "matter of historical timing" in that "there was a fortuitous match between the experience and skills of Jewish immigrants, on the one hand, and the manpower needs and opportunity structures, on the other."[53]

Unlike Jewish American immigrants at the beginning of the century, the current movement of Asians into sweatshop labor is explained by the fundamental transformation of the global economy in the era of U.S. economic and military dominance. Placed under pressure by the World Bank and the International Monetary Fund, underdeveloped or so-called Third World countries have been given no choice but to allow transnational corporations and agribusiness to displace local rural economies, thereby disrupting traditional social relations of production. The heavy flow of nonskilled immigrant workers into metropolitan core areas such as represented by the flourishing garment industry in New York and Los Angeles is symptomatic of the larger transformation of the global economy. Third World women in particular have borne the brunt of the severe social and economic dislocations that have forced many into the "sex tourism" industry, as is the case in Thailand and the Philippines, or created a new stratum of easily exploitable "cheap" labor in a number of labor-intensive industries such as clothing manufacture.[54] Less visibly, the high-tech glamor of the electronics industry that has taken root in the "Silicon Valley" of California or along Route 128 outside of Boston are also direct beneficiaries of large-scale emigration from Asia and Latin America. According to Annette Fuentes and Barbara Ehrenreich, as in the U.S. garment industry, immigrant female labor composes fully 40 percent of the workforce in the electronics industry. "On the west coast," write Fuentes and Ehrenreich, "Filipinas, Thais, Samoans, Mexicans and Vietnamese have made the electronics assembly line a microcosm of the global production process."[55]

Drawing dubious comparisons between immigrant groups of widely divergent social class and occupational backgrounds serves only to reinforce reigning myths concerning the differential moral or cultural "fitness" of select ethnic or racial minorities who have attained a relative degree of success in American society. The principle of ethnic succession purports to "explain" objectively why some ethnic minorities succeed and others do not. If, therefore, Jews in the United States have attained high-income professional status, then it must be because of their superior cultural and intellectual attributes.

The same line of reasoning has been applied to Asian Americans (a diverse group) *in toto*. As for the current crop of Asian American sweatshop laborers who do not fit the standard profile, the prevailing assumption is that if they pay their dues and put in their time, then they too will gain admission into middle-class society. Unfortunately, such moralistic arguments do not take cognizance of far-reaching political and economic decisions and strategies that have created a global division of labor that cuts across the lines of ethnicity, race, and nationality. Unlike earlier arrivals, the Asian immigrant proletariat of today is faced with the prospect of remaining at or near the bottom of the social system beyond the first and second generation, thus confounding the rosy optimism implied in the model of ethnic succession.

America the Bountiful

Mutually opposed interpretations of the new Asian immigration to the Southern California region have been debated by Joel Kotkin and Mike Davis on the innovative local program produced by Community Television of Southern California, *Life and Times*.[56] Opening the segment titled "Double Vision," Kotkin restates a familiar argument: that the "future of L.A. really rests on how we integrate the immigrants and can we tap their tremendous energy." Kotkin points to Safi U. Qureshey—a cofounder of AST Research, Inc., of Irvine, California—as an example of how large-scale businesses created by Asian immigrants in turn create employment for other immigrants.

Along with Hong Kong-born partners Thomas C. K. Yuen and Albert C. Wong, the Pakistani American Qureshey and company not only have created hundreds of jobs in a dynamic new industry, but serve as a "shining example" to other immigrants. Yuen, for example, was the son of an impoverished chauffeur. He emigrated from Hong Kong in 1970 to study at a community college in California and later became an engineer. After being laid off a $12,000-a-year job at Hughes Aircraft and realizing that the "glass ceiling" would prevent an Asian American from rising to a top position with an established company, Yuen cofounded AST Research in 1980 and developed it into a Fortune 500 corporation.

The Asian immigrant saga of the trio who once described themselves as the "Three Musketeers," however, seems to have come to a distasteful end. In late June 1992, Thomas C. K. Yuen was ousted from his position as "cochairman" at AST as the result of a corporate power struggle that saw cofounder Safi U. Qureshey emerge as victor.[57] Qureshey is the last remaining member of the "Three Musketeers," as Albert C. Wong resigned in 1988 after a conflict with Yuen over a product launch. Now that the high-risk entrepreneurial spadework has been done, the successful Asian immigrants have been replaced by a predominantly Euro-American cadre of professional managers and board members who will now guide AST's entry into the national economy via Wall Street.

In contrast to Joel Kotkin, social critic Mike Davis, author of the darkly elegiac meditation on contemporary Los Angeles *City of Quartz*, discusses symptoms of "social breakdown" and "economic decline" that have become manifest throughout the region.[58] Davis investigates the myth of Asian American entrepreneurial success by conducting a tour of L.A.'s Chinatown. He is guided by local Chinese American attorney Sharon Lowe, who represents a number of small-business owners and handles immigration cases. Their destination is a typical mall in Chinatown, Mandarin Plaza. "It looks like a ghost town," says Davis. "Where is everybody?" Lowe explains that Mandarin Plaza "typifies the entire Chinatown community" and that high vacancy rates plague similar malls in the community.

"But I thought Chinatown's supposed to be booming?" Davis asks, disingenuously. The visitor's question elicits an amused laugh from Lowe. "Oh, a wonderful myth about Asian Pacifics," she answers. " 'Booming' in the sense of high land values, high rents, but for the small business entrepreneurs . . ." Images of closed family-run stores with soaped-out windows and vacancy signs reinforce the bleak picture of a community that has historically served as the center of the Los Angeles Chinese American community.

Davis takes leave of Chinatown by noting the difficulties faced by small businesses owned and operated by Asian Americans in an ethnic enclave economy already glutted by "nail parlors, doughnut shops, Chinese restaurants." The economic recession that has ravaged Southern California over the past several years will no doubt make matters doubly worse for failed Asian American business owners, family members, and employees who hope to enter into the mainstream economy. In 1991 alone, Los Angeles County lost a total of 208,400 jobs, making the prospects for future employment dim indeed.[59]

No-Money-Down Capitalism

The politics of the Reagan-Bush era were such that the state was relegated to a secondary role as handmaiden to the freebooting practices of oligopoly capitalism. In this neoclassical conception of a minimalist state presiding over a laissez-faire economy, individuals, families, and local communities were made to bear the heavy costs exacted by what Seymour Melman refers to as "military state capitalism."[60] By definition, it is understood that the state assumed only incidental responsibility in the amelioration of persistent social problems caused by the unequal distribution of basic resources within a capitalist political economy.

In this context, the Asian American family has often been extolled by liberal/conservative commentators as a model of economic self-sufficiency. Among Asian Americans, a high level of participation in the labor force, better-than-average family income, and superior educational attainment are cited as evidence that liberal democracy does indeed work. Underlying the false celebration of the Asian American family as a paragon of self-reliant success is the implicit denigration of other nonwhite groups who have not reached similar levels of achievement.

To rationalize the increased polarization of rich and poor, the laissez-faire economics of the Reagan-Bush era invoked such watchwords as *deregulation, privatization, small government, entrepreneurialism,* and the *free market* economy. This helped further strengthen control by the capitalist plutocracy of America's heavily leveraged social wealth. At the opposite end of the class structure, young families, racial minorities, women, and children fell victim to the "Reagan revolution."

A cult of wealth creation via "entrepreneurialism" reached a fevered pitch during the hollow boom years of the 1980s. The myth of the self-made man enjoyed a populist revival as a grab bag of junk bond arbitrageurs, real estate speculators, savings and loan bust-out artists, and takeover specialists marched on the bastions of inherited wealth to stake their claim to personal fortunes. Added to this decidedly antielitist feeding frenzy was a newly discovered social type: the Asian immigrant entrepreneur. As political analyst Kevin Phillips has observed, "outsider access" to the economy made possible by the "Reagan revolution" was "ethnically spiced by Vietnamese-American shrimp wholesalers, Korean greengrocers and Asian high-tech entrepreneurs."[61]

This theme is no better illustrated than by the Gospel of No Money Down Real Estate preached by Tom Vu on television "infomercials" that tout his free wealth-acquisition seminars.[62] Arriving in the United States a penniless Vietnamese immigrant with minimal English skills, Vu claims that he was able to parlay modest profits made from the buying and selling of "distressed property" into a vast real estate empire. As he stands next to luxury automobiles or lounges on a yacht surrounded by buxom, bikinied beauties, Vu offers to share his secrets of wealth to those willing to join him in the pursuit of personal riches. According to a former Vu instructor, the majority of Vu's students are men in their late twenties to thirties who hope to earn money enough to buy fancy cars and attract women.

Clearly a large part of Tom Vu's appeal stems from his mythic rise from humble origins. Tom Vu—born Tuan Ahn Vu—along with his parents and nine siblings, fled South Vietnam after the communist takeover in 1975. They first arrived at a refugee camp in Florida and then worked at a variety of menial jobs in order to survive. Vu followed the example of his father, who had traded in real estate in Saigon, and bought his first house in Orlando, Florida, for $20,000. Vu claims to have made the bulk of his personal fortune from real estate investments, but since 1983 he has conducted seminars across the country to share the secret of wealth creation. As reported on the TV newsmagazine *48 Hours,* the Vietnamese American real estate tycoon has now moved into the field of higher education with the founding of the "Tom Vu Wealth Creation University."[63] From there he will spread the gospel of entrepreneurial capitalism in courses of one, two, or five days' duration.

"I think people like me because my advice is simple and because I'm entertaining," Vu claims. "People tell me that watching my show is better than going to the movies."[64] But there are storm clouds looming over Tom Vu's real estate seminar empire. The Florida attorney general is investigating accusations of deceptive trade practices lodged by a number of former students who were promised financial partnership in select transactions. In addition, the attorney general is also trying to determine whether Vu has broken any laws by neglecting to register his businesses with the state of Florida.

Resurrection of Fu Manchu

There is perhaps no other contemporary Asian figure more recognizable to the American public than the Reverend Sun Myung Moon of the Unification Church. During the 1970s, scenes of mass weddings between couples who had been handpicked by the founder of the Holy Spirit Association for the Unification of World Christianity were regularly reported on network television news broadcasts. At a well-publicized Unification ceremony held in 1975, 120 American couples were wed among a convocation of 1,800 church adherents.[65] By the end of the 1980s, the term *Moonies* had entered the language and become synonymous with individuals who had fallen under the hypnotic sway of the Unification Church. Moonies were regarded as having succumbed to insidious mind-control or "brainwashing" techniques practiced by church members. Like Dr. Fu Manchu before him, the power possessed by the Reverend Sun Myung Moon threatened to enslave the Western mind.

During the Cold War, a journalist and CIA operative named Edward Hunter introduced the concept of brainwashing to the American public. In an article published in the *Miami News* (September 1950) titled " 'Brain-Washing' Tactics Force Chinese into Ranks of Communist Party," the Chinese concept of *hsi-nao* (to cleanse the mind) was given a more sinister connotation by Hunter. The CIA agent popularized the notion of "brainwashing" to account for the fact that fully 70 percent of the 7,190 U.S. prisoners of war held in China either confessed to various crimes or called for an end to the American military presence in Asia.

Among U.S. POWs, 15 percent collaborated with their Chinese captors. The high rate of confession and mass denunciation of U.S. war crimes in Asia by the POWs (including the alleged practice of germ warfare) was an embarrassment to the U.S. government and cried out for explanation. Rather than recant once they returned home to the United States, many former POWs refused to disavow their confessions. "Puzzled and dismayed by this wholesale collapse of morale among the POWs," writes John Marks, "American opinion leaders settled in on Edward Hunter's explanation: The Chinese had somehow brainwashed our boys."[66]

The esteemed Robert Jay Lifton, who had worked in a U.S. military program to study the effects of "brainwashing," lent scientific respectability to the concept in his study *Thought Reform and the Psychology of Totalism* (1961).[67] Lifton's observations, however, were but a scientific recasting and updating of the deep-seated Euro-American fear of the inscrutable Oriental Mind that has its roots in the abhorrence of the "yellow peril" dating back to the mid-nineteenth century. In the popular culture, brainwashing techniques are held to be the unique property of Asians, from the evil Dr. Fu Manchu to the Reverend Sun Myung Moon. Other Asian-derived "cults" such as the Rajneeshis in Oregon, Nichiren Shoshu of America, and the International Society for Krishna Consciousness have been accused of employing similar methods to win converts and expand the numbers of zombielike adherents. In some instances, anticult organizations have been enlisted to "deprogram" converts to nontraditional Asian religious organizations. In the mid-1970s, for example, the Freedom of Thought Foundation based in Tucson, Arizona, attempted to win court-ordered conservatorships for the parents of five adult members of the Unification Church in California so that they could undergo "reality therapy" administered by mental health professionals.[68]

For all the social hysteria that has attended the rise of cult activity in recent years, a PBS *Frontline* documentary—*The Resurrection of Reverend Moon* (1992)—reveals that the American public has less to fear from Asian masters of mind control than it does from the U.S. government itself, which routinely subverts democratic processes with help from overseas political clients.[69] The documentary gathers an impressive array of information, evidence, and personal interviews that points to the complicity of government agencies, including the U.S. Department of Justice, in allowing the Unification

Church to execute its right-wing political agenda in direct violation of federal law, specifically, the Foreign Agent's Registration Act.

This tale of religiopolitical intrigue began with the mysterious appearance of a little-known organization that identified itself as the American Freedom Coalition (AFC) in Rapid City, South Dakota. The coalition offered to help a local organization sponsor a "support our troops" march and rally for Operation Desert Storm in 1990. Unbeknownst to rally organizers, the American Freedom Coalition was linked to the Unification Church. Douglas Weed, a special assistant to President George Bush who served as liaison to conservative groups, asserts that the AFC was heavily involved in the 1988 presidential campaign. At its own expense, the organization printed and distributed a massive volume of campaign literature in support of presidential candidate George Bush. Moreover, the AFC over the years has supported right-wing initiatives and policies by funneling tens of millions of dollars through a wide array of conservative think tanks, publishing concerns, and political action committees.

In 1977, the Reverend Sun Myung Moon attracted the attention of a congressional investigation committee headed by Representative Donald M. Fraser, a Minnesota Democrat. In the so-called Koreagate investigation, which in part probed the relationship between the Unification Church and the Korean Central Intelligence Agency, the Fraser Committee concluded that Moon's international organization "had systematically violated U.S. tax, immigration, banking, currency and Foreign Agents Registration Act laws." In 1982, Moon was convicted and imprisoned for thirteen months in federal prison on charges of conspiracy and filing false tax returns.

Despite his checkered past, the Reverend Sun Myung Moon has become a major player in Washington, D.C., political circles. His organization has contributed generously to a number of conservative causes, including the Nicaraguan Freedom Fund headed by National Security Council staffer Lieutenant Colonel Oliver North. The privately raised funds were to be used in support of the contras after Congress had cut off (but subsequently restored) financial assistance in October 1984. The American Freedom Coalition even picked up the $200,000 expense of producing a 1950s-vintage nuclear attack fantasy titled *One Incoming*. The film was designed to win support for the Strategic Defense Initiative ("Star Wars") being promoted by President Ronald Reagan at the time. Author Tom Clancy wrote the scenario for the film (which aired on more than 400 television stations), and archconservative diehard Charlton Heston was pressed into service to do voice-overs.

Through Unification Church ownership of the *Washington*

Times, the New Right was given an ideological forum previously denied to them in the nation's capital because of the overwhelming influence wielded by the *Washington Post.* New Right columnist Patrick Buchanan brought the newspaper much-needed credibility and respect by appearing regularly as a commentator on the Cable News Network. But former editor and publisher James Whelan soon decried the lack of his paper's journalistic independence under Moon's ownership. Whelan complained that Moon and his chief associate, a former South Korean military officer named Bo Hi Pak, had turned the *Washington Times* into a "Moonie newspaper."

In his rise from poverty and triumph over adversity, the unlikely career of the Reverend Sun Myung Moon is an Asian American success story. But there is more to the tale. It seems that since the early 1960s, Moon has maintained close ties with right-wing political and business interests in Japan. Their shared anticommunist agenda served as a means of enforcing postwar social solidarity while rebuilding monopoly capitalist institutions. One of Moon's more prominent sponsors was a "Class A" war criminal named Ryoichi Sasakawa, who controls a $14-billion-a-year legal gambling monopoly in the sport of motorboat racing. Two of Sasakawa's closest associates have been fellow suspected war criminals: Yoshio Kodama, perhaps best known in the United States for his role in the Lockheed bribery scandal, became a prominent *yakuza* leader after the war and enjoyed direct access to the highest reaches of the Japanese government; Nobusuke Kishi, imprisoned by U.S. authorities as a suspected war criminal but never brought to trial, later became prime minister of Japan and an ardent supporter of the United States and its policies of anticommunist military containment combined with the economic development of Southeast Asian countries along capitalist lines.

The Resurrection of Reverend Moon makes it obvious that the Far Eastern Messiah has used his religious infrastructure and allied businesses to build and maintain a bridge between the postwar Japanese power elite and the American political establishment, including the New Right. At present, the U.S. Department of Justice remains singularly uninterested in investigating whether the American Freedom Coalition and the Unification Church might be in violation of the Foreign Agent's Registration Act. Neither is the U.S. Congress willing to convene an investigatory panel to look into possible illegal activity committed by Moon's multifarious business empire. It might well be that the right-wing, anticommunist religiopolitical might of the Unification Church and its spin-offs provides crucial services to a government that routinely engages in antidemocratic, covert activity both at home and abroad.[70] Not only was the Reverend Sun Myung Moon's Unification Church "plugged into Reagan's conservative Washington," but several staff writers for the *Washington Times* had also worked for the National Security Agency.[71] It is no mere coincidence that the *Washington Times* under editor Arnaud de Borchgrave contributed $100,000 to Oliver North's Nicaraguan Freedom Fund to assist the so-called freedom fighters in their counterrevolution against the Sandinistas.

Yellow Martyrdom

The Reverend Sun Myung Moon presents a dilemma for the Asian American community: although Moon is portrayed on television as the latter-day embodiment of the diabolical Asian evil genius Dr. Fu Manchu, the nature and scope of Moon's religiopolitical enterprise poses a very real threat to basic democratic processes. During a $75 million "New Birth Campaign" designed to restore a public image tarnished by criminal convictions and a subsequent prison term, Moon exploited his Asianness by claiming racial and religious persecution at the hands of U.S. government authorities who put him behind bars. Yet well-organized white Christian evangelists collect vast sums of money each year with impugnity, operate large media companies such as the Reverend Pat Robertson's Christian Broadcasting Network (CBN), and attempt to influence government policy.[72] Given the history of intolerance toward Asians in American society, there is good reason to believe that in the case of the Reverend Sun Myung Moon there might indeed be a racial double standard at work.

But the issue of Moon's being persecuted on the basis of "race" is of only secondary importance within the larger context of postwar international power politics. That is, Moon appears to be a minor player in a much more Byzantine scenario. Since the end of World War II, South Korea has been one of the key U.S. client states in East Asia, along with Taiwan, the Philippines, Thailand, and Indonesia (under General Suharto).[73] South Korea, with its repressive U.S.-backed political regime, is very much the product of U.S. business investment, economic aid, and military occupation. As an installment of the excellent PBS series *The Pacific Century* (1992) explains, since the time of the Korean War the United States has played a key role in supporting an authoritarian state capitalist system that has pursued rapid industrial development at the expense of human rights and democratic freedoms.[74]

The militaristic right-wing anticommunist agenda of Moon and the Unification Church also has been of vital strategic importance to Japan, whose postwar economic recovery to a large extent was made possible by heavy U.S. military spending during the Korean War. U.S. sponsorship of the Vietnam War further relieved Japan from shouldering the burden of nonproductive military expenditures, expenditures that have weakened, perhaps irreparably, the American economy. In his magisterial historical survey that both chronicles and explains the "rise and fall" of the great modern nation-states, Paul Kennedy observes that the U.S.-maintained defensive perimeter has worked to the advantage of the Japanese economy. In living behind the shield of American nuclear and conventional military might, Japan has been be able to "redirect its national energies from militaristic expansion and its resources from high defense spending" and instead has pursued economic growth through the manufacture and export of consumer goods.[75]

Authors George Friedman and Meredith Lebard, in *The Coming War with Japan* (1991), make a similar claim that the Korean War was instrumental in the "resurrection" of the Japanese economy, which had grown moribund before the manufactured hostilities began. The megamultinational Japanese corporations that have come to dominate the world economy "were saved from extinction by the Korean War," write Friedman and Lebard.[76] It is no small wonder, then, that the Japanese capitalist *zaibatsu* (corporate oligopolies) that reemerged after the war relatively intact found the high level of U.S. military spending compatible with their own economic goals. The perceived threat posed by the Soviet Union and their East Asian communist allies provided the necessary justification for both the United States and Japan to forge a "co-prosperity sphere" of their own in a postwar world order keyed to a permanent war economy. That U.S. military spending quadrupled from $13.7 billion in 1950 to $52.8 billion in 1953 demonstrates the material efficacy of the "red scare" campaign waged, again, on media such as network television.[77]

As in the case of Japan, the precipitous growth of the South Korean economy commenced from the period of heavy U.S. military involvement in Vietnam. For South Korea, Noam Chomsky notes, the Vietnam War generated "some 20% of its foreign exchange earnings," which included meeting the payroll for "300,000 mercenaries introduced from January 1965 to 'defend South Vietnam' by terrorizing its population."[78] More dispassionately, Ivan Light and Edna Bonacich document the massive amounts of financial support extended by the United States to South Korea in the form of civilian grants-in-aid, public loans, and military assistance. In military aid alone, South Korea received a total of $6.5 to $7 billion from 1945 to 1975 and continues to be one of the chief recipients of U.S. strategic largesse.[79]

The Reverend Sun Myung Moon and his Unification Church are but the "spiritual" manifestation of the concrete political-economic relationship between the United States and its partner in Asia, Japan. South Korea, as one of the capitalist newly industrializing countries, or "Little Tigers," is to be a junior partner in the grand arrangement.[80] Moon's divine mission on earth has been to convince both the American public and the military-corporate-governmental power elite of its duty to protect God-fearing nations from the maleficent intentions of the communist scourge to the north. Moon and his organization have undertaken this daunting task by using their extensive media holdings to spread their message of Christian anticommunism. As Bo Hi Pak emphasized in a 1984 television interview, the use of the media by the Unification Church is crucial to the anticommunist crusade: "It is a total war. Basically, a war of ideas. War of mind. The battlefield is the human mind. . . . That is what the Third World War is all about. The war of ideology." It is a war in which Moon and his presumed "enemies" in the mainstream media share strikingly similar objectives.

Chapter 7

Counterprogramming

They All Look Alike

When represented at all, Asian Americans on network television programs exist primarily for the convenience and benefit of the Euro-American lead players. By and large, TV Asians are inserted in programs chiefly as semantic markers that reflect upon and reveal telling aspects of the Euro-American characters alone. Rarely are the lives of Asian American characters examined on their own merit, and the problems they face in daily life are not considered to be of intrinsic interest. On most of network television, as in the larger social world, meaning begins and ends with the cares and concerns of the dominant group and its members. All other subordinate groups, including Asian Americans, are held in close orbit to Euro-American "stars," revolving around the heliocentric universe of the dominant white figures.

At first glance, African Americans seem to be the one nonwhite group to have overcome marginalization on network television. African American sports figures, newscasters, talk-show hosts, entertainers, and actors are by now fixtures on television. Moreover, a number of network TV shows have featured African Americans, many of which have been enormously popular with the general audience. But even then, the story lines and characters are evaluated and accepted on the basis of how they relate to mainstream television programs and to the dominant society at large. That is, the popular appeal of programs such as *The Cosby Show* (1984–92) and *Fresh Prince of Bel Air* (1990–present) stems from their congruity with upper-middle-class Euro-American values, but given an African American tinge.[1]

Rare is the case where Asian or Asian American characters are portrayed in an overtly racist manner. Indeed, Euro-American lead characters unfailingly go out of their way to ensure that no physical or emotional harm befalls their darker brothers through acts of prejudice or racist hate. Rather, television portrayals of Asian Americans operate on the basis of what Stuart Hall has described as "inferential racism." Hall refers to the "apparently naturalised representations of events and situations relating to race . . . which have racist premises and propositions inscribed in them as a set of *unquestioned assumptions*."[2] Such assumptions allow a racist subtext to be communicated without indulging in the explicit rhetoric characteristic of demogogues or hate groups.

Network television has been singularly incapable of representing the full humanity of Asian Americans. This is not necessarily because individual writers, producers, or executives are racist. Indeed, many if not most of the creative people working in network television probably exhibit higher tolerance for racial and other forms of diversity than the general public. But because network television is a creature of the supranational interests of media oligopolies, one of its implicit functions is to provide ideological legitimacy for an unstable, crisis-ridden advanced capitalist social order that ever threatens to fragment along class, gender, age, and racial lines. Network television personnel must therefore adhere to the "basic entertainment creed" as articulated by David L. Paletz and Robert M. Entman: "Hew to the familiar social values and practices, long-socialized by all cultural institutions (including the media themselves). This awakens recognition and identification (and prevents disturbance) of the widest possible audience."[3] So long as network television maintains its structural relationship to the inner workings of oligopoly capitalism, there is little hope that Asian American representations will change for the better.

Given the inherent inability of the market-driven, for-profit networks to service the competing needs of a racially and ethnically diverse audience, it has been primarily public-sector television that has given nondominant groups such as Asian Americans the wherewithal to represent the lives of their own communities. Since its creation by the Public Broadcasting Act of 1967, the Corporation for Public Broadcasting (CPB) has served as a nongovernmental entity that allocates federal monies to individual radio and television stations whose constituency comprises underserved groups such as the poor, minorities, and children. Established by the CPB, the Public Broadcasting Service (PBS) and National Public Radio (NPR) are responsible for maintaining the network of noncommercial stations on a nationwide basis.

Though woefully underfunded in comparison to the networks, the Corporation for Public Broadcasting through PBS has done much to support programming that depicts the fullness of ethnic minority life, including that of Asian Pacific Americans. The Corporation for Public Broadcasting, however, is not immune to external political pressures. Conservative congressmen such as Robert Dole (R-Kansas) and John McCain (R-Arizona), for example, have sided with right-wing interest groups in contending that PBS, especially in its public affairs programming, exhibits a "leftist bias." The conservative Heritage Foundation has even argued for the elimination of public-supported television, which is budgeted for a paltry $275 million in 1994.[4]

Nor is the Corporation for Public Broadcasting without its detractors on the left. An editorial published in *The Nation* went so far as to lump the CPB with "propaganda voices of the cold war" such as Radio Liberty, Radio Free Europe, Radio and TV Martí, Worldnet T.V., and Voice of America. Apparently, the partial corporate sponsorship of such programs as *The MacNeil/Lehrer NewsHour*, *Wall Street Week*, and *Morning Edition* is enough to discredit the CPB in its entirety. As a cost-saving measure under the Clinton administration, the editors of *The Nation* suggest that the federally funded CPB be made to "run foreign as well as domestic propaganda services."[5] PBS was further criticized by filmmaker Barbara Trent, whose *Panama Deception* won an Academy Award for best feature-length documentary. During an acceptance speech at the 1993 award ceremonies, Trent dedicated her Oscar to the "millions of Americans who may or may not get to see this film now that public TV has refused to broadcast it."[6] Executive producer Ellen Schneider of *P.O.V.*, a PBS program that features independently produced documentaries, rejected *Panama Deception* for airing without providing an explanation. The selection committee, however, was said to have had serious reservations about authorizing such a politically sensitive documentary to air.

War of Meaning

One of the early challenges to the "leftist bias" of public television was posed by the conservative media watchdog group Accuracy in Media (AIM) in reaction to the PBS series *Vietnam: A Television History* (1983). Veteran journalist Stanley Karnow served as chief correspondent for the series and also wrote the best-selling companion volume *Vietnam: A History*, which was advertised as "The First Complete Account of Vietnam at War."[7] Funded in part by the National Endowment for the Humanities, *Television's Vietnam* (1985) was a 120-minute two-part rebuttal to the PBS series and was hosted by none other than Charlton Heston.[8]

Produced by WGBH-TV Boston at a cost of $5 million, the Emmy Award-winning (six total) multipart *Vietnam: A Television History* was the brainchild of Lawrence Grossberg, who, as president of PBS, hatched the idea in 1978.[9] With the authoritative tenor voice of narrator Will Lyman accompanied by the eerie percussion-dominated score by Grateful Dead drummers Micky Hart and Billy Kreutzmann, filmed images of "history's first television war" were brought into brutal relief. One of the thirteen installments covered the 1968 Tet offensive, during which North Vietnamese guerrillas breached the U.S. embassy compound in Saigon.[10] Trying to maintain an outward show of calm as soldiers root out the last remaining communist infiltrators, General William Westmoreland is visibly startled by an explosion while being interviewed on camera. The general smiles nervously and tries to downplay the seriousness of the assault on the once-inviolable embassy compound, an incident that many observers view as the turning point in the Vietnam War.

A scene showing an ARVN soldier stealing money from a Viet Cong corpse and laughing with glee at his good fortune seems emblematic of the disdain many GIs felt for their South Vietnamese allies, who were viewed as being militarily ineffectual, corrupt, and generally undeserving of U.S. support. Shots of elderly Vietnamese civilians being burned in their homes and atrocities committed during the Battle of Hue completely demolish the veracity of sanitized network news reports and documentaries that were produced for domestic consumption during the war.

Produced by Accuracy in Media, Inc., *Television's Vietnam* was aired in the summer of 1985 with the stated intention of "setting the historical record straight," according to narrator Charlton Heston.[11] Douglas Pike, director of the Indochina Archive at the University of California, Berkeley, claims to have served as a consultant to the PBS program. But Pike condemns *Vietnam: A Television History* for being being flawed methodologically and for its distortion of history through its "kaleidoscope of images." Most important, there is "nothing in the series that an American can be proud of," says Pike.

Reed Irvine, chairman of Accuracy in Media, appears on camera to denounce the PBS series for its failure to connect U.S. military involvement in Vietnam with the "imposition of communist rule over all of Indochina." The bulk of Part 1, "The Real Story," is devoted to the observations of assorted experts who mouth the conventional wisdom of the contempory American right. Stephen Morris, attached to the University of California's Institute of East Asian Studies, contends that Ho Chi Minh was no mere "nationalist," but a "communist" internationalist who therefore posed a "security threat" to the United States. Dolf Droge of the infamous Agency for International Development condemns Ho Chi Minh for the ruthlessness of his dealings with Vietnamese nationalists.

A number of South Vietnamese refugees now living in the United States were offended by the PBS series, claims Nguyen Ngoc Bich of the Georgetown University Center for Bilingual Education. Charlton Heston protests that "our friends" the South Vietnamese are depicted as the bad guys in the series. Especially unflattering is the portrayal of Prime Minister Ngo Dinh Diem. Heston, however, neglects to mention that President Kennedy, through U.S. Ambassador to South Vietnam Henry Cabot Lodge, assisted in the coup d'état that did away with Diem. Ever the anticommunist Cold War crusader, Heston often lapses into rhetorical flourishes reminiscent of the 1950s: "Through all this PBS melodrama of heroes and villains, there's no hint that two ways of life—one based on freedom the other on communism—were struggling for the future of Indochina."

Heston also criticizes the PBS documentary series for having painted a "pretty dark picture of the American military in Vietnam." Again, the U.S. military mission in Southeast Asia is defended by the well-worn themes and images invoked to blunt objective analysis and excuse American genocide. Captain John McCain, a Naval aviator and former POW who now represents the state of Arizona in the U.S. Congress, claims that there were only "isolated" instances of American brutality in the field. The obligatory film clip of "Hanoi" Jane Fonda touring North Vietnam is shown as McCain castigates the former social activist, Ramsey Clark, and other antiwar protesters for giving comfort to the enemy.

Shortly before the conclusion of Part 1, a parallel is drawn between the debacle in Vietnam and the more recent U.S. involvement in Central America. This time around, important lessons have been learned that will allow the United States to hold the line against communism. But the battle can be won only if the free press is somehow squelched. Says Irvine, "One of the great lessons of the Vietnam War was that the enemy was able to use our free uncontrolled media to achieve their own objective." Heston concludes by denying that military weakness decided the outcome of the war. Rather, "words—disinformation, deception—were the deciding factors in the Vietnam War," says Heston.

Part 2, "The Impact of the Media," features a parade of right-wing and neoconservative observers who blame the messenger for the U.S. defeat in Vietnam. These figures include the neoconservative editor of *Commentary*, Norman Podhoretz, and editor in chief of the *Washington Times* (the "Moonie" newspaper) Arnaud de

Borchgrave, whose sympathy for right-wing causes is well known. "Many believe that our will to win was eroded by the way our media – especially television – reported the war," says Heston.[12]

The dubious notion that the print media and television were responsible for the U.S. defeat in Vietnam appeared in *The Big Story* (1977) by Peter Braestrup, a detailed analysis of the Tet offensive and its coverage by the press.[13] A 1981 *Commentary* article by novelist and *Los Angeles Times* correspondent Robert Elegant later echoed the argument. In particular, the pessimistic reportage of CBS news anchor Walter Cronkite is singled out as having helped turn the tide of public opinion against the war.

The mass slaughter of Vietnamese civilians is explained away by "military historian" Tom Carhart, who dismisses the My Lai massacre as simply a "tragic accident of war." Irvine asks why the communist killing of civilians at the battle of Hue was underreported yet the My Lai massacre was given extensive news coverage. Heston speaks of the "horrendous communist atrocity" at Hue as being "downplayed" by the U.S. media. Ben Wattenberg of the ultraconservative American Enterprise Institute calls attention to acts of "genocide" (his term) committed by the Soviet Union in Afganistan. He observes that while the Soviets safely escape domestic criticism because state-run media institutions exercise control and censorship of the news, the U.S. press enjoys no such constraints. Because of this disparity between the two systems, Wattenberg concludes that the U.S. press is responsible for nothing less than changing the "balance of power" in international relations.

PBS has on occasion bowed to pressure exerted by right-wing advocacy groups, as in the case of the documentary *Stop the Church* (1991). *P.O.V.*, the left-leaning showcase for independent films, withdrew the documentary from the national schedule in late 1991 after being urged to do so by PBS.[14] But for the most part, PBS has managed to preserve its autonomy and commitment to quality public sector television whose mandate is to present programming that is free of the limitations imposed by the commercial marketplace. It would be inconceivable, for example, that the networks would dare broadcast a full-length documentary on the public health disaster created by the U.S. bombing of Iraq as shown in *The War We Left Behind* (1991), reported by Andrew and Leslie Cockburn.[15] Nor is it likely that the fundamental issues of race and sexuality would ever be so honestly addressed as in *Tongues Untied* (1989) by Marlon Riggs, also aired as part of the innovative series *P.O.V.*[16] Despite the formidable pressure applied by various and sundry right-wing religious and political advocacy groups during the Reagan-Bush era,

PBS has done remarkably well in supporting programs that allow nondominant groups to represent themselves in both dramatic and nonfiction television forms.

Asian American Playhouse

For more than a decade, PBS has produced the exemplary dramatic anthology series *American Playhouse* (1982–present). The series has presented the work of the finest talent in American letters, including Mark Twain, Eugene O'Neill, James Baldwin, and John Cheever. With the airing of the KCET-TV Los Angeles coproduction *Hot Summer Winds* in 1991, a previously little-known *Nisei* writer named Hisaye Yamamoto joined the pantheon of American literary giants whose works have been anthologized by *American Playhouse*.[17] Based upon two short stories that convey the subtle shadings and textures of prewar rural Japanese American life, *Hot Summer Winds* was adapted for television by writer-director Emiko Omori.[18]

Hot Summer Winds is narrated by the adult child of an emotionally estranged farm couple. Yoneko (Jeanne Mori) harkens back to her childhood during the summer of 1934 and tells of the tension between her barely literate father Takahashi "Tex" Hosoume (Sab Shimono) and his wife Hatsu (Natsuko Ohama), who is well educated and holds literary aspirations. The harshness of farm life and dissimilar social backgrounds leave an isolated Takahashi alone at night in the tool shed finding solace in the bootleg liquor he produces, while Hatsu—writing under the *nom de plume* Hanamoto Ume (Plum Blossom)—loses herself in the poetry enjoyed in the company of country aesthetes who gather at the Hosoume home to critique one another's work.

One day a well-traveled Filipino laborer named Marpo (Pepe Serna) breezes into the lives of the Hosoumes to help with the seasonal harvest. He is a worldly man of many talents who even builds the Hosoume children a crude radio receiver from scratch. Tex and Marpo get along famously at first, more like boon companions than boss and employee. They drink, play cards, and share liquor-fueled dreams of a better life as shots of Hatsu luxuriating in a steaming hot *furo* (Japanese bathtub) are intercut with scenes of the two men carrying on through the night. Marpo rhapsodizes that his ideal life would include owning a farm, having a Japanese wife, and employing a Chinese cook.

As the family prepares the season's crop for market, Teruo Kuroda (Yuji Okumoto), the poetry editor of a Japanese-language newspaper, arrives at the Hosoume farm seeking Hanamoto Ume. Kuroda announces that she has won a poetry competition and presents Hatsu with a scroll as a prize. All the while, Tex looks on with resentment. As Tex and the children are crating produce for shipment, Hatsu invites the hot and sweaty editor inside for refreshments. Fuming mad by now, Tex sends the journalist packing and then gathers Hatsu's writing instruments along with the scroll and sets them on fire.

An act of nature assists Marpo in realizing at least one of his dreams when an earthquake strikes and, unbeknownst to the Hosoume family, Tex is stranded in town after being slightly injured. After having dinner with Hatsu and the children, Marpo shows off the radio he has built. He invites Hatsu to don the headset and listen to the barely audible music coming over the airwaves. They sit side by side, sharing a single earphone, straining to hear a weak broadcast signal that keeps drifting in and out. Suddenly, they become aware of each other's physical closeness and quickly move apart.

That same sultry summer evening, Hatsu walks by Marpo's shack on her way to the *furo*. In a highly eroticized scene, Hatsu takes a long, slow bath, languorously laddling the soothingly warm water over her tired body. As she washes herself, fleeting images of Hatsu wearing a fresh *yukata* (a light cotton summer garment) and happily drinking tea with Marpo in his room punctuate the bathhouse tableau. When the scene shifts to Hatsu and Marpo engaged in lovemaking, a skillfully executed cinematic prolepsis leaves it unclear whether the actual deed has been done or if it has been realized in the mind of the wife/poet alone.

Tex, who has suffered an injury to his arm, is brought home the next day by the grocer Yosh Oka (Dennis Sakamoto). Upon his return, Tex observes a new level of intimacy shared between Marpo and Hatsu. As Hatsu washes her hair, a passing Marpo stops to pour the water that rinses the soap away. Soon thereafter, Tex sends Marpo packing when the farmhand intervenes in an argument between the boss and his wife. The young Yoneko (Tricia Joe) and her brother Seigo (Rand Takeuchi) are sad to see their engaging friend leave.

It is not too long after Marpo's forced departure that Hatsu informs her husband that she is pregnant. Tex is incredulous, knowing full well that he is not the father of the child. After the family makes a surreptitious visit to a doctor in town, Hatsu remains bedridden for a long while, implying that she has submitted to an abortion. Tex makes the children swear that they will tell no one about the incident. After Hatsu's crisis, the typically autocratic, emotionally distant, patriarchal *Issei* farmer's attitude toward his wife appears to soften. This is seen when Tex surprises Hatsu with a new writing set ordered from a catalog. The adult narrator Yoneko recalls fondly how she could hear her mother's pen scratching against paper late into the night as the household slept.

What strikes the viewer most about *Hot Summer Winds* is that the Japanese American community it portrays is self-contained and exists without reference to the larger white society. Only the transient Marpo links the Hosoume household with the wider world. Nor is there a single Euro-American intercessor in evidence to ensure mainstream "audience identification" and confer meaning upon the tale. The characters speak for themselves without external mediation. Indeed, the outside world does not seem to exist within the isolated confines of Japanese American farm life save for the music of distant radio broadcasts or the occasional rural route delivery of a mail-order purchase. While the travails of the Hosoume family may not be of earth-shattering magnitude so far as U.S. national history is concerned, the small truths laid bare in *Hot Summer Winds* nonetheless convey the poetry of rural Japanese American community life before the coming of the war that was to tear this world asunder.

Lethal Aid

The willful ignorance of even the most well-intentioned of liberals is the subject of the *American Playhouse* presentation *Lethal Innocence* (1991).[19] Unlike most feature-length network productions, *Lethal Innocence* establishes the historical basis of the personal story being dramatized, that of a Cambodian refugee who has been adopted by an altruistic Vermont couple. Even more noteworthy, the program rips through the usual liberal pieties and takes the American people to task for their tacit acceptance of U.S. military policy in Southeast Asia.

The program opens with a series of photographs that document the devastating effects of the U.S. "secret" bombing of Cambodia, which began in March 1969 on orders from President Richard M. Nixon in collusion with his national security adviser, Dr. Henry Kissinger. By the end of the air war against Cambodia, a total of 110,000 tons of bombs had been dropped on a supposedly neutral country on the pretext of incapacitating NVA supply lines and encampments. Photographs of B-52s releasing their twenty- to thirty-ton payloads are juxtaposed with shots of desolate cities emptied by the Khmer Rouge and pictures of Cambodian holocaust victims, whose numbers totaled an estimated one million.

Lethal Innocence at first leads the viewer to assume that the program is but another self-congratulatory exercise applauding American humanitarian aid to the "Third World" peoples the United States has been responsible for displacing. The opening scene, with British relief worker Vinnie Moore (Brenda Fricker) jumping out of an International Red Cross vehicle on a mission of mercy at a Khmer Rouge-controlled refugee camp, seems to confirm all suspicions. But as it turns out, Vinnie Moore unflinchingly blames the United States of America and its lethally innocent citizens for the Cambodian holocaust.

Sally Hatch (Blair Brown) and husband Mark (Kevin Coleman) are representative of the many Americans who suffer from the "lethal innocence" that prevents them from understanding the root causes of the Cambodian holocaust and the refugee population it created. Sally and Mark Hatch are persuaded to care for a Cambodian teenager named Sirik Nheth (Vathana Biv) after he is rejected by his original adoptive parents because of his antisocial behavior. Margaret (Amy Wright) and Dave Stokely (Neil Maffin) are unaware that Sirik's outbursts are caused by the guilt he feels at having left his family behind in a Thai refugee camp.

Vinnie Moore works to reunite Sirik with his family, but is hampered by new racially based laws limiting the number of Cambodians entering the United States. "It seems like your country is afraid the whole country is just being overrun with immigrants," Moore explains to Sally and Mark Hatch. "And so very, very few—I mean, yes, especially Asians—are getting in now." To gain admission to the country, one must either be classified as a "political refugee" or have a "sponsor" who can provide a place to live and extend financial support.

Moore's anger at the hypocrisy of the U.S. government spills over into a heated exchange with Sally. "You'd think Washington would take some responsibility for a situation they helped create in the first place, wouldn't you?" says Moore. Sally is quick to defend her country, arguing that "we've done more than most. . . . All the boat people and the children we've taken in." "Well, measure that against the thousands of lives destroyed and you come up a little short, don't you?" Moore snaps.

Sally responds with a mealymouthed excuse for her government's role by explaining that the war in Vietnam "sort of spilled over" into Cambodia. "That's what happens in war." Digusted by Sally's insouciant naïveté, Moore sarcastically comments, "How inconvenient if you just happen to be in the neighborhood of an American war." Moore bluntly suggests that Sally do more reading about Cambodia and the part the United States actively played in the holocaust. Sally walks off in a huff and sulks over the encounter.

Vinnie Moore and Sally Hatch manage to patch things up and later begin a joint effort to have the entire town of Meeker, Vermont, "sponsor" Cambodian refugees. Even so, Moore is loath to absolve Sally Hatch of personal responsibility in the silent acceptance of government policy in Southeast Asia. "You make it seem as if it's my fault and I could barely vote when what happened in Cambodia happened," says Sally. Moore responds with an impassioned speech that strikes at the heart of the issue:

> Sally, since you *could* vote, your country has provided money and arms and training to fuel a civil war in Cambodia in which hundreds of thousands of people have been killed. And do you want to know which side you've been helping for the last twelve years? You've been helping the Khmer Rouge. The Khmer Rouge; the Khmer Rouge who are guilty of the worst genocide since Hitler. And you didn't care enough to find out about that, did you? . . . Sally, it's just too easy to blame the government. It's too easy to point the finger at the Richard Nixons and the Henry Kissingers who wage their secret wars and kill millions of people. But who elects these people? Who votes for those people and lets them do those things unchecked?

Moore's speech is a harsh indictment of the United States, which even today officially recognizes the legitimacy of the Khmer Rouge. As early as 1979, William Shawcross specifically had named Nixon and Kissinger as the principal architects of the Cambodian holocaust, who, in acting "without care," were responsible for the "catastrophe" that resulted from large-scale bombing attacks.[20] It is inconceivable, however, that such views as articulated by Vinnie Moore would ever find expression on network television, in fictional form or otherwise. And if a minority of powerful conservative lobbies and political interest have their way, public television would also be prevented from airing observations and ideas that depart from state-approved orthodoxy.

Vinnie Moore, Sally Hatch, and the citizens of Meeker achieve their goal of reuniting Sirik with his family. Mark Hatch goes so far as to search for Sirik's sister in Thailand after she had been sold into sex slavery to a Thai gangster. Although the reunion between Sirik Nheth and his family is an occasion for joy, a superimposed message reminds the viewer of the many more refugees whose lives remain in limbo: "Today, Sirik Nheth and his family live in Vermont. They are thriving. 350,000 other Cambodians are not."[21]

Family Doughnut Ties

The lives of three different Cambodian American refugee families are the subject of the award-winning documentary *Cambodian Doughnut Dreams* (1990).[22] Aired on KCET-TV Los Angeles during the station's "Asian Pacific American Month," the film was written and directed by Charles Davis and produced by the students at the University of Southern California School of Cinema-Television. Davis, a medical doctor by profession who works at an East Los Angeles clinic, first had the notion of making a film about the urban underclass and started frequenting doughnut shops as a first step in the project. Instead, Davis became intrigued by the proprietors of the doughnut stores, who were overwhelmingly Cambodian American. As he gradually came to learn about their lives, the subject of the original film shifted. "Then I thought, 'Maybe I'll make a *shoah*,' " Davis explains, "a film about the holocaust."[23] The forty-six-year-old physician had spent time with the Peace Corps in Thailand during 1969–70 and observed firsthand the consequences of U.S. military intervention in Southeast Asia. "I related to the Cambodian holocaust because I was born Jewish and I had read a good deal about the Holocaust in Europe," says Davis. Because the United States formally supports the Khmer Rouge, Davis is concerned that the genocide might well begin anew.

As the film opens, narrator Davis states that more than 80 percent of the doughnut shops in Los Angeles are either owned or managed by Cambodian Americans. Amidst the daily struggle to earn a living in their new homeland, the doughnut shop operators must also grapple with the memory of family members who perished during what they refer to as the "Pol Pot time." After having faced starvation, the shop owners are now ironically in the position of serving their customers the ultimate in American junk food, the humble doughnut. Cambodian refugees followed the lead of a coethnic entrepreneur named Bontek "Ted" Ngoy into the doughnut business. Ambassador to Thailand during the Lon Nol regime, Ngoy fled Cambodia for the United States prior to the arrival of Pol Pot.[24] After arriving in the United States, Ngoy established a number of successful family-based doughnut operations and now maintains a low-profile existence in the affluent seaside community of Laguna Beach, California.

One of the interviewees is Bunna Men, co-owner of Daily Donuts. He finds little that is appealing about making doughnuts as such, but says, "I have to do for a living." Despite his apparent distaste for the business, Bunna Men is grateful for having been given the opportunity to make his way in the United States. As he expresses it, "Lives of a dog or cat over here is better than a human being over there during the Pol Pot time." Like many an immigrant before him, Bunna Men echoes the belief in upward economic mobility by dint of individual effort: "If you work hard," says he, "you depend on yourself, you will get something in the United States." Bunna Men is shown driving his Nissan 280Z through an automatic car wash as he expresses the desire to one day own his dream car, a Jaguar.

Sokkun Kimpau has a much better chance at the brass ring than Bunna Men. Having come to the United States as a child, she is more acculturated than older Cambodian refugees and is not handicapped by the lack of English-language skills. Indeed, as a medical student attending the University of California, Los Angeles, Sokkun Kimpau is well on the way to high-income professional status. When not attending classes, however, she is required to work the counter at Donut Star. Like Bunna Men, Sokkun Kimpau would rather not have to work in the doughnut shop owned by her brother, but family obligations require her to help out whenever she can. During a private moment at home, Sokkun Kimpau weeps as she tells of witnessing her father being taken away by the Khmer Rouge, never to return.

The subject of the final profile is the owner of Super Donuts, Leng Hing. The Khmer Rouge imprisoned her husband in 1976 and he is presumed to be dead. Leng Hing's life conists of a seven-day workweek, keeping hours from 5:00 a.m. to 10:00 p.m. Apart from Super Donuts, Leng Hing has devoted herself to her children, vowing that she will not remarry until they have completed college. Leng Hing's twenty-one-year-old son Roger sometimes lends a hand at the store when not working his regular job at a "fashion shop." He invites the interviewer into his bedroom, where posters of personal icons adorn the walls: supermodel Cindy Crawford, Elvis Presley, and Bruce Lee.

As is the case with most Asian immigrants, the family plays a central role in both the affective and material spheres of life for Cambodian Americans. Family members serve as cheap or unpaid labor that helps marginal business enterprises survive on slim profit margins. In elevating group needs over the inclinations of the individual, Asian refugee families make a virtue of necessity. It is not that Asians cherish "the family" and "family values" any more than other ethnic or racial groups, as conservative apologists would have it. Rather, the family stands at the center of the social relations of production for those excluded from the primary labor market and serves as an emotional refuge from a heartless world.

Cambodian Americans, like most refugees, are deeply thankful for the opportunity to eke out an existence in the United States. However, there are hidden psychic costs that must be borne. For example, Celia Vann Noup, a former high school teacher in Phnom Penh and currently the owner of a small doughnut shop in Lawndale, California, speaks of the personal sacrifices she makes for the sake of relatives. She also alludes to ever-present intrafamily tensions that keep the web of reciprocity stretched to the breaking point.[25] Still, Celia Vann Noup voices profound gratitude for the freedoms she now enjoys. She hopes to sponsor other Cambodian refugees for resettlement in the United States so that they too will be able to share in the bounty of America.

Perhaps one day the entertainment industry will memorialize the Cambodian holocaust with a situation comedy that takes a doughnut shop as its focus, just as *Hogan's Heroes* (1965–71) was set in a Nazi POW camp. This is not as far-fetched as it seems. According to Charles Davis, creator of *Family Ties* (1982–89) Gary David Goldberg was interested in *Cambodian Doughnut Dreams* as a sitcom and pitched the premise to president of CBS Entertainment Jeff Sagansky, where the idea mercifully expired. In the age of television, all manner of historical tragedy becomes the premise for a potential sitcom.

U.S. Chaos in Laos

The year 1959 marked the beginning of U.S. covert military operations in Laos, when the Central Intelligence Agency first organized Meo tribesmen to fight the communist Pathet Lao. The clandestine army was assisted by civilian "relief" organizations such as the Agency for International Development, which functioned as a parallel government that managed U.S. interests in Laos. International Volunteer Service, Inc. – a "fundamentalist Protestant organization dedicated to relief work for refugees" – was contracted by the CIA to provide "crucial intelligence and logisitical support" and "cover" for its operatives.[26] What religion and a secret army could not accomplish was bolstered by a massive U.S. bombing campaign waged against the civilian population of Laos. Between 1964 and 1969 alone, anywhere from 74,000 to 150,000 tons of bombs were dropped on a region known as the Plain of Jars, killing countless thousands and displacing more than 25 percent of the Laotian population.[27]

One such displaced Laotian ethnic group was the subject of the publicly funded documentary *Moving Mountains: The Story of Yiu Mien* (1989).[28] Along with the Hmong and other ethnic groups, the

Mien were enlisted by the U.S. government in the undeclared war against the communist Pathet Lao. In 1962, the Mien began serving as a counterinsurgency force under the direction of the CIA. When the war ended in 1975, the Mien were left out in the cold by their U.S. benefactors, who reneged on their promise never to abandon the fiercely independent mountain people, whose origins can be traced to China.

The title of the documentary derives from the wisdom of Mien elders, who observe that "moving mountains is easier than moving your mind." The film explores the problems of sociocultural adjustment encountered by the Saelee family, living in Portland, Oregon. The titular leader of the clan, Ay Choy Saelee, was employed in Laos as a forward air controller for the U.S. military. In that capacity, Saelee enjoyed high status. He speaks knowledgeably about the "culture shock" experienced by the Mien and works in a public agency that assists Laotian refugees. Ay Choy Saelee is somewhat bitter over the abandonment of the Mien by the United States. Not only are most Americans ignorant of the Mien contribution to the U.S. war, says Saelee, they resent the refugees as well.

Ay Choy Saelee's elderly parents joined the family in 1979 and have experienced great difficulty in making the transition to an alien society. Family patriarch Fou Choy Saelee was formerly a village elder and a shaman, which means he once held a position of high importance within traditional Mien society. Today, he complains of the weakening generational bonds his family has suffered since transplantation to the United States. Although Fou Choy Saelee has learned to drive an automobile and presides over occasional Cambodian American ritual ceremonies, his alienation is profound: "We don't belong to American; we don't belong to Mien. We are just nothing."

The marital relationship between Ay Choy Saelee and his wife, Farm Yoon, is given extended treatment in *Moving Mountains*. It is this section of the documentary that is most revealing about changing gender roles among Laotian refugees. As a teenager, Farm Yoon Saelee was given in marriage to Ay Choy as arranged by their respective families. Within village society, her role was carefully circumscribed by traditions arising out of the constraints of an agriculturally based subsistence economy. But in the United States, Farm Yoon works outside the home as a skilled technician, making her paycheck and insurance benefits central to the survival of the Saelee extended family. Farm Yoon's position as a wage earner elevates her individual status within the family. Although she remains deferential to her in-laws, Farm Yoon no longer occupies a subordinate position within the household as dictated by tradition.

Ay Choy Saelee registers both surprise and trepidation at how quickly Farm Yoon has become Americanized. She is outgoing, likes to dance and socialize, jokes heartily with her non-Asian coworkers, and has almost completely shed the trappings of her former existence as a rural peasant living in a remote region of Laos. As a soldier of fortune under the employ of the U.S. military, it was Ay Choy who had been the worldly-wise seeker of pleasure. Now the roles have been reversed. Farm Yoon enjoys dancing and socializing with friends, whereas Ay Choy has become somewhat of a homebody. Divorce is unheard-of in traditional Mien society, observes Ay Choy, but not so in the United States as women seek to assert the independence and equality they now enjoy as wage earners. Ay Choy, however, has made a few concessions to changed circumstances. He now believes the dowry system to be obsolete and would like to see the practice abandoned.

Moving Mountains does much to dispel some of the popular perceptions concerning Southeast Asian refugees in the United States. For one, the opening sequence of this documentary makes it clear that the situation of political refugees such as the Mien is far removed from that of European immigrants who settled in the United States on a voluntary basis. The responsibility of the United States in creating vast numbers of Southeast Asian refugees is duly noted as well. The "immigrant analogy," then, simply does not apply to Southeast Asian refugees. Second, Southeast Asian refugees pose virtually no threat to the economic health of the nation by "taking" jobs away from "real" Americans. Many refugees lack the professional experience and language skills that allow them to compete for high-paying jobs. Third, the idealized Asian American family as glorified by the political Right is seen in this film as fraught with debilitating internal tensions. Farm Yoon Saelee, for example, maintains a strained relationship with her in-laws and bridles against the expectations and duties imposed by traditional Mien cultural practices. The quotidian struggles endured by the Saelee family do indeed bear out the adage "Moving mountains is easier than moving minds."

Casualties of Childhood

In 1968, a twelve-year-old Vietnamese boy named Phan Thanh was severely wounded and his family killed by a U.S. Army patrol that attacked their village while in search of the Viet Cong. His esophagus was severed by a grenade, but he was airlifted to a provincial army hospital and rendered emergency medical aid. During the ride, Thanh thought that he would be pushed from the helicopter, as was often done with suspected Viet Cong sympathizers. Only four years before, Thanh's home had been destroyed by fire. He and his family subsequently were relocated to a "strategic hamlet," which the villagers actually considered a concentration camp. *Thanh's War* (1990), a documentary produced by PBS affiliate KQED-TV (San Francisco) provides a glimpse into the life of just one of the "hundreds of thousands of children" who were killed or wounded during the Vietnam War.[29] The story of the juvenile casualties of war is largely unknown.

Dr. George Roth, with the Committee of Responsibility, is credited with bringing wounded Vietnamese children to the United States for medical treatment. After undergoing extensive surgery in San Francisco, the bewildered Phan Thanh was taken in by Episcopalian priest Father James Jones and his wife, Virginia. Now employed by a high-tech company that manufactures artificial hearts, Thahn is struck by the central irony of his life: The Americans killed his family and inflicted serious injury upon him, yet they spared no effort to keep him from death. "Today I'm an American too," Thahn says. "Is that make me crazy?"

Thanh is not content to let fade the memory of his slain family and devastated country. Haunted by survivor's guilt, he has returned to Vietnam five times since 1980. During his first visit, Thanh was particularly intent on learning the fate of his sister. Villagers informed Thanh that his sister was killed in 1969 by a shell fired by U.S. soldiers as they sought to engage Viet Cong troops thought to have been in the area.

Thanh's War depicts the events of June 1990, when Thanh travels to Vietnam and marries a woman from his village. His adoptive father and stepmother attend the traditional Vietnamese ceremony, a chaotic affair involving every significant member of the community, including a drunken local official who brags of fighting the Americans during the war. Once married, the couple will be separated for at least a year while Thanh returns to his job in the United States, for the United States and the Socialist Republic of Vietnam do not maintain diplomatic relations. Thanh therefore must leave his bride behind. Out of the desire to punish their former adversary, the United States has erected barriers to immigration that have put the couple's life together in America on indefinite hold.[30] Thus the country responsible for killing his family but saving the young boy from death has subjected Thanh to one final indignity: keeping him apart from his wife. "I don't hate being a citizen of the United

States," says Thanh, "I just hate the history of what it's done to this land, to this people, to me, to my family."

Childhood Reeducation

Among the neglected victims of the Vietnam War are the approximately 100,000 "Amerasian" children sired by GIs during the U.S. occupation. Over the past ten years, more than 40,000 Amerasian children have left Vietnam for the United States, although few are ever reunited with their biological fathers. Spanning almost four years, *The Story of Vinh* chronicles the failure of one such Amerasian child to find his way in the country of his unknown father's birth.[31]

Funded as part of a cooperative arrangement between the National Asian American Telecommunications Association (NAATA), National Endowment for the Arts, New York State Council on the Arts, and the Corporation for Public Broadcasting, the documentary captures the very moment fifteen-year-old Vinh Dinh arrives at JFK Airport on September 11, 1986. A child-care agency has already arranged to place Vinh with the Lynch family of Long Island. Vinh is to be the Lynches' second Vietnamese foster son.

Through a Vietnamese American social worker it is learned that Vinh's biological father was stationed at a U.S. air base while consorting with his mother. Later in the film, the documentary crew travels to Vietnam and interviews Vinh's biological mother, who now works on a "coffee cooperative" in the Dalat Highlands north of Ho Chi Minh City. During the interview, his mother reveals that she lived with Vinh's father for a period of six months while he was stationed at the Binh Thuy air base. One day he returned to the base and never came back. Between tubercular coughs, she recalls that Vinh's father was in his 20s and had worked as a medical officer before abandoning her. "Do you have a message for Vinh?" asks the interviewer. Weeping, his mother says, "I'd like to talk to him, send him my love." As Vinh's grandmother peers into the camera as if to "see" Vinh inside, she wishes her grandson "good health and good luck," wiping away tears with fingers gnarled by years of pain and hardship.

The tattoo on Vinh's arm betrays his years of street life before joining the Lynch household. He explains that the initials tattooed on his arm stand for "Young Man Without Love." Despite the best efforts of his domineering foster mother and somewhat passive father, Vinh fails to mesh with Lynch family life. He is also out of his element at Rocky Point High School, where he freely wanders the hallways and takes extended restroom breaks when not ignoring exasperated teachers and administrators. There are mounting suspicions that perhaps Vinh is older than was originally claimed and that this might account for his "problem with authority" and rebelliousness.

Slightly more than a month later, the Lynches are back at the foster care agency to turn Vinh back in. Mr. Lynch says that the problems they encountered with Vinh were evident from the beginning. A dental examination does indeed bear out the suspicion that Vinh is older than his stated age. The dentist puts Vinh's age at no younger than eighteen years. Next, an "agency psychologist" has a go at the recalcitrant foster child and, after a battery of tests, concludes that Vinh's "social judgment is poor."

A Filipino American couple, the Amantes, agree to take Vinh into their home despite his past problems. A portent of the ill-fated attempt to reform the young man is seen during their very first encounter. Vinh extends his hand to greet Mrs. Amante, but she ignores the gesture and instead hugs him lightly and gives the young man a perfunctory peck on the cheek. The new foster father (who, like Mr. Lynch, is exceptionally passive) follows suit. Mrs. Amante tries to hold Vinh's hand, but it drops limply from her insincere grasp. The family matriarch asserts that while her children are being raised "American," they are being taught to respect their elders in the "Oriental" manner.

The Amantes are a fairly well-off Staten Island couple who enjoy ruling over their brood of Vietnamese adoptees, including "Junior," an assimilated teenager who sports a hairdo characteristic of suburban middle-class pubescent male devotees of hard rock or "metal." Junior teaches foster brother Vinh a bit of English and helps him adjust to the new surroundings. Mrs. Amante is very much the prima donna, flailing away at a white baby grand piano as her young captive audience looks on. In contrast to the rococo splendor of the living room, Vinh's cell-like, windowless room adjoins the laundry room. Vinh spends countless hours watching television while smoking the pilfered cigarettes that lead to his eventual banishment from the Amante home.

Before being sent to a "group home for troubled youths," Vinh attends a Vietnamese New Year's party in Chinatown. His former foster mother Mrs. Lynch is there with her "new boy" and a girl who are both younger and cuter than was the uncommunicative and sullen Vinh. As Vinh sits at the other end of the room smoking with some of the older boys, Mrs. Lynch speaks glowingly of her smiling foster children and is plainly pleased with her new acquisitions.

Once Vinh joins the tough-looking young men at the group home, his downward spiral accelerates. From there, Vinh becomes involved in a series of petty crimes that result in his being in and out of jail. The budding tough guy's arrest record mounts and becomes marked by increasingly violent crimes, with strong-arm robberies and a shooting topping his rap sheet. In time, representatives of the criminal justice system attempt to take Vinh off the street. An assistant district attorney at the Manhattan Criminal Court argues that as an "incorrigible recidivist" Vinh should be sentenced to a four- to twelve-year term in state prison. "He came to the United States and he was given an opportunity to start a new life here, judge," pleads the white district attorney. "He was placed in this group home in Staten Island where he wound up going AWOL from, he committed a shooting in Staten Island." Finally, the D.A. plays upon the fears and prejudices of the court by accusing Vinh of belonging to an Asian gang called BTK ("Born to Kill").

Vinh's Asian American lawyer explains to the judge that he is a child of a U.S. serviceman, a refugee who probably turned to crime out of desperation. Unmoved by the argument, the white judge sentences Vinh to five years in state prison with a minimum two years to be served. He also denies the "youthful offender" provision requested by Vinh's legal counsel. Vinh's attorney attributes his stiff sentence to the sensationalistic "publicity of Asian gangs and the fear that people have of them." Even though no proof was offered to identify Vinh positively as a gang member, the mere mention by the public prosecutor of a possible link was enough to have a "negative effect on the court."

At the conclusion of a tortuous four-year odyssey, the documentary film crew visits Vinh at the Cayusa Correctional Facility, where he is known as "Danny" to an older white woman who is tutoring him in English. The bravado that Vinh once displayed seems to have vanished. The Amerasian convict tells how prison has changed him for the better. Vinh draws a telling parallel between prison life in the United States and that of Vietnam. "It's not really prison," says Vinh. "It's like our reeducation camps. You can change your way of life and thinking."

Postcolonial Hawai'i

South Pacific exotica as represented on network television reproduces and naturalizes the servitude of native Hawaiians. They are almost without exception portrayed as childlike wards of a white patriarchal social order. Rarely are Hawaiians seen as autonomous social actors engaged in self-activity. Nor are indigenous philosophical, religious, and scientific systems understood as being fully appropriate to the conditions of Hawaiian communal existence prior to contact with the West.[32] Rather, the indigenous peoples of Hawai'i serve only as amusing adjuncts or attendants to the Euro-American colonizer. Moreover, never are native Hawaiians shown actively challenging their social, cultural, and economic subordination at the hands of the *haole* (white) elite that now controls almost every aspect of life in Hawai'i. The systematic denial of their rights as indigenous Hawaiian peoples is represented on network television programs as being nonproblematic.

Once more, it is PBS that has done the most to help correct the gross distortions in television imagery as it concerns Hawai'i. The one-hour documentary *Troubled Paradise* (1991) subverts the denigrating conventions of network television Hawaiiana by recording the aggressive efforts of cultural and political groups organized to resist both state and corporate capitalist attempts at the further exploitation of the native population and its ancestral lands.[33] The false romanticism of the Hawaiian islands reproduced in the popular culture has provided a disarmingly seductive cover for the misery and degradation inflicted upon the land and its native peoples since they first came into contact with the West.

In Part 1, "Love of the Land," the material and spiritual relationship between native Hawaiians and the *aina* (land) is told by a number of community activitists who have banded together to halt a $325 million resort project headed by local developer Tom Yamamoto in partnership with a Japanese firm, Nansay Hawaii, Inc. A coalition of surfers and native Hawaiian activists formed Protect Kohanaiki 'Ohana to oppose the planned tourist resort, which the group claims will desecrate what remains of an ancient village and destroy the habitat of an endangered species. The expansionary requirements of the tourist economy, whose seven million visitors each year generate $10 billion in revenues, is in direct conflict with the religious and economic needs of the approximately 210,000 "pure or part Hawaiians" living in the islands. Although they represent almost 20 percent of the population, native Hawaiians are the poorest of all racial and ethnic groups in the state.

Once the sugar cane and pineapple industries abandoned Hawaii for South America and the Philippines, many of the locals went to work in factories or hotels. But quite a number of Hawaiians became chronically unemployed and welfare dependent, even though the Hawaiian Homes Commission created by the U.S. Congress in 1921 was to "provide land for the native population." Attorney Mililani Trask of the indigenous peoples' rights organization Ka Lahui Hawai'i describes the dismal living conditions of Hawaiians such as Vietnam veteran Louis Pelekani, Jr. After losing his job on a sugar plantation, Pelekani was unable to gain state assistance. In response, Pelekani and nine other families "have taken a stand against the state and the Hawaiian Homes Commission" by creating their own settlement near the Hilo Airport called King's Landing.

The unofficial leader of King's Landing is Vietnam War veteran Skippy Ioane. His gradual radicalization began with an illuminating encounter with Vietnamese villagers as they gathered together to share a meal. They observed that Ioane, like the Vietnamese, squatted while eating. This compelled the villagers to raise the question of his origins. Ioane tried to explain that he was an American by drawing in the dirt a map of Asia and North America with the Hawaiian Islands in the middle. The map confirmed for the villagers that Ioane was not really an "American." From this pivotal moment on, their naive but dead-on accurate insight began transforming Ioane's consciousness. "From talking to these people in war," Ioane says, "I slowly but surely started unmasking the whiteness of me and bringing out the brown."

Ioane draws a parallel between the plight of Hawaiians and that of Native Americans, an indigenous people also engaged in the struggle for political sovereignty. As Ioane observes, "To be an American you had to have left someplace that you had a hard life to seek a better life. The opposite happened to us. We was here first and then we got squeezed out." He speaks of the "hypocrisy of democracy" that has sparked his refusal to "die humbly" at the hands of a bureaucracy that cares nothing about the Hawaiian people. Ioane lays much of the blame for Hawaiians' wretched condition on their ideological domination by the Christian faith that was imposed upon them. Although raised a Catholic, he "never quite believed" what he was taught, and now shares the animistic religious values of his Hawaiian ancestors.

The fight to reclaim native lands is also linked with the revitalization of native Hawaiian cultural institutions, indigenous expressive forms, and preliterate modes of discourse that are instrumental to the project of "decolonization" as described by such postcolonial critics as Homi K. Bhabha, Gayatri C. Spivak, and Abdul R. JanMohamed.[34] For instance, the burgeoning number of classes in hula comprising all age groups is indicative of the renewed interest in traditional Hawaiian culture. Similarly, in the lush Waipio Valley on the "big island" of Hawaii, *Troubled Paradise* shows a taro farmer named Kia Fronda who reacquaints a new generation with the food value and medicinal properties of the taro root, a staple crop for native Hawaiian people. As Professor Haunani-Kay Trask of the University of Hawaii emphasizes, *aloha aina* means literally "love of the land." "The land feeds us and our responsibility is to care for the land," says Trask.

Part 2, "Pele's Children," documents the efforts of native Hawaiians to block a $2–5 billion state-approved geothermal energy project that will tap volcanic steam to generate electricity. The Pele Defense Fund protests the location of a drill site in the Wao Kele O' Puna forest as "an act of sacrilege." Opponents also argue that the geothermal project is "toxic, costly, and a potential ecological disaster." Pele Defense Fund principals Davianna McGregor, Noa Aluli, and Palikapu Dedman have attempted to obtain injunctions against the project on "religious and cultural grounds as protected by the First Amendment."

By acting in concert with such environmentalist groups as the Rainforest Action Network and through mobilizing broad-based public support, the movement has made substantial progress in its battle against the state of Hawaii and True/Mid-Pacific Geothermal. In 1991, the U.S. district court ordered a "comprehensive environmental impact study" before more federal money could be spent on the geothermal energy project. "These are our ancestral lands," asserts Haunani-Kay Trask. "We have identifiable lands that in American law belong to us. We are not using them, we are not controlling them, we should have those lands under our control and non-Hawaiians should respect that."

In addition to raising substantive legal and moral issues, *Troubled Paradise* does a superlative job of capturing the dialectical relationship that exists between culture and politics. Native Hawaiians are shown drawing from their precolonial cultural heritage as a living resource deployed in the struggle against transnational capital and as a means to forge a collective identity as *political* subjects. Indeed, the very structure of this documentary is formed by the use of traditional Hawaiian folk songs (*kanikapila*) rendered by local artists playing the "slack key" guitar style unique to the islands. Music such as featured in *Troubled Paradise* "celebrates the traditions of native Hawaiians, in opposition and reaction to the cultural domination of the mainland United States and the entertainment needs of the booming tourist industry of the 1970s and 1980s."[35] As a politicized social collectivity for itself, the Hawaiian indigenes featured in the documentary have tapped into the power of oral tradition, folk music, and ancient forms of hula (*hula kahiko*) combined with a pantheistic cosmology that restores the land and its people to a position of centrality as against the abstracted commodity relations of an international tourist economy that markets a debased and denatured Hawaiiana to the millions of visitors each year who seek to regenerate themselves during vacations from routinized work by purchasing two-week stays in an ersatz utopian paradise complete with man-made dolphin pool (as featured at the $360 million Hyatt Regency Waikoloa), ready-made "beaches" formed with sand shipped from California, and golf courses implanted upon ancient lava flows.

All Talk

Asian Americans fare a bit better on network-level and independent commercial television when it comes to news, documentaries, and other nonfiction forms such as the many popular afternoon talk shows modeled on the format pioneered by Phil Donahue in 1967. Although news and information programs are highly structured and controlled, these particular television forms are ontologically dependent upon political controversy, social conflict, and cultural heterodoxy. Although the issues presented are often trivialized, syndicated shows such as *Sally Jessy Raphael* (1985–present), *The Oprah Winfrey Show* (1986–present), and *Geraldo* (1987–present) flirt with sociocultural taboos and expose the multiplicity of lived experience before amused, shocked, and sometimes outraged audiences.

Nonfiction television forms – syndicated (nonnetwork) talk shows in particular – permit a certain degree of ideological "leakage" and allow for a wider range of expression to be voiced by traditionally underrepresented groups, movements, or sodalities. But by failing to link personal problems and group oppression with larger social structures and processes, the otherwise provocative ideas, issues, and arguments raised on talk shows remain at a prepolitical level of sophistication, which delays and perhaps even contains sociocultural and political transformation. Still, contemporary talk shows expose the fragility of a social order divided along class, gender, and racial lines while highlighting the myriad discrepant worlds inhabited by a panoply of normative minorities, occupational groupings, single-interest advocacy organizations, and crackpots with ideological axes to grind.

In the era of oligopoly capitalism, the network television news divisions no longer even pretend to function as a traditionally adversarial fourth estate. The institutional memory of figures such as Murrow, Severeid, and Cronkite grow ever more faint as extravagantly paid celebrity journalists assume center stage. The 1993 resignation of Michael Gartner, president of the NBC news division, in the wake of a highly publicized faked truck-crash story appearing on the TV magazine *Dateline NBC* is symptomatic of the downward slide afflicting network news divisions in recent times. News programs have become just another profit center, a "cash cow" where simulations and reenactments of "real" events are considered to be standard practice.[36] Current television newsmagazines such as *60 Minutes* (1968–present), *20/20* (1978–present), and *48 Hours* (1988–present) are tepid affairs that more closely resemble family dinner-table discussions (but with visuals and expert opinion) than hard reportage. For better or worse, it is talk shows such as *Donahue* (1970–present) that take the risks the networks are unwilling to assume.

During each program, Phil Donahue devotes a full hour of discussion and dialogue to a complex issue in a manner that would be unthinkable on the networks save for infrequent *ABC News Nightline* (1980–present) "town meetings" hosted by Ted Koppel. That is, the very concept of *Donahue* makes it highly participatory. Not only does the show accommodate in-person guests, but a studio audience and viewers calling from home are encouraged to ask questions and offer comments. Phil Donahue does not sit behind an anchor desk, but roams freely among the audience, blurring the line between authority and audience.

On one particular show, J. Philippe Rushton, Ph.D., professor of psychology at the University of Western Ontario, presents his theory on the relationship between race and intellect.[37] Alluding to research findings, Rushton contends that because of measurable differences in cranial capacity, African Americans on average are less intelligent than whites, who in turn are less intelligent than "Orientals" (meaning Asians, presumably). As a corollary to this observation, Professor Rushton states that the larger genitals of African Americans predispose them to promiscuity and larger families.

The *Donahue* audience almost to a person rejects the assertions of Professor Rushton and instead sides with a guest who holds an opposing view. Barry Mehler, Ph.D., a professor at Ferris State University, Michigan, observes that Rushton's claims are symptomatic of neo-Nazi ideology that is currently enjoying a resurgence worldwide. Alarmingly, although the ideological racism spouted by Rushton is rejected by the audience, they do accept the notion that Asians might indeed be "superior" to whites. Apparently, the research findings of Professor Rushton square with their own nonscientific observations. Audience members speak of how Asians persevere, sacrifice, and "clique together" in order to advance themselves, whereas other groups (Blacks perhaps?) are not as disciplined and ambitious. As a Euro-American woman in the studio audience expresses it, "Maybe the whites and the Blacks should try to measure up to the Asians; people reflect the culture and ideology they live in." By their vocal responses to the guests, the audience appears to share the belief that racism represents an unpleasant *departure* from the normal processes of American society rather than being *basic* to it.

Because many Asians have been able to excel in certain portions of standardized tests and are therefore admitted to elite universities in disproportional numbers, the notion has taken root that their better-than-average academic performance must be the result of a special genetic endowment.[38] How else, the reasoning goes, could Asians possibly outperform whites – they must hold an inherent biological advantage. The high academic achievement of many Asian Americans has by now become such a cliché within the popular culture that this theme found its way into an episode of the crime show *Law & Order* (1990–92), wherein an MIT-bound Chinese American high school honor student named Tim Chong (Stephen Xavier Lee) is murdered by a white competitor who could no longer tolerate his standing as academic second fiddle.[39] Superior academic or athletic performance by individual members of nonwhite racial minorities seems predictable when other avenues of opportunity and achievement are restricted or blocked.

Oddly enough, this new twist on scientific racism only reinforces the assumption of white superiority, because it confers unfair biological advantage to competing groups. The material effects of racism as such are never acknowledged. Among all those in attendance – the guest experts, telephone callers, and audience members – no one but host Phil Donahue himself gets to the heart of the matter by alluding to America's racist past. Donahue reminds the audience that "we live in the same country that interned thousands and thousands of people in the forties because they were Japanese." The audience, however, basking in their collective sense of moral superiority over Rushton, fails to understand the connection between their brand of ideological racism and that of the Canadian professor.

The racist purport of Professor Rushton's assertions is partially obscured by the seemingly value-free tenor of his research. By adopting the discourse of the hard sciences and transcoding social issues into biologistic rhetoric, the ideological racism of Rushton and his ilk takes on the veneer of truth for those predisposed to belief. But at bottom, as Professor Mehler states, the hidden agenda of scientific racism is to suggest "biosocial solutions to social problems." That is, the false appeal to biological "nature" is offered as an explanation for a host of problems in society that can be more properly attributed to structured social inequality. As Marvin Harris notes in his critical history of anthropological theory, scientific racism and the notion of racial determinism is the cornerstone of modern social science. "It was in this guise that anthropology first achieved a positive role alongside of physics, chemistry, and the life sciences, in the support and spread of capitalist society," writes Harris.[40]

For all the genre's limitations, television talk shows such as *Donahue* provide a forum for the airing of issues that do not otherwise receive much play in the media. The specific program discussed above might be criticized for its oversimplification of complex arguments, and there is an overriding tendency to prefer moralistic judgment over concrete social analysis, but the show does serve a valuable function by exposing a large national audience of nonspecialists to the practical consequences of arcane theories being argued by cloistered academics. At minimum, the *Donahue* episode alerts viewers to the dangers associated with the resurgence of scientific racism within the academic community—a warning that few network news and information programs would dare issue.

Black Korea

Of the estimated 820,000 Koreans living in the United States, more than 164,000 reside in Los Angeles County. One in five Koreans lives in the district of Los Angeles known as Koreatown. Koreans represent 10 percent of the population of Koreatown, with African Americans and Latinos predominating.[41] Along with South-Central Los Angeles, Crenshaw, Hollywood, Mid-Wilshire, Echo Park, and Silver Lake, the Koreatown community bore the brunt of the urban uprising that occurred following the April 29, 1992, acquittal of the Los Angeles police officers charged in the beating of African American motorist Rodney G. King on March 3, 1991.

Prior to 1965, when discriminatory barriers against Asian immigration were lifted, the Korean population in the United States was small. But from 1970 to 1990 the numbers of Koreans soared, from 70,598 to 820,000. Since 1980, 33,000 Koreans have entered the country each year, a rate of growth exceeded only by Filipinos and Hispanics. Middle-class in origin and highly educated as a group, Korean immigrants have made their mark on the Los Angeles economy. Although composing only 10 percent of the Koreatown population, Koreans own 42 percent of the commercial lots, 40 percent of the office buildings, and 41 percent of all the shopping centers within an area ten times larger than Chinatown and Little Tokyo combined.[42] Throughout the 1970s to present, the Korean American ethnic subeconomy in Los Angeles has flourished in comparison to the sluggish performance of the nation at large. But such economic strides have earned the enmity of many Blacks and Latinos, while winning the praise of conservative commentators who point to Korean Americans as a shining example of entrepreneurial capitalism at work.

Koreans are the most geographically dispersed of all Asian American groups, with the exception of Asian Indians, and Black-Korean conflict has been reported in almost every major urban area in the country, including Los Angeles. In October 1991, Korean-born grocer Soon Ja Du was convicted of voluntary manslaughter in the shooting death of Black teenager Latasha Harlins.[43] The following month, Judge Joyce A. Karlin handed Du a suspended ten-year sentence and placed her on probation for five years. The Black community was understandably outraged. "I think we've got to come together very quickly," Los Angeles City Councilman Nate Holden said after Du was granted probation. "The wrong signal could be sent out with this sentence. No one should be given the impression that they could take a person's life and not be held accountable."[44]

The shooting death of Latasha Harlins only exacerbated longstanding tensions between Korean American shopkeepers and African Americans in Los Angeles. In the aftermath of Soon Ja Du's sentencing, Korean-owned stores were boycotted and several stores were firebombed. Only one week after the killing of Latasha Harlins, the nine-year-old daughter of a Korean American minimarket owner was shot in the chest during an early morning holdup. According to the police, the girl had been watching TV in a room at the rear of the store when a Black man armed with a handgun jumped over the counter and took more than $500 from the cash register and then shot the child without provocation. Korean American shopkeepers did not blame the Black community for the shooting, but cited the incident as an example of the danger they face each day. Nineteen Korean American merchants have been killed at work over the past ten years.

President of the Brotherhood Crusade Danny Bakewell condemned the shooting incident but confirmed that his organization would continue to apply pressure against Korean American merchants. "It's a terrible tragedy and my heart goes out to the family," Bakewell said. "I am not about to be silenced just because it was a young Korean girl."[45] Bakewell had been leading a boycott against Chung's Liquor Market, where forty-two-year-old Lee Arthur Mitchell was shot and killed by Kumoch Park in self-defense, according to police.[46] After Du's sentencing, Bakewell attended a gathering of more than 300 community activists at the Bethel African Methodist Episcopal Church. The community leaders met to discuss ways of improving Black-Korean relations and how they might exercise more political and economic power in their community. But Bakewell called on the group to inflict "economic paralysis" on Korean American store owners who do not deal with Black customers in good faith.[47]

From New York to Los Angeles, the Korean American shopkeeper has been portrayed as the principal antagonist of an ethnic underclass composed of Blacks and Hispanics. A classic example of what sociologists refer to as a "middleman minority," Korean American small business owners act as a buffer between absentee Euro-American capitalist owners and nonwhite residents living in core urban areas. The Korean American businessperson is often held up as "proof" of upward mobility in a class-bound society, a living denial that race prejudice stands as a barrier to economic success. Yet it is a combination of social discrimination and the lack of English-language competence that forces Korean immigrants into the ethnic enclave economy in the first place.

The self-sufficiency of Korean American businesses is deceptive. As Ivan Light and Edna Bonacich observe in their exhaustive study *Immigrant Entrepreneurs: Koreans in Los Angeles 1965–1982*, large-scale U.S. capital looms in the background through the sales and service of national business franchises and the subcontracting of piecework to Korean American manufacturing concerns. The highly competitive garment manufacturing industry is but one example of unequal economic exchange relations between Korean small business and large U.S. corporations. More important, Korean American small businesses provide indirect benefits to large-scale capital by distributing national brand-name products to underserved urban populations, reducing labor standards and costs, pioneering new areas of enterprise for eventual takeover by big capital, and perpetuating the myth of ethnic entrepreneurial success within class society.[48]

The Los Angeles rebellion gives lie to the myth of Asian American entrepreneurial dynamism currently being trumpeted by a number of journalists and academics, including Joel Kotkin, James Fallows, and Thomas Sowell. Koreatown was especially hard hit by firebomb attacks and looting, two days and nights of terror that were interpreted by the news media as the almost inevitable result of ongoing conflict between Blacks and Korean Americans. The destruction of several hundred Korean-owned businesses worth an estimated $300 million illustrates the risks assumed by merchants who do business in urban areas deemed too risky and unprofitable by corporate chains.

In the popular culture, the tension-fraught relationship between the Korean store clerk Sonny (Steve Park) and his Black clientele in

Spike Lee's *Do the Right Thing* (1989) is emblematic of the Black-Korean conflict. That film's climactic scene prefigured the much greater conflagration that was later to engulf large sections of Los Angeles, except that Sonny managed to prevent his store from being set on fire. Rap artist Ice Cube voiced the anti-Asian hostility of many African Americans in his forty-seven-second diatribe "Black Korea" on *Death Certificate* (1991). The cut expressed the common sentiment among many Black customers of Korean-owned businesses that they have been treated with suspicion and disrespect. The narrator even goes so far as to threaten a Korean shopkeeper with burning down his store unless more respect is shown to Black patrons. Ice Cube made it plain to the yellow objects of his wrath that they "can't turn the ghetto into Black Korea."

Self-Evident Truths

Unlike the networks, whose news-gathering and documentary operations have been cut back over the past few years in favor of the sports and entertainment side of the business, independently produced talk shows devote a good deal of time to a variety of pressing social issues.[49] The nationally syndicated *Oprah Winfrey Show*, for example, devoted a number of programs to the theme "Racism in 1992." One installment of the yearlong series took up the racist subtext of the "Buy American" campaign, in which president of the Japanese American Citizens League, Dennis Hayashi, squared off with a certain Dan Porter, identified as being "Hostile Towards Japanese Americans."[50]

The ashes left by the spring rebellion had barely cooled when Oprah Winfrey brought her Chicago-based program to Los Angeles. The program described here involves an extremely agitated audience composed of African Americans, Korean Americans, and a smattering of whites.[51] At the show's opening, superimposed upon successive images of the U.S. flag, the March on Washington, and a KKK cross burning, is the noble sentiment, "There is but one race, Humanity," which is in turn followed by the immortal lines drawn from the Declaration of Independence: "We hold these truths to be self-evident: That all men are created equal." Shown in ironic contrast to these pieties are videotaped scenes that include a helicopter shot of Blacks assaulting a motorist, rioters smashing the glass doors of government offices, a clip of the attack on Reginald O. Denny, and the now-famous George Holliday videotape footage of Rodney King being beaten by officers of the Los Angeles Police Department.

Among those in the audience are self-identified "looters," Black middle-class business owners, and a large contingent of very vocal

Korean Americans. There is only one "expert" among the attendees, essayist Ralph Wiley (*Why Black People Tend to Shout*), who manages to sneak in an all-too-brief comment blaming "media politics and the American justice system" for precipitating the riots.[52] But for the most part, the program is a barely contained free-for-all with accusations and counteraccusations flying freely between Black and Korean American members of the audience. What strikes the viewer most about the live program is the lack of order and control Oprah is able to exercise over the proceedings. The tension in the studio is palpable. At times, Oprah struggles to maintain possession of the microphone as audience members grasp it tightly while speaking with impassioned eloquence.

In the midst of the finger-pointing, a young Korean American man says with emphasis, "We're not your oppressors." When he mentions that a large percentage of destroyed businesses were Korean-owned, light audience applause is heard. "We cannot justify 300 years of your oppression. We've been here twenty years and you expect us to solve all your problems?" he shouts to no one in particular. A Black woman says that the Koreans are "rude" in "*my* neighborhood" and a young man echoes her sentiment by demanding respect: "I don't want you to come out from behind your counter and follow me around your store assuming I'm gonna steal from you."

The live in-studio discussion periodically breaks away to taped interviews with riot victims and now-familiar news footage of the spring disturbance. Most gripping is the sight of Korean American merchants — one wearing a bullet-proof vest — firing their weapons at attackers. In most television drama, Asian Americans submit passively to their brutalization and are utterly dependent upon white police/legal authority for help. But in this live, uncensored scene of Korean shopkeepers defending their stores with firearms, the LAPD is nowhere to be seen. Born of racial tensions and class conflict, the random nonnarrativized videotaped record of urban rebellion *in medias res* rips a wide hole in prefabricated television mythologies whose very composition depends upon racist assumptions. One such tacit assumption in network television is that Asian American characters can never be shown as autonomous social actors and can function only as servants to white power. Beyond the Los Angeles rebellion, news footage of Korean shopkeepers maintaining order in a social space vacated by white civil authority will leave a lasting impression in the mind of the public and might even begin to alter the manner in which Asian Americans are portrayed on network television.

In the epilogue, Oprah solemnly intones, "It's a time for healing."

A video montage of riot activity is followed by clips of the Reverend Martin Luther King, Jr., uttering the classic phrases that have entered into the lexicon of liberal amelioration. "Let's try to work it out," Rodney King says haltingly at a news conference hastily assembled after the rebellion broke out. Suddenly, the heavenly saxophone introduction to Marvin Gaye's "What's Going On" (1971) breaks through the cloud of gloom that has settled over the fractious assembly. In the studio, a camera zooms in on a weeping young Black man. He had been one of the more outspoken and aggressive self-described "looters." It is a powerful moment for all its spontaneity. Hunched over like a penitent reprobate, the young man wipes away tears of rage as the strains of Marvin Gaye's soulful lament brings the program to a close.

Despite the unstable meanings generated by the heated live in-studio group encounter, this special edition of *The Oprah Winfrey Show* applies an ameliorative gloss to the ever-worsening problems of contemporary class society. Even as Oprah calls for understanding between Blacks and Koreans, the very format of the program is calculated to incite overt conflict between the two groups. Nothing illuminating is said about the underlying causes of interethnic hostility. Neither is intraethnic class conflict dealt with, although Black business owners in attendance voice their anger at having had their establishments looted and destroyed by fellow African Americans. Instead, the conflict between the African American community and Korean Americans is kept at the forefront while the unseen structures of political economic control and domination go unmentioned. No matter what potentially subversive meanings might have been loosed during the show, the liberal ideological underpinnings of commercial television are reaffirmed in the closing montage. Images of the Reverend Martin Luther King, Jr.—not those of Malcolm X or the Reverend Louis Farrakhan—are selected to contain lingering traces of dissidence. It is only appropriate that Marvin Gaye's conciliatory "What's Going On" and not Public Enemy's "Fight the Power" (1990) be used as a musical counterpoint to the concluding imagery, for it is liberal amelioration and not radical opposition that is being implicitly offered as a solution to racial and class conflict.

Chapter 8

Epilogue

Constructing Orientals

In a film and television career that spanned a period of fifty years, beginning with the "Charlie Chan" film series during the 1930s and running through the TV-movie reprise of *Kung Fu* (1986), Keye Luke (1904–1991) was probably the Asian American actor best known to the general public. Born in Canton, China, but raised in Seattle, where he attended the University of Washington, Luke appeared in scores of feature films prior to his entry into television. He made his film debut in *The Painted Veil* (1934), starring Greta Garbo. "I was lucky," said Luke in a 1986 interview with the *Los Angeles Times*, "I started at the top."[1] Not only did he costar in dozens of individual television episodes, TV movies, and miniseries, Luke also performed as a regular on such network programs as *Kentucky Jones* (1964–65), *Anna and the King* (1972), *Kung Fu* (1972–75), *Harry-O* (1974–76), and *Sidekicks* (1986–87). With few exceptions, Keye Luke's outstanding career was predicated upon his ability to portray the stock array of Asian domestic servants, laundrymen, mystics, gangsters, and enemy soldiers. In this, Keye Luke was the prototypical "Oriental" as constructed by the implicit racism of network television standards and practices.

In his very first appearance on television, for example, the ambiguity of Keye Luke's Asian ethnicity serves as the comedic premise for two sketches featured in *The Milton Berle Show* (1948–67).[2] Often cited as a seminal program in the history of commercial television, *The Milton Berle Show* (earlier, *Texaco Star Theater*) relied heavily upon conventions drawn from the vaudeville tradition. "Uncle Miltie" would usually join guests in song, dance, skits, and stage patter rather than simply stand by as master of ceremonies. The "double act" and "cross talk" employed in the program originated in the "banter developed between the clown and master in the circus, and between the 'Interlocutor' and 'Endmen' (Tambo and Bones) in the opening section of the minstrel show."[3] Similarly, throughout the entire encounter with Keye Luke, Berle presides over the racial and ultimately social meaning of his guest's identity.

The March 1950 broadcast demonstrates the way in which a multiform and diverse Asian American social identity is controlled, fixed, and contained through the discursive strategies of commercial television, itself drawing from earlier entertainment forms such as vaudeville and the cinema. The containment of Asian American social identity is only partial, however, as seen in the mock frustration and bemused reactions of onstage interlocutor and host Milton Berle as he struggles, in a comedic vein, with the contradictions posed by the cultural collision between the "Orient" and the "West."

Berle introduces Keye Luke as "Charlie Chan's Number One Son." By this introduction, Berle is already conflating Luke's private identity with a socially constructed "Oriental" persona as summoned by the honorific phrase, "Number One" (son), an ordinal descriptor used to connote "Asianness." The orchestra strikes up a pentatonic ("Oriental") fanfare as a dynamic Keye Luke, resplendent in a double-breasted suit ("Western" attire), strides to center stage with a sense of purpose and command. Luke's vibrant presence and physical attitude stand in marked contrast to the obsequious Chinaman body language he was made to assume for most of his career. As Berle turns to greet Luke, the host extends his hand for a "Western"-style handshake and bows deeply in the "Oriental" fashion. To make doubly sure that no breaches in cross-cultural etiquette have occurred, Berle bows deeply once more.

Berle speaks haltingly to Luke in loose approximation of a "Chinese" accent. His demeanor and stilted speech betray the cloying hyperpoliteness of the "Oriental" people: "Keye Luke, pleasure to have you, here, this evening, for *Texaco Star Theater*, we have very wonderful audience, here, everybody love you in screen, and very happy to welcome you here." Berle looks at his guest anxiously, wondering whether the introduction was adequately comprehended. In response, Luke launches into a perfectly inflected rhetorical flourish that elicits the trademark Berlean double take. "This glorious moment," says Luke, gesturing broadly, "I'll remember it to the end of time." "He speaks with a broken Chinese accent, I think," says Berle to the audience. Turning to Luke, Berle says, "You fooled me, I didn't even know you spoke English." Not missing a beat, Luke responds, "Well, I didn't know you did either." Luke then delivers a series of deftly timed ripostes that deflate Berle's braggadocio.

"This gentleman is an Oriental Henny Youngman, this man," says Berle to the audience, taking Luke's hand as a parent would a child's.

Berle exits the stage, leaving Luke to introduce a second sketch that will cast him back into the role of socially constructed Chinaman, subordinating his briefly glimpsed "Western" identity. The "Texaco Servicemen," who open each program singing their sponsor's jingle before musically introducing Berle, appear on stage dressed in "Chinese" costume. The quartet harmonizes in a monotone, clipped, singsong ("Oriental") manner before introducing Milton Berle as the top television star in China. Dressed in a "coolie" outfit and eye makeup that "Asianizes" him, Berle trots onto the stage pulling Luke in a rickshaw, whereupon they perform a song together delivered with a "Chinese" accent.

In a corny skit that has obvious ties to vaudeville, Berle and Luke engage in brisk repartee that, in addition to being rich in wordplay, draws its humor from the clash of meaning among dissimilar language systems, including Standard English, Yiddish, Cantonese, and macaronic Chinese-English. Not only is Berle's humorous "Chinese" speech sprinkled liberally with "Yiddishisms," but jokes arise from the perceived inability of Asians to articulate the *l* sound in English, or to substitute it for the *r* sound (lambdacism). "Who was that Mandarin I saw you with last night?" asks Luke. "That was no Mandarin," replies Berle, "that was a ukelele."

Although the skits featuring Keye Luke self-reflexively play against common controlling images of Asian Americans, the privilege of constructing ethnic and racial identity nevertheless remains with the white interlocutor, Milton Berle. Luke's real-life nontheatrical demeanor, appearance, and speech are so at odds with common expectations that, rather than allow him to perform in mufti, Berle quickly forces the veteran actor back into the role of the more familiar "Chinaman" figure as constructed by the popular arts of previous decades, reaching back to the nineteenth century. It is a role that Keye Luke was to occupy with amazing consistency for the next thirty-five years of his professional life.

Considering that Luke's career paralleled the civil rights struggles of the 1950s, the cultural nationalism of the 1960s, and the search for primordial ethnic "roots" during 1970s, it might seem baffling that he would be restricted to such a narrow range of Asian American roles. But if the underlying anti-Asian racism of U.S. society is acknowledged and understood, the acting career of Keye Luke can be viewed as emblematic of the dilemmas confronted by Asian Americans at large. Although select Asian American groups have attained a relative degree of success in liberal democratic society as measured by educational level, occupational status, and income, it remains the case that access to the key political, economic, and cultural institutions governing the lives of diverse peoples of Asian origins is severely limited.[4] Keye Luke did indeed enjoy steady employment subsequent to his television debut on *The Milton Berle Show*. But thereafter, he was rarely allowed to exhibit the full scope and depth of his abilities, imprisoned as he was by his success at representing controlling images of Asian Americans conceived by the white male elite that dominate the television industry with the tacit approval and support of the liberal racial state. *Los Angeles Times* arts editor Charles Champlin paid tribute to Keye Luke shortly after the actor's death. Champlin thought it only fitting that after such a long career occupying "stereotypical roles" in Hollywood films that Luke's final role would be that of Mia Farrow's confidant in *Alice* (1990), directed by Woody Allen. "And so it is possible to remember Keye Luke, not simply as Chan's impetuous No. 1 Son," wrote Champlin, "but as a distinguished actor always capable of doing more than Hollywood—during so much of his career—dared ask him to do."[5]

Strangers in the Night

Television in its first full decade revealed the almost total acceptance of white ethnic performers, who filled the ranks of variety shows, situation comedies, and dramas. Second-generation Jewish Americans such as Jack Benny, George Burns, Milton Berle, and Sid Caesar enjoyed enormous popularity on television during the 1950s. In interpreting the "dispersion" of Jewish American comedians into the national culture via television and the accompanying "Yiddishization of American humor," Irving Howe observes that the open expression of what was once considered "Jewish vulgarity" reflected a certain level of confidence and security attained by a middle-class Jewish audience residing in urban areas. Moreover, the "systematic flaunting of Yiddish" in television humor implied the acceptance of Jewish Americans by the larger society to the point where it was *"no longer necessary to be careful"* and it was *"no longer necessary to be defensive."*[6]

Like other white ethnic groups who were initially excluded from WASP-dominated institutions, Italian Americans have also made a mark in television entertainment. Second-generation Italian Americans such as Perry Como (*The Perry Como Show*, 1948–63), Frank Sinatra (*The Frank Sinatra Show*, 1950–52), Julius LaRosa (*The Julius LaRosa Show*, 1955), Frankie Laine (*Frankie Laine Time*, 1955–56), and Dean Martin (*The Dean Martin Show*, 1965–74) have starred in network television programs since the 1950s. Irish Americans have also been well represented as stars of their own shows, including Ed Sullivan (*The Ed Sullivan Show*, 1948–71), Jackie Gleason (*The Jackie Gleason Show*, 1952–55), and Dennis O'Keefe (*The Dennis O'Keefe Show*, 1959–60). Even Arab Americans have enjoyed a degree of prominence on network television. Lebanese American Danny Thomas, born Muzyad Yaghoob in Deerfield, Michigan, starred in the beloved *The Danny Thomas Show* (1953–71) (*Make Room for Daddy* in its first three seasons) and *The Danny Thomas Hour* (1967–68).

African Americans have had a tougher time of it. Although not the first Black to do so, Nat "King" Cole hosted an eponymously titled musical variety show for two years (1956–57) before it was canceled owing to the inability of the program to attract a national sponsor. In accounting for the failure of a program that regularly featured many of the best musical artists of the day, Cole bitterly accused "Madison Avenue" and "their big clients" of not wanting "their products associated with Negroes."[7] It would not be until the mid-1960s that African Americans would again appear on network television in featured or costarring roles, which in turn set the stage for the effloresence of Black-oriented situation comedies during the 1970s and *The Cosby Show* phenomenon of the mid-1980s to early 1990s.

In comparison with white ethnics and Blacks, Asian Americans have had few opportunities to display their talents in the performing arts on television. And even when the likes of entertainer Pat Suzuki makes a guest appearance on *The Frank Sinatra Show* (also known as *Bulova Watch Time*, 1957–58), she is made out to be racial oddity.[8] Upon being introduced by Frank Sinatra, Suzuki delivers a popular song in a powerful singing voice similar to that of the great Dinah Washington. Sinatra joins Suzuki onstage after she finishes the tune and warmly puts his arm around her.

As in the pairing of Keye Luke and Milton Berle, Sinatra and Suzuki exchange seemingly innocent quips that problematize their respective ethnicities. Sinatra begins the routine by jokingly mistaking Suzuki for being Italian. When she identifies herself as being a Japanese American from Seattle, Sinatra says, "You can't get anyplace as a singer unless you're an Italian. . . . And even if you're not, you've gotta pretend you are, look what it did for Perry Como." Sinatra claims that Como is a "Swedish lad," while Dean Martin is actually a "Hawaiian beach boy." As for Sinatra, he makes light of his Italian ethnicity, claiming to be "Eskimo." "My real name is Blubber Nanook," says Sinatra. "Now that doesn't make any difference to you Pat?" "Oh no, my best friends are Eskimos," says Suzuki, "but I like you just the way you are."

Unlike white ethnics, Asian Americans are viewed as being forever "strangers" in their own country. As such, both Keye Luke and Pat Suzuki are made to engage in ritualistic apologies to explain and justify their appearance on television rather than being simply allowed to perform as they are. Although Milton Berle and Frank Sinatra banter with their Asian American guests in a lighthearted and humorous way, the utterly alien social identity of Keye Luke and Pat Suzuki must first be normalized and regulated before the audience can begin to appreciate their *individual* identities. Once having demonstrated their familiarity and congruence with the dominant Euro-American culture, both Luke and Suzuki are granted the modicum of artistic expression that finally establishes that "they" are passably acceptable to the social audience.

Rice-Capades

The example of Kristi Yamaguchi illustrates that the inferential anti-Asian racism faced by entertainers such as Keye Luke and Pat Suzuki is alive and well. Millions of Americans watched twenty-year-old Kristi Yamaguchi figure-skate to victory in the 1992 Winter Olympics broadcast by CBS. Like Peggy Fleming and Dorothy Hamill before her, Yamaguchi was expected to reap huge financial rewards from endorsement deals offered by major companies, especially since no American competitor had won the gold medal since 1976. Her face appeared on boxes of Kellogg's Special K cereal and she secured endorsement contracts with Evian, Bausch & Lomb, Campbell Soup, and Kraft. But as of March 1992, Yamaguchi had no other major offers. Coke and Pepsi shied away from the Northern California figure skater, as did Nutrasweet, which had used Hamill as a spokesperson for five years.

A March 9, 1992, article in *Business Week* bluntly stated that "companies may be shying away from Yamaguchi because her surname and looks are Japanese."[9] Advertising executive Jay Coleman, whose company had signed Michael Jackson to a Pepsi campaign for the third time, stated that the current anti-Japanese mood in the United States limits Yamaguchi's "earning potential." The article stated that although Yamaguchi has a two-year contract with Bausch & Lomb, the optical firm is using Olympians Jackie Joyner-Kersee and Matt Biondi in its television advertisements.

A later *Los Angeles Times* article was dismissive of the controversy set into motion by the *Business Week* piece. The piece denied that "subtle racism" and the anti-Japanese climate had an adverse effect on Yamaguchi's ability to attract lucrative endorsements. Instead, the *Times* article argued that the economic recession made advertisers leary of "spending big money on anybody."[10] New York talent agent Martin Blackman, however, conceded that Yamaguchi's marketability would have been better had she been "blonde and blue-eyed and from Greenwich, Connecticut," and had the country not been in a "Japan-bashing mood."

Beginning in late 1992, Yamaguchi's face began appearing in print ads for DuraSoft Colors contact lenses (made by Wesley Jensen, not Bausch & Lomb). "When I want a little change I go green, violet, or gray," read the ad copy. Given that her Asian physical appearance probably prevented Yamaguchi from fully cashing in on her Olympic victory, perhaps a "subtle to dramatic" change in eye color "even if you don't need visual correction" might be the best she can do in a society that prefers the antics of superannuated white athletes like tennis player Jimmy Connors or highly overrated media darling Andre Agassi to the consistently superior performance of a Michael Chang. During two separate appearances on *The Arsenio Hall Show* (1989–present), Yamaguchi, despite gentle prodding by the host, politely declined to voice her resentment for having been discriminated against by corporate America.

Connie Chung Syndrome

The one area where Asian Americans are allowed to display a sense of mastery and expertise is in television news, the most prominent figure being Connie Chung of CBS. Paying her an annual salary in the neighborhood of $2 million, CBS devised the personality-driven program *Saturday Night with Connie Chung* (1989–90) for their new acquisition, who had been lured away from rival NBC. In addition to being a ratings failure, the program was criticized for its use of dramatic reenactments that blurred the line between reportage and entertainment. "I'm angry at the critics and their holier-than-thou attitude about an innovative way of telling a story," Chung remarked at the time.[11] The *Saturday Night with Connie Chung* fiasco was followed by the celebrity interview program, *Face to Face with Connie Chung* (1990). Less than three months after the program's debut, Chung withdrew into the arms of husband and fellow television personality Maury Povich (*A Current Affair*) to "take a very aggressive approach to having a baby."[12] It was also an opportune moment to win public support as she calculated her next career move.

The following August, Connie Chung was scheduled to deliver the keynote address at a convention of the Asian American Journalists Association. Instead, Chung sent a videotaped message apologizing for not being able to attend the event. Her no-show at the convention helped feed the already-existing perception that Chung was professionally uncomfortable with being identified with the Asian American community. A short profile in an Asian American publication, for example, described Chung as having "shown ambivalence about being identified with her Asian heritage."[13]

Connie Chung can be credited with setting off a boom in female Asian American network newscasters; by now virtually every major metropolitan market across the nation features at least one anchor who fits the mold. Humorist Harry Shearer has described the phenomenon as the "one-Asian-woman-per-station rule that has prevailed in TV news."[14] Novelist Gish Jen observes that in the wake of Connie Chung's media success, the popular culture has absorbed the female Asian American television anchorperson as a novel social type.[15] In Michael Cimino's *Year of the Dragon* (1985), for example, international model Ariane plays the part of a TV news reporter named Tracy Tzu who invites rape by a hard-boiled detective (Mickey Rourke) who is waging a personal war against the Chinese American Mafia in New York.

The overrepresentation of female Asian American anchorpersons and the near-total absence of their male counterparts—the Connie Chung syndrome—is the material outcome of a complementary system of racism and sexism. But in journalistic accounts of the syndrome, the roles that racism and sexism play in the casting of TV news anchors is rarely alluded to. A December 1991 *Los Angeles Times* article, for example, tiptoed around the twin taboos by reporting the "difficult to prove" accusations made by "minorities in the field" that the "white, male hiring Establishment feels more comfortable seeing a white male sitting next to a minority female at the anchor desk than the reverse."[16] One of only a handful of male Asian Americans currently working as television news anchors in the entire country, Stephen Tschida of WDBJ-TV (Roanoke, Virginia), was informed early in his career that he should concentrate on reporting because he did not have the proper "look" to qualify for the top job. In the meantime, such broadcast news veterans as Ken Kashiwahara, Mario Machado, and Sam Chu Linn, who began their careers in the early 1970s, have been passed over for younger, more beauteous, female Asian American objects of desire. For although those in TV news management would never admit to it, there is a belief that "Asian women are exotic looking and thus more appealing to white audiences, while Asian men are not."[17]

News anchor at KCBS-TV Los Angeles Tritia Toyota somewhat disingenuously explains away the phenomenon as a historical accident. "Initially, because there were Asian-American women like myself and Connie Chung on television," says Toyota, "that made a difference who subsequently went into the business. If I had been a man, I think it might have been very different." Moreover, Toyota blames Asian American men for not being "willing to take the risk" in entering a profession that offers little job security and possibilities for career advancement.[18] CBS-TV news correspondent James Hattori (currently based at the Tokyo bureau), however, is less generous in his assessment of the network double standard. He remains critical of decision makers who profess sympathy for the plight of Asian American male talent but are unwilling to offer more than lip service in correcting the gross gender imbalance of on-camera talent.

The prevalence of Asian American women functioning as TV anchors is rooted in a sexual politics that harks back to the era of European imperialism continuing through to the more recent U.S. wars of conquest in Asia. As David Henry Hwang shrewdly dramatized in the Tony Award-winning play *M. Butterfly* (1988), the relationship between colonized Asia and the Euro-American world is shot through with fundamental issues of power as expressed through sexuality in all its real and imagined manifestations.[19] Asia itself stands as a sign-symbol for a passive and compliant femininity as constructed under the imperial regime of Euro-American patriarchy, an Asia meant to be possessed by force and ravaged at will. Once subdued and wrested from her male defenders, the fantasy-ideal of the Asian woman can then take her rightful place at the side of the Euro-American conqueror as war bride, as mail-order wife, as whore, as TV news anchor. Ti-Hua Chang, who works as a reporter for WCBS-TV New York, was once told by a "friend" that "when I see an Asian male, I get negative thoughts. I see a Japanese soldier during World War II. I see a karate expert. But when I see an Asian female, I feel good. I see a geisha girl. I see Suzy [*sic*] Wong."[20]

The apotheosis of Connie Chung came in May 1993, when she ascended the dais to join Dan Rather as coanchor of the *CBS Evening News*. Only the second woman (after Barbara Walters) and the first Asian American to head a network news program, Chung has been positioned as the living affirmation of a meritocratic society that elevates its best and brightest to positions of prominence. Where else but in America could the daughter of a former intelligence officer for Jiang Jie-shi rise through the ranks of a highly compititive, male-dominated profession to attain its most coveted prize? Skeptics within the news industry, however, dismissed Chung's promotion as mere "window dressing." Her hiring was viewed widely by critics as a "cosmetic change to bolster the ratings and demographics of CBS' No. 2-rated newscast" and as a calculated move to stimulate viewer interest in her prime-time newsmagazine *Eye to Eye,* which premiered on June 17.[21]

Lost in Discursive Space

In an interview promoting the spring 1992 PBS airing of the seriously flawed *Thousand Pieces of Gold* on *American Playhouse,* actress Rosalind Chao mentioned that while she was growing up, the "only positive role models were (TV anchorwomen) Connie Chung and Tritia Toyota."[22] In a separate interview, Chao revealed that she began college as an English literature major, but later transferred to the University of Southern California and switched to a journalism major. In doing so, Chao hoped to "capitalize in the Asian American female newscaster rush," according to reporter Barry Koltnow.[23] Instead, Chao moved into acting while still attending college and most recently has appeared on *Star Trek: The Next Generation* (1987–present) as *Enterprise* botanist Keiko Ishikawa O'Brien, the wife of Transporter Chief Miles Edward O'Brien (Colm Meaney). Both have now joined the cast of the spin-off series *Star Trek: Deep Space Nine* (1993–present) as the same characters.

Whether in the rough-and-tumble late nineteenth-century frontier setting of *Thousand Pieces of Gold,* the free-floating twenty-fourth-century galactic peregrinations aboard the *Enterprise* in *Star Trek: The Next Generation,* or on the frontier space station in *Deep Space Nine,* the characters played by Rosalind Chao occupy the socially circumscribed role of white man's helpmeet. Although approximately half a millennium of fictional time and space separate these programs, it is quite telling that the Chinese immigrant Holly Bemis (Chao) who is married by a kindly white man in *Thousand Pieces of Gold* and Keiko of *Star Trek: The Next Generation* and *Deep Space Nine* occupy an almost identical discursive space. The problem lies not with the limitations of television as a medium, but in racialized discursive practices that have taken on an opaque and naturalized obduracy through repetition and redundancy.

Hackneyed approaches to the depiction of Asian Americans are in large part the result of the exclusionary, hermetically enclosed world of network television and its allied production companies. For example, a 1989 report commissioned by the Writers Guild of America, west, found that minorities constitute only 2 percent of members employed by major film and television companies. When asked at a news conference whether the lack of minority participation in the field could be attributed to "racism," Writers Guild executive director Brian Walton answered, "It's difficult to come to a contrary conclusion."[24] Opportunities for minority writers at major studios increased slightly during the 1970s under the threat of class-action lawsuits and for fear of losing government contracts. But under the procorporate deregulatory regime of President Ronald Reagan during the 1980s, the incentive to correct the underrepresentation of minority writers voluntarily through affirmative action programs was removed. As Ronald Reagan enjoyed the considerable financial and political support of Hollywood power brokers such as Lew Wasserman of MCA, he was probably not inclined to intervene in entertainment industry concerns, particularly labor matters.[25]

If Asian American groups are to be depicted on television in a fair, realistic, and nonderogatory manner, this will require their greater representation among the ranks of professional writers. Toward this end, there must be equal access to writing jobs and pay equity as well. If labor and production companies do not take positive, measurable steps in this direction, then perhaps government intervention and the active involvement of civil rights organizations will be needed to break the gentlemen's agreement that prevents Asian Americans and other nonwhite minorities from working as writers in the television and film industries. The failure of labor and management to correct the problem, according to the Writers Guild report, "implicitly endorses employment practices that keep minority, female, and older writers from participating fully in the writing of feature films and television programming."[26]

A 1993 update of the *Hollywood Writers' Report* covering employment trends from 1987 through 1991 pointed to "pockets of promise" for minorities writing for television. In particular, Warner Bros. Television was cited for having increased its representation of minority writers from four in 1987 to twenty-eight by 1991 through its "effective minority access program."[27] However, the progressive steps taken by Warner Bros. to integrate the ranks of its writers hardly makes a dent in the vast overrepresentation of majority group members. "While there have been modest gains in employment of minority writers in television in general and substantial improvement at a few companies," write the authors of the study, "nonminority writers still account for over 95% of employment in television."[28] The film and television industries would do well to note the findings of an August 1993 *Los Angeles Times* poll that posed the following question to residents of Southern California: "What is the portrayal of Asians in television and movies?" The vast majority of respondents (72 percent) observed that such portrayals are "distorted."[29] Given the large percentage of the viewing public that acknowledges the disparity between image and reality, the film and television industries should take aggressive action to remedy the historical pattern of calumny and misrepresentation. The employment and involvement of Asian American writers in the production process would go a long way toward redressing this plainly unacceptable situation.

Although a de facto protective covenant excludes Asian Americans from the writing trade, a select few are making slow but steady inroads into the Hollywood film and television industries. A chatty article appearing in *Buzz* magazine referred to the growing ranks of prominent Asian American entertainment executives as "The Chan Clan," after Hanna-Barbera's animated *The Amazing Chan and the Chan Clan* (1972–74) (in which former Number One Son Keye Luke supplied the voice of his fictional father, Charlie Chan).[30] The piece breathlessly describes the career paths of various Asian American television producers, writers, actors, and executives, the most prominent probably being Scott Sassa, president of Turner Entertainment Networks since 1990. "He's got so much money, so much power. He's definitely the one to watch," gushes one Asian American executive.[31] Sassa is credited with being one of the principal architects of the Fox Broadcasting Company under Barry Diller before leaving for Turner in 1987.[32]

It is doubtful that the individual power of a few well-placed media executives will translate into the more equitable representation of Asian Americans on network television. Although it provokes optimism that a select few Asian American movers and shakers are able to wield a measure of power in a tough and competitive business, at a more fundamental level the problem resides in the larger relationship between the private, for-profit, market-centered television networks and the overriding tendency for ethnic loyalties to assume secondary importance in favor of long-term career survival.

Despite the almost complete control of television by capitalist oligopolies, cable and satellite technologies have formed the possibility for furthering democratic access to news, information, and entertainment. Edward S. Herman suggests that those interested in realizing a democratic media "be alert to and take advantage of every technological innovation."[33] Similarly, Douglas Kellner proposes that cable and satellite television be used to make available "new public broadcasting channels open to groups currently excluded from national communication."[34]

Any and all challenges to the private, for-profit system of network television doubtless will be vigorously resisted by various sectors of corporate America. Nonetheless, it is not too soon to begin envisioning a radically restructured system of television that will better serve the requirements of a functioning democracy. Whatever shape a transformed television system finally assumes, it should be informed by the values of diversity, dissent, self-activity, and a good measure of *jouissance*. With James Curran, I agree that programs produced and distributed by a democratized media system would allow citizens to "reinterpret their social experience, and question the assumptions and ideas of the dominant culture."[35] Such a democratized media system would better allow programming that reflects the ethnic and racial diversity of an American society composed of a multiplicity of regional, age, gender, language, and class differences.

Bold Journeys

Other than the abhorrence of Asian peoples as ingrained in the dominant popular culture, there is no compelling reason Asian Americans should have been restricted in the roles they have occupied in network television. As early as 1951, the great actress Anna May Wong (Wong Lui-Tsong) starred in her own program, *The Gallery of Mme. Lui-Tsong* (1951). In this ill-fated program, which aired on the now-defunct DuMont network, Wong played the part of an international art gallery owner whose occupation engaged her in detective work as well.

Near the end of her career (Wong died of a heart attack in 1961, at age fifty-four) she appeared as a guest on the travel/adventure program *Bold Journey* (1956–59).[36] In that episode, the Los Angeles-born actress narrates a documentary film that recorded her "first and last" visit to China. Reunited with an aged father who returned to China during the 1930s to run the family farm, Wong takes the viewer through Shanghai and a brief tour of the "Forbidden City" in Beijing. As she describes her travels, Wong's sense of pride in her Asian background is conveyed in a softly understated fashion. Seen through the eyes of the thoroughly cosmopolitan Wong, the Chinese people are neither freakish nor quaint "Oriental" specimens.

The travelogue is freshingly free of the revulsion or condescension toward China expressed by other television programs of this vintage, which were usually rabidly anticommunist in tone. However, host John Stephenson takes care to reassure the viewer that the film footage was shot in the prerevolutionary China of old. But when Stephenson errs by exoticizing Wong's encounter by observing, "Well, they're a very wonderful and interesting people, the Chinese of the old country, aren't they?" Wong smiles wanly and deflects his mildly patronizing tone by simply replying, "I'm very glad that I'm of Chinese extraction."

Throughout the program, Anna May Wong is seen as a thoughtful, articulate individual who is fully capable of defining and interpreting the social world for herself. So accustomed is the viewer to the intellectual equivalent of "foot binding" inflicted upon Asian performers that at times it is startling to hear this former "Oriental" femme fatale of the American cinema speaking uninterruptedly in complete, intelligent, syntactically correct English sentences. Only in the twilight of her career was the full humanity of Anna May Wong allowed to come into being. As an older woman, no longer could she be mistaken for the yellow temptress who could lure decent white men into unspeakable acts of debauchery with only a slight parting of her ruby-red lips (for, according to American sexual lore, it is Chinese women who were said to have introduced the practice of fellatio to the United States).

Another Asian American idol of the silent screen, Sessue Hayakawa (1889–1973), made occasional appearances on TV once his financially rewarding film career had fallen into decline. According to editor and filmmaker Yoshio Kishi, between 1914 and 1922 Hayakawa appeared in fifty-three films, twenty-five of which were produced by his own company. In a span of only four years, Hayakawa himself claims to have earned $2 million in the days before the federal taxation of personal income.[37] At the height of his box-office popularity in 1920, Hayakawa earned $7,500 per week. His earning power placed him among such elite silent-era film stars as Francis X. Bushman, Rudolph Valentino, and Mary Pickford, all of whom Hayakawa counted as both friends and professional peers.[38]

Apart from his costarring role in David Lean's epic film *The Bridge on the River Kwai* (1957), Hayakawa appeared as a guest in a number of television programs from the late 1950s to the mid-1960s, ranging from the "Golden Age" drama of *Kraft Theatre* (previously *Kraft Television Theatre*, 1947–58) and *Studio One* (1948–58) to the popular Western *Wagon Train* (1957–65) and the innovative "road" adventure *Route 66* (1960–64). In addition, the comedy variety programs *The Red Skelton Show* (1951–71) and *The Steve Allen Show* (1956–61) featured the aged matinee idol in guest spots.[39]

On *World Theatre*, a program following a format similar to that of *Bold Journey*, Sessue Hayakawa serves as on-camera narrator of a documentary that explores the forms of traditional Japanese theatre. Series host Dr. Charles Lee of the University of Pennsylvania rather pedantically introduces the general topic before turning the program over to Hayakawa.[40] With grace and erudition, the actor describes such rarefied Japanese aesthetic forms as *bugaku* (ancient court dance), *gagaku* (ancient court music and dance), *bunraku* (classical puppet theater), *noh*, and *kabuki*. Now in his seventies, Hayakawa cannot be mistaken for the hypersexual Asian predator who threatened to defile white womanhood in his early films. Like Anna May Wong, the elderly Hayakawa is finally permitted the luxury of expressing himself without being subjected to external mediation or control.

The performances of Anna May Wong and Sessue Hayakawa demonstrate that Asian Americans are fully capable of representing their lives and experiences for themselves, without obsessive Euro-American intervention and control. By revisiting these two programs featuring respected Asian American figures of an earlier era, the inevitability of degrading and discriminatory network television practices is thrown into question. Other than for cynical purposes of social control, there is no reason Asian Americans should continue to suffer the indignities usually spared other nonwhite groups and white ethnics. In denying the humanity of Asian Americans by restricting them to narrowly defined social roles, the gatekeepers of network television deprive the larger American public of the vitality and genius of the diverse Asian groups whose contributions to both U.S. society and world culture have been substantial.

If a cosmopolitan, multiracial internationalism is indeed the future of U.S. society, then those who control the content of network television programming would be be well advised to begin tapping the talent and energy of the many Asian American communities.[41] What with their rapidly growing numbers and trans-Pacific ties to the extraordinarily dynamic newly industrialized economies of East Asia, Asian Americans will play a central role in the globally integrated society of the twenty-first century.[42] Their representation among the managerial ranks in network and public television, in creative sectors, and in the pool of on-camera talent will provide much-needed specialized insight into the epochal demographic, cultural, and political-economic changes that are taking place on a worldwide scale.

Moral suasion alone, however, has never been a sufficient goad to the corporate media leviathan. Network self-reform rarely comes about without intense external pressure. Required most immediately are the sustained creative efforts of public-supported independent film and video artists, vastly improved access to existing commercial media institutions, and aggressive legal-political challenges to discriminatory employment practices in the television industry. As strategic battles are waged on these three primary fronts, it must also be kept in mind that the fair, equitable, and just representation of Asian Americans on television is linked to the larger political struggles against racism, sexism, nationalism, homophobia, and economic inequality. If the inclusionary imperative of liberal democratic principles stand as the philosophical denial of discrimination and racism, then the issue of equitable Asian American representation on television constitutes nothing less than a referendum on the legitimacy of society that is maintained by multiple forms of inequality. The yellow presence on television, then, raises fundamental questions as to the meaning of American democracy. These are questions too precious to be left to the supposedly impersonal "market forces" of private sector network television alone.

Notes

Preface

1. Elaine H. Kim, "Home Is Where the *Han* Is: A Korean American Perspective on the Los Angeles Upheavals," in *Reading Rodney King Reading Urban Uprising*, ed. Robert Gooding-Williams (New York: Routledge, 1993), 221.

2. Ibid., 218. In the documentary *Sai-I-Gu*, aired September 12, 1993, on PBS affiliates, Elaine Kim, Christine Choy, and Dai Sil Kim-Gibson captured the anguish of three Korean women struggling to put their lives back in order after having experienced personal tragedy during the Los Angeles rebellion.

3. For a survey of theory concerning film, television, and video, see Steven Connor, *Postmodernist Culture: An Introduction to Theories of the Contemporary* (Cambridge, Mass.: Basil Blackwell, 1989), 158–83.

4. Douglas Kellner refers to Baudrillard as a "new McLuhan" whose media theory suffers from a formalist bias, technological determinism, and theoreticism. See Douglas Kellner, *Jean Baudrillard: From Marxism to Postmodernism and Beyond* (Stanford, Calif.: Stanford University Press, 1989), 60–92.

5. See Tim Dant, *Knowledge, Ideology and Discourse: A Sociological Perspective* (New York: Routledge, 1991).

6. Steven Best and Douglas Kellner write, "In discourse politics, marginal groups attempt to contest the hegemonic discourses that position individuals within the straitjacket of normal identities to liberate the free play of differences." See Steven Best and Douglas Kellner, *Postmodern Theory: Critical Interrogations* (New York: Guilford, 1991), 57.

7. The renewed obsession with preserving a Judeo-Christian religious, Anglo-Saxon monoculture is seen in Allan Bloom, *The Closing of the American Mind* (New York: Touchstone, 1987); E. D. Hirsch, Jr., *Cultural Literacy: What Every American Needs to Know* (New York: Vintage, 1988); and Dinesh D'Souza, *Illiberal Education: The Politics of Race and Sex on Campus* (New York: Free Press, 1991).

8. The concept of "racial meanings," and its broader implications for power relations in U.S. society, is developed in Michael Omi and Howard Winant, *Racial Formation in the United States: From the 1960s to the 1980s* (New York: Routledge, 1986), 57–60. See also the underappreciated work of Oliver C. Cox, *Caste, Class, and Race: A Study in Social Dynamics* (New York: Modern Reader, 1948).

9. Don T. Nakanishi, "Minorities and International Politics," in *Counterpoint:*   *255*

Perspectives on Asian America, ed. Emme Gee (Los Angeles: UCLA Asian American Studies Center, 1976), 81–85.

Chapter 1. White Christian Nation

1. Lucie Cheng and Edna Bonacich, eds., *Labor Immigration under Capitalism: Asian Workers in the United States before World War II* (Berkeley: University of California Press, 1984).

2. Sucheng Chan, *This Bitter-Sweet Soil: The Chinese in California Agriculture, 1860–1910* (Berkeley: University of California Press, 1986).

3. Among the social characteristics of elites in the United States, "WASPs are preeminent in America's institutional structure," according to Thomas R. Dye. He cites empirical studies that note approximately 79.4 percent of top business leaders and 72.4 percent of congressional members are Protestant English Americans. The inclusion of non-Protestant "white ethnics" pushes these percentages even higher. See Thomas R. Dye, *Who's Running America? The Bush Era,* 5th ed. (Englewood Cliffs, N.J.: Prentice Hall, 1990), 193.

4. Keith Osajima, "Asian Americans as the Model Minority: An Analysis of the Popular Press Image in the 1960s and 1980s," in *Reflections on Shattered Windows: Promises and Prospects for Asian American Studies,* ed. Gary Y. Okihiro et al. (Pullman: Washington State University Press, 1988), 165–74.

5. Darrell Y. Hamamoto, *Nervous Laughter: Television Situation Comedy and Liberal Democratic Ideology* (New York: Praeger, 1989).

6. Patricia Hill Collins, *Black Feminist Thought: Knowledge, Consciousness, and the Politics of Empowerment* (Boston: Unwin Hyman, 1990), 69.

7. "Mammy" figures appeared on the television programs *Beulah* (1950–53), *The Great Gildersleeve* (1955), and *Make Room for Daddy/The Danny Thomas Show* (1953–71); *The Jeffersons* (1975–85) put a post-civil rights-era spin on the stock character by placing her in a Black middle-class household.

8. Donald G. Baker, *Race, Ethnicity and Power: A Comparative Study* (London: Routledge & Kegan Paul, 1983), 37.

9. Pierre L. van den Berghe, *Race and Racism: A Comparative Perspective* (New York: John Wiley & Sons, 1967), 11.

10. Dennis H. Wrong, *Power: Its Forms, Bases, and Uses* (Chicago: University of Chicago Press, 1988), 33.

11. Stuart Hall, "The Whites of Their Eyes: Racist Ideologies and the Media," in *The Media Reader,* ed. Manuel Alvarado and John O. Thompson (London: BFI, 1990), 12.

12. Kenneth Thompson, *Social and Gender Boundaries in the United States* (London: Tavistock, 1986), 103.

13. See Russell Leong, ed., *Moving the Image: Independent Asian Pacific American Media Arts* (Los Angeles: UCLA Asian American Studies Center and Visual Communications, Southern California Asian American Studies Central, 1991).

14. Raymond Williams, *The Politics of Modernism: Against the New Conformists* (London: Verso, 1989), 134.

15. Evelyn Nakano Glenn, *Issei, Nisei, War Bride: Three Generations of Japanese Women in Domestic Service* (Philadelphia: Temple University Press, 1986).

16. Ibid., 11.

17. See Nathan Glazer, *The Limits of Social Policy* (Cambridge, Mass.: Harvard

University Press, 1988); William Julius Wilson, *The Truly Disadvantaged: The Inner City, the Underclass, and Public Policy* (Chicago: University of Chicago Press, 1987); Charles Murray, *Losing Ground: American Social Policy 1950–1980* (New York: Basic Books, 1984). Though not without serious flaws of its own, a survey and critique of the conservative reaction is found in Christopher Jencks, *Rethinking Social Policy: Race, Poverty, and the Underclass* (New York: Harper Perennial, 1993).

18. E. San Juan, Jr., "Multiculturalism vs. Hegemony: Ethnic Studies, Asian Americans, and U.S. Racial Politics," *Massachusetts Review* 32 (1991): 468.

19. The rigidity of class-based analysis in traditional Marxian theory at the expense of racial and gender issues has been addressed recently by Stanley Aronowitz, *The Crisis of Historical Materialism: Class, Politics and Culture in Marxist Theory*, 2d ed. (Minneapolis: University of Minnesota Press, 1990), 123–35. The growing body of work in the Marxian tradition that theorizes race is surveyed in John Solomos, "Varieties of Marxist Conceptions of 'Race,' Class and the State: A Critical Analysis," in *Theories of Race and Ethnic Relations*, ed. John Rex and David Mason (London: Cambridge University Press, 1986), 84–109.

20. Michael Novak, *The Rise of the Unmeltable Ethnics* (New York: Macmillan, 1972).

21. Peter Steinfels, *The Neoconservatives: The Men Who Are Changing America's Politics* (New York: Touchstone, 1979).

22. Elaine H. Kim, *Asian American Literature: An Introduction to the Writings and Their Social Context* (Philadelphia: Temple University Press, 1982); Eugene Franklin Wong, *On Visual Media Racism: Asians in the American Motion Pictures* (New York: Arno, 1978).

23. Ronald Takaki, *Strangers from a Different Shore: A History of Asian Americans* (Boston: Little, Brown, 1989), 31–33.

24. Chan, *This Bitter-Sweet Soil*, 387.

25. Ronald Takaki, *Iron Cages: Race and Culture in 19th-Century America* (New York: Oxford University Press, 1990), 237.

26. "Although the once lopsided ratio between men and women had narrowed, from 15 to 1 in 1910 to 3 to 1 in 1950, a disproportionate number of Chinese men still lived without wives and families." Shih-Shan Henry Tsai, *The Chinese Experience in America* (Bloomington: Indiana University Press, 1986), 147.

27. See Alexander Saxton, *The Rise and Fall of the White Republic: Class Politics and Mass Culture in Nineteenth-Century America* (New York: Verso, 1990), 294–303.

28. See David R. Roediger, *The Wages of Whiteness: Race and the Making of the American Working Class* (New York: Verso, 1991). The author examines the role of nineteenth-century minstrelsy in constructing white racial identity.

29. *Raven*, "Return of the Dragon" (24 June 1992). Created by Frank Lupo. Writer: Frank Lupo. Director: Craig R. Baxley.

30. Cast members gathered for a heartfelt tribute to Jack Soo, who costarred in eighty episodes. *Barney Miller* (1979). Created by Danny Arnold and Theodore J. Flicker. Executive producer: Danny Arnold. Producers: Tony Sheehan and Reinhold Weege. Director: Noam Pitlik.

31. Sulu's given name, Hikaru, was revealed in the movie *Star Trek VI: The Undiscovered Country* (1992). His birthplace was identified as San Francisco in *Star*

Trek IV: The Voyage Home (1986). Michael Okuda and Denise Okuda, *Star Trek Chronology: The History of the Future* (New York: Pocket Books, 1993), 152.

32. Nelson George, *In Living Color: The Authorized Companion to the Fox TV Series* (New York: Warner, 1991), 3.

33. *In Living Color*, "The Wrath of Farrakhan" (1990). Executive producer: Keenen Ivory Wayans. Producer: Tamara Rawitt.

34. Mary Ann Doane, *Femme Fatales: Feminism, Film Theory, Psychoanalysis* (New York: Routledge, 1991), 217.

35. Yuji Ichioka, *The Issei: The World of the First Generation Japanese Immigrants, 1885–1924* (New York: Free Press, 1990), 172.

36. Ibid., 253.

37. Another noteworthy Asian American in the variety arts on television was Laurie Ichino, a child performer who was a regular on *The Danny Kaye Show* (1963–67) from 1964 to 1965.

38. *Ohara*, "Seeing Something That Isn't There" (30 Apr. 1988). Created by Michael Braverman, Pat Morita, and John Kuri. Executive producers: Roderick Taylor, Tony Wharmby, and Brian Grazer. Writers: Jeff Mandell and Bruce A. Taylor.

39. *The Tonight Show* (8 May 1969).

40. Jon Matsumoto, "Faces: Comic Henry Cho Cashes in on His Down-Home Tennessee Drawl," *Los Angeles Times*, 25 July 1992, Orange County ed., F4.

41. Amado Cabezas, Larry H. Shinagawa, and Gary Kawaguchi, "New Inquiries into the Socioeconomic Status of Pilipino Americans in California," *Amerasia Journal* 13.1 (1986–87): 1–21.

42. Fred Cordova, *Filipinos: Forgotten Asian Americans* (Dubuque, Iowa: Kendall/Hunt, 1983), 139.

43. *E/R* (1984). Executive producers: Saul Turteltaub and Bernie Orenstein. Producer: Eve Brandstein. Writer: Gary Gilbert. Director: Peter Bonerz.

44. *The United States and the Philippines: In Our Image*, "Colonial Days" (8 May 1989). Executive producer: Andrew Pearson. Producer: Andrew Pearson and Eric Neudel. Writers: Stanley Karnow and Andrew Pearson. Chief correspondent: Stanley Karnow.

45. *The United States and the Philippines: In Our Image*, "Showcase of Democracy" (1989). Executive producer: Andrew Pearson. Producers: Andrew Pearson and Eric Neudel. Writers: Stanley Karnow and Andrew Pearson. Chief correspondent: Stanley Karnow.

46. Yayori Matsui, *Women's Asia* (Atlantic Highlands, N.J.: Zed, 1989), 72.

47. Susan Essoyan, "First Hawaiians Seek Return to Some Sovereignty," *Los Angeles Times*, 22 July 1992, Orange County ed., A5.

48. Alexander Cockburn, "Hawaiians Want Their Land Returned," *Los Angeles Times*, 24 Aug. 1993, Orange County ed., B9.

49. Haunani-Kay Trask, "Politics in the Pacific Islands: Imperialism and Native Self-Determination," *Amerasia Journal* 16.1 (1990): 11.

50. *Hawaii Five-O*, "Two Doves and Mr. Heron" (1971). Writer: Anthony Lawrence. Director: Charles Dubin.

51. That this relationship between the white boss and his nonwhite subordinates is a common theme in U.S. popular culture is borne out in the television cartoon series *Dick Tracy* (1960–62), produced by United Productions of America. At the

beginning of each episode, Dick Tracy would assign an ethnic detective such as Go Go Gomez (Mexican) or Joe Jitsu (Japanese) to solve a crime. Only after the difficult work had been done would Tracy arrive to make the arrest. This never varied from episode to episode.

52. Paul Jacobs and Saul Landau, with Eve Pell, *To Serve the Devil*, vol. 2, *Colonials and Sojourners* (New York: Vintage, 1971), 28.

53. *Hawaii Five-O*, "Killer Bee" (21 Jan. 70). Producer: Leonard Katzman. Writer: Anthony Lawrence. Director: Paul Stanley.

54. Christopher Anderson, "Reflections on *Magnum, P.I.*," in *Television: The Critical View*, 4th ed., ed. Horace Newcomb (New York: Oxford University Press, 1987), 116.

55. A program that tried to capitalize on the success of the film adventure *Raiders of the Lost Ark* (1981), *Tales of the Gold Monkey* (1982–83) was set in the South Pacific on the fictional Marivella Islands.

56. *ABC News Nightline*, "Pearl Harbor +50" (6 Dec. 1991). Executive producer: Shunchi Itaya. Producer: Taeki Takahashi.

57. Philip Agee, "Producing the Proper Crisis," *Z Magazine*, Nov. 1990, 53–60.

58. *P.O.V.*, *Homes Apart: The Two Koreas* (28 May 1992). Filmmakers: J. T. Takagi and Christine Choy. Writer: David Henry Hwang. Narrator: Christine Choy.

59. James T. Fawcett and Benjamin V. Cariño, "International Migration and Pacific Basin Development," in *Pacific Bridges: The New Immigration from Asia and the Pacific Islands*, ed. James T. Fawcett and Benjamin V. Cariño (Staten Island, N.Y.: Center for Migration Studies, 1987), 11.

60. *M*A*S*H* (1972). Developed for television by Larry Gelbart. Producer: Gene Reynolds. Writer: Larry Gelbart. Director: Gene Reynolds.

61. *M*A*S*H* (1972). Developed for television by Larry Gelbart. Producer: Gene Reynolds. Executive script consultant: Larry Gelbart. Writer: Laurence Marks. Director: Hy Averback.

62. "Moose" is short for *musume*, the Japanese term for a young unmarried woman or daughter, probably adopted during the U.S. occupation of Japan after World War II. The designation "moose," then, is rooted in the material relationship between the conquerer and the vanquished. During the Vietnam War, the "hootch maid" filled the same function.

63. *AfterMASH*, "Klinger vs. Klinger." Script dated 29 June 1983. Writers: Ken Levine and David Isaacs.

64. *AfterMASH*, "Thanksgiving of '58." Script dated 11 July 1983. Writers: Ken Levine and David Isaacs.

65. Paul Frederick Cecil, *Herbicidal Warfare: The RANCH HAND Project in Vietnam* (New York: Praeger, 1986), 109.

66. The explanatory concept of "technowar" is central to the study by James William Gibson, *The Perfect War: The War We Couldn't Lose and How We Did* (New York: Vintage, 1988).

67. William Shawcross, *The Quality of Mercy: Cambodia, Holocaust and Modern Conscience* (New York: Simon & Schuster, 1984), 405.

68. William P. O'Hare and Judy C. Felt, "Asian Americans: America's Fastest Growing Minority Group," *Population Trends and Public Policy*, Feb. 1991, 2.

69. Andrew Lam, "My Vietnam, My America," *The Nation*, 10 Dec. 1990, 724.

70. David Dellinger, *Vietnam Revisited: From Covert Action to Invasion to Recon-*

struction (Boston: South End, 1986), 163. In late 1992, the U.S. government began showing signs of normalizing relations with Vietnam in response to the urging of American corporations, who view the country as the "last great untapped business opportunity in Asia." Philip Shenon, "For Vietnam, Settling the Past Could Be Good Business," *New York Times*, 22 Nov. 1992, sec. 4, p. 5.

71. James Fallows, *More Like Us: Making America Great Again* (New York: Houghton Mifflin, 1990), 99–109.

72. Sucheng Chan, *Asian Americans: An Interpretive History* (Boston: Twayne, 1991), 170.

73. Thanh Van Tran, "The Vietnamese American Family," in *Ethnic Families in America: Patterns and Variations*, 3d ed., ed. Charles H. Mindel, Robert W. Habenstein, and Roosevelt Wright, Jr. (New York: Elsevier, 1988), 290.

74. *ABC Movie, Earth Angel* (4 Mar. 1991). Executive producers: Leonard Hill and Joel Fields. Producer: Ron Gilbert. Writer: Nina Shengold. Director: Joe Napolitano.

75. Based on the 1986 movie of the same title, the sitcom *Gung Ho* took as its premise the clash of cultures between American autoworkers and the Japanese management team at Assan Motors Company. Executive producer: John Rappoport. Producer: George Sunga. Based on characters created by Edwin Blum, Lowell Ganz, and Babaloo Mandel.

76. *Down Home* (4 May 1991). Created by Barton Dean. Executive producers: Barton Dean, Dan Fauci, and Ted Danson. Producers: Christopher Lloyd and Jace Richdale. Writer: Ken Kuta.

77. *Down Home* (11 May 1991). Created by Barton Dean. Executive producers: Barton Dean, Dan Fauci, and Ted Danson. Producers: Christopher Lloyd and Jace Richdale. Writer: Jace Richdale.

78. U.S. Commission on Civil Rights, *Recent Activities against Citizens and Residents of Asian Descent* (Washington, D.C.: U.S. Government Printing Office, 1986), 50–52.

79. Stanley Sue and James K. Morishima, *The Mental Health of Asian Americans* (San Francisco: Jossey-Bass, 1988), 91.

80. Stanley Karnow and Nancy Yoshihara, *Asian Americans in Transition* (New York: Asia Society, 1992), 42.

Chapter 2. Asians in the American West

1. Eric R. Wolf, *Europe and the People without History* (Berkeley: University of California Press, 1982), 354–83.

2. Edna Bonacich and Lucie Cheng, "Introduction: A Theoretical Orientation to International Labor Migration," in *Labor Immigration under Capitalism: Asian Workers in the United States before World War II*, ed. Lucie Cheng and Edna Bonacich (Berkeley: University of California Press, 1984), 31.

3. Sucheng Chan, *This Bitter-Sweet Soil: The Chinese in California Agriculture, 1860–1910* (Berkeley: University of California Press, 1986), 16.

4. George Anthony Peffer, "Forbidden Families: Emigration Experiences of Chinese Women under the Page Law, 1875–1882," *Journal of American Ethnic History* 6.1 (1986): 28–46.

5. J. Fred MacDonald, *Who Shot the Sheriff? The Rise and Fall of the Television Western* (New York: Praeger, 1987), 97–98.

6. *Bonanza*, "Amigo" (1967). Producer: David Dortort. Story by Jack Turley. Teleplay by John Hawkins and Jack Turley. Director: William F. Claxton.

7. *Bonanza*, "A Christmas Story" (1966). Producer: David Dortort. Writer: Thomas Thompson. Director: Gerd Oswald.

8. *Bonanza*, "The Fear Merchants" (1970). Producer: David Dortort. Story by Frank Unger. Teleplay by Frank Unger and Thomas Thompson. Director: Lewis Allen.

9. George M. Blackburn and Sherman L. Ricards, "The Chinese of Virginia City, Nevada: 1870," *Amerasia Journal* 7:1 (1980): 51–71.

10. Ibid., 68.

11. Morrison G. Wong, "The Chinese American Family," in *Ethnic Families in America: Patterns and Variations* 3d ed., ed. Charles H. Mindel, Robert W. Habenstein, and Roosevelt Wright, Jr. (New York: Elsevier, 1988), 239.

12. *Gunsmoke*, "Gunfighter, R.I.P." (1966). Executive producer: Philip Leacock. Producer: John Mantley. Teleplay by Hal Sitowitz. Director: Mark Rydell. Story consultant: Paul Savage.

13. *How the West Was Won*, "China Girl" (1979). Executive producer: John Mantley. Producer: John G. Stephens. Executive story consultant: Calvin Clements. Writer: Calvin Clements, Jr. Director: Joseph Pevney.

14. *American Playhouse, Thousand Pieces of Gold* (29 Apr. 1992). Producers: Kenji Yamamoto and Nancy Kelly. Writer: Anne Makepeace. Director: Nancy Kelly.

15. See Michele Wallace, *Black Macho and the Myth of the Superwoman* (New York: Verso, 1990). These two essays discuss the legacy of racism and sexism and their implications for African American male-female relationships.

16. Lucie Cheng, "Free, Indentured, Enslaved: Chinese Prostitutes in Nineteenth-Century America," in *Labor Immigration under Capitalism: Asian Workers in the United States before World War II*, ed. Lucie Cheng and Edna Bonacich (Berkeley: University of California Press, 1984), 425.

17. Stanford M. Lyman, *Chinese Americans* (New York: Random House, 1974), 187.

18. American Social History Project. *Who Built America? Working People and the Nation's Economy, Politics, Culture, and Society*, vol. 1 (New York: Pantheon, 1990), 516.

19. Ronald Takaki, *Strangers from a Different Shore: A History of Asian Americans* (Boston: Little, Brown, 1989), 85.

20. *Yancy Derringer*, "Two Tickets to Promontory" (4 June 1959). Created by Mary Loos and Richard Sale. Executive producers: Don W. Sharpe and Warren Lewis. Producers: Mary Loos and Richard Sale.

21. *Gunsmoke*, "The Queue" (3 Nov. 1955). Producer: Charles Marquis Warren. Story by John Meston. Teleplay by Sam Peckinpah. Director: Charles Marquis Warren.

22. Sucheng Chan, *Asian Americans: An Interpretive History* (Boston: Twayne, 1991), 48.

23. *Cowboy G-Men*, "Chinaman's Chance" (syndicated 1952). Producer: Henry B. Donovan. Director: Thor Brooks. Based on an original story by Henry B. Donovan.

24. See, for example, such classic studies as Michael Banton, *Race Relations* (London: Tavistock, 1967); Pierre L. van den Berghe, *Race and Racism: A Comparative Perspective* (New York: John Wiley & Sons, 1967); Robert Blauner, *Racial Oppression in America* (New York: Harper & Row, 1972).

25. Laura Mulvey, "Visual Pleasure and Narrative Cinema," in *Feminism and Film Theory*, ed. Constance Penley (New York: Routledge, 1988), 57–68.

26. Jane Gaines, "White Privilege and Looking Relations," in *Issues in Feminist Film Criticism*, ed. Patricia Erens (Bloomington: Indiana University Press, 1990), 202.

27. bell hooks, *Black Looks: Race and Representation* (Boston: South End, 1992), 125.

28. Evelyn Nakano Glenn, *Issei, Nisei, War Bride: Three Generations of Japanese American Women in Domestic Service* (Philadelphia: Temple University Press, 1986), 192.

29. Jane Hunter, *The Gospel of Gentility: American Women Missionaries in Turn-of-the-Century China* (New Haven, Conn.: Yale University Press, 1984), 176.

30. Ibid., 205.

31. *Annie Oakley*, "Annie and the Chinese Curse" (1955). Producer: Louis Gray. Teleplay by Maurice Tombragel. Director: Ray Nazarro.

32. The notion of the "social bandit" is developed by E. J. Hobsbawm in the classic work *Primitive Rebels: Studies in Archaic Forms of Social Movement in the 19th and 20th Centuries* (New York: W. W. Norton, 1959), 13–29.

33. Maxine Hong Kingston, *Tripmaster Monkey: His Fake Book* (New York: Vintage, 1990), 27.

34. *Have Gun Will Travel* (1959). Producer: Ben Brady. Writer: Donn Mullally. Created by Herb Meadow and Sam Rolfe.

35. Kareem Abdul-Jabbar and Peter Knobler, *Giant Steps* (New York: Bantam, 1983), 188–89.

36. Verina Glaessner, *Kung Fu: Cinema of Vengeance* (New York: Bounty, 1974), 91.

37. Peter Rainer, " 'Dragon,' Jason Scott Lee: They Have the Chops," *Los Angeles Times*, 7 May 1993, Orange County ed., F1.

38. *Kung Fu*, pilot (1972). Producer: Jerry Thorpe. Story by Ed Spielman. Teleplay by Ed Spielman and Howard Friedlander. Director: Jerry Thorpe.

39. Alexander Saxton, "The Racial Trajectory of the Western Hero," *Amerasia Journal* 11.2 (1984): 68.

40. An older, slower, but no less taciturn Kwai Chang Caine recently returned to television in the syndicated series *Kung Fu: The Legend Continues* (pilot, 27 Jan. 1993). Producer: Susan Murdoch. Coproducers: David Carradine, Phil Bedard, and Larry LaLonde. Based on a character created by Ed Spielman. Story by Michael Sloan and Ed Waters. Teleplay by Michael Sloan. Director: Jud Taylor.

Chapter 3. War against Japanese America

1. Daniel Patrick Moynihan, *The Negro Family: The Case for National Action* (Washington, D.C.: U.S. Department of Labor, Office of Family Planning and Research, 1965).

2. Roger Daniels and Harry H. L. Kitano, *American Racism: Exploration of the Nature of Prejudice* (Englewood Cliffs, N.J.: Prentice Hall, 1970), 89–90.

3. William Petersen, *Japanese Americans: Oppression and Success* (New York: Random House, 1971), ix.

4. Ibid., 231–32.

5. Sucheng Chan, "New Studies in Ethnicity, Gender, and Political Inequality," in *Social and Gender Boundaries in the United States,* ed. Sucheng Chan (Lewiston, N.Y.: Edwin Mellen, 1989), 4.

6. William Petersen, "Chinese Americans and Japanese Americans," in *Essays and Data on American Ethnic Groups,* ed. Thomas Sowell (Washington, D.C.: Urban Institute, 1978), 93.

7. *Farewell to Manzanar* (1976). Executive producer: George J. Santoro. Producer: John Korty. Teleplay by Jeanne Wakatsuki Houston, James D. Houston, and John Korty. Director: John Korty. Technical advisers: Edison Uno and Karl Yoneda.

8. Greta Chi provides the voice-over narration for Jeanne Wakatsuki Houston. Nobu McCarthy plays the roles of both Misa Wakatsuki and Jeanne Wakatsuki Houston as an adult.

9. Yuji Ichioka, "JERS Revisited: Introduction," in *Views from Within: The Japanese American Evacuation and Resettlement Study,* ed. Yuji Ichioka (Los Angeles: Asian American Studies Center, 1989), 12.

10. The intensity of the division within the Japanese American community over the issue of "loyalty" registration was dramatized in the novel by John Okada, *No-No Boy* (Rutland, Vt.: Charles Tuttle, 1957).

11. Raymond Okamura, "Farewell to Manzanar: A Case of Subliminal Racism," in *Counterpoint: Perspectives on Asian America,* ed. Emma Gee (Los Angeles: UCLA Asian American Studies Center, 1976), 280–83.

12. Ibid., 282.

13. Karl G. Yoneda, *Ganbatte: Sixty-Year Struggle of a Kibei Worker* (Los Angeles: UCLA Asian American Studies Center, 1983), 197–98.

14. See Thomas Sowell, *The Economics and Politics of Race: An International Perspective* (New York: William Morrow, 1983).

15. Burton Yale Pines, *Back to Basics: The Traditionalist Movement That Is Sweeping Grass-Roots America* (New York: William Morrow, 1982), 131.

16. Richard Drinnon, *Keeper of Concentration Camps: Dillon S. Myer and American Racism* (Berkeley: University of California Press, 1987), xxiii.

17. Ibid., 266.

18. William H. Warren, "Maps: A Spatial Approach to Japanese American Communities in Los Angeles," *Amerasia Journal* 13.2 (1986–87): 137–51.

19. Roger Daniels, *Asian America: Chinese and Japanese in the United States since 1850* (Seattle: University of Washington Press, 1988), 210.

20. Elaine H. Kim, *Asian American Literature: An Introduction to the Writings and Their Social Context* (Philadelphia: Temple University Press, 1982), 156.

21. Karl Schoenberger, "Public's View of Japan Mixed, Contradictory," *Los Angeles Times,* 12 Feb. 1992, Orange County ed., A8.

22. George White, "Poll Shows a Hardening on Trade," *Los Angeles Times,* 13 Sep. 1991, Orange County ed., D1.

23. Quoted in Leslie Helm, "Japan's Rising Scorn for America," *Los Angeles Times,* 25 Oct. 1991, Orange County ed., A1.

24. *Frontline, Who Is David Duke?* (3 Mar. 1992). Executive producer: David

Fanning. Producer: Elena Mannes. Writers: Elena Mannes and Hodding Carter. Correspondent: Hodding Carter. Reporter: Jason Berry.

25. Sonni Efron, "Japanese Roots Still Ignite Bias," *Los Angeles Times*, 5 Dec. 1991, Orange County ed., A1, A36, A38.

26. Ibid., A38.

27. *Nightline*, "Pearl Harbor +50" (5 Dec. 1991).

28. Jane Hall and Leslie Helm, "Clouds across the Pacific," *Los Angeles Times*, 24 Nov. 1991, Orange County ed., Calendar, p. 90.

29. *Frontline, Losing the War with Japan* (19 Nov. 1991). Executive producer: David Fanning. Producer: Martin Koughan. Writer: Martin Koughan. Reporter: Martin Koughan.

30. See Clyde Prestowitz, Jr., *Trading Places: How We Are Giving Our Future to Japan and How to Reclaim It* (New York: Basic Books, 1989); Karel van Wolferen, *The Enigma of Japanese Power: People and Politics in a Stateless Nation* (New York: Vintage, 1990); and Pat Choate, *Agents of Influence: How Japan Manipulates America's Political and Economic System* (New York: Touchstone, 1991).

31. *60 Minutes* (30 Sep. 1990).

32. Quoted in Amy Harmon, "NAACP Urges Blacks to Boycott Japanese Cars," *Los Angeles Times*, 12 Feb. 1922, Orange County ed., D1, D15.

33. Pat Choate, *Agents of Influence: How Japan Manipulates America's Political and Economic System* (New York: Touchstone, 1991).

34. As of mid-1992, the video game business in the United States was worth $3.5 billion annually. Since "Losing the War with Japan" was produced, Nintendo's market share has slipped to 30.1 percent, on par with that of Japanese rival Sega at 31.2 percent. The volatility of the industry and anticipated entry of established large-scale corporations such as Sony and Matsushita have allowed many U.S. video game software companies to enter this highly competitive field. See Leslie Helm, "Sega Muscles in on Nintendo," *Los Angeles Times*, 25 May 1992, Orange County ed., D1, D2.

35. Quoted in Cristina Lee, "County's Japanese Firms Taking Heat," *Los Angeles Times*, 23 Feb. 1992, Orange County ed., B1, B13.

36. Shintaro Ishihara, *The Japan That Can Say No* (New York: Simon & Schuster, 1991), 28.

37. U.S. Commission on Civil Rights, *Civil Rights Issues Facing Asian Americans in the 1990s* (Washington, D.C.: U.S. Government Printing Office, 1992), 191.

38. Quoted in Sam Fulwood III, "Japan-Bashing Condemned by Rights Panel," *Los Angeles Times*, 26 Feb. 1992, Orange County ed., A1, A13.

39. Kevin Starr, "A Protectionist Elite with a Multiethnic Face Is Still Dangerous," *Los Angeles Times*, 14 June 1992, Orange County ed., M6.

40. Jane Fritsch, "Time Was Ripe for Reversal of Japanese Company's Green Line Contract," *Los Angeles Times*, 23 Jan. 1992, Orange County ed., A26.

41. Quoted in ibid.

42. *Life and Times* (13 Jan. 1992). Executive producer: Jim Kennedy. Senior producer: Martin Burns. Producer: Saul Gonzalez. Series producer: Nancy De Los Santos. Hosts: Hugh Hewitt, Patt Morrison, John Ochoa.

43. Quoted in Fritsch, "Time Was Ripe," A26.

44. *Frontline, Coming from Japan* (18 Feb. 1992). Writers: Shuichi Kato and Thomas Lennon. Narrator: Sab Shimono.

45. *Power in the Pacific*, Part 2, *Japan Comes First* (3 June 1991). A coproduction of the Australian Broadcasting Corporation and KCET/Los Angeles. Producer: Tony Barrell. Series producer: Bruce Belsham. Executive producer KCET: Blaine Baggett. Executive Producer ABC: Harry Bardwell. Writer: Tony Barrell. Narrator: Ken Kashiwahara.

46. *20/20* (6 Oct. 1990).

47. John Balzer, "U.S. Grazing Subsidies Aid Japanese-Owned Ranches," *Los Angeles Times*, 26 May 1991, Orange County ed., A1, A18, A20.

48. John Balzer, "Mariners Needed a Save, So Seattle Drafted Nintendo," *Los Angeles Times*, 25 Jan. 1992, Orange County ed., A1, A21.

49. Quoted in ibid., A21.

50. Quoted in Ross Newhan, "Japanese Get Approval to Purchase Mariners," *Los Angeles Times*, 12 June 1992, Orange County ed., C5.

51. *Northern Exposure* (1991). Created by Joshua Brand and John Falsey. Executive producers: Joshua Brand and John Falsey. Producer: Robert T. Skodis. Writer: Sean Clark. Director: Dan Lerner.

52. *Northern Exposure* (1992). Executive producers: Joshua Brand and John Falsey. Producers: Matthew Nodella and Rob Thompson. Writer: Jeffrey Vlaming. Director: Tom Moore.

53. *Inside Edition* (24 Feb. 1992).

54. Loni Ding, "Strategies of an Asian American Filmmaker," in *Moving the Image: Independent Asian Pacific American Media Arts*, ed. Russell Leong (Los Angeles: UCLA Asian American Studies Center and Visual Communications, Southern California Asian American Studies Central), 47.

55. *The Color of Honor: The Japanese American Soldier in WWII* (1988; KCET 1991). Producer: Loni Ding. Associate producer: Beth Hyams. Writer: Loni Ding. Director: Loni Ding. Narrator: Joseph Miksak.

56. *History and Memory* (27 June 1992). Writer: Rea Tajiri. Director: Rea Tajiri, with Noel Shaw and Sokhi Wagner.

Chapter 4. Asian Americans and U.S. Empire

1. Roger Daniels, *Asian America: Chinese and Japanese in the United States since 1850* (Seattle: University of Washington Press, 1988), 285–88.

2. John Lewis Gaddis, *The Long Peace: Inquiries into the History of the Cold War* (New York: Oxford University Press, 1987), 74.

3. Richard Reeves, "A Land of Widows and Orphans Remains U.S. Enemy," *Los Angeles Times*, 31 Mar. 1991, Orange County ed., M2.

4. *Vietnam: A Television History*, "Cambodia and Laos" (1983). Writer: Bruce Palling. Executive producer: Richard Ellison. Producers: Bruce Palling, Martin Smith. Chief correspondent: Stanley Karnow. Director of media research: Lawrence Lichty. Narrator: Will Lyman.

5. The POW/MIA issue allowed President Richard Nixon to prolong the war for four more years by blunting the efforts of the antiwar movement and forestalling the Paris peace talks. See H. Bruce Franklin, *M.I.A. or Mythmaking in America* (New York: Lawrence Hill, 1992), 74.

6. *48 Hours*, "Missing in Action" (4 Nov. 1992). Executive producer: Andrew Heyward. Producers: Nancy Duffy, David Schneider, Thomas Flynn, and Mary Murphy. Director: Eric Shapiro. Host: Dan Rather.

7. J. Fred MacDonald, *Television and the Red Menace: The Video Road to Vietnam* (New York: Praeger, 1985), 101.

8. *Korean Legacy* (24 Dec. 1964). Producer: Baldwin Baker, Jr. Writers: Edward Spiegel and Jules Maitland. Director: Baldwin Baker, Jr. Narrator: Dana Andrews.

9. See Christopher Robbins, *Air America* (New York: Avon, 1990).

10. Harry H. L. Kitano and Roger Daniels, *Asian Americans: Emerging Minorities* (Englewood Cliffs, N.J.: Prentice Hall, 1988), 111.

11. *Sons and Daughters*, "Crime and Punishment" (1991). Executive producers: Brad Buckner and Eugenie Ross-Leming. Producer: Peter Levin. Story by Ronald Rubin and Ken Carlton. Writer: Ronald Rubin. Director: Bill Bixby.

12. Mary Jo McConahay, "The Baby Trade," *Los Angeles Times Magazine*, 16 Dec. 1990, 14.

13. *This Is Your Life*, "Dr. Tom Dooley" (1960). Created by Ralph Edwards. Producer: Axel Gruenberg. Writer: Paul C. Phillips. Director: Richard Gottlieb. Host: Ralph Edwards. Announcer: Bob Warren.

14. An entire chapter devoted to "The Orphanage of Madame Ngai" is found in Thomas A. Dooley, *Deliver Us from Evil* (New York: Farrar, Straus & Cudahy, 1956), 156–72.

15. Diana Shaw, "The Temptation of Tom Dooley," *Los Angeles Times Magazine*, 15 Dec. 1991, 45.

16. *Ted Mack's Original Amateur Hour*, "The Original Amateur Hour in Korea" (1952).

17. *Propaganda: L'image et son pouvoir*, "America" (1987). Réalisation: Philippe Collin.

18. *Navy Log*, "A Guy Named Mickey" (26 Dec. 56). Executive producer: Leslie Harris. Producer: Sam Gallu. Writer: Max Ehrlich. Director: Oscar Rudolph.

19. *Navy Log*, "Incident at Formosa" (5 Dec. 1956). Executive producer: Leslie Harris. Producer: Sam Gallu. Writer: Max Ehrlich. Director: Oscar Rudolph.

20. *Navy Log*, "Bishop of the Bayfield" (1955). Created by Sam Gallu. Producer: Sam Gallu. Writer: Max Ehrlich. Director: Reginald LeBorg.

21. Frances FitzGerald, *Fire in the Lake: The Vietnamese and the Americans in Vietnam* (New York: Vintage, 1989), 105.

22. William Blum, *The CIA: A Forgotten History* (London: Zed, 1986), 141. Murrow's biographer implies that his bout with lung cancer distracted him from the USIA activities in Vietnam, but does not exonerate the newsman for his part in heading the "agency charged with selling U.S. policy in South Vietnam." Joseph E. Persico, *Edward R. Murrow: An American Original* (New York: Dell, 1990), 486.

23. Robert J. Donovan and Ray Scherer, *Unsilent Revolution: Television News and American Public Life, 1948–1991* (New York: Woodrow Wilson International Center for Scholars and Cambridge University Press, 1992), 102.

24. *CBS News Special*, "The Face of Red China" (1950). Producer: Leslie Midgley. Associate producer: Av Westin. Director: Av Westin. Cameraman: Rolf Gilhausen. Commentator: Gerald Clark. News associate: Alice Weel. Host and narrator: Walter Cronkite.

25. *Adventures of the Falcon*, "Backlash" (1954). Executive producer: Buster Collier. Teleplay by Herb Purdum. Director: Ralph Murphy.

26. *The Adventures of Dr. Fu Manchu*, "The Prisoner of Dr. Fu Manchu" (1955). Writer: Barry Shipman. Director: Franklin Adreon.

27. Cay Van Ash and Elizabeth Sax Rohmer, *Master of Villainy: A Biography of Sax Rohmer* (Bowling Green, Ohio: Bowling Green University Popular Press, 1972), 75.

28. Ibid., 214.

29. Rear Admiral Ellis M. Zacharias, U.S. Navy (ret.), in collaboration with Ladislas Farago, *Behind Closed Doors: The Secret History of the Cold War* (New York: G. P. Putnam's Sons, 1950).

30. *Behind Closed Doors*, "Mightier Than the Sword" (12 Mar. 1959). Producer: Sidney Marshall. Story by Tony Barrett. Teleplay by Robert Leslie Bellem and Tony Barrett. Director: John Peyser.

31. Roger Daniels, *Asian America: Chinese and Japanese in the United States since 1850* (Seattle: University of Washington Press, 1988), 308.

32. *Behind Closed Doors*, "The Quemoy Story" (12 Feb. 1959). Producer: Sidney Marshall. Story by Alan Caillou. Teleplay by Donn Mullally and Arthur Fitz-Richard. Director: John Peyser.

33. A television commercial for Timex watches (1992) features two overweight white actors in yellowface playing *sumo* wrestlers. They both have the purportedly indestructible timepieces taped to their ample bellies as they clash.

34. *Behind Closed Doors*, "The Gamble" (19 Mar. 1959). Producer: Sidney Marshall. Story by Stanley H. Silverman. Teleplay by Robert Leslie Bellem and Stanley H. Silverman. Director: John Peyser.

35. *Crossroads*, "Calvary in China" (1956). Writer: George Bruce. Director: Ralph Francis Murphy.

36. *Crossroads*, "Chinese Checkers" (1956). Writer: Herb Purdum. Director: Tim Whelan.

37. *TV Reader's Digest*, "The Brainwashing of John Hayes" (Nov. 1955). Teleplay by George Bruce, based on an article by Frederic Sondern, Jr. Director: Harry Horner. Host: Hugh Reilly.

38. Jon Heitland, *The Man from U.N.C.L.E. Book: The Behind-the-Scenes Story of a Television Classic* (New York: St. Martin's, 1987), 17.

39. *I Spy*, "An American Empress" (1967). Executive producer: Sheldon Leonard. Producers: David Friedkin and Morton Fine. Writers: Elick Moll and Joseph Than. Director: Earl Bellamy.

40. Donna McCrohan, *The Life and Times of Maxwell Smart* (New York: St. Martin's, 1988), 5–8.

41. *Front Page Detective*, "The Deadly Curio" (1951). Executive producer: Jerry Fairbanks. Teleplay by Gene Levitt and Robert Mitchell. Director: Arnold Wester.

42. See Paul C. P. Siu, *The Chinese Laundryman: A Study of Social Isolation* (New York: New York University Press, 1987).

43. *The Children of An Lac* (1980). Executive producer: Charles Fries and Malcolm Stuart. Producer: Jay Benson. Writer: Blanche Hanalis. Based on a story by Ina Balin. Director: John Llewellyn Moxey.

44. Stanley Karnow, *In Our Image: America's Empire in the Philippines* (New York: Ballantine, 1990), 209.

45. Gil Loescher and John A. Scanlan, *Calculated Kindness: Refugees and America's Half-Open Door, 1945 to the Present* (New York: Free Press, 1986), 106.

46. Noam Chomsky and Edward S. Herman, *After the Cataclysm: Postwar Indochina and the Reconstruction of Imperial Ideology* (Boston: South End, 1989), 29, 313.

47. Gail Fisher, "O.C. Women Reach Out in Third World," *Los Angeles Times*, 30 Aug. 1992, A1. According to the article, World Vision is based in Monrovia, California.

48. *One to One* (15 Dec. 1975). Executive producer: Bob Screen. Producer: Warren G. Stitt. Writer: Buz Kohan. Director: Bill Davis.

49. Linkletter also hosted the popular audience participation program *People Are Funny* (1954–61), *The Art Linkletter Show* (1963), and *Hollywood Talent Scouts* (1965–66), and was a trusted television personality.

50. *When Will the Dying Stop?* (1982). Producers: Lynn Doerschuk and William P. McKay. Writer: Robert C. Larson. Director: Tom Ivy. Narrator: Mason Williams. Host: Charlton Heston.

51. James E. Fowler, "Adventist Preacher to Appear on Soviet TV," *Los Angeles Times*, 5 May 1991, Orange County ed., A3, A50.

52. *It Is Written*, "Good News from China." Recorded 3 Oct. 1989.

53. Reginald Horsman, *Race and Manifest Destiny: The Origins of American Anglo-Saxonism* (Cambridge, Mass.: Harvard University Press, 1981), 288.

54. James C. Thompson, Jr., Peter W. Stanley, and John Curtis Perry, *Sentimental Imperialists: The American Experience in East Asia* (New York: Harper & Row, 1981), 44.

55. Jane Hunter, *The Gospel of Gentility: American Women Missionaries in Turn-of-the-Century China* (New Haven, Conn.: Yale University Press, 1984), 3.

Chapter 5. Southeast Asian America

1. Lloyd Gardner, "America's War in Vietnam: The End of Exceptionalism?" in *The Legacy: The Vietnam War in the American Imagination*, ed. D. Michael Shafer (Boston: Beacon, 1990), 11.

2. Marilyn B. Young, *The Vietnam Wars: 1945–1990* (New York: Harper Perennial, 1991), 301–2.

3. Gabriel Kolko, *Anatomy of War: Vietnam, the United States, and the Modern Historical Experience* (New York: Pantheon, 1985), 200.

4. The networks provided ideological support for Operation Desert Storm through their cheerfully distorted reportage, including blow-by-blow expert commentary by former high-level military officers in mufti. The extensive losses inflicted upon the civilian population of Baghdad were reported on PBS's *Frontline*, *The War We Left Behind* (29 Oct. 1991). Executive producer: David Fanning. Reported by Leslie Cockburn and Andrew Cockburn. Narrated by Leslie Cockburn. Written and produced by Leslie Cockburn, Andrew Cockburn. Directed by Leslie Cockburn.

5. John J. Fialka, *Hotel Warriors: Covering the Gulf War* (Washington, D.C.: Woodrow Wilson Center Press, 1991), 62. See also Daniel C. Hallin, *The "Uncensored War": The Media and Vietnam* (Berkeley: University of California Press, 1989), 128.

6. *The Pacific Century*, "Sentimental Imperialists" (17 Dec. 1992). Executive producer: Alex Gibney. Producer: Al Levin. Director: Marc Levin. Narrator: Peter Coyote.

7. Richard Drinnon, *Facing West: The Metaphysics of Indian-Hating and Empire-Building* (New York: Schocken, 1990), 463–64.

8. Patricia Nelson Limerick, *The Legacy of Conquest: The Unbroken Past of the American West* (New York: W. W. Norton, 1987), 36–37.

9. Edward S. Herman, "The Judeo-Christian Ethic," *Z Magazine*, Oct. 1990, 71.

10. Walter H. Capps, *The Unfinished War: Vietnam and the American Conscience*, 2d ed. (Boston: Beacon, 1990), 169. The author even cites *The American Adam* by R. W. B. Lewis in affirming the supposed "loss of American innocence" (p. 145) in the aftermath of the Vietnam War.

11. Daniel Miller, "Primetime Television's Tour of Duty," in *Inventing Vietnam: The War in Film and Television*, ed. Michael Anderegg (Philadelphia: Temple University Press, 1991), 186.

12. Carolyn Reed Vartanian, "Women Next Door to War: *China Beach*," in *Inventing Vietnam: The War in Film and Television*, ed. Michael Anderegg (Philadelphia: Temple University Press, 1991), 195. It can also be observed that most of the producers, directors, art directors, and writers of *China Beach* and *Tour of Duty* were women.

13. Quoted in Sharon Bernstein, "The Women of TV's Vietnam: Females on Front Lines of 'Tour of Duty' and 'China Beach' Wage Battle against Male-Dominated Network TV," *Los Angeles Times*, 18 Feb. 1990, Orange County ed., Calendar, p. 9.

14. Todd Gitlin, *Inside Prime Time* (New York: Pantheon, 1985), 228–31.

15. Rick Berg, "Losing Vietnam: Covering the War in an Age of Technology," in *From Hanoi to Hollywood: The Vietnam War in American Film*, ed. Linda Dittmar and Gene Michaud (New Brunswick, N.J.: Rutgers University Press, 1990), 47.

16. Morley Safer, *Flashbacks: On Returning to Vietnam* (New York: St. Martin's, 1991), 177.

17. "Donut Dollies" also referred to women attached to the USO or to women in the Special Services. There is a strong suggestion that Donut Dollies also provided GIs with sexual favors on a per fee basis. See Bruce E. Jones, *War without Windows* (New York: Berkley Books, 1990), 44–45.

18. William Broyles, Jr., *Brothers in Arms: A Journey from War to Peace* (New York: Alfred A. Knopf, 1986), 173, 174.

19. *China Beach*, pilot (26 Apr. 1988). Created by William Broyles, Jr., and John Sacret Young. Writer: John Sacret Young. Director: Rob Holcomb. John Sacret Young gained experience in narrativizing the Vietnam War in writing the screenplay for *A Rumor of War* (1980), an adaptation of Philip Caputo's (1977) excellent autobiographical account.

20. A "cherry girl" is GI slang for a virgin. It was commonly joked among American soldiers in Vietnam that "the only cherry you're gonna get while you're here's the one you get in your drink." Dan Cragg, "Viet-Speak," in *The Best of Maledicta*, ed. Reinhold Aman (Philadelphia: Running Press, 1987), 156.

21. Evelyn Yoshimura, "G.I.'s and Asian Women," in *Roots: An Asian American Reader*, ed. Amy Tachiki, Eddie Wong, and Franklin Odo (Los Angeles: UCLA Asian American Studies Center, 1971), 28.

22. Safer, *Flashbacks*, 177.

23. *China Beach*, "Through and Through" (16 July 1991). Created by William Broyles, Jr., and John Sacret Young. Executive consultant: William Broyles, Jr. Producers: Carol Flint and Lydia Woodward. Writer: Carol Flint. Director: Mimi Leder.

24. A *chi ba* is an older unrelated woman who lives in the household and is viewed as almost part of the family, in contrast to a *nguoi lam* or maid.

25. Born in Hanoi to a wealthy family, since 1957 Kieu Chinh has appeared in more than forty feature films in Vietnam, numerous Asian countries, and the United States. In 1972, she was selected Most Popular Actress of Asia. Since settling in the United States, Chinh has appeared in both films and network television programs. See Nha Ca, Alison Leslie Gold, and Le Van, *Kieu Chinh: Hanoi Saigon Hollywood* (Orange, Calif.: Than Huu, 1991).

26. *China Beach*, "Rewind" (9 July 1991). Created by William Broyles, Jr., and John Sacret Young. Executive consultant: William Broyles, Jr. Producers: Carol Flint and Lydia Woodward. Writers: Carol Flint and John Wells. Director: Mimi Leder.

27. *China Beach*, "The Always Goodbye" (18 June 1991). Created by William Broyles, Jr., and John Sacret Young. Executive consultant: William Broyles, Jr. Producers: Carol Flint and Lydia Woodward. Writer: Lydia Woodward. Director: Gary Sinise.

28. *China Beach*, "100 Klicks Out" (1991). Created by William Broyles, Jr., and John Sacret Young. Executive consultant: William Broyles, Jr. Producers: Carol Flint and Lydia Woodward. Writer: Susan Rhinehart. Director: Mimi Leder.

29. *China Beach*, "Hello Goodbye" (22 July 1991). Created by William Broyles, Jr., and John Sacret Young. Executive consultant: William Broyles, Jr. Producers: Carol Flint and Lydia Woodward. Story by John Sacret Young, John Wells, Lydia Woodward, and Carol Flint. Teleplay by John Wells. Director: John Sacret Young.

30. Al Santoli, *Everything We Had: An Oral History of the Vietnam War by Thirty-Three American Soldiers Who Fought It* (New York: Ballantine, 1982), 144.

31. Keith Walker, *A Piece of My Heart: The Stories of 26 American Women Who Served in Vietnam* (Novato, Calif.: Presidio, 1985), 82.

32. Ibid., 156.

33. Elizabeth M. Norman, *Women at War: The Story of Fifty Military Nurses Who Served in Vietnam* (Philadelphia: University of Pennsylvania Press, 1990), 40.

34. Lynda Van Devanter, *Home before Morning: The Story of an Army Nurse in Vietnam* (New York: Warner, 1984), 157.

35. For a critique of "difference feminism" see Katha Pollitt, "Are Women Morally Superior to Men?" *The Nation*, 28 Dec. 1992, 799–807. Although Pollitt does not properly credit her, Susan Faludi's insightful critique of "difference" feminism appears in *Backlash: The Undeclared War against American Women* (Garden City, N.Y.: Doubleday, 1992), 327–31.

36. Quoted in Rick Du Brow, " 'China Beach' Puts Star on New Paths," *Los Angeles Times*, 28 May 1991, Orange County ed., F6.

37. Among the misfit members of Squadron 214 in *Baa Baa Black Sheep* was Captain Tommy Harachi (Byron Chung). It is fairly unlikely that a Japanese American would have been commissioned as a pilot during World War II. Byron Chung also played the part of "Kuroda" in *Search* (1972–73), a one-hour adventure program about a high-tech private security agency.

38. Clayton R. Koppes and Gregory D. Black, *Hollywood Goes to War: How Politics, Profits and Propaganda Shaped World War II Movies* (Berkeley: University of California Press, 1987), 248–77.

39. *Tour of Duty*, "I Wish It Would Rain" (14 Feb. 1989). Created by L. Travis Clark and Steve Duncan. Produced by Vahan Moosekian and Jim Westman. Story by Rick Husky, Dennis Cooper, Stephen Phillip Smith. Teleplay by Robert Burns Clark. Directed by Bradford May.

40. "Viet Cong," from "Viet Cong San" is a catchall term of derision employed by the Diem regime against Vietnamese communists and the National Liberation Front.

41. Douglas Valentine, *The Phoenix Program* (New York: William Morrow, 1990), 13.

42. Elayne Rapping, *The Looking Glass World of Nonfiction TV* (Boston: South End, 1987), 159.

43. *Shooter* (11 Sep. 1988). Executive producers: Stephen Kline and David Hume Kennerly. Producer: Barry Berg. Writers: Stephen Kline and David Hume Kennerly. Director: Gary Nelson.

44. Harry W. Haines, " 'What Kind of War?': An Analysis of the Vietnam Veterans Memorial," *Critical Studies in Mass Communication* 3 (1986): 9.

45. Quoted in Barry Koltnow, "Wings of War – and Love," *Orange County Register*, 22 May 1990, F6.

46. *To Heal a Nation* (29 May 1988). Executive producers: Frank von Zerneck, Stu Samuels, and Lionel Chetwynd. Producer: Robert M. Sertner. Writer: Lionel Chetwynd. Director: Michael Pressman.

47. John Wheeler, "Perot's War against the Vets' 'Wall,' " *Los Angeles Times*, 3 June 1992, Orange County ed., B11.

48. Peter Tauber, "Monument Maker," *New York Times Magazine*, 24 Feb. 1991, 53.

49. Jan C. Scruggs and Joel L. Swerdlow, *To Heal a Nation: The Vietnam Veterans Memorial* (New York: Harper & Row, 1985), 77.

50. Quoted in Sal Lopes, *The Wall: Images and Offerings from the Vietnam Veterans Memorial* (New York: Collins, 1987), 16.

51. *Inside Edition* (25 Dec. 1991). Segment producers: Greg Chisholm and Samantha Greene.

52. *K*I*D*S*, "Tien's Story" (1984). Created by Terry Carter. Producer: Terry Carter. Writer: Daryl G. Nickens. Director: Terry Carter.

53. *In the Heat of the Night*, "My Name Is Hank" (24 Dec. 1991). Developed for television by James Lee Barrett. Executive producers: Fred Silverman and Carroll O'Connor. Producer: Edward Ledding. Writer: Edward De Blasio. Based on characters from the novel by John Ball. Director: Harry Harris.

54. Neil Sheehan observes, "Hopeful Asians who looked to the United States for protection also did not understand that American attitudes toward them were influenced by a racism so profound that Americans usually did not realize they were applying a racist double standard in Asia." Neil Sheehan, *A Bright Shining Lie: John Paul Vann and America in Vietnam* (New York: Vintage, 1989), 153.

55. *Highway to Heaven*, "Choices" (1988). Executive producer: Michael Landon. Producer: Kent McCray. Writer: Parke Perine. Director: Michael Landon.

56. Robert Jay Lifton, *Home from the War: Learning from Vietnam Veterans*, 3d ed. (Boston: Beacon, 1992), 189–216.

57. Following the definition provided by longtime critic of U.S.-sponsored terror Edward Herman, the term *atrocity* as used in these pages refers to "acts of direct and deliberate violence against civilians" and "acts against civilian populations or enemy troops that violate international rules of war, as in the use of gas, deliberate attacks on enemy hospitals, or torturing and killing prisoners." Edward S. Herman, *Atrocities in Vietnam: Myths and Realities* (Philadelphia: Pilgrim, 1970), 13.

58. *Frontline* (8 Jan. 1991), *Remember My Lai* (1989). Executive producer: David Fanning. Producers: Kevin Sim and Michael Bilton. Executive producer for Yorkshire Television: Grant McKee. Director: Kevin Sim. Narrator: Will Lyman.

59. Vietnam Veterans Against the War, *The Winter Soldier Investigation: An Inquiry into American War Crimes* (Boston: Beacon, 1972), xiii.

60. Mark Baker, *Nam: The Vietnam War in the Words of the Men and Women Who Fought There* (New York: Berkley, 1981), 187.

61. Ibid.

62. Wallace Terry, *Bloods: An Oral History of the Vietnam War by Black Veterans* (New York: Ballantine, 1985), 248.

63. Michael Lee Lanning, *Inside the LRRPS: Rangers in Vietnam* (New York: Ivy, 1988), 91.

Chapter 6. Contemporary Asian America

1. *Who Killed Vincent Chin?* (1988). Producer: Renee Tajima. Director: Christine Choy.

2. Bill Nichols, *Representing Reality: Issues and Concepts in Documentary* (Bloomington: Indiana University Press, 1991), 47.

3. Quoted in Eric Lichtblau, "Surge in O.C. Hate Crimes Raises New Concerns, Fear," *Los Angeles Times*, 15 July 1991, Orange County ed., A1, A22.

4. Quoted in Victor Merina, "Success, Then Tragedy: Family of Refugee Lost Store and Loved One in Riots," *Los Angeles Times*, 17 Aug. 1992, Orange County ed., A25.

5. Mike Clary, "Rising Toll of Hate Crimes Cited in Slaying," *Los Angeles Times*, 10 Oct. 1992, Orange County ed., A1, A9.

6. "Sentence in Slaying of Asian-American," *Los Angeles Times*, 9 Dec. 1992, Orange County ed., A28.

7. Gregory Crouch, Leslie Earnest, and Len Hall, "Police Say Laguna Beach Beating Was Hate Crime," *Los Angeles Times*, 11 Jan. 1993, Orange County ed., A1, A24.

8. Michael Moore, "Scapegoats Again," *The Progressive*, February 1988, 25–27.

9. Scott Jaschik, "U.S. Finds Harvard Did Not Exclude Asian Americans," *Chronicle of Higher Education*, 17 Oct. 1990, A1, A37. For a full account of the controversy over university admissions policies concerning Asian Americans, see Dana Y. Takagi, *The Retreat from Race: Asian-American Admissions and Racial Politics* (New Brunswick, N.J.: Rutgers University Press, 1992).

10. U.S. Commission on Civil Rights, *The Economic Status of Americans of Asian Descent* (Washington, D.C.: U.S. Government Printing Office, 1988), ch. 7, p. 15.

11. Roger Daniels, *Coming to America: A History of Immigration and Ethnicity in American Life* (New York: HarperCollins, 1990), 368.

12. James Fallows, *More Like Us: Making America Great Again* (Boston: Houghton Mifflin, 1990).

13. Ibid., 200.

14. *Trends in the Nineties*, "The First Universal Nation" (22 June 1992). Producers: Marilyn Weiner and Hal Weiner. Director: Hal Weiner. Essayist/host: Ben Wattenberg.

15. Peter Skerry, "Individualist America and Today's Immigrants," *The Public Interest* 102 (1991): 113–14.

16. *KNBC News*, "Home in L.A. Hearts in Saigon" (22 May 1985).

17. *The American Promise*, "Wanting It All" (1987). Producer: Frank Kwan. Associate producers: Yvonne Guevara and Stan Morita. Director: Frank Kwan.

18. Renee E. Tajima, "Lotus Blossoms Don't Bleed: Images of Asian Women," in *Making Waves: An Anthology of Writings by and about Asian American Women*, ed. Asian Women of California (Boston: Beacon, 1989), 309.

19. Barbara Ehrenreich, *Fear of Falling: The Inner Life of the Middle Class* (New York: Harper Perennial, 1990), 248.

20. *Asian America* (1984). Producers: Frank Kwan and Stan Kawakami. Writer: Tritia Toyota. Directors: Erwin Rosen and Gene Leong.

21. There was a 56.6 percent increase in the Asian Pacific American population in Los Angeles County between 1980 and 1990. In 1990, Asian Pacifics numbered 954,485, which represents 10.8 percent of the total county population. Paul M. Ong and Tania Azores, *Asian Pacific Americans in Los Angeles: A Demographic Profile* (Los Angeles: UCLA Asian American Studies Center, 1991), 7, 14.

22. See Dennis Baron, *The English-Only Question: An Official Language for Americans?* (New Haven, Conn.: Yale University Press, 1990).

23. Dave Lesher, "GOP See Ideological Link to Asian-Americans," *Los Angeles Times*, 16 June 1991, Orange County ed., B6.

24. Eric Bailey, "President's Visit Fixes Spotlight on Asians," *Los Angeles Times*, 16 June 1991, Orange County ed., B7.

25. John H. Lee, "Grocer Sells Brooklyn Store That Was Target of a Boycott," *Los Angeles Times*, 30 May 1991, Orange County ed., A5.

26. *Equal Justice* (1991). Created by Christopher Knopf, David A. Simons, and Thomas Carter. Executive producer: Thomas Carter. Producer: Ian Sander. Writer: Frank Abatemarco. Director: Barbara Amato.

27. Quoted in Steve Weinstein, " 'Equal Justice' Targets Black-Korean Strife," *Los Angeles Times*, 4 Apr. 1991, Orange County ed., F12.

28. Earl Ofari Hutchinson, "Fighting the Wrong Enemy," *The Nation*, 4 Nov. 1991, 555.

29. *Shannon's Deal*, "Strangers in the Night" (1991). Created by John Sayles. Co-executive producer: Marvin Kupfer. Producer: Gareth Davies. Associate producer: Peter Chomsky. Creative consultant: David Greenwalt. Legal consultant: Alan Dershowitz. Theme and music by Wynton Marsalis. Writer: Tom Richman.

30. Quoted in Richard Reyes Fruto, "Guilty Verdict in 'Buddhaheads' Trial," *Korea Times*, 4 Nov. 1992, English ed., 1.

31. *In Living Color* (9 Feb. 1992). Created by Keenen Ivory Wayans. Executive producer: Keenen Ivory Wayans. Producer: Tamara Rawitt. Director: Terri McCoy.

32. Shih-Shan Henry Tsai, *The Chinese Experience in America* (Bloomington: Indiana University Press, 1986), 41.

33. Elmer Clarence Sandmeyer, *The Anti-Chinese Movement in California* (Urbana: University of Illinois Press, 1991), 52, 74.

34. Noam Chomsky, *Deterring Democracy* (New York: Hill & Wang, 1992), 107–37.

35. Gerald L. Posner, *Warlords of Crime — Chinese Secret Societies: The New Mafia* (New York: Penguin, 1990), xvii.

36. *Gideon Oliver*, "Tongs" (13 Mar. 1989). Created by Dick Wolf. Executive producers: William Sackheim and Dick Wolf. Producer: Keven Donnelly. Writer: Jack Richardson. Director: Alan Metzger. *Gideon Oliver* was one of the police/detective dramas that appeared on a rotating basis with other programs as part of *The ABC Mystery Movie* (1989–90).

37. *The New Godfathers* (20 Jan. 1993). Executive producer: John Parsons. Producer: Phil Eigner. Writers: Geraldo Rivera, John Parsons, Wayne Darwen, and Phil Eigner. Director: Don McSorley.

38. See Geraldo Rivera with Daniel Paisner, *Exposing Myself* (New York: Bantam, 1992).

39. The *Wally George Show* began on KCOP-TV in 1979 and moved to KDOC in 1982, but *Hot Seat* did not debut until 1983. Jan Herman, "He Won't Sit Still for Anything," *Los Angeles Times*, 11 July 1992, Orange County ed., F1, F3.

40. *Asian Gangs: Terror in the Streets*, "A Newswatch Special" (9 Mar. 1992). Executive producer: Chuck Velona. Producer: Beth Bingham. Writer: Beth Bingham. A follow-up report — *Asian Gangs*, Part 2, *When Will the Violence End?* — was broadcast on 12 Aug. 1992.

41. Randy Lewis, "KDOC Turns Cameras on Asian Gangs in Little Saigon," *Los Angeles Times*, 9 Mar 1992, Orange County ed., F3.

42. *Your Family Matters, Jennifer's in Jail* (26 Aug. 1992). Host: Susan Dey. A Renee Tajima Christine Choy Production for Lifetime Television. Executive producers: Dalton Delan and Donna Harris. Senior producer: Christine Choy. Producer: Quynh Thai. Executive in charge of production: Lauren Gray. Writer: Renee Tajima. Directors: Renee Tajima and Christine Choy.

43. James Diego Vigil and Steve Chong Yun, "Vietnamese Youth Gangs in Southern California," in *Gangs in America*, ed. C. Ronald Huff (Newbury Park, Calif.: Sage, 1990), 146–62.

44. *Tequila and Bonetti*, "Language of the Heart" (28 Feb. 1992). Created by Donald P. Bellisario. Executive producer: Donald P. Bellisario. Writer: Robin Jill Bernheim. Director: Christopher Hibler.

45. *MacGyver*, "The Coltons" (14 Oct. 1991). Created by Lee David Zlotoff. Executive producers: Henry Winkler, John Rich, and Stephen Downing. Story by Stephen Downing and Michael Greenburg, teleplay by Stephen Downing. Director: William Gereghty.

46. Andrew Hacker, *Two Nations: Black and White, Separate, Hostile, Unequal* (New York: Charles Scribner's Sons, 1992), 10.

47. *Wiseguy*, "All or Nothing" (11 Jan. 1989). Created by Stephen J. Cannell and Frank Lupo. Executive producer: Stephen J. Cannell. Producers: Alfonse Ruggiero, Jr., and Alex Beaton. Writer: Suzanne Oshry. Director: Gus Trikonis.

48. The process of "ethnic succession" is described as the "historical pattern of

one group replacing another in neighborhoods, jobs, leadership, schools, and other institutions." Thomas Sowell, *Ethnic America: A History* (New York: Basic Books, 1981), 277.

49. Stuart Silverstein, "Clothes Industry a Huge and Vital Economic Force," *Los Angeles Times,* 21 July 1991, Orange County ed., D10.

50. Quoted in ibid., D11.

51. David Rieff, *Los Angeles: Capital of the Third World* (New York: Touchstone, 1991), 173.

52. Stephen Steinberg, *The Ethnic Myth: Race, Ethnicity, and Class in America,* 2d ed. (Boston: Beacon, 1989), 97.

53. Ibid., 103.

54. See Thanh-Dam Truong, *Sex, Money and Morality: Prostitution and Tourism in South-East Asia* (London: Zed, 1990).

55. Annette Fuentes and Barbara Ehrenreich, *Women in the Global Factory* (Boston: South End, 1983), 54.

56. *Life and Times,* "Double Vision" (1992). Executive producer: Jim Kennedy. Producer: Arthur Dong.

57. Dean Takahashi, "Power Struggle Led to Ouster of AST's Yuen, Insiders Say," *Los Angeles Times,* 3 July 1992, Orange County ed., D1, D6.

58. Davis is particularly adept at analyzing the relationship of Asian (particularly Japanese) capital to the economic and political life of Los Angeles. Mike Davis, *City of Quartz: Excavating the Future in Los Angeles* (New York: Vintage, 1992), 136.

59. Jonathan Peterson and Patrick Lee. " '91 State Job Loss Was 6 Times That Estimated." *Los Angeles Times,* 3 Apr. 1992, Orange County ed., A3, A12.

60. Seymour Melman, "Military State Capitalism," *The Nation,* 20 May 1991, 649, 664–68.

61. Kevin Phillips, *The Politics of the Rich and Poor: Wealth and the American Electorate in the Reagan Aftermath* (New York: Harper Perennial, 1991), 68.

62. *Tom Vu Quick Money Making System* (1991). Paid programming.

63. *48 Hours,* "Get Rich Quick"/"The Harder They Fall" (30 Dec. 1992). "Only in America," reported by Bernard Goldberg. Executive producer: Andrew Heyward. Writer: Thomas Flynn. Host: Dan Rather.

64. Jube Shiver, Jr., "Despite Florida Probe, Real Estate Promoter Tom Vu Still Wows Crowds," *Los Angeles Times,* 16 Feb. 1992, Orange County ed., D3.

65. David G. Bromly and Anson D. Sharp, Jr., *"Moonies" in America: Cult, Church, and Crusade* (Beverly Hills: Sage, 1979), 135.

66. John Marks, *The Search for the "Manchurian Candidate": The CIA and Mind Control* (New York: Times Books, 1979), 126.

67. Robert J. Lifton, *Thought Reform and the Psychology of Totalism* (New York: W. W. Norton, 1961). See also Edward Hunter, *Brainwashing* (New York: Pyramid, 1958).

68. David Chidester, *Patterns of Power: Religion and Politics in American Culture* (Englewood Cliffs, N.J.: Prentice Hall, 1988), 252–53.

69. *Frontline, The Resurrection of Reverend Moon* (21 Jan. 1992). Executive producer: David Fanning. Producer: Rory O'Connor. Writer: Rory O'Connor. Director: Rory O'Connor. Reporter: Eric Nadler. Narrator: Will Lyman.

70. See Jai Hyon Lee, "The Activities of the Korean Central Intelligence

Agency in the United States," in *The Politics of Reverend Moon and the Unification Church*, ed. Irving Louis Horowitz (Cambridge: MIT Press, 1978), 120–47. See also Chong Sun Kim, *Rev. Sun Myung Moon* (Washington, D.C.: University Press of America, 1978).

71. Bob Woodward, *Veil: The Secret Wars of the CIA 1981–1987* (New York: Pocket Books, 1988), 429.

72. Robertson, a 1988 presidential candidate and active in the 1992 Republican campaign, oversees a multimillion-dollar television empire that includes the Family Channel, a highly profitable offshoot of CBN that is on the verge of going global with the planned $74 million acquisition of TVS Entertainment, a British firm that will provide access to the European market. See Jeff Kaye, "Global Vision: Pat Robertson's $74-Million Bid May Link MTM Parent and Family Channel," *Los Angeles Times*, 31 Dec. 1992, Orange County ed., D1, D2.

73. See John G. Taylor, *Indonesia's Forgotten War: The Hidden History of East Timor* (London: Zed, 1991).

74. *The Pacific Century*, "The Fight for Democracy" (4 Dec. 1992). Executive producer: Alex Gibney. Producer: Carl Byker. Writer: Carl Byker. Director: Carl Byker. Narrator: Peter Coyote.

75. Paul Kennedy, *The Rise and Fall of the Great Powers: Economic Change and Military Conflict from 1500 to 2000* (New York: Vintage, 1989), 459.

76. George Friedman and Meredith Lebard, *The Coming War with Japan* (New York: St. Martin's, 1991), 118.

77. Tim Weiner, *Blank Check: The Pentagon's Black Budget* (New York: Warner, 1991), 31.

78. Noam Chomsky, *The Culture of Terrorism* (Boston: South End, 1988), 31–32. South Korean mercenaries known as "ROKs" (for Republic of Korea) struck fear even in the hearts of hardened GIs for acts of utter barbarism committed against the Vietnamese.

79. Ivan Light and Edna Bonacich, *Immigrant Entrepreneurs: Koreans in Los Angeles 1965–1982* (Berkeley: University of California Press, 1991), 41.

80. Peter L. Berger points to the so-called East Asian Little Tigers as examples of the capitalist triumph. Yet even Berger concedes that the East Asian countries such as South Korea provide "weak support for the thesis that successful capitalist development generates pressures toward democracy." Peter L. Berger, *The Capitalist Revolution: Fifty Propositions about Prosperity, Equality, and Liberty* (New York: Basic Books, 1986), 161.

Chapter 7. Counterprogramming

1. See Herman Gray, "Television, Black Americans, and the American Dream," *Critical Studies in Mass Communication* 6 (1989): 376–86.

2. Stuart Hall, "The Whites of Their Eyes: Racist Ideologies and the Media," in *The Media Reader*, ed. Manuel Alvarado and John O. Thompson (London: BFI, 1990), 12.

3. David L. Paletz and Robert M. Entman, *Media Power Politics* (New York: Free Press, 1981), 171.

4. Sharon Bernstein, "Senate Stalls PBS Money, Blames 'Bias,' " *Los Angeles Times*, 20 Jan. 1992, Orange County ed., F1.

5. "Voices of America," editorial, *The Nation*, 22 Mar. 1993, 361.

6. Quoted in Terry Pristin, " 'Deception': Oscar Victor, PBS Reject," *Los Angeles Times*, 31 Mar. 1993, Orange County ed., F1.

7. Stanley Karnow, *Vietnam: A History* (New York: Penguin, 1984).

8. *Television's Vietnam*, "The Real Story"/"The Impact of Media" (1985). Producer: Peter Rollins, Ph.D. Director: William E. Crane. Narrator: Charlton Heston.

9. Erik Barnouw, *Tube of Plenty: The Evolution of American Television*, 2d rev. ed. (New York: Oxford University Press, 1990), 517.

10. *Vietnam: A Television History*, "Tet 1968" (1983). Executive producer: Richard Ellison. Producer: Austin Boyd. Associate producer: Marilyn Hornbeck. Writer: Austin Boyd. Director of media research: Lawrence Lichty. Chief correspondent: Stanley Karnow. Narrator: Will Lyman. The series was a coproduction of WGBH-TV Boston, Central Independent Television of the United Kingdom, and Antenne-2, France, in association with LRE Productions.

11. AIM was founded in 1969 and is funded by large corporations and foundations. According to Edward S. Herman and Noam Chomsky, "The function of AIM is to harass the media and put pressure on them to follow the corporate agenda and a hard-line, right-wing foreign policy." Edward S. Herman and Noam Chomsky, *Manufacturing Consent: The Political Economy of the Mass Media* (New York: Pantheon, 1988), 27.

12. Podhoretz was responsible for one of the early comprehensive attempts on the part of right-wing intellectuals to rationalize U.S. military involvement in Vietnam. See Norman Podhoretz, *Why We Were in Vietnam* (New York: Simon & Schuster, 1982).

13. See Peter Braestrup, *Big Story: How the American Press and Television Reported and Interpreted the Crisis of Tet in Vietnam and Washington* (Garden City, N.Y.: Anchor, 1978).

14. Howard Rosenberg, " 'P.O.V.' Answers Criticism from Conservatives," *Los Angeles Times*, 25 Oct. 1991, Orange County ed., F1, F31.

15. *Frontline, The War We Left Behind* (29 Oct. 1991). Executive producer: David Fanning. Producers: Leslie Cockburn and Andrew Cockburn. Writers: Leslie Cockburn and Andrew Cockburn. Director: Leslie Cockburn. Narrator: Leslie Cockburn.

16. *P.O.V., Tongues Untied* (7 Oct. 1991). Featuring Essex Hemphill. Executive producer: Marc N. Weiss. Executive director: David M. Davis. Director: Marlon Riggs. Copresentation with the National Black Programming Consortium.

17. *American Playhouse, Hot Summer Winds* (22 May 1991). Executive producer: Ricki Franklin. Producer: Wendy Blair Slick. Teleplay by Emiko Omori, after two short stories by Hisaye Yamamoto. Director: Emiko Omori.

18. The pieces have been collected and reprinted in Hisaye Yamamoto, *Seventeen Syllables: And Other Stories* (Latham, N.Y.: Kitchen Table – Women of Color Press, 1988).

19. *American Playhouse, Lethal Innocence* (13 Nov. 1991). Producers: Frank Doelger and Howard Meltzer. Coproducer: Nan Bernstein-Freed. Writer: Bruce Harmon. Director: Helen Whitney.

20. William Shawcross, *Sideshow: Kissinger, Nixon and the Destruction of Cambodia* (New York: Simon & Schuster, 1979), 396.

21. In 1992, a wire service reported that a 22,000-member U.N. peacekeeping

force would be deployed to Cambodia. Their mission would be to enforce a cease-fire between warring parties, monitor human rights, repatriate refugees, and help rebuild a country where an "estimated 75,000 died in the fighting and as many as 1 million died under the radical Communist Khmer Rouge government of the late 1970s." Associated Press, "U.N. Approves Cambodia Peacekeeping Mission," *Los Angeles Times*, 29 Feb. 1992, Orange County ed., A11.

22. *Cambodian Doughnut Dreams* (1990). Writer: Charles Davis. Director: Charles Davis.

23. Charles Davis, personal interview, 13 Nov. 1991.

24. Daniel Akst, "Cruller Fates: Cambodians Find Slim Profit in Doughnuts," *Los Angeles Times*, 9 Mar. 1993, Orange County ed., D1, D6.

25. See Al Santoli, *New Americans: An Oral History* (New York: Ballantine, 1990), 207–33.

26. James William Gibson, *The Perfect War: The War We Couldn't Lose and How We Did* (New York: Vintage, 1988), 388.

27. Marilyn B. Young, *The Vietnam Wars: 1945–1990* (New York: Harper Perennial, 1991), 235.

28. *Moving Mountains: The Story of Yiu Mien* (24 May 1991). Producer: Elaine Velazquez. Director: Elaine Velazquez. Released in 1989, the documentary was broadcast in May 1991 as part of the KCET-TV Los Angeles "Asian Pacific Heritage Month."

29. *Thanh's War* (May 1991). Executive producer: Michael Schwarz. Producer: Elizabeth Farnsworth. Directors: Elizabeth Farnsworth and John Koop. Narrator: Elizabeth Farnsworth.

30. Jim Mann, "Pressure to Alter Hanoi's Political System Urged," *Los Angeles Times*, 30 Oct. 1992, Orange County ed., A4.

31. *The Story of Vinh* (22 Oct. 1991). Producers: Quang Nguyen, Patricia Sides and Keiko Tsuno. Writers: Quang Nguyen and Patricia Sides. Narrator: Gene Galusha.

32. See George Hu'eu Sanford Kanahele, *Ku Kanaka Stand Tall: A Search for Hawaiian Values* (Honolulu: University of Hawaii Press, 1986).

33. *Troubled Paradise* (5 Aug. 1991). Producer: Steven Okazaki. Associate producer: Zand Gee. Writer: Steven Okazaki. Director: Steven Okazaki. Narrator: Amy Hill.

34. Bill Ashcroft, Gareth Griffiths, and Helen Tiffin, *The Empire Writes Back: Theory and Practice in Post-Colonial Literatures* (New York: Routledge, 1989), 177–80.

35. George H. Lewis, "Don' Go Down Waikiki: Social Protest and Popular Music in Hawaii," in *Rockin' the Boat: Mass Music and Mass Movements*, ed. Reebee Garofalo (Boston: South End, 1992), 179.

36. Neil Postman and Steve Powers, *How to Watch TV News* (New York: Penguin, 1992), 88–89.

37. *Donahue* (1991). Executive producer: Patricia McMillen. Senior producer: Lorri Antosz Benson. Director: Bryan Russo.

38. See Stanley Sue and Sumie Okazaki, "Asian-American Educational Achievements: A Phenomenon in Search of an Explanation," *American Psychologist* 45 (1990): 913–20.

39. *Law & Order* (19 Apr. 1992). Created by Dick Wolf. Executive producer:

Dick Wolf. Producers: Robert Palm and Daniel Sackheim. Writers: Robert Nathan and Sally Nemeth. Director: Steven Robman.

40. Marvin Harris, *The Rise of Anthropological Theory: A History of Theories of Culture* (New York: Thomas Y. Crowell, 1968), 80–81.

41. Eui-Young Yu, *Korean Community Profile: Life and Consumer Patterns* (Los Angeles: Korea Times/Hankook Ilbo, 1990), 1–4.

42. Ibid., 4.

43. It should be noted that the Dus have been robbed three times and burglarized forty times during the two years they have owned Empire Liquor Market. Tim Rutten, "Politics and the Du Verdict," *Los Angeles Times*, 22 Nov. 1991, Orange County ed., E6.

44. Quoted in Tracy Wilkinson and Frank Clifford, "Korean Who Killed Black Teen Gets Probation," *Los Angeles Times*, 16 Nov. 1991, Orange County ed., A34.

45. Quoted in Jesse Katz, "Anguished Merchant Returns to Work after His Daughter, 9, Is Shot by Robber," *Los Angeles Times*, 21 Oct. 1991, Orange County ed., A25.

46. Rick Holguin and John H. Lee, "Groups Urge Boycott of Store Where Black Man Was Killed," *Los Angeles Times*, 18 June 1991, A22.

47. Jesse Katz and Stephanie Chavez, "Blacks Seek to Channel Anger over Sentence," *Los Angeles Times*, 17 Nov. 1991, Orange County ed., A38.

48. Ivan Light and Edna Bonacich, *Immigrant Entrepreneurs: Koreans in Los Angeles 1965–1982* (Berkeley: University of California Press, 1991), 392.

49. Ken Auletta chronicles and laments the recent erosion of network television news in *Three Blind Mice: How the TV Networks Lost Their Way* (New York: Vintage, 1992).

50. *The Oprah Winfrey Show*, "Racism in 1992." Executive producer: Debra DiMaio.

51. *The Oprah Winfrey Show* (4 May 1992). Executive producer: Debra DiMaio. Supervising producer: Oprah Winfrey.

52. See Ralph Wiley, *Why Black People Tend to Shout: Cold Facts and Wry Views from a Black Man's World* (New York: Penguin, 1992).

Chapter 8. Epilogue

1. Burt A. Folkart, "Keye Luke, Charlie Chan's 'No. 1 Son,' Is Dead at 86," *Los Angeles Times*, 15 Jan. 1991, Orange County ed., A24.

2. *The Milton Berle Show* (22 Mar. 1950).

3. Steve Neale and Frank Krutnik, *Popular Film and Television Comedy* (New York: Routledge, 1990), 182.

4. See Leadership Education for Asian Pacifics (LEAP), *The State of Asian Pacific America: Policy Issues to the Year 2020* (Los Angeles: LEAP Asian Pacific American Public Policy Institute and UCLA Asian American Studies Center, 1993).

5. Charles Champlin, "Keye Luke Was No. 1 in Every Role," *Los Angeles Times*, 16 Jan. 1991, Orange County ed., F8.

6. Irving Howe, *The World of Our Fathers: The Journey of the East European Jews to America and the Life They Found and Made* (New York: Touchstone, 1976), 569, emphasis his.

7. Quoted in J. Fred MacDonald, *Blacks and White TV: African Americans in Television since 1948*, 2d ed. (Chicago: Nelson-Hall, 1992), 68.

8. *The Frank Sinatra Show* (1958). Producer: William Self. Writers: Ray Singer and Dick Chevillat. Director: Jack Donohue. Musical director: Nelson Riddle.

9. Laura Zinn, "To Marketers, Kristi Yamaguchi Isn't as Good as Gold," *Business Week*, 9 Mar. 1992, 40.

10. Thomas S. Mulligan, "Yamaguchi's Endorsement Deals Prove Good as Gold," *Los Angeles Times*, 17 Mar. 1992, Orange County ed., D6.

11. Quoted in Jane Hall, "The 'Connie Chung' Concept," *Los Angeles Times*, 4 May 1990, Orange County ed., F32.

12. Quoted in Susan Schindehette et al., "Waking Up Late to the Biological Clock," *People Weekly*, 20 Aug. 1990, 74.

13. Cindy Hsu, "100 Greats: A Showcase of the People, Places and Things That Make Us Proud to Be Asian," *Transpacific*, Nov./Dec. 1991, 32.

14. Harry Shearer, "Man Bites Town: Anchors Away," *Los Angeles Times Magazine*, 21 July 1991, 4.

15. Gish Jen, "Challenging the Asian Illusion," *New York Times*, 11 Aug. 1991, sec. 2, p. 13.

16. Jon Krampner, "Anchored Out of the Mainstream," *Los Angeles Times*, 15 Dec. 1991, Orange County ed., Calendar, p. 6.

17. David Rosenthal, "The Asian Few: A Growing Minority Still Goes Mostly Unrepresented on TV," *Chicago Tribune*, 6 May 1989, sec. 1, p. 16.

18. Quoted in Krampner, "Anchored Out," 92. In a separate article, Toyota attributes the relative absence of male Asian American newscasters to white male managers "who tend to want to hire women more than men, partly because we fill two slots." Quoted in Steve Weinstein, "Toyota Quality: Broadcast Veteran Marks 19 Years on Southland Airwaves While Serving as a Role Model for Minority Journalists," *Los Angeles Times*, 9 Jan. 1991, Orange County ed., F6.

19. David Henry Hwang, *M. Butterfly* (New York: Plume, 1989).

20. Quoted in Lilian Huang, "A Newsroom of Our Own," *A Magazine* 1.3 (1992): 21.

21. Jane Hall, "Chung's Making News Tonight," *Los Angeles Times*, 1 June 1993, Orange County ed., F1.

22. Quoted in Ron Miller, "Actress Rosalind Chao Finds the Golden Rule," *San Jose Mercury News*, 1 May 1992, 4D. Compare *Thousand Pieces of Gold* with the theatrical feature *Come See the Paradise* (1990), directed by Alan Parker, in which the white-male-rescues-yellow-female formula also obtains.

23. Barry Koltnow, "OC Actress Discovers Her Roots," *Orange County Register*, 12 Sept. 1991, F1.

24. Quoted in Nina J. Easton, "Who *Isn't* Writing Hollywood's Stories: Writers Guild Study Hiring Picture Still Poor for Women, Minorities, Older Writers," *Los Angeles Times*, 25 May 1989, Orange County ed., sec. 6, p. 1.

25. See Ronald Brownstein, *The Power and the Glitter: The Hollywood-Washington Connection* (New York: Vintage, 1992), 219–22.

26. William T. Bielby and Denise D. Bielby, *The 1989 Hollywood Writers' Report: Unequal Access, Unequal Pay* (West Hollywood, Calif.: Writers Guild of America, west, 1989), 24.

27. William T. Bielby and Denise D. Bielby, *The 1993 Hollywood Writers' Report: A Survey of the Employment of Writers in the Film, Broadcast, and Cable Indus-*

tries for the Period 1987–1991 (West Hollywood, Calif.: Writers Guild of America, west, 1993), 1.

28. Ibid., 2.

29. K. Connie Kang, "Separate, Distinct – and Equal," *Los Angeles Times*, 20 Aug. 1993, Orange County ed., A22.

30. Stuart Fischer, *Kids' TV: The First 25 Years* (New York: Facts on File, 1983), 266.

31. Alison Dakota Gee, "The Yellowing of Hollywood," *Buzz* July/Aug. 1992, 59.

32. Alex Ben Block, *Out-Foxed: The Inside Story of America's Fourth Television Network* (New York: St. Martin's, 1991), 160–62.

33. Edward Herman, "Democratic Media," *Z Papers* 1.1 (1992): 30.

34. Douglas Kellner, *Television and the Crisis of Democracy* (Boulder, Colo.: Westview, 1990), 218.

35. James Curran, "Mass Media and Democracy: A Reappraisal," in *Mass Media and Society*, ed. James Curran and Michael Gurevitch (London: Edward Arnold, 1991), 103.

36. *Bold Journey*, "Native Land" (c. 1956). Producer: Julian Lesser. Host: John Stephenson.

37. Yoshio Kishi, "Final Mix: Unscheduled," in *Moving the Image: Independent Asian Pacific American Media Arts*, ed. Russell Leong (Los Angeles: UCLA Asian American Studies Center and Visual Communications, Southern California Asian American Studies Central, 1991), 165.

38. Akemi Kikumura, *Issei Pioneers: Hawaii and the Mainland 1885 to 1924* (Los Angeles: Japanese American National Museum, 1992), 74.

39. David Inman, *The TV Encyclopedia* (New York: Perigee, 1991), 398.

40. *World Theatre*, "Japan: The Frozen Moment" (c. 1964). Information is sketchy, but this program is probably a production of National Educational Television (NET), the predecessor to PBS. Producer: Bert Lawrence. Director: Robin Hardy. Consultant: Donald Keene. Poetry and drama translated by Donald Keene, Kenneth Rexroth, and Arthur Waley.

41. Robert B. Reich, *The Work of Nations: Preparing Ourselves for 21st-Century Capitalism* (New York: Vintage, 1992), 301–15.

42. Paul Kennedy, *Preparing for the Twenty-First Century* (New York: Random House, 1993), 196–202.

Bibliography

Abdul-Jabbar, Kareem, and Peter Knobler. *Giant Steps*. New York: Bantam, 1983.

Alvarado, Manuel, and John O. Thompson, eds. *The Media Reader*. London: BFI, 1990.

Aman, Reinhold, ed. *The Best of Maledicta*. Philadelphia: Running Press, 1987.

American Social History Project. *Who Built America? Working People and the Nation's Economy, Politics, Culture, and Society*, Vol. 1. New York: Pantheon, 1990.

Anderegg, Michael, ed. *Inventing Vietnam: The War in Film and Television*. Philadelphia: Temple University Press, 1991.

Aronowitz, Stanley. *The Crisis of Historical Materialism: Class, Politics and Culture in Marxist Theory*, 2d ed. Minneapolis: University of Minnesota Press, 1990.

Ash, Cay Van, and Elizabeth Sax Rohmer. *Master of Villainy: A Biography of Sax Rohmer*. Bowling Green, Ohio: Bowling Green University Popular Press, 1972.

Ashcroft, Bill, Gareth Griffiths, and Helen Tiffin. *The Empire Writes Back: Theory and Practice in Post-Colonial Literatures*. New York: Routledge, 1989.

Asian Women of California, ed. *Making Waves: An Anthology of Writings by and about Asian American Women*. Boston: Beacon, 1989.

Auletta, Ken. *Three Blind Mice: How the TV Networks Lost Their Way*. New York: Vintage, 1992.

Baker, Donald G. *Race, Ethnicity and Power: A Comparative Study*. London: Routledge & Kegan Paul, 1983.

Baker, Mark. *Nam: The Vietnam War in the Words of the Men and Women Who Fought There*. New York: Berkley, 1981.

Banton, Michael. *Race Relations*. London: Tavistock, 1967.

Barnouw, Erik. *Tube of Plenty: The Evolution of American Television*, 2d rev. ed. New York: Oxford University Press, 1990.

Baron, Dennis. *The English-Only Question: An Official Language for Americans?* New Haven, Conn.: Yale University Press, 1990.

Berger, Peter L. *The Capitalist Revolution: Fifty Propositions about Prosperity, Equality, and Liberty*. New York: Basic Books, 1986.

Best, Steven, and Douglas Kellner. *Postmodern Theory: Critical Interrogations*. New York: Guilford, 1991.

Bielby, William T., and Denise D. Bielby. *The 1989 Hollywood Writers' Report: Unequal Access, Unequal Pay*. West Hollywood, Calif.: Writers Guild of America, west, 1989.

_____ . *The 1993 Hollywood Writers' Report: A Survey of the Employment of Writers in the Film, Broadcast, and Cable Industries for the Period 1987–1991.* West Hollywood, Calif.: Writers Guild of America, west, 1993.

Blauner, Robert. *Racial Oppression in America.* New York: Harper & Row, 1972.

Block, Alex Ben. *Out-Foxed: The Inside Story of America's Fourth Television Network.* New York: St. Martin's, 1991.

Bloom, Allan. *The Closing of the American Mind.* New York: Touchstone, 1987.

Blum, William. *The CIA: A Forgotten History.* London: Zed, 1986.

Braestrup, Peter. *Big Story: How the American Press and Television Reported and Interpreted the Crisis of Tet in Vietnam and Washington.* Garden City, N.Y.: Anchor, 1978.

Bromly, David G., and Anson D. Sharp, Jr. *"Moonies" in America: Cult, Church, and Crusade.* Beverly Hills: Sage, 1979.

Brownstein, Ronald. *The Power and the Glitter: The Hollywood-Washington Connection.* New York: Vintage, 1992.

Broyles, William, Jr. *Brothers in Arms: A Journey from War to Peace.* New York: Alfred A. Knopf, 1986.

Ca, Nha, Alison Leslie Gold, and Le Van. *Kieu Chinh: Hanoi Saigon Hollywood.* Orange, Calif.: Than Huu, 1991.

Capps, Walter H. *The Unfinished War: Vietnam and the American Conscience,* 2d ed. Boston: Beacon, 1990.

Cecil, Paul Frederick. *Herbicidal Warfare: The RANCH HAND Project in Vietnam.* New York: Praeger, 1986.

Chan, Sucheng. *This Bitter-Sweet Soil: The Chinese in California Agriculture, 1860–1910.* Berkeley: University of California Press, 1986.

_____ , ed. *Social and Gender Boundaries in the United States.* Lewiston, N.Y.: Edwin Mellen, 1989.

_____ . *Asian Americans: An Interpretive History.* Boston: Twayne, 1991.

Cheng, Lucie, and Edna Bonacich, eds. *Labor Immigration under Capitalism: Asian Workers in the United States before World War II.* Berkeley: University of California Press, 1984.

Chidester, David. *Patterns of Power: Religion and Politics in American Culture.* Englewood Cliffs, N.J.: Prentice Hall, 1988.

Choate, Pat. *Agents of Influence: How Japan Manipulates America's Political and Economic System.* New York: Touchstone, 1991.

Chomsky, Noam. *The Culture of Terrorism.* Boston: South End, 1988.

_____ . *Deterring Democracy.* New York: Hill & Wang, 1992.

Chomsky, Noam, and Edward S. Herman. *After the Cataclysm: Postwar Indochina and the Reconstruction of Imperial Ideology.* Boston: South End, 1989.

Collins, Patricia Hill. *Black Feminist Thought: Knowledge, Consciousness, and the Politics of Empowerment.* Boston: Unwin Hyman, 1990.

Connor, Steven. *Postmodernist Culture: An Introduction to Theories of the Contemporary.* Cambridge, Mass.: Basil Blackwell, 1989.

Cordova, Fred. *Filipinos: Forgotten Asian Americans.* Dubuque, Iowa: Kendall/Hunt, 1983.

Cox, Oliver C. *Caste, Class, and Race: A Study in Social Dynamics.* New York: Modern Reader, 1948.

Curran, James, and Michael Gurevitch, eds. *Mass Media and Society*. London: Edward Arnold, 1991.

Daniels, Roger. *Asian America: Chinese and Japanese in the United States since 1850*. Seattle: University of Washington Press, 1988.

———. *Coming to America: A History of Immigration and Ethnicity in American Life*. New York: HarperCollins, 1990.

Daniels, Roger, and Harry H. L. Kitano. *American Racism: Exploration of the Nature of Prejudice*. Englewood Cliffs, N.J.: Prentice Hall, 1970.

Dant, Tim. *Knowledge, Ideology and Discourse: A Sociological Perspective*. New York: Routledge, 1991.

Davis, Mike. *City of Quartz: Excavating the Future in Los Angeles*. New York: Vintage, 1992.

Dellinger, David. *Vietnam Revisited: From Covert Action to Invasion to Reconstruction*. Boston: South End, 1986.

Dittmar, Linda, and Gene Michaud, eds. *From Hanoi to Hollywood: The Vietnam War in American Film*. New Brunswick, N.J.: Rutgers University Press, 1990.

Doane, Mary Ann. *Femme Fatales: Feminism, Film Theory, Psychoanalysis*. New York: Routledge, 1991.

Donovan, Robert J., and Ray Scherer. *Unsilent Revolution: Television News and American Public Life, 1948–1991*. New York: Woodrow Wilson International Center for Scholars and Cambridge University Press, 1992.

Dooley, Thomas A. *Deliver Us from Evil*. New York: Farrar, Straus & Cudahy, 1956.

Drinnon, Richard. *Keeper of Concentration Camps: Dillon S. Myer and American Racism*. Berkeley: University of California Press, 1987.

———. *Facing West: The Metaphysics of Indian-Hating and Empire-Building*. New York: Schocken, 1990.

D'Souza, Dinesh. *Illiberal Education: The Politics of Race and Sex on Campus*. New York: Free Press, 1991.

Dye, Thomas R. *Who's Running America? The Bush Era*, 5th ed. Englewood Cliffs, N.J.: Prentice Hall, 1990.

Ehrenreich, Barbara. *Fear of Falling: The Inner Life of the Middle Class*. New York: Harper Perennial, 1990.

Erens, Patricia, ed. *Issues in Feminist Film Criticism*. Bloomington: Indiana University Press, 1990.

Fallows, James. *More Like Us: Making America Great Again*. Boston: Houghton Mifflin, 1990.

Faludi, Susan. *Backlash: The Undeclared War against American Women*. Garden City, N.Y.: Doubleday, 1992.

Fawcett, James T., and Benjamin V. Cariño, eds. *Pacific Bridges: The New Immigration from Asia and the Pacific Islands*. Staten Island, N.Y.: Center for Migration Studies, 1987.

Fialka, John J. *Hotel Warriors: Covering the Gulf War*. Washington, D.C.: Woodrow Wilson Center Press, 1991.

Fischer, Stuart. *Kids' TV: The First 25 Years*. New York: Facts on File, 1983.

FitzGerald, Frances. *Fire in the Lake: The Vietnamese and the Americans in Vietnam*. New York: Vintage, 1989.

Franklin, H. Bruce. *M.I.A. or Mythmaking in America*. New York: Lawrence Hill, 1992.

Friedman, George, and Meredith Lebard. *The Coming War with Japan*. New York: St. Martin's, 1991.

Fuentes, Annette, and Barbara Ehrenreich. *Women in the Global Factory*. Boston: South End, 1983.

Gaddis, John Lewis. *The Long Peace: Inquiries into the History of the Cold War*. New York: Oxford University Press, 1987.

Garofalo, Reebee, ed. *Rockin' the Boat: Mass Music and Mass Movements*. Boston: South End, 1992.

Gee, Emma, ed. *Counterpoint: Perspectives on Asian America*. Los Angeles: UCLA Asian American Studies Center, 1976.

George, Nelson. *In Living Color: The Authorized Companion to the Fox TV Series*. New York: Warner, 1991.

Gibson, James William. *The Perfect War: The War We Couldn't Lose and How We Did*. New York: Vintage, 1988.

Gitlin, Todd. *Inside Prime Time*. New York: Pantheon, 1985.

Glaessner, Verina. *Kung Fu: Cinema of Vengeance*. New York: Bounty, 1974.

Glazer, Nathan. *The Limits of Social Policy*. Cambridge, Mass.: Harvard University Press, 1988.

Glenn, Evelyn Nakano. *Issei, Nisei, War Bride: Three Generations of Japanese Women in Domestic Service*. Philadelphia: Temple University Press, 1986.

Gooding-Williams, Robert, ed. *Reading Rodney King Reading Urban Uprising*. New York: Routledge, 1993.

Hacker, Andrew. *Two Nations: Black and White, Separate, Hostile, Unequal*. New York: Charles Scribner's Sons, 1992.

Hallin, Daniel C. *The "Uncensored War": The Media and Vietnam*. Berkeley: University of California Press, 1989.

Hamamoto, Darrell Y. *Nervous Laughter: Television Situation Comedy and Liberal Democratic Ideology*. New York: Praeger, 1989.

Harris, Marvin. *The Rise of Anthropological Theory: A History of Theories of Culture*. New York: Thomas Y. Crowell, 1968.

Heitland, Jon. *The Man from U.N.C.L.E. Book: The Behind-the-Scenes Story of a Television Classic*. New York: St. Martin's, 1987.

Herman, Edward S. *Atrocities in Vietnam: Myths and Realities*. Philadelphia: Pilgrim, 1970.

Herman, Edward S., and Noam Chomsky. *Manufacturing Consent: The Political Economy of the Mass Media*. New York: Pantheon, 1988.

Hirsch, E. D., Jr. *Cultural Literacy: What Every American Needs to Know*. New York: Vintage, 1988.

Hobsbawm, E. J. *Primitive Rebels: Studies in Archaic Forms of Social Movement in the 19th and 20th Centuries*. New York: W. W. Norton, 1959.

hooks, bell. *Black Looks: Race and Representation*. Boston: South End, 1992.

Horowitz, Irving Louis, ed. *The Politics of Reverend Moon and the Unification Church*. Cambridge: MIT Press, 1978.

Horsman, Reginald. *Race and Manifest Destiny: The Origins of American Anglo-Saxonism*. Cambridge, Mass.: Harvard University Press, 1981.

Howe, Irving. *The World of Our Fathers: The Journey of the East European Jews to America and the Life They Found and Made.* New York: Touchstone, 1976.

Huff, C. Ronald, ed. *Gangs in America.* Newbury Park, Calif.: Sage, 1990.

Hunter, Edward. *Brainwashing.* New York: Pyramid, 1958.

Hunter, Jane. *The Gospel of Gentility: American Women Missionaries in Turn-of-the-Century China.* New Haven, Conn.: Yale University Press, 1984.

Hwang, David Henry. *M. Butterfly.* New York: Plume, 1989.

Ichioka, Yuji, ed. *Views from Within: The Japanese American Evacuation and Resettlement Study.* Los Angeles: Asian American Studies Center, 1989.

_____ . *The Issei: The World of the First Generation Japanese Immigrants, 1885–1924.* New York: Free Press, 1990.

Inman, David. *The TV Encyclopedia.* New York: Perigee, 1991.

Ishihara, Shintaro. *The Japan That Can Say No.* New York: Simon & Schuster, 1991.

Jacobs, Paul, and Saul Landau, with Eve Pell. *To Serve the Devil,* vol. 2, *Colonials and Sojourners.* New York: Vintage, 1971.

Jencks, Christopher. *Rethinking Social Policy: Race, Poverty, and the Underclass.* New York: Harper Perennial, 1993.

Jones, Bruce E. *War without Windows.* New York: Berkley, 1990.

Kanahele, George Hu'eu Sanford. *Ku Kanaka Stand Tall: A Search for Hawaiian Values.* Honolulu: University of Hawaii Press, 1986.

Karnow, Stanley. *Vietnam: A History.* New York: Penguin, 1984.

_____ . *In Our Image: America's Empire in the Philippines.* New York: Ballantine, 1990.

Karnow, Stanley, and Nancy Yoshihara. *Asian Americans in Transition.* New York: Asia Society, 1992.

Kellner, Douglas. *Jean Baudrillard: From Marxism to Postmodernism and Beyond.* Stanford, Calif.: Stanford University Press, 1989.

_____ . *Television and the Crisis of Democracy.* Boulder, Colo.: Westview, 1990.

Kennedy, Paul. *The Rise and Fall of the Great Powers: Economic Change and Military Conflict from 1500 to 2000.* New York: Vintage, 1989.

_____ . *Preparing for the Twenty-First Century.* New York: Random House, 1993.

Kikumura, Akemi. *Issei Pioneers: Hawaii and the Mainland 1885 to 1924.* Los Angeles: Japanese American National Museum, 1992.

Kim, Chong Sun. *Rev. Sun Myung Moon.* Washington, D.C.: University Press of America, 1978.

Kim, Elaine H. *Asian American Literature: An Introduction to the Writings and Their Social Context.* Philadelphia: Temple University Press, 1982.

Kingston, Maxine Hong. *Tripmaster Monkey: His Fake Book.* New York: Vintage, 1990.

Kitano, Harry H. L., and Roger Daniels. *Asian Americans: Emerging Minorities.* Englewood Cliffs, N.J.: Prentice Hall, 1988.

Kolko, Gabriel. *Anatomy of War: Vietnam, the United States, and the Modern Historical Experience.* New York: Pantheon, 1985.

Koppes, Clayton R., and Gregory D. Black. *Hollywood Goes to War: How Politics, Profits and Propaganda Shaped World War II Movies.* Berkeley: University of California Press, 1987.

Lanning, Michael Lee. *Inside the LRRPS: Rangers in Vietnam.* New York: Ivy, 1988.

Leadership Education for Asian Pacifics (LEAP). *The State of Asian Pacific America: Policy Issues to the Year 2020.* Los Angeles: LEAP Asian Pacific American Public Policy Institute and UCLA Asian American Studies Center, 1993.

Leong, Russell, ed. *Moving the Image: Independent Asian Pacific American Media Arts.* Los Angeles: UCLA Asian American Studies Center and Visual Communications, Southern California Asian American Studies Central, 1991.

Lifton, Robert J. *Thought Reform and the Psychology of Totalism.* New York: W. W. Norton, 1961.

Lifton, Robert Jay. *Home from the War: Learning from Vietnam Veterans,* 3d ed. Boston: Beacon, 1992.

Light, Ivan, and Edna Bonacich. *Immigrant Entrepreneurs: Koreans in Los Angeles 1965–1982.* Berkeley: University of California Press, 1991.

Limerick, Patricia Nelson. *The Legacy of Conquest: The Unbroken Past of the American West.* New York: W. W. Norton, 1987.

Loescher, Gil, and John A. Scanlan. *Calculated Kindness: Refugees and America's Half-Open Door, 1945 to the Present.* New York: Free Press, 1986.

Lopes, Sal. *The Wall: Images and Offerings from the Vietnam Veterans Memorial.* New York: Collins, 1987.

Lyman, Stanford M. *Chinese Americans.* New York: Random House, 1974.

MacDonald, J. Fred. *Television and the Red Menace: The Video Road to Vietnam.* New York: Praeger, 1985.

_____. *Who Shot the Sheriff? The Rise and Fall of the Television Western.* New York: Praeger, 1987.

_____. *Blacks and White TV: African Americans in Television since 1948,* 2d ed. Chicago: Nelson-Hall, 1992.

Marks, John. *The Search for the "Manchurian Candidate": The CIA and Mind Control.* New York: Times Books, 1979.

Matsui, Yayori. *Women's Asia.* Atlantic Highlands, N.J.: Zed, 1989.

McCrohan, Donna. *The Life and Times of Maxwell Smart.* New York: St. Martin's, 1988.

Mindel, Charles H., Robert W. Habenstein, and Roosevelt Wright, Jr., eds. *Ethnic Families in America: Patterns and Variations,* 3d ed. New York: Elsevier, 1988.

Moynihan, Daniel Patrick. *The Negro Family: The Case for National Action.* Washington, D.C.: U.S. Department of Labor, Office of Family Planning and Research, 1965.

Murray, Charles. *Losing Ground: American Social Policy 1950–1980.* New York: Basic Books, 1984.

Neale, Steve, and Frank Krutnik. *Popular Film and Television Comedy.* New York: Routledge, 1990.

Newcomb, Horace, ed. *Television: The Critical View,* 4th ed. New York: Oxford University Press, 1987.

Nichols, Bill. *Representing Reality: Issues and Concepts in Documentary.* Bloomington: Indiana University Press, 1991.

Norman, Elizabeth M. *Women at War: The Story of Fifty Military Nurses Who Served in Vietnam.* Philadelphia: University of Pennsylvania Press, 1990.

Novak, Michael. *The Rise of the Unmeltable Ethnics.* New York: Macmillan, 1972.

Okada, John. *No-No Boy*. Rutland, Vt.: Charles Tuttle, 1957.

Okihiro, Gary Y., et al. *Reflections on Shattered Windows: Promises and Prospects for Asian American Studies*. Pullman: Washington State University Press, 1988.

Okuda, Michael, and Denise Okuda. *Star Trek Chronology: The History of the Future*. New York: Pocket Books, 1993.

Omi, Michael, and Howard Winant. *Racial Formation in the United States: From the 1960s to the 1980s*. New York: Routledge, 1986.

Ong, Paul M., and Tania Azores. *Asian Pacific Americans in Los Angeles: A Demographic Profile*. Los Angeles: UCLA Asian American Studies Center, 1991.

Paletz, David L., and Robert M. Entman. *Media Power Politics*. New York: Free Press, 1981.

Penley, Constance, ed. *Feminism and Film Theory*. New York: Routledge, 1988.

Persico, Joseph E. *Edward R. Murrow: An American Original*. New York: Dell, 1990.

Petersen, William. *Japanese Americans: Oppression and Success*. New York: Random House, 1971.

Phillips, Kevin. *The Politics of the Rich and Poor: Wealth and the American Electorate in the Reagan Aftermath*. New York: Harper Perennial, 1991.

Pines, Burton Yale. *Back to Basics: The Traditionalist Movement That Is Sweeping Grass-Roots America*. New York: William Morrow, 1982.

Podhoretz, Norman. *Why We Were in Vietnam*. New York: Simon & Schuster, 1982.

Posner, Gerald L. *Warlords of Crime—Chinese Secret Societies: The New Mafia*. New York: Penguin, 1990.

Postman, Neil, and Steve Powers. *How to Watch TV News*. New York: Penguin, 1992.

Prestowitz, Clyde, Jr. *Trading Places: How We Are Giving Our Future to Japan and How to Reclaim It*. New York: Basic Books, 1989.

Rapping, Elayne. *The Looking Glass World of Nonfiction TV*. Boston: South End, 1987.

Reich, Robert B. *The Work of Nations: Preparing Ourselves for 21st-Century Capitalism*. New York: Vintage, 1992.

Rex, John, and David Mason, eds. *Theories of Race and Ethnic Relations*. London: Cambridge University Press, 1986.

Rieff, David. *Los Angeles: Capital of the Third World*. New York: Touchstone, 1991.

Rivera, Geraldo, with Daniel Paisner. *Exposing Myself*. New York: Bantam, 1992.

Robbins, Christopher. *Air America*. New York: Avon, 1990.

Roediger, David R. *The Wages of Whiteness: Race and the Making of the American Working Class*. New York: Verso, 1991.

Safer, Morley. *Flashbacks: On Returning to Vietnam*. New York: St. Martin's, 1991.

Sandmeyer, Elmer Clarence. *The Anti-Chinese Movement in California*. Urbana: University of Illinois Press, 1991.

Santoli, Al. *Everything We Had: An Oral History of the Vietnam War by Thirty-Three American Soldiers Who Fought It*. New York: Ballantine, 1982.

————. *New Americans: An Oral History*. New York: Ballantine, 1990.

Saxton, Alexander. *The Rise and Fall of the White Republic: Class Politics and Mass Culture in Nineteenth-Century America*. New York: Verso, 1990.

Scruggs, Jan C., and Joel L. Swerdlow. *To Heal a Nation: The Vietnam Veterans Memorial.* New York: Harper & Row, 1985.

Shafer, D. Michael, ed. *The Legacy: The Vietnam War in the American Imagination.* Boston: Beacon, 1990.

Shawcross, William. *Sideshow: Kissinger, Nixon and the Destruction of Cambodia.* New York: Simon & Schuster, 1979.

———. *The Quality of Mercy: Cambodia, Holocaust and Modern Conscience.* New York: Simon & Schuster, 1984.

Sheehan, Neil. *A Bright Shining Lie: John Paul Vann and America in Vietnam.* New York: Vintage, 1989.

Siu, Paul C. P. *The Chinese Laundryman: A Study of Social Isolation.* New York: New York University Press, 1987.

Sowell, Thomas, ed. *Essays and Data on American Ethnic Groups.* Washington, D.C.: Urban Institute, 1978.

———. *Ethnic America: A History.* New York: Basic Books, 1981.

———. *The Economics and Politics of Race: An International Perspective.* New York: William Morrow, 1983.

Steinberg, Stephen. *The Ethnic Myth: Race, Ethnicity, and Class in America,* 2d ed. Boston: Beacon, 1989.

Steinfels, Peter. *The Neoconservatives: The Men Who Are Changing America's Politics.* New York: Touchstone, 1979.

Sue, Stanley, and James K. Morishima. *The Mental Health of Asian Americans.* San Francisco: Jossey-Bass, 1988.

Tachiki, Amy, Eddie Wong, and Franklin Odo, eds. *Roots: An Asian American Reader.* Los Angeles: UCLA Asian American Studies Center, 1971.

Takagi, Dana Y. *The Retreat from Race: Asian-American Admissions and Racial Politics.* New Brunswick, N.J.: Rutgers University Press, 1992.

Takaki, Ronald. *Strangers from a Different Shore: A History of Asian Americans.* Boston: Little, Brown, 1989.

———. *Iron Cages: Race and Culture in 19th-Century America.* New York: Oxford University Press, 1990.

Taylor, John G. *Indonesia's Forgotten War: The Hidden History of East Timor.* London: Zed, 1991.

Terry, Wallace. *Bloods: An Oral History of the Vietnam War by Black Veterans.* New York: Ballantine, 1985.

Thompson, James C., Jr., Peter W. Stanley, and John Curtis Perry. *Sentimental Imperialists: The American Experience in East Asia.* New York: Harper & Row, 1981.

Thompson, Kenneth. *Social and Gender Boundaries in the United States.* London: Tavistock, 1986.

Truong, Thanh-Dam. *Sex, Money and Morality: Prostitution and Tourism in South-East Asia.* London: Zed, 1990.

Tsai, Shih-Shan Henry. *The Chinese Experience in America.* Bloomington: Indiana University Press, 1986.

U.S. Commission on Civil Rights. *Recent Activities against Citizens and Residents of Asian Descent.* Washington, D.C.: U.S. Government Printing Office, 1986.

———. *The Economic Status of Americans of Asian Descent.* Washington, D.C.: U.S. Government Printing Office, 1988.

_____ . *Civil Rights Issues Facing Asian Americans in the 1990s*. Washington, D.C.: U.S. Government Printing Office, 1992.

Valentine, Douglas. *The Phoenix Program*. New York: William Morrow, 1990.

van den Berghe, Pierre L. *Race and Racism: A Comparative Perspective*. New York: John Wiley & Sons, 1967.

Van Devanter, Lynda. *Home before Morning: The Story of an Army Nurse in Vietnam*. New York: Warner, 1984.

van Wolferen, Karel. *The Enigma of Japanese Power: People and Politics in a Stateless Nation*. New York: Vintage, 1990.

Vietnam Veterans Against the War. *The Winter Soldier Investigation: An Inquiry into American War Crimes*. Boston: Beacon, 1972.

Walker, Keith. *A Piece of My Heart: The Stories of 26 American Women Who Served in Vietnam*. Novato, Calif.: Presidio, 1985.

Wallace, Michele. *Black Macho and the Myth of the Superwoman*. New York: Verso, 1990.

Weiner, Tim. *Blank Check: The Pentagon's Black Budget*. New York: Warner, 1991.

Wiley, Ralph. *Why Black People Tend to Shout: Cold Facts and Wry Views from a Black Man's World*. New York: Penguin, 1992.

William, Raymond. *The Politics of Modernism: Against the New Conformists*. London: Verso, 1989.

Wilson, William Julius. *The Truly Disadvantaged: The Inner City, the Underclass, and Public Policy*. Chicago: University of Chicago Press, 1987.

Wolf, Eric R. *Europe and the People without History*. Berkeley: University of California Press, 1982.

Wong, Eugene Franklin. *On Visual Media Racism: Asians in the American Motion Pictures*. New York: Arno, 1978.

Woodward, Bob. *Veil: The Secret Wars of the CIA 1981–1987*. New York: Pocket Books, 1988.

Wrong, Dennis H. *Power: Its Forms, Bases, and Uses*. Chicago: University of Chicago Press, 1988.

Yamamoto, Hisaye. *Seventeen Syllables: And Other Stories*. Latham, N.Y.: Kitchen Table – Women of Color Press, 1988.

Yoneda, Karl G. *Ganbatte: Sixty-Year Struggle of a Kibei Worker*. Los Angeles: UCLA Asian American Studies Center, 1983.

Young, Marilyn B. *The Vietnam Wars: 1945–1990*. New York: Harper Perennial, 1991.

Yu, Eui-Young. *Korean Community Profile: Life and Consumer Patterns*. Los Angeles: Korea Times/Hankook Ilbo, 1990.

Zacharias, Ellis M., with Ladislas Farago. *Behind Closed Doors: The Secret History of the Cold War*. New York: G. P. Putnam's Sons, 1950.

Index

Darrell Y. Hamamoto has served as lecturer in the Program in Comparative Culture at the University of California, Irvine. He was the 1990–91 recipient of a Rockefeller Research Fellowship at the Asian American Studies Center at UCLA. Professor Hamamoto has also taught in the School of Film and Television at UCLA as a visiting professor. His previous book is *Nervous Laughter: Television Situation Comedy and Liberal Democratic Ideology* (1989). In 1993, Professor Hamamoto received a Fulbright Fellowship to lecture at Hiroshima University, Japan, on the subjects of media, popular culture, and U.S. racial and ethnic relations.